Republican Women

Republican

CATHERINE E. RYMPH

FEMINISM AND

CONSERVATISM

FROM SUFFRAGE

THROUGH THE

RISE OF

THE NEW RIGHT

The University of

North Carolina Press

Chapel Hill

© 2006
The University of North Carolina Press
All rights reserved
Set in Scala and Poplar types
by Tseng Information Systems, Inc.
Manufactured in the United States of America

Publication of this book was assisted by a grant from the University
of Missouri Research Council.

The paper in this book meets the guidelines for permanence and
durability of the Committee on Production Guidelines for Book
Longevity of the Council on Library Resources.

Library of Congress Cataloging-in-Publication Data
Rymph, Catherine E.
Republican women : feminism and conservatism from suffrage
through the rise of the new right / by Catherine E. Rymph.
    p. cm. — (Gender & American culture)
Includes bibliographical references and index.
ISBN 0-8078-2984-6 (cloth : alk. paper) —
ISBN 0-8078-5652-5 (pbk. : alk. paper)
1. Republican Party (U.S. : 1854–)—History. 2. Women in
politics—United States. 3. Conservatism—United States—History.
4. Feminism—United States—History. 5. Women political
activists—United States. I. Title. II. Series.
JK2356.R96 2006
324.2734'082—dc22   2005018338

Portions of this work appeared earlier, in somewhat different form,
in "'Keeping the Political Fires Burning': Republican Women's
Clubs and Female Political Culture in Small-Town Iowa, 1928–
1938," *Annals of Iowa* 56 (Winter–Spring 1997): 99–127, reprinted
by permission; and "Neither Neutral nor Neutralized: Phyllis
Schlafly's Battle against Sexism," in *Women's America: Refocusing the
Past*, ed. Linda K. Kerber and Jane Sherron De Hart, 5th ed., 501–7
(copyright 2000 Oxford University Press, Inc.), used by permission
of Oxford University Press, Inc.

Contents

Illustrations

Acknowledgments

This book has been a long time in the making. For its origins, I thank Karen Mason, of the Iowa Women's Archives for assigning me the task of processing Mary Louise Smith's papers when I worked for her in 1993. That collection sparked my initial interest in the intersection of feminism, conservatism, and partisanship. This project has transformed itself considerably since those days and I have incurred a long list of debts, both personal and professional, along the way.

I would like to thank the Iowa Sesquicentennial Grant, the Colonial Dames of America, the Dwight D. Eisenhower Foundation, the Gerald R. Ford Foundation, the Graduate College of the University of Iowa, and the University of Missouri Research Council for the timely grants and fellowships that enabled me to complete my research.

Historians are dependent on the work of archivists and staff who manage the various manuscript collections that we use. I am indebted to archivists at Arizona State University's Hayden Library, the Historical Society of Pennsylvania, the Hoover Presidential Library, the Iowa Women's Archives, the Manuscripts Division of the Library of Congress, the Nixon Presidential Materials at the National Archives, the Rare and Manuscripts Divisions at Cornell University, the Special Collections Department of the University of Iowa, the State Historical Society of Iowa, and the Western Historical Manuscripts Division of the University of Missouri, who have helped me locate materials and who, in many cases, have continued to answer questions and look up information for me long after I had returned home. Also of great help have been the staff members at various other archives, including the Minnesota Historical Society, the Archives of Appalachia, the Margaret Chase Smith Library, and the Special Collections Department at the University of Maine, who have provided me with photocopies of materials from their collections by mail, thus reducing the amount of travel necessary. Geir Gunderson at the Ford Library and Herb Pankratz at the Eisenhower Library have been especially helpful in guiding me through their collections. I am also grateful to Karen Jania of the Bentley Historical Library for accommodating me during a research trip when the library was closed for renovation.

Certain individuals and organizations allowed me access to their own materials and thus added a richness to my sources that would have been unavailable had I been confined to what was collected in the archives. Jane Hamilton Macauley and Joyce Weise were generous enough to lend me their personal scrapbooks; William Martin provided me with clippings and photographs related to his aunt, Marion Martin; and the National Federation of Republican Women allowed me to rummage through the old records and scrapbooks stored at its headquarters.

As much time as historians spend in the archives, poring in solitude over our documents, we are never actually alone in our endeavors. A long list of individuals have read and commented on parts of this manuscript in its various forms. Members of my dissertation committee, Colin Gordon, Arthur Miller, and Allen Steinberg provided excellent suggestions for going further with this project. Ken Cmiel not only read the entire dissertation manuscript, but in subsequent years has continued to be generous with his sage advice, his intellect, and his ability to keep everything in perspective. Anyone who has worked with Linda Kerber knows of the deep commitment she makes to her graduate students and to the broader historical profession. From my first attempts to formulate this project, she has expressed consistent faith in its merits and in my ability to see it through. A supportive, encouraging adviser, she has become a valuable friend and colleague.

I have been the beneficiary of the generosity of friends, teachers, and colleagues at the University of Iowa, the University of Missouri, and in the wider historical profession who have read my work as this project developed over the years and helped point me in new directions. Although listing their names does none of them justice, I would like to thank Marv Bergman, Sierra Bruckner, Jennifer Delton, Jason Duncan, John Evelev, Sarah Hanley, Charles Hawley, Ellis Hawley, Glen Jeansonne, Sharon Kennedy-Nolle, Jon Lauck, Maurice Lee and the rest of the Missouri Americanist Group, Marjorie Levine-Clark, Kim Nielsen, John Skrentny, Michael Struebin, and LeeAnn Whites. Conversations with Suzanne Schenken about our mutual interest in Mary Louise Smith were invaluable. A special thanks is due to Jane De Hart and Susan Ware, who carefully read this manuscript toward the end of its completion and who did their best to show me how to make it stronger. I hope I have succeeded. Thanks also to Chuck Grench and Amanda McMillan of the University of North Carolina Press for shepherding the manuscript through its final stages.

Colleagues in the History Department at the University of Missouri, including Carol Anderson, Bob Collins, Mary Neth, Linda Reeder, Steve Watts, and LeeAnn Whites, have supplied me with valuable advice, encouragement, and friendship. I am also deeply appreciative of the assistance supplied by members of the department's support staff, including Patty Eggleston, Sandy Kietzman, Melinda Lockwood, and Karen Pecora.

In the course of pursuing this project, several Republican women activists were kind enough to take the time to talk with me about their activities. Although I have written about Republican women from the position of an outsider, I have developed a great respect and appreciation for the commitment, thoughtfulness, and goodwill of those I have met. In particular, I would like to thank Rosalind Bovey, Jane Hamilton Macauley, the late Mary Louise Smith, and Joyce Weise.

Over the years, I have been sustained in this project, either directly or indirectly, by the friendship of many individuals, including Jason Duncan, Kim Nielsen, Christy Prahl, Rick Nagy, Paul Hockenos, and John Skrentny. And I would have been simply lost without Sierra Bruckner, Charles Hawley, Marjorie Levine-Clark, Kathleen Mills, and Amy Peterson. Thanks also for the encouragement of my parents, Raymond and D-D Rymph, and my brother Georg Rymph. My children, Polly and Linus, arrived toward the end of the completion of this project and have supplied me with many marvelous distractions. Vanessa Palmer provided the necessary childcare that enabled me to meet my final deadlines. Finally, I cannot begin to thank Scott Southwick for all that he has done to bring this project to a close. Not only has he read every word more than once, helped me with technological malfunctions, and taken care of our children, he has added the joy, humor, and friendship to my life that helps everything else make sense.

Abbreviations

AFL	American Federation of Labor
CIO	Congress of Industrial Organizations
DAR	Daughters of the American Revolution
DNC	Democratic National Committee
DO Committee	
	Delegates and Organization Committee of the RNC
ERA	Equal Rights Amendment
Federation	
	National Federation of Women's Republican Clubs/
	National Federation of Republican Women
GOP	Grand Old Party (Republican Party)
ICRW	Iowa Council of Republican Women
LWV	League of Women Voters
NAACP	National Association for the Advancement of Colored People
NACW	National Association of Colored Women
NARW	National Association of Republican Women
NAWSA	National American Woman Suffrage Association
NLRCW	National League of Republican Colored Women
NWP	National Woman's Party
NWPC	National Women's Political Caucus
RNC	Republican National Committee
RWP	Republican Women of Pennsylvania
RWTF	Republican Women's Task Force (of the NWPC)
WCTU	Woman's Christian Temperance Union
WJCC	Women's Joint Congressional Committee
WNRC	Women's National Republican Club
WPAB	Women's Policy Advisory Board (to the 1980 Reagan campaign)

Republican Women

Introduction

In 1975 Republican feminists seemed to be everywhere. The Republican president, Gerald Ford, supported the Equal Rights Amendment; his wife Betty toured the country campaigning for its ratification and speaking in support of abortion rights. Republicans sympathetic to a women's rights agenda were serving as governors of several states, including Iowa, Michigan, and Missouri. A proud feminist, Mary Louise Smith, chaired the Republican National Committee. Audrey Rowe Colom, an African American Republican, was serving as president of one of the most important feminist organizations of the seventies, the National Women's Political Caucus. Even the GOP's staid auxiliary, the National Federation of Republican Women, had endorsed the ERA.

In the mid-1970s the second-wave feminist movement was becoming broadly, if not universally, accepted. Although the political component of the new feminism quickly became more identified with the Democratic Party, a core group of Republican women responded positively to the insights and objectives of the emerging women's movement and pressed the GOP to embrace a particular women's rights agenda. The Republican Party, floundering in the wake of the Watergate scandal, appeared ready to adopt that agenda as part of its rebuilding strategy.

In reality, the hold that Republican feminists had on the Grand Old Party was far more tenuous than they liked to believe. Already in 1975, a new movement of social conservatism within the Republican Party was ascending, one that would marginalize Republican feminists and succeed in moving the party away from its traditional support for women's rights. In 1980 delegates affiliated with the New Right dominated the Republican presidential convention, nominated Ronald Reagan for president, and approved new platform planks explicitly at odds with many of the goals of Republican feminists, including ERA and abortion rights.

Mobilized by their opposition to feminism and empowered by the social transformations that were bringing women onto the political stage, socially conservative women became a critical component of the rising New Right coalition. As their allies gained strength within the party, these women saw their views on feminist issues increasingly reflected in the Republican Party's official positions. These antifeminist activists were led by Phyllis Schlafly, a former officer of the National Federation of Republican Women. Schlafly's emergence as America's most famous antifeminist had its roots in her frustration with the Republican Party in the mid-1960s as both an ideological conservative within a party dominated by moderates and, paradoxically, as an ambitious woman within a party dominated by men. Over the course of the 1970s, Phyllis Schlafly came to represent, in many minds, The Republican Woman—an image that made Republican feminism seem more and more like an oxymoron. It was antifeminists of the New Right who, by the end of the decade, proved successful in winning the Republican Party in the war over feminism.

Conflicts between feminists and antifeminists were an important part of the process by which the Republican Party remade itself in the 1970s and 1980s. This fact emphasizes the significance of female actors and of gender issues to the developments of American political history. Although at odds in many ways, Schlafly and the feminists were each products of decades of efforts to advance women's power and influence within the party. In the 1970s each offered different women's political agendas, different models of how women could be politically effective, different visions of their party, and, indeed, different models of Republican womanhood. Their stories are part of a longer history of women's efforts to engage with the Republican Party, the origins of which date back to the ways women were integrated into the GOP after the ratification of the Nineteenth Amendment in 1920. It is that history that this book unravels.

★ In considering the political and social history of Republican women's activism from 1920 to 1980, this book focuses on the thousands of women who volunteered for their party through the Republican women's club movement ("clubwomen") and the smaller number who served the GOP as party officials ("party women"). These women wrestled with different approaches to political involvement. Though mostly unknown today, they did much to create and project the party's image to neighbors and to persuade others to vote Republican.[1] Yet for most of the period this book addresses, few had much of a voice in party affairs.

Republican women in the 1920s had expressed greater ambitions for the generations of voting women to come. As American women contemplated the new political status that accompanied women's suffrage, many saw good reasons for joining the parties, yet were still ambivalent about the partisan route. Their efforts to engage with partisan politics reveal some of the dilemmas surrounding the integration of previously excluded groups into mainstream politics. Republican women wrestled with the question of whether enfranchised women would use party politics to advance a women's agenda, or whether partisan women's work would be used to advance the party. Although some Republican women in the 1920s entered the all-male party councils, many more approached party politics from the periphery—through separate women's clubs.

These options led to different strategies, which in turn nurtured often conflicting ideas about gender, power, and politics. Simply put, Republican women (like other partisan women) confronted a choice between trying to integrate into their party on the same terms as men or organizing separately as women. The apparent choice between integration and separation was in many ways a false one, as even those who pursued "integration" could never, as women, fully escape their status as "separate." Still this "choice" was a critical component of what would distinguish the different models of Republican womanhood this book explores.[2] As Melanie Gustafson, Kristie Miller, and Elizabeth Israels Perry note in the introduction to their collection of essays on women in political parties, "[a]ny story of women in politics must take into account women's struggle to resolve the tensions between these two strategies or risk ignoring the complexity of women's political experience."[3] The particular ways these struggles played out in the GOP during the twentieth century also illuminates the relationship of women's rights and gender consciousness to the changing political ideologies and organizational structures of the Republican Party.

During the period this book examines, a few Republican women pursued integration into the party's official bodies and sought power sharing with men. As these women were drawn deeper into the party and given positions of authority, like other party professionals they developed a commitment to the party's success that led them to accept compromise and negotiation as fundamental to a vital party and to a functioning political system.[4] As party officials, they tended to express careful, moderate views on political issues of the day. These party women were often unmarried, viewed politics as a career, and were in some cases paid for their work. Although few called themselves feminists before the 1970s, party women challenged sex discrimination in their chosen profession, while trying to assimilate to the profession's norms. They served as party officials, often as organizers of women, achieving their positions in the party based on their ability to mobilize women's partisan activism and votes.

A much larger number of women chose to work within separate all-female Republican clubs, pursuing their own forms of partisanship. Clubwomen believed they could engage with party politics while retaining the separate women's institutions and distinct women's agendas that had served them in the past. Volunteer clubwomen tended to view politics as an act of love or of civic duty, rather than as a career. They were often drawn to notions of political purity that left them bewildered and angered by what they viewed as the hypocrisy, corruption, and weakness of party professionals.[5] Initially, the targets of their anger were men, but as party women became increasingly visible, they too earned the wrath of those clubwomen preferring a "purer" form of politics.

Through the club movement, thousands of women developed a devotion to the party, a passion for politics, and a respect for their own contributions to American political life. Clubwomen in the twenties, thirties, and forties established programs, literature, spaces, and rituals to bring women into the world of partisan politics. Male party leaders did not always embrace clubwomen's organizing efforts and instead variously mocked, feared, or overlooked them. After World War II, however, the GOP increasingly turned to women's grass-roots organizing partly as a means of countering political organizing by labor unions on behalf of the Democrats. Local Republican organizing and fundraising in the 1950s became clearly identified as women's work (what I call the "housework of government"). The party relegated the work of local party organizing to clubwomen, while not treating them as an interest group with legitimate claims on patronage or power. There had always been clubwomen who expressed frustration with this arrangement and who wanted to work for a particular agenda within the party. In the 1960s, this frustration would finally result in an organized revolt, first during Goldwater's presidential campaign in 1964, and again in 1967 during Phyllis Schlafly's bid to become leader of the National Federation of Republican Women.

Although there were Republican clubwomen who heeded the advice of their leaders and began to downplay differences between male and female politics as the decades wore on, many continued to emphasize women's unique contributions to political life. These women embodied a political style that borrowed from the traditions of nineteenth-century middle-class women's activism. This style stressed women's political independence and their differences from men and framed political issues as moral crusades that women were particularly prepared to lead. This political style nurtured an outsider politics that many Republican women's organizations in the 1920s used on behalf of progressive Republicanism, but which carried through the next fifty years to form the building blocks of a reactionary women's politics. Notably, for most of the period under consideration it was the party's more right-wing women who demanded an independent voice for women.

One important feature that came to distinguish clubwomen from party women was the particular form of gender consciousness many clubwomen displayed. Depicting politics as an urgent, moral crusade, these women argued that the superiority of women made them uniquely equipped to pursue these crusades. The conception of women's politics as a moral crusade had been refined by nineteenth-century mass women's organizations like the Woman's Christian Temperance Union, which summoned ordinary women into political life through the imperatives of their Protestant faith and their position as women.[6] Many of the women who were active in the Republican club movement, as well as the male politicians who wooed them, carried the rhetoric of women as uncompromising political crusaders deep into the twentieth century. Women leaders who embraced the crusading style tried to encourage women to participate in politics by convincing them that only women's moral superiority could adequately confront the issues at hand. Republican women hoped that politics framed in such dire terms would resonate with those women who were skeptical of political participation.

Women were not necessarily more "moral" than men, and individual men themselves certainly described politics as a crusade of good against evil. Indeed, as James Morone has recently argued, the fight against sin and the search for salvation have framed much of American political history.[7] Women's proclivity to describe their activism as part of a moral crusade, however, suggests the ways in which citizenship and public activism have been differently justified and understood for women historically. The rhetoric of the female political crusade offered women a kind of political legitimacy that they otherwise found hard to earn. While this language may have been ideal for the outsider politics that women by necessity developed while they were without the vote, it was a more problematic strategy for helping women adapt to the norms of formal politics.

In arguing that clubwomen conceived of politics as a moral crusade, I do not mean to suggest that they were concerned merely with issues of social morality (drinking or prostitution, for example). Rather, I mean to evoke the ways in which women described the politics they cared about as a crusade of good against evil. Sometimes social evils were indeed their target; at other times, however, they attacked, in similar language, what they saw as political or economic evils, such as the growth of the state or challenges to U.S. sovereignty. What these different crusades shared was an approach to political issues that was uncompromising, urgent, and often deeply gendered.

For those party women who pursued integration into the party's official bodies, this rhetoric of female superiority and of female political crusades was a liability as it emphasized their differences from the men with whom they were trying to work as equals and presented women as uncompromising in their politics and therefore as unreliable partisans. Beginning in the late 1930s, Marion Martin, who served as both the founding head of the National Federation of Women's Republican Clubs as well as the Republican National Committee (RNC) assistant chairman in charge of women's activities, encouraged party loyalty in women both to help the party and to advance women in politics.[8] Martin promoted a view distinct from that of many of the clubwomen she organized, insisting that both women and the party would benefit if women ceased to present their interests as separate from men's. Martin sought to eradicate this female Republican style and replace it with one that more closely resembled what she considered to be a male standard of partisanship. She hoped doing so would create an army of reliable party workers, thus helping the party as well as women themselves. She was partly successful, as the Federation did create party machinery that would be expanded upon after the war. Yet her success was never complete.

Martin made a tacit bargain with party leaders, in which the loyalty of Republican women was offered in exchange for future access to leadership. Martin recognized that many men in her party were ready to dismiss women as a group. She therefore called for women to develop forms of female partisanship that were subservient and cooperative. This was a curious strategy for empowerment, because it discouraged Republican women's independent voices in the hope of ultimately increasing their power. Some women who pursued this strategy did become party leaders, but theirs was a leadership whose internal logic required political compromises that were at times quite profound.

This was a strategy that not all Republican clubwomen would accept. Conflicts between those who championed loyalty and assimilation and those who asserted women's political uniqueness and independence would mark the Federation in the 1950s and 1960s. When

Federation members succeeded in freeing the organization from the leadership of the RNC in the 1950s, the RNC assistant chairman had a less clear relationship to the Federation. Yet Bertha Adkins, RNC assistant chairman during the Eisenhower administration, raised the ire of many Federation women because of her moderate politics and because she represented a competing model of women's party work that many clubwomen rejected.

Indeed there were times when tensions erupted between these two visions of Republican womanhood, partly because integrationists like Martin and Adkins were assigned to lead and organize volunteer clubwomen whose political views and thoughts about proper partisan behavior and roles for women were quite different from their own. Conflicts between different models of Republican female activism waxed and waned through the twentieth century, as Republican women attempted to carve a place for themselves in party politics. By the 1970s both party women and clubwomen had grown frustrated with their place in the party. At that time, the civil rights movement, second-wave feminism, and other social and political movements were reconfiguring American politics, including the Republican Party. Republican women wanted a voice as their party came to terms with these transformations. The new political attention to women's issues engendered by the feminist movement provided women a clout within the GOP they had not had in decades. Yet Republican women would themselves be deeply divided over these issues.

★ This book explores the evolving efforts of women to establish themselves in the GOP, the political socialization efforts and cultural practices of grass-roots women's organizations, and the relationship between women's thinking about power and their thinking about party ideology over the course of sixty years. In this sense it is part of the history of the feminist struggle to expand women's access to the political process. Until recently, neither women's historians nor political historians have shown much interest in women's partisan activities. It was once widely assumed that women played no significant role in party organizations before the ratification of the Nineteenth Amendment and that, with the exception of a few noteworthy figures such as Democratic activists Eleanor Roosevelt and Molly Dewson, women's decisions to leave their female political organizations in favor of trying to enter male-dominated political parties after 1920 represented regrettable (or not very interesting) choices. New work by political scientists and historians is undermining these assumptions. We now know that women did not suddenly become interested in partisan politics for the first time upon national enfranchisement in 1920.[9] And through new histories of individual party activists and of state and city organizations, we have learned that those who entered party politics in the early twentieth century did so with a variety of goals, varying degrees of gender consciousness, different strategies for ensuring their effectiveness in party politics, and different degrees of success.[10]

Much of the new historical work on women's partisanship, however, remains weighted toward the decades just before and after national enfranchisement. These decades, overlapping as they do with the Progressive movement and women's suffrage movement, coincided with a period of particularly intense political activity by women. We know much less about how women continued to work within the constraints of party politics once the heyday of women's activism was over.[11] Taking the story of women's party activism well into the twentieth century not only enriches and complicates our picture of women's partisanship and of women's political work in general. Doing so also addresses the ways in which the expansion of women's political rights has helped alter American politics in more recent decades.

By focusing on women's organizing within the GOP in particular, this book places themes of female partisanship in the distinctive context of the twentieth-century Republican Party and therefore addresses questions different from those considered in other works on women and the political parties. This book explores not only the challenges associated with women's entry into male institutions in general, but also what occurred when women entered a specific male institution, a dynamic one marked by its particular history, personalities, ideological traditions, and organizational structure. Republican women, especially those who pursued the integrationist approach, were choosing to work in a party of men. Sharing similar worldviews with some men in the party more than others, and needing political allies, they often developed ties to particular factions in the party. When women achieved positions of leadership, it was often the case that they would not have done so were it not for their alliances with particular factions and with individual men. Although I do not address these relationships in a thoroughgoing way, I have tried, where possible, to show the important intersections and alliances between men and women in the party.

The Republican Party in the twentieth century did not speak with one voice. Progressives and business Republicans in the twenties and thirties, black and white Republicans in that same period, isolationists and interventionists before the Second World War, conservatives and "modern" Republicans during the Eisenhower years, Goldwater supporters and Rockefeller Republicans in the 1960s, and Southern Strategy advocates and supporters of the "Party of the Open Door" during the early 1970s all disagreed profoundly over their visions of what the party should stand for, whom it should reach out to, and on what terms.[12] Contention among female Republicans at times mirrored these conflicts. At other times, debates about women's political nature and their roles in the party and society in fact helped to shape the development of those internal party debates, a point to which historians have so far directed little attention. Interpreting the history of Republican women's partisanship in light of the party's own history helps us to understand the choices partisan women made and to expand our grasp of the party's history itself.

Although a considerable number of GOP women adhered to a progressive, moderate, or liberal brand of Republicanism, this book is also part of the effort to analyze women's relationship to conservative and right-wing politics. Early women's historians often assumed that U.S. women's politics were reliably liberal, progressive, or radical. U.S. women's historians have charted women's efforts to advance women's legal equality and on behalf of progressive social changes. Historians more recently have begun to acknowledge that American women have also organized on behalf of more-conservative or reactionary causes that have employed their own forms of woman-centered rhetoric. In recent years, historians have produced a number of important books dealing with various aspects of women's right-wing activism and the connections of gender to right-wing politics, thus greatly expanding our understanding of the meanings of gender consciousness and women's activism.[13]

The literature on gender and the American Right is not sufficient, however, to explain the full range of women's activism within the Republican Party. As Kim Nielsen reminds us, our understanding of what comprises the Right is "partially contextual," defined in relation to other prevailing political views on an ever-shifting continuum of political thought.[14] "Republican" has never been reliably synonymous with the political Right, as the party contained an influential and often dominant moderate wing during much of the period this book addresses. Furthermore, in Republican women's clubs, ideas considered conservative during their time (such as opposition to the New Deal, opposition to the United Nations, or support for Barry Goldwater) intersected with ideas not immediately understood to be conservative in any traditional sense—that is, with the ideas of grass-roots empowerment and the empowerment of women. Thus this book highlights the particular forms of political conservatism and feminism that developed during the twentieth century in the United States.

★ This book is not a chronicle of the drama of Republican nominating conventions and presidential races nor does it provide a thorough analysis of the battles among competing party factions. Other historians and political scientists have ably tackled such projects, and their work has been of great value to me.[15] I pick up their stories where relevant to my own but remain primarily wedded to an exploration of women's political power and activism.

This project spans the period between the ratification of the Nineteenth Amendment and the rise of the New Right. Beginning in 1920 risks perpetuating the notion that the Nineteenth Amendment was "an absolute dividing point" in the political activities of women, a view Nancy Cott has rightly cautioned historians to avoid.[16] American women in several states could vote before 1920, and many participated in partisan politics even when they did not possess voting rights. Other historians have begun the important work of documenting the rich history of women's partisan activities before 1920. As I argue, women's political strategies and style in the twentieth century were strongly informed by their experiences in public life before 1920. Although I begin in 1920, it is with the understanding that I am joining a story already long in progress.

Ronald Reagan's presidential campaign provides a dramatic conclusion for this narrative. Just as Reagan's election in 1980 had "profound effects . . . on the strategy of the women's movement vis-à-vis political institutions," so too did it profoundly affect the position of feminists and women's issues in the party.[17] Although conflicts between the feminist and antifeminist impulses within the party certainly did not end that year, Reagan's nomination marked a clear defeat for Republican feminism, as well as a defeat for party loyalty as a strategy for women achieving influence. Although important ideological battles would continue to be waged within the GOP over the next two decades, 1980 clearly marked the end of an important historical moment. By the 1980s, "[m]oderate or liberal Republicanism . . . , had vanished as if [it] had never been a force in party affairs."[18]

This book's eight chapters are ordered chronologically and thematically. Chapter 1 examines the challenges women and the Republican Party faced when they tried to incorporate women into the party's official bodies after 1920. This chapter focuses on the strategies used by Republican women leaders who already had ties to the party's institutions. The dilemmas party women faced in 1920 (of whether to articulate concerns within the party as women or to deny that women were a distinct political group) recur throughout this book. Chapter 2 explores the other major means by which women entered party politics—through forming independent female Republican clubs, both black and white. It examines the different forms independent Republican women's clubs took in the 1920s and 1930s and argues that, despite significant differences among these organizations, they shared elements of a common political style.

Chapter 3 chronicles Marion Martin's efforts from 1938 to 1946 to form the National Federation of Women's Republican Clubs as an organization that would turn the hundreds of independent women's Republican clubs into disciplined party machinery. Inhibiting Martin's efforts were racial and social differences, conflicting conceptions of partisanship, and skepticism about party loyalty. Yet she did succeed in building a solid organization. This chapter argues that Martin's conservative methods represented a strategy for women's empowerment that historians and feminists should incorporate into understandings of the spectrum of twentieth-century feminism.

Chapter 4 demonstrates the ways in which the Federation, in its efforts to expand after the Second World War, departed from Martin's emphasis on assimilation and discipline and reintroduced themes of women's moral and religious nature and women's separatism. In doing so, the Federation leadership unwittingly nurtured the Federation's right wing, which it ultimately was unable to control. Chapter 5 explores the increasing dependence of the Republican Party on women's work at the grass roots. Women accepted a role for themselves as political "housekeepers" whose work for the party conformed to popular ideas about domesticity. This chapter also explores the growing tensions between the Federation and the RNC's assistant chairman Bertha Adkins.

In 1964 women in the Federation finally went against the party's professional leadership and channeled their work on behalf of the presidential ambitions of Barry Goldwater, a candidate who conformed to many of its members' conservative sensibilities. Chapter 6 examines the role of women and gender in this campaign and explores its consequences for the National Federation of Republican Women. One significant outcome of the Goldwater movement was the emergence of Phyllis Schlafly, who took her conservative followers out of the Federation, eventually building her powerful antifeminist movement.

Chapter 7 explores how the Republican Party and Republican women responded to the new women's movement of the 1970s. Second-wave feminism, along with the civil rights movement and other social movements of the day, transformed American politics, offered new avenues for women's political participation, and brought a host of new gender issues to the political arena. Republican feminists worked as part of a broader American women's movement to promote feminist goals in the party. Their efforts did not go uncontested. During the 1970s the long-simmering conflicts between different models of Republican womanhood erupted, as women with conflicting views sought to influence the ways in which the party would remake itself during a critical rebuilding period. Chapter 8, then, addresses the challenge to Republican feminism posed by women of the New Right, led by Phyllis Schlafly.

★ In adjusting to the new reality of women's suffrage, male and female partisans looked for ways to bring women into the Grand Old Party. Old Guard Republican men in the 1920s hoped this could be achieved without substantively affecting politics as usual. Republican women activists, by contrast, hoped their presence would transform the party and American politics. Neither hope was entirely fulfilled. The weight of party traditions, the desire of men in power to stay there, the struggles of women leaders to negotiate the tension between women's equality and women's difference, the political apathy of large numbers of American women, and the very real differences among Republican women themselves limited the efforts of Republican women leaders to make their mark on politics. Together, these factors meant that the particular ways some women were able to access positions of party leadership produced a cohort of female leaders whose feminism would be circumscribed by the logic of party loyalty. These factors also nurtured among other women a deeply felt conservatism, an anti-elitism, and a particular kind of gender consciousness that would eventually produce a constituency of right-wing women with considerable influence on the party and on American politics. Thus the various efforts of women to engage with the Republicans produced a party that, by the end of the twentieth century, contained critical constituencies of active women deeply at odds with each other. This fact remains a continuing source of instability in the GOP.

Republican women over the course of the twentieth century were by no means a monolithic group speaking with one voice. Some Republican women have been wealthy; others have come from more modest financial means (although few were actually poor). The overwhelming majority of Republican women have been white; yet the Party of Lincoln remained the political home of many middle-class African American women well into the 1940s. Some Republican women were sympathetic to the party's right wing; others shared a commitment to progressive, moderate, or liberal Republicanism. Many Republican women were content to remain on the periphery of politics; yet others fought for a way into the center. Some thought women could achieve the most in party politics by demonstrating their party loyalty and their ability to assimilate to male political styles; others insisted that women in the party should articulate an independent women's voice and fight party insiders on those issues about which they cared deeply. This book traces the tensions between these various constituencies and impulses over sixty years as Republican women attempted to carve a place in partisan politics in the twentieth century.

PARTY WOMEN AND THE DILEMMAS OF WOMEN'S SUFFRAGE

On a sweltering Chicago day in early June 1920, 4,000 members of the National Woman's Party (NWP) picketed outside the national Republican nominating convention, holding a purple and gold banner that read "Vote against the Republican Party as Long as it Blocks Suffrage."[1] The NWP was not playing partisan favorites. In 1916 the NWP (then called the Congressional Union) had campaigned against all Democratic candidates because the head of the ticket, Woodrow Wilson, had refused to endorse women's suffrage.[2] Now it was the Republicans the National Woman's Party demonstrators denounced as the major obstacle to the amendment's success. Alice Paul, chairman of the NWP, insisted that the Republican convention had the power to force Delaware, Vermont, or Connecticut (each with Republican-controlled legislatures) to ratify. Paul accused national GOP leaders of deliberately blocking ratification because of fears that the GOP's opposition to the League of Nations would cause female voters to rally behind the Democrats.[3] Chairman of the Republican National Committee Will Hays denied the National Woman's Party's claim that the Republican Convention had the power to force any state legislature to ratify. Hays suggested instead that the suffragists' attacks revealed their lack of experience in "practical politics." The convention did go on record urging the recalcitrant states to ratify, but without effect.[4] The Republicans were able to prevent neither the NWP picket nor the steady publicity the protesters attracted.

While NWP suffragists demonstrated against the Republican Party outside the convention hall, more than a hundred female partisans ignored the picket and participated in the party's proceedings, hoping to influence the outcome. They were building on several decades of women's work with the national Republican Party, dating back to 1888 when Ellen Foster began the Women's National Republican Association to assist during campaigns, to educate women about politics, and to advise the party in the interim.[5] In 1920, in addition to the League of Nations, significant issues such as the Volstead Act (legislation to enforce Prohibition) and proposed progressive legislation concerning women and children were at stake. Republican women who participated in the convention wanted to secure a place of influence for women in the party, something their leaders had been pondering since 1916.[6] Indeed, Will Hays and other prominent convention delegates anticipated correctly that women would have the vote in time for the November elections. Consequently, they solicited Republican women's recommendations for party reforms that would reflect the changes in the electorate that woman suffrage would bring.

On Sunday, 6 June, the female delegates and alternates to the Republican convention ("some of the brainiest women in America") met to discuss their goals and demands.[7] Two of the most prominent of these women were Mary Garrett Hay and Ruth Hanna McCormick, both well known as suffragists and Republicans. Hay and McCormick were members of the original Republican Women's Executive Committee formed by the RNC Executive Committee in 1918 as an advisory committee on women.[8] The sixty-three-year-old Hay had begun her political work decades earlier in the Woman's Christian Temperance Union (WCTU) and had been an active suffragist since the 1880s. Hay was also a close friend of suffragist Carrie Catt, with whom she had shared a home since the death of Catt's husband in 1905. In 1917 Hay was named chairman of the New York Republican Party's platform committee and succeeded in convincing the committee to endorse suffrage for women. That same year, the National American Woman Suffrage Association (NAWSA) sent Hay to Washington as its "Republican steer" to work with congressional Republicans on behalf of suffrage.[9] McCormick, who was forty in 1920, was the daughter of the powerful Republican boss, the late Mark Hanna, and wife of a Republican senator from Illinois, Medill McCormick. Ruth McCormick had been involved with various progressive reform movements in Chicago and had lobbied the Illinois legislature on behalf of the Illinois Consumers' League. Along with her husband, she had taken an active part in the 1912 Progressive Party campaign. She lobbied for passage of the 1913 suffrage bill in Illinois and later headed the Congressional Committee of NAWSA.[10]

In contrast to the NWP picketers, Hay and McCormick wanted to work from inside their party. Yet the two Republicans differed over strategy in ways that reflected conflicting understandings of the meaning and promise of women's new rights. Hay, wanting action that was both visible and meaningful, advocated that the party set up a separate, parallel women's organization that would move women quickly into the official party organization. For every existing male position, Hay proposed that a female position be created. McCormick was wary of this approach. If women insisted on parallel or equal representation, McCormick feared, they might find themselves segregated within the party, without any substantive power. She believed women should seek committee chairmanships and other positions as individuals and proposed that the party women demand "adequate" rather than equal representation.[11] To demand equal representation, McCormick's reservations implied, might ironically undermine hopes for equality.

Both arguments had appeal, indicating that Hay and McCormick were confronting difficult questions about difference and political power that were not neatly answered. Political women faced the lasting impossibility of dissolving "women" into the larger humanity (or, in this case, simply into a political party) without losing the potential for some women to identify common interests and needs.[12] Woman suffrage required new understandings of women's citizenship. Did enfranchised women now possess (with men) an ungendered, public identity as "citizens" that was separate from their private, female identities? Were women special kinds of citizens, marked by their sex, with different concerns and sensibilities, requiring different political appeals? Did the full citizenship promised by the Nineteenth Amendment mean women should stop articulating their needs and interests separately or was women's citizenship still something unique and different from men's? Did the Woman Citizen speak with one voice?

The difficulties in answering these questions were particularly apparent when women tried to enter male-dominated political institutions such as parties. These issues were not just typical of the 1920s but persisted (although not always in the same form) throughout the twentieth century, indicating the enormous obstacles to fully integrating women into party politics. Entering party politics, of course, was not an option pursued by all political women. After gaining the right to vote in 1920, many women activists thought they would be wise to stay out of male political institutions altogether and instead continue channeling their political activism—as they had for decades—through all-female reform organizations. Alva Belmont of the National Woman's Party urged women to reject both major political parties and thereby "refus[e] to consort with admitted evils." Women voters could form a powerful new political force, Belmont predicted, but only if they worked together in common cause. She cautioned women against succumbing to the enticements that the two parties were likely to offer in pursuit of women's votes. Do not let the parties "use you as catspaws," Belmont admonished women. "Ignore their flattery. Be strong and self-respecting. Hand back to the wily leaders the empty honors offered bribing for your servitude. They are but crumbs from the bosses' table."[13]

Other leading suffragists did not think women should shun party politics. Carrie Chapman Catt urged women to eschew separatism and join the parties "after intelligent reflection."[14] Catt argued that women would not achieve full political equality until they were as "independent within the party as men."[15] She realized it would be difficult for women to work their way into influential positions within the historically male political parties. But she feared that voting women would have no real political influence unless they did so. Catt herself never joined a political party, but many other politically active women did. These women considered acceptance into the major political parties to be the necessary next step toward full integration into American political life and the best way to achieve their political and personal goals as women and as citizens. In contrast to Belmont's strategy, pursuing partisan politics required that women change their traditional tactic of forming separate organizations and instead that they enter male institutions.

This strategy posed a unique set of problems. Women partisans debated the best ways to create a visible presence of women in the party. They also had to reconcile the competing goals of political advancement within male-dominated organizations with the desire to remain true to whatever legislative agendas and political principles had driven them to politics in the first place. In other words, they had to determine whether women's long-term goals were best achieved through loyalty to party or to principle. A less acknowledged problem concerned appeals to universal womanhood in a politics framed by partisanship and in a party that claimed African American women as among its most loyal constituents. How male and female Republicans thought about post-suffrage party reforms reveals much about the challenges woman suffrage posed to American party politics. As male and female partisans sought to reshape the political parties in response to woman suffrage, they did not merely confront problems of institutional reform. They also wrestled with complex questions about the nature of men and women and about the meanings of equality and power. For women who chose to work within the party organization, balancing gender and party interests would present ongoing problems over the next decades.

★ Although Ruth McCormick's concerns about institutionalized difference would prove to be persistent ones for Republican women, it was Mary Hay's viewpoint that prevailed in 1920. The resolution the women delegates presented to the Republican convention illustrated the general strategy and goals that most partisan women (of both parties and at all levels) would pursue for decades. Republican women demanded the creation of new seats designated for women on the party's committees. The RNC consisted of a national committeeman from each state and territory; ten RNC members formed the Republican National Executive Committee. The women's resolution called for doubling the size of both committees (with women filling the new seats) and installing a woman as assistant secretary of the RNC. The women delegates were only partially successful in 1920. The convention did increase the size of the Executive Committee to include seven women out of fifteen members. The convention rejected what many considered the more important proposal to double the size of the RNC, however.[16] No national committeewomen would be joining the RNC in 1920.

Mary Hay and other Republican women were disappointed. It only exacerbated their frustration when, several weeks later, the Democratic convention easily passed a measure doubling the size of its National Committee in order to include a woman from each state. Mrs. Francis Shinn of the Democratic Women's National Committee was pleased with the RNC's recalcitrance, suggesting that the GOP's inaction had made her committee's job of securing women's votes for the Democrats "as easy as possible."[17] During the presidential campaign that fall, Democratic women compared their party favorably with the opposition on the issue of women's integration. Republican Harriet Upton retorted publicly that the Executive Committee was more important than the full National Committee and that Democratic women did not have seats on the DNC's Executive Committee.[18] Later, however, she complained privately that the Executive Committee was "simply a servant of the National" and that women had to move onto the RNC if they were going to be effective.[19]

Although they disappointed many of the party's leading women, GOP officials were indeed courting powerful women, while hoping to control them by bringing them into the inner circle of party regulars. Fears that enfranchised women might vote as a bloc prompted Democratic

Do You Believe in Equality?

Republican National Committee	Democratic National Committee
Men 50	Men 50
Women 0	Women 50

Intelligent women believe in the ability of their sex. They believe that the woman's point of view, equally with the man's, should be represented in government.

In December, 1916, the Democratic National Committee had admitted a woman to membership. It made the Woman's Bureau an integral part of itself.

The Republican Organization accorded women no such recognition.

In February, 1919, after the close of hostilities had released women from war occupations and restored them to suffrage and political work, the Democratic National Committee doubled itself by receiving into its membership an associate national committeewoman from every state.

At the Democratic National Convention in San Francisco in July of this year a resolution was adopted making regular and permanent election of national committee women to the National Democratic Committee. What had been before a courtesy was thus established a legal right. On the Executive Committee of the National Democratic Committee at that Convention, there were the same number of women as of men, seventeen of each.

The Republican Party, which invites women to work for it, to raise money for it, and to vote for it, HAS NOT ONE WOMAN on its National Committee.

Intelligence demands authority commensurate with responsibility and effort.

That is what the Democratic Party has given women.

That is what the Republican Party has denied them.

If you want to vote for the party which allows you to work not merely FOR it, but WITH it and IN IT,

Vote the Democratic ticket Nov. 2.

Photo (C) Baker

Governor James M. Cox
Democratic Nominee for President

Photo (C) Baker

Franklin D. Roosevelt
Democratic Nominee for Vice-President

Vote the Democratic ticket November 2nd

Democratic National Committee

Democratic Party advertisement targeted to suffragists.
(Woman Citizen 5 [11 September 1920]: 399.)

and Republican party leaders to pursue women's support vigorously in the early 1920s.[20] Leaders of both parties were interested not only in preempting a women's party, but also in ensuring that women would cast their new votes to each party's respective advantage. The women named to the newly expanded Republican Executive Committee in 1920 were not ornamental figureheads beholden to male leaders. They gener-

WOMEN MEMBERS OF REPUBLICAN NATIONAL
EXECUTIVE COMMITTEE

The Republican National Committee was the first national committee of either party to grant official representation to women. They placed women on the *REAL COMMITTEE* that does the work and controls the management of the biggest transaction in American politics—the Presidential Election.

Mrs. Harriet Taylor Upton of Ohio is Vice-Chairman of this *REAL COMMITTEE* which is called the REPUBLICAN NATIONAL EXECUTIVE COMMITTEE. She is one of the active forces at the Mid-West Headquarters in Chicago where she is directing National organization.

Mrs. Christine Bradley South of Kentucky, is Assistant Secretary of the National Committee, as well as a member of the Executive Committee. She is a daughter of the late W. O. Bradley, the first Republican Governor of Kentucky. The organization campaign is being carried on in the Mid-West section under her leadership.

Mrs. Arthur Livermore of New York is Regional Director of the Eastern States. She is in charge of the work of organizing and is conducting the campaign from the New York headquarters of the National Committee.

Mrs. Jeannette Hyde of Utah, Regional Director of the Rocky Mountain States, has headquarters at Salt Lake City. She is personally visiting the Mountain States, having just completed a speaking tour in Montana and Wyoming.

Mrs. Corinne Roosevelt Robinson of New York is in great demand as a speaker. Her engagements cover a wide range of States and she will be actively in the field until Election Day.

Mrs. Medill McCormick of Illinois is Director of Publicity in the Mid-West headquarters. In addition to this big task she is filling many speaking engagements.

Mrs. Manley L. Fosseen of Minnesota is Co-Chairman of the National Speaker's Bureau and is also one of the National's popular campaign speakers. She is at the Chicago headquarters.

Mrs. Katherine Philips Edson of California, Regional Director of the Pacific Coast States, is known as a " Political Leader " among the women of the west. She is carrying on her work from the San Francisco headquarters.

The difference between the kind of recognition given the Republican women and that accorded the Democratic women is marked. The Democratic women have been given places on the Democratic National Committee which meets only once in four years, and then only to fix the date and place of the next convention. It is the National *Executive* Committee which actually conducts the presidential campaign, and on this *REAL COMMITTEE* of real *power* the Republican party appointed women who work side by side with the men in the greatest of all American political responsibilities—WINNING THE ELECTION.

Harriet Taylor Upton

Republican Party advertisement targeted to suffragists.
(Woman Citizen 5 [9 October 1920]: 513.)

ally were nationally or regionally prominent and politically experienced. Like McCormick, Christine Bradley South of Kentucky had served on the original Republican Women's Executive Committee. The other six women were Katherine Philips Edson of California, Carrie Fosseen of Minnesota, Jeannette Hyde of Utah, Henrietta Livermore of New York, Corinne Roosevelt Robinson of New York, and Harriet Upton of Ohio. Most had connections to the suffrage movement, either nationally or in their home states. Upton and Fosseen had been active also in the WCTU.

Together these women represented an effort to balance regional and factional divisions within the party; they came from all regions of the country (except the Deep South, where the party had little meaningful presence). Harriet Upton, a native of Harding's home state of Ohio, became vice chairman of the RNC Executive Committee and she headed the women's campaign for Harding. McCormick and Edson (who had been a member of the California State Committee of the Progressive Party) were brought on to the committee explicitly to represent the Progressive wing of the party. That wing was also represented at least symbolically by Robinson, who was Theodore Roosevelt's sister.[21] Each of the new Executive Committee members was white. In the fall, a black woman, Lethia Fleming of Cleveland, was selected to head a separate black women's advisory committee that was assembled for the 1920 presidential campaign.[22]

The RNC was careful to modify its desire to include nationally prominent women with the demand that they display party loyalty. Mary Hay, although she worked inside the party during the 1920 convention, quickly found she could not go along with these constraints. A committed suffragist, she lent her energies to a campaign to quash the reelection hopes of unrepentant antisuffragist James W. Wadsworth of New York. As Wadsworth was a Republican, party leaders attacked Hay. She responded not by towing the party line but by announcing she would resign her position on the RNC to concentrate on her suffrage work and on the anti-Wadsworth campaign. In effect, Hay was forced out.[23] Other organization women were more able to adapt to the demands of party loyalty. National Executive Committee member Henrietta Livermore (who was also chairman of the New York Republican Women's State Executive Committee) used a standard partisan argument to urge Republican women in New York to support Wadsworth, despite his poor record on suffrage. Republican control of the Senate, the fifty-six-year-old Livermore argued, would be essential to Harding's administration if he became president. Women should therefore support the party as a whole by voting for even its less ideal candidates.[24]

To Mary Hay, principle was not worth sacrificing for the sake of partisanship.[25] Yet for others who had cast their lot with the Republican Party, the choice between principle and partisanship was not so simple. Leading Republican women muffled their dissatisfaction with the institutional reforms accepted at the convention and did their jobs as partisans to sell their party to other women. For women who sincerely sought victory for the GOP and who, furthermore, wanted to prove to male leaders that they could play the game of partisanship, it was necessary to demonstrate this kind of loyalty. The *New York Times* recognized the dilemma of Republican women leaders. Women at the Republican National Convention, the paper reported, put the "soft pedal on expressions of discontent and tried to prevent the spreading of an impression . . . that the male masters of the party machinery were grudging or parsimonious in yielding equal place to the new voters."[26] Balancing the demands of party interest with women's interests *as women* would confound women partisans for decades, culminating in the battle over Ronald Reagan's presidential nomination in 1980.

★ Support for increased representation of women in the party came to rest on arguments about the need to *appeal* to women on the one hand and the need to *reward* women on the other. The National Committee believed it had to convey to women across the country its enthusiasm for women's participation in party affairs, although it often fell short of the expectations of its own women members. During the fall campaign there was much discussion about the efforts of the two parties to appeal to women and about how the new voters would behave. This discussion generated speculation about "women's interest." Neither party seemed to dispute that a "women's interest" existed; each simply presented its own positions as best embodying that interest. Spokeswomen for both parties did this as well, implying the existence of a unified women's interest, yet needing to accommodate the reality that some women were working hard for the other party. Did women in the other party not understand the issues, did they not have women's best interests at heart, or were they dupes of empty promises by male leaders? Women who tried to portray women's issues in partisan terms had to explain the opposition in these ways. Meanwhile, women like Alva Belmont believed women in both parties to be the dupes.

Perhaps the single most important national issue of the campaign was the League of Nations. When journalists and party leaders discussed women's votes, it was often in terms of the League. After ratification of the Nineteenth Amendment, Wall Street betting odds in favor of Harding reportedly dropped from 3 to 1 to 2 to 1, probably because of the League issue.[27] Both parties seemed to agree that women were inherently opposed to war. But would women's allegedly peaceful tendencies mean they would support the League that, according to the Democrats, would reduce the risk of war? Or would they reject the League because it would compel their sons to fight and die in endless foreign disputes, as the Republicans claimed? These different appeals were not merely opportunistic on the part of the parties. Women (particularly progressive women) may have shared certain values, but the connections between those values and ideas about the state and national interest were not monolithic and could be made compatible with different political ideologies.

The League of Nations was not the only women's campaign issue in 1920. The League of Women Voters certainly tried to insert a progressive women's agenda into the political discussion. An LWV delegation led by Maude Wood Park had presented both party conventions in the summer with a set of planks concerning women's citizenship and the protection of women and children. The Democratic Convention adopted twelve of the LWV's fifteen proposals, including support for the abolition of many forms of child labor, a minimum wage for working women, and a plan for federal and state cooperation in promoting care for pregnant women and infants. Although leading Republican women had spoken in favor of the LWV planks at the GOP convention, only five of the planks were included in the Republican platform. Later in October, responding to the criticisms of Republican women, Harding held a "Social Justice Day" during which he declared his support for almost every part of the LWV program. In the view of historian Blanche Wiesen Cook, Harding's move persuaded the overwhelming majority of those progressive women who voted in November to choose Harding.[28] Once elected, however, Harding did not follow through with this program.

Northern black women responded enthusiastically to their new political status, and their loyalty to the Party of Lincoln was solid. The South, however, was dominated by the Democrats, and blacks were largely denied the right to vote. Still, Republicans did attempt to secure the votes of African American women in parts of the South where the party felt it had something to gain by doing so. Southern whites feared the potential of woman suffrage to disrupt white rule, in some cases believing that black women would be more difficult to disenfranchise than black men. Republican efforts were limited to those areas where local competition between Democrats and Republicans was tight enough to give Republicans a reason to court African American voters.[29]

In November, Harding carried the day, winning 404 electoral votes to Cox's 127. It is impossible to know exactly how women voted, since accurate polling data are not available. Contemporary observers and historians generally have agreed that, although women did not vote in high numbers, the majority of those who did vote for president chose the Republican Harding. Scholars usually do not understand Harding's edge with new voters in 1920 as a preference of women in general for Republicans. Rather, they see it as a reflection of the greater inclination of native-born, Protestant, northern women (who tended to be Republicans) to register to vote initially when compared with immigrant, Catholic, or southern women.[30] Furthermore, as Freeman notes, the Republican Party was also historically the party of reform, retaining that association "even when it became dominated by a business elite," as occurred in the 1920s.[31]

Women members of the Republican Executive Committee used the consensus that women had voted for Harding to press their case for increased representation in the party.[32] Indeed, at the first meeting of the RNC Executive Committee after Harding's victory, the women members called for women's advancement in terms of the good of the party. Because American women clearly were "eager for political activity," Harriet Upton and her colleagues argued, the RNC needed to ensure that it would be the GOP that continued to benefit from that enthusiasm. The women proposed that the RNC maintain a headquarters for women with its own budget (a Women's Division), that it appoint two national women's organizers, and that three members of the RNC be appointed as liaisons between the women members of the Executive Committee and the still all-male RNC.[33] The motion carried.

Yet women organizers had reason to be skeptical of the RNC's commitment to them. The women Executive Committee members still were not members of the full Republican National Committee and so continued to be left out of important meetings.[34] Although the RNC passed a resolution in June 1921 calling for the RNC to include an associate national committeewoman from each state and territory, this gesture was fairly empty since the associates could not vote. Not until the next presidential convention, in 1924, was the status of the women on the National Committee upgraded to full membership, with voting privileges.[35] Furthermore, Upton's efforts to plan for women's activities were handicapped by the RNC's urgent need to pay bills incurred from the 1920 campaign; any new expenses were not welcome.[36] The party in the 1920s did not typically carry out partisan activities during off years. Women like Upton, however, recognized that winning female voters would require sustained, year-round efforts at political socialization. Efforts along those lines would not be initiated by the Republican National Committee, however, but by local party organizations and by women acting outside the party.

Other efforts to increase the participation of women in official party affairs focused on women as convention delegates and state and local party officials. In keeping with its pragmatic interest in increasing the visibility of women within the party, the RNC wanted to ensure women's presence at the 1924 presidential convention. Democrats in 1920 had made much of the fact that more women delegates and alternates had participated in their convention than had participated in the Republican proceedings.[37] But efforts to increase the number of Republican women delegates produced limited results. Traditionally, delegates to the Republican National Convention had been allotted to the states proportionally, according to population. Each state sent four at-large delegates and two from each congressional district to the convention. Delegates were not elected democratically by state party members but were selected by state party leaders. These delegates tended to be prominent local Republicans who had made significant contributions to the party. Senators or governors typically held at-large seats. Being a delegate was an indication of prestige, and men held their status as delegates for decades. As one committeeman later observed, district delegateships were "only infrequently surrendered by the men."[38] Short of democratizing the entire process or forcing prominent, longtime supporters to surrender their seats, the sole way that large numbers of women would attend the 1924 convention as delegates was if the number of delegates itself was increased.

In fact, in the early 1920s the party was undertaking a change that would indeed increase the number of delegates. The party put delegate allotment formulas in place that rewarded those states successful in electing Republicans by awarding them additional delegate slots. Because this reform involved creating new delegate slots, some of its supporters presented it as a pro-woman reform—to increase the participation of women in party affairs, which would be both just and a boon to the party.[39] Its real purpose, however, was to decrease what proponents saw as the undue and corrupt influence of the southern states on the party. Supporters of the change viewed southern black delegates as an embarrassment to the party. Because their states had no real Republican Party organizations and did not deliver Republican victories on election day, southern delegates to the conventions were considered to be for sale. In other words, whichever candidate for the nomination was able to offer the most to a southern delegate (in terms of patronage or money) would be assured of that delegate's support. Having abandoned the idea that African Americans represented a potential for the GOP in the South, many white Republicans had for decades wanted to reduce the power of the southern states at the national conventions to something more in line with the region's performance in elections.[40] In 1923 the RNC finally acted.

This controversial proposal did not pass without objection. Several African American committeemen from the southern states argued that the RNC was unfairly punishing southern blacks (among the most loyal of all Republicans) for the poor performance of the GOP in the South. Henry Lincoln Johnson of Georgia described in poignant detail the impossible situation faced by African American men and women who tried to register to vote in his home state. Why punish black voters for not being able to produce Republican victories in places where they were not able to vote? Johnson protested. In suggesting that the Republican Party could better address the problem by working to enforce the civil rights of African Americans in the southern states, Johnson asked, "Why not the Republican Party first give me the chance to vote, and then if I fail penalise [sic] me?"[41] Most of the members of the RNC, anxious as they were to appease the demands of white women, remained unconcerned about possible black defections. The creation of "women's seats" on the RNC from all states did mean the addition of two African American women, Mary Booze of Mississippi and Mamie Williams of Georgia, to the committee. The influence of black Republicans overall, however, was diminishing. By the late 1920s, when it became apparent that the "women's vote" was not the powerful force that many had anticipated, white women nonetheless had institutionalized their representation within the party. Black RNC members, however, had not attempted to solidify their presence on the RNC as a special constituency marked by difference as women had. Instead, members like Johnson argued their cause in the language of regional representation. And they did this at a time when the party considered southern black voters to be expendable.

Despite Johnson's objections, the reform was passed, creating 111 new

delegate slots for 1924 and providing the possibility of women delegates being selected. It was apparently understood that state committees would select women to fill those new seats, although that understanding was not mandated. This reform does seem to have had at least
a temporary effect. In 1924, 120 women sat as delegates at the Republican Convention, or 11 percent of the total. As with other matters
pertaining to the representation of women in the party, however, the
states did not always adhere to the suggestions of the RNC. New Jersey
selected 2 women as delegates to the 1924 convention. After a bitter
fight, Pennsylvania selected 1. Seven states sent no women delegates at
all. After 1924 the perception that political parties needed to increase
women's representation waned. The percentage of women delegates at
the GOP convention dropped considerably beginning in 1928 and would
not reach 1924 levels again until 1952.[42]

Male and female party reformers also wanted to see women move
onto local party councils. The RNC encouraged state, district, county,
and precinct committees to appoint female vice chairmen to serve with
the male chairmen as the heads of these organizations. The RNC had no
authority over state organizations, however; state parties did not embrace the national model unless they felt it served their particular interests. Due to the peculiar nature of the party system in place since the
1890s, the Democratic and Republican Parties were typically not competitive at the local level. A dominant local party (of either persuasion),
assured of future victories, had little reason to disrupt the status quo
voluntarily by admitting women into its ranks. One Pennsylvania observer noted that state party committees easily passed measures mandating equal representation in states where the two parties were evenly
matched. In solidly Republican states like her own, she complained,
as well as in the Democratic South, such measures did not pass without a struggle.[43] Harriet Upton described the situation somewhat differently. Upton believed women encountered the greatest difficulty in
states where political parties were divided into factions, each faction
being afraid women's votes would help the other and so preferring to
exclude women altogether.[44]

In either case, the basic problem was clear: women could not force
men to set aside tradition and open the party councils to women. Their
choice was to convince male party members that the move was expedi-
ent or to get state legislatures to pass 50-50 laws mandating equal representation for women on state party committees. The League of Women
Voters, and women active in the Democratic and Republican Parties,

pursued so-called 50-50 laws at the state level. Throughout most of the nineteenth century, parties had been essentially private organizations. Beginning in the 1890s states had begun passing laws transforming the parties into public institutions subject to laws and regulations (a process not completed until 1943 when the Supreme Court finally struck down the all-white primaries conducted in many southern states).[45] In the 1920s women activists were able to pursue legal solutions to women's exclusion from party counsels by seeking state laws that would have made compulsory the equal representation of men and women on state party committees. By 1929, eighteen states had some form of 50-50 law governing both parties.[46]

Although Republican women did achieve equal representation on the National Committee as well as on some state and local committees, they quickly became frustrated with the results of this much-sought reform. Their frustration suggests an additional problem with the "seats for women" strategy. Women party officials and convention delegates, although intended to be representatives of women, usually were not elected through a democratic process—neither Republican women nor Republicans as a whole had the privilege of choosing these leaders. Rather, they were selected by existing committee members. After passage of the resolution doubling the size of the RNC, each committeeman was told to pick a woman as his counterpart. Although in some states the committeewoman was selected in consultation with prominent GOP women leaders, often she was chosen because she was in sympathy with whatever state political faction the committeeman was allied. In many cases these women were socially prominent—wives of business or political leaders or of newspaper editors. Creating women's seats on the party committees gave ordinary women no more input into the party organization than ordinary men had.

Republican women leaders regularly complained (sometimes openly, sometimes under a veil of polite deference) about the lack of respect, influence, representation, and power the party accorded women. They advocated such reforms as equal representation of women on all subcommittees of the RNC, consultation by the chairman with women members concerning women appointments, 50-50 rules for the makeup of state committees, and increased budgets for women's activities. At times success was forthcoming; on other occasions, the concerns of women were referred to committees and ignored. In 1965, forty-five years after suffrage, Republican women leaders were still suggesting to the RNC that the "gentlemen in this Party would be very smart if they would take the ladies into their confidence and utilize them on policy-making boards and committees."[47]

Mandated seats for women on Republican Party committees and as delegates, preferably in numbers equal to men, was a rallying point for party organization women who were active in GOP politics after 1920. Partisan women generally appear to have agreed on the importance of these goals; when given the opportunity to make demands on the party, these are the types of reforms women promoted. As Ruth McCormick had predicted, however, this strategy of pursuing separate, new positions for women ultimately ghettoized women's activities within the party. Because the party created *new* positions for women, women did not vie for positions within the party that held real authority. As a member of the New Jersey Republican State Central Committee, Miriam Lippincott found that the committee hardly met and that, when it did meet, "a few resolutions of no importance were passed, and a motion made to adjourn." Afterward, the men met without the women, conducted the real business, and later handed their decisions to the entire committee "on a silver salver, as it were."[48] Historians have generally agreed that women on both parties' committees had relatively little power, particularly by the end of the 1920s when it became clear that women's votes were not going to be as decisive as initially thought.[49] Why, then, did partisan women pursue this strategy for entering party politics?

★ Certainly there were other strategies in circulation. One alternative was identified with Alice Paul. Her National Woman's Party was not actually a political party in the traditional sense. It was instead an interest group whose purpose was to use its influence and voting power to support candidates who favored the full equality of women and to defeat those who opposed it.[50] The Women's Joint Congressional Committee, an umbrella organization of women's reform organizations, also pursued sex-defined interest group lobbying. But some women activists thought they could not really influence politics if they chose these strategies. GOP women partisans denied that women working exclusively within separate women's organizations could facilitate women's entry into formal political life. They viewed equal representation on the party committees as critical, believing that, once on these committees, women would have a voice in writing platform planks and in selecting the candidates who received official and financial backing from the party. Representation on party committees, partisan women hoped, would move women candidates onto the ballot and "women's issues" onto the platforms. A separate women's party would not do that. Nor would nonpartisan study groups like the League of Women Voters. Although partisan women's evaluation of the influence of party committees may have been exaggerated, it did influence the political strategies they chose to pursue.

While championing women's advancement and the need to institutionalize their presence, partisan women routinely went on record as opposed to "sex antagonism" in politics—something they implied advocates of a separate women's party supported. Alma Lorimer of Philadelphia, despite being an independent-minded Republican who was not hesitant to voice her differences with the party, declared "sex antagonism" and the idea of a women's party to be "the negation of the ideal for which most of us have been working."[51] Did demands for the designation of separate female positions on party committees constitute "sex antagonism"? Apparently not, since many of the same women who supported the creation of these positions were also foes of "sex antagonism." Yet the justifications for women's seats did rest on assumptions about essential differences between men and women.

A belief that women were fundamentally different from men was widespread in the 1920s. A related idea, that women had a special, gender-defined role to play in politics, had been promoted by many suffrage advocates before 1920. If women's biology or social roles made them inherently more peaceful, more nurturing, and less corrupt than men, as voters they could perhaps end war, pass needed social legislation, stamp out alcohol abuse, and clean up the dirtiness of male politics. This rhetoric of difference influenced the RNC's assessment of how women could—or should—be incorporated into the party after suffrage.

Creating a "separate sphere" for women within the party was comprehensible to both men and women. This strategy had certain advantages for women, although many would grow disillusioned with it. If women voters were understood to be different from their male counterparts, then reaching them, appealing to them, and persuading them to vote for Republican candidates would require special strategies, distinct from the traditional methods of appealing to male voters. Who better to run these efforts than women themselves? In this sense, insisting that women be given separate campaign headquarters and their own positions on committees *because they were women* was a useful tactic: it led the RNC to create offices, positions, campaigns, and budgets specifically for women. Moreover, it would provide a means for a small number of organization women, based in the RNC Women's Division, to gain influence over the next decades as the mobilizers of critical party constituencies.

If women had insisted on a fungible equality of women with men, it would have been more problematic to argue that women needed special representatives on the RNC. And without that argument, women simply would not have moved onto the committee in large numbers. The strategy of creating separate positions for women meant that women would not need to challenge the seats of the national committeemen, many of whom had held their seats for years. Doubling the size of the party committees produced quick, visible, painless results.

Women based their arguments for creating separate positions within the party not only on beliefs about women's difference but also on arguments about the justice of expanding opportunities for other women. Yet women members did what they could to deny that this was the case. To be *too much* an advocate of women's advancement was to slip into the dreaded "sex antagonism." Difference was not the same as "sex antagonism." Difference was natural and could include a proper notion of gender equality. "Sex antagonism" was equality run amok. It implied competition rather than cooperation between the now equal sexes. Women who wanted to enter a male bastion like the Republican Party had to be careful to insist that they would do nothing to create "sex antagonism."

At the same time, some women considered the real source of "sex antagonism" to be men's unwillingness to accord women the influence they deserved. Miriam Lippincott of New Jersey made this complaint in an address before the Republican Women of Pennsylvania in 1924. "At first the men were afraid of us and gave us what we wanted, but during this last election they gave us little or nothing. Turning us down did more to inspire us than anything they could have done." Lippincott went on to assert that "sex antagonism" was arising because men "refuse[d]" to put women on committees, councils, and boards. "We must," she insisted, "work shoulder to shoulder."[52]

After suffrage, partisan women argued for women's seats on party committees because it would help the party at the polls (by demonstrating to the female electorate that the party supported women's advancement) and because women were different from men (requiring their own party representatives). Yet the acquisition of suffrage supposedly had leveled the playing field and enabled women to compete fairly with men as equals. There was something unsettling about championing women's new equality brought on by suffrage while wanting simultaneously to see immediate and *visible* results of that equality.

Harriet Hubbs, a reporter on women's topics for Philadelphia's *Evening Public Ledger*, expressed this tension in an essay she wrote for a Republican women's magazine. In 1923 state senator Frank Smith had introduced a bill prepared by the Pennsylvania League of Women Voters that would have required equal representation of men and women on both of Pennsylvania's state party committees. Hubbs supported this 50-50 law but was aware of the reasons why some might oppose it. "Ordinarily," she allowed, "it might be said, that in view of the fact that men and women now have equal voting rights, it was not necessary to provide for equal representation on state committees and that such provision represented a kind of favoritism or discrimination." The reasons why Hubbs nevertheless gave unqualified support to the Smith bill are worth quoting at length because their awkwardness demonstrates her struggle to articulate an intricate and nuanced understanding of what equality should mean:

> Practically, however, such legislation is required so that women may have not only equal representation, but also an equal chance and an equal voice in the councils of the party. . . . The state committee represents the men and the women of the party. Unlike branches of the government, the state committee does not represent all of the people; it represents only the men and women voters in the party. Consequently it seems clear to me that the men and women voters should be represented equally on the state committee, otherwise it is conceivable that only men would be selected, just as it is conceivable, of course, that only women would be selected. The number chosen in each district compared to the whole number of voters in the district is exceedingly small, and unless the law makes provision for equal representation, the result would be exceedingly unequal representation. With unequal representation, the views of one element in the party would be dominated by the views of another.[53]

For Hubbs, there was something unequal, or unrepresentative, about a political committee consisting only of men (or only of women). She made her argument based on difference: men and women were different; therefore, any committee consisting of one or the other sex was not representative. But she alluded also to power, recognizing that women's acquisition of the vote did not mean necessarily that they had "an equal chance" or "an equal voice" within politics. Women would not break into previously all-male institutions like political parties simply because they now had the right to vote. Individual men would not freely give up their committee seats to make room for women. The allocation of those seats was rooted in traditions that equal suffrage for women alone could not affect. Thus Hubbs, and many other women in the state, supported legislation that would force the political parties to accept women into their decision-making bodies. Although her focus was political parties rather than employers or educational institutions, Hubbs was articulating, in a rather tortured way, what affirmative action advocates fifty years later would develop into a powerful legal argument.

Hubbs only went so far as to advocate equal representation on party committees. She did not suggest that women also required their own designated representatives in state legislatures, Congress, or the White House. The "representation of women on the committees," Hubbs concluded, was "a political problem separate and distinct from the general question of the right of men and women to participate in political and governmental functions on the same footing."[54] Neither did she suggest that any other "element in the party" (blacks, Jews, or German Americans, for example) also ought to have mandated representation to avoid "unequal representation." Women and men apparently were different from each other in such a unique way that equality between them could not involve one sex standing in for the other (whereas providing fair representation for other "element[s] in the party" did not present this problem).

Hubbs did not explain this unique difference in any greater detail. Alma Lorimer, however, offered clues as to how at least some women understood the relationship of men and women in politics. Lorimer's vision of equality in party politics was one based not on the ideal of an ungendered public sphere but on a model of modern marriage. In this modern family, women were not subservient to men but did have different strengths and roles from those of their husbands. Both woman's and man's place was in the home, according to Lorimer, for "a home is not the affair of one person, either man or woman. It can only be established and perpetuated by working in harmony toward a common goal." In Lorimer's view, the concerns of the home were political concerns, and all politics ultimately concerned the home. Woman's special responsibility for children meant only that she (following Lorimer's own example) should wait until her children were grown before pursuing her political responsibilities. "Just as man is needed in the home," Lorimer argued, "woman is needed in politics" because women brought to politics a realism, common sense, and resistance to sentimentality that men lacked.[55] The analogy between politics and marriage was something that male politicians had not yet grasped, Lorimer complained elsewhere. She pointed out that "the House of Bishops recently decided to omit the word 'obey' from the marriage service." Yet the male politician "still expects the woman that he has taken as his partner in political life to love, honor, and obey him without question. She is still far from being his confidant and his helpmate though he is willing that she should help to pay the household expenses."[56]

By the 1950s the analogy between modern marriage and political parties would become a common metaphor describing Republican women's relationship to their party. In the 1920s Alma Lorimer expressed this analogy more directly than did other women who struggled to articulate new meanings of equality. But much of what seemed contradictory in other party women—for example, the rejection of sex antagonism while insisting on the distinct needs and qualifications of women—makes more sense when understood in terms of this model. Men and women partisans were not to be antagonistic to each other, but each was to respect and recognize the unique contributions of the other toward their common political goals—goals whose roots were in the home and the family. Viewing these ideas about political equality in terms of a marriage model also illuminates one way in which white Republican women generally were able to ignore questions of differences among women. If women related to men in their parties as they did to men in their homes, then questions of white women's relationship to black women in the party were simply irrelevant.

They were not irrelevant, however, to black women themselves, large numbers of whom were highly active in Republican Party politics. As the party reorganized itself in the 1920s, questions about the relationship of black women to white women mirrored questions about white women's relationship to the party's male leaders. Nannie Burroughs, prominent black club leader, suffragist, and Republican, turned the rhetoric of white women's demands back on itself. "In the fight for reforms," Burroughs said in a 1923 article, white Republican women were "overlooking or undervaluing their greatest moral asset—the Negro woman." In language that directly echoed many of white women's criticisms of male party leaders, Burroughs urged white Republican women, for their own sake, to accept black women into their councils. In addition, she criticized white women for preferring to select African American women as leaders who were not the choice of black women themselves.[57]

The Republican Party did engage African American women organizers in its campaign work. In 1924 and 1928 respectively, Hallie Q. Brown and Daisy Lampkin led the black women's campaigns for the Republican Party. Both were leaders in the National Association of Colored Women (NACW) and thus ideal for the job of mobilizing middle-class black women.[58] These campaigns were conducted under the auspices of the Republican Women's Division, rather than the Colored Division campaign. African American women had a logical home in both organizations but were not welcomed as full partners in either.

In 1928 black women worked hard on Herbert Hoover's campaign. As recognition for their part in Hoover's victory, Burroughs wanted the RNC, among other things, to establish a permanent headquarters for African American women in Washington. In her request, which she channeled through her ally at the RNC Women's Division, Sallie Hert, Burroughs compared her appeal with the demands that white women had made earlier. She urged Hert to consider how white women would feel if "they were not given any group consideration when they have group needs." As did Ruth McCormick, Harriet Hubbs, and others, Burroughs recognized that there were traps embedded in this line of argument. Like the white women who insisted that their demands were not motivated by "sex antagonism," Burroughs maintained that black women were not seeking "any special consideration because we are colored." Yet, like white women, Burroughs also feared that the alternative to "special" consideration might be no consideration at all.[59]

This uncertainty about whether reforms targeting women's representation in the party really indicated equality or whether they reified sexual (or racial) difference in ways that undermined women's attempts to be taken seriously illustrates what Nancy Cott has called the "dual legacy" of the suffrage campaign. Advocates of woman suffrage had argued their cause in terms of *both* women's difference from men and their equality to men; residue of both arguments lingered after suffrage.[60] As they had during the suffrage movement, many women activists simultaneously maintained that women should be understood as equal to *and* different from men. The same was true of partisan women who struggled to carve a place for their sex in party politics.[61] African American women partisans, like Nannie Burroughs, complicated the problem further by raising troubling questions about differences in status and interests among women. These observations do not suggest that partisan women were confused or naively inconsistent. Rather, they suggest that they perceived the complexity of realizing their new rights in a society that held up individualism and equality as fundamental ideals, but that also clung to equally powerful notions concerning the superiority of whites to nonwhites and about women's fundamental differences from men.[62]

★ The need for the political parties to appeal to the newly enfranchised suggests some of the dilemmas inherent to democratization. The Nineteenth Amendment increased the number of individuals who had the right of franchise. The extension of suffrage to women, however, did not increase the numbers of some abstract, ungendered electorate. To assess, or to demonstrate, the effects of suffrage reform, those citizens had to be understood not as individuals but in terms of their group characteristics: Were *women* voting? Were *women* holding elected office? Were *women* being accepted into the councils of the political parties? Unlike, for example, the large number of citizens who were registered to vote under the 1993 "motor-voter" law, those enfranchised by the Nineteenth Amendment were readily identifiable as different from the older electorate. The extent of women's integration into political life was something that could be visually experienced and, in some cases, counted and measured. Both male and female Republicans had reasons to promote visible signs that the party accepted women.

Central to the effect of woman suffrage on political life, according to Kristi Andersen, was the renegotiation of gender boundaries. Although woman suffrage erased one boundary defining political rights and appropriate political behavior, new boundaries emerged after 1920. For example, women were more likely to serve as political officeholders at the local or state level than at the national level, partly because they could do so without appearing to abandon their traditional ties to the home. Certain government offices (state superintendent of schools) became "women's" positions, whereas others (state attorney general) did not. Women in political office were expected to "remain womanly, to avoid displaying political ambition, and to be interested primarily in a narrow range of women's issues."[63] Existing beliefs that women's political concerns stemmed from family responsibilities and a disinterested commitment to the public good (rather than personal ambition) influenced the configuration of new gender boundaries of appropriate political behavior. So too did men's efforts to ensure that "real" politics remained a male province. These new boundaries would remain more or less in place until the 1970s.

Gender boundaries were also redrawn within political parties. As the gender boundaries that had kept women off party committees eroded, new boundaries distinguishing male and female partisanship arose. One crucial way in which these boundaries were redrawn was around the concept of party loyalty. If one were truly a party loyalist (which men presented to women as a vital component of partisanship and advancement), it was necessary to transcend one's personal views or agendas (to sacrifice one's "independence") for the good of the party as a whole. While insisting that women did not want to become members of the RNC merely to enhance their own "dignity and honor," Henrietta Livermore offered some cautiously critical observations of the position of women on the RNC in the 1920s. Men had a tendency, Livermore suggested politely, to select for party positions "women of more or less inferior ability because they feel more safe with those women . . . than they do with those women of greater ability who have more [independence]."[64] What to Livermore was women's "independence" was to many men—particularly those already resistant to women's entry into formal politics—women's lack of party discipline and loyalty.

To be sure, male partisans frequently feuded among themselves and the party already contained bitter, opposing factions before women's suffrage. But concerns about undisciplined behavior and lack of party loyalty came to focus on women after 1920. Women threatened to disrupt the functioning of the party if they took sides in intraparty disputes or pursued their own agenda. Republican women expressing "group concerns" risked being accused of "sex antagonism" or of lacking loyalty. Mary Hay concluded that the benefits of party involvement were not great enough to merit the compromises demanded by party loyalty. Other women, like Harriet Upton, decided that such a bargain was justified and accepted positions as party officials. For women on party committees, concerns about being labeled disloyal were real. Even the most committed to women's equality would be generally diplomatic and restrained in their demands once they had aligned their interests with those of the party. In holding out an elusive standard of "party loyalty" as the key to admission to the inner circles of party politics, male Republicans found an effective tool for ultimately muting the voices of women who served on party committees. But certain women partisans continued to see this route as desirable and formed a base in the party organization as committeewomen and sometimes as paid RNC staffers.

From those positions they concentrated on a strategy that emphasized women's partisan loyalty and the importance of women to electoral victories, and that pursued demands for further institutional consideration based on those claims. They were often frustrated.

Other Republican women, however, pursued an independent route they thought could combine partisanship with their own political values, including a tradition of independence. These women in the 1920s created their own understandings of partisanship not always recognizable or appealing to Old Guard party leaders. Party loyalty and discipline were new concepts for those women who had worked outside formal political institutions during their earlier public activism. Some women had difficulty understanding, Henrietta Livermore noted, why they should have party loyalty. Indeed many women believed that there was "something not quite so desirable among those who have party loyalty and regularity as there is in those who exercise more independence."[65] To Livermore, it was imperative that the RNC confront women's concerns about party loyalty by giving women real, rather than token, responsibilities.

Yet there was more to women's doubts about partisanship than Livermore's complaints that the official organizations failed to give a few women meaningful duties. While many female party leaders had been involved with the GOP for some time, this was not the case for the mass of potential Republican women voters. For most women, the very idea of party politics connoted political machines, corruption, unsavory public spaces, and issues and rituals they did not understand. The world of party politics appeared as a thoroughly masculine culture of which many American women wanted no part. Instead, Republican women interested in politics formed their own partisan organizations. This was something Democratic women did as well. Emily Newell Blair, Harriet Upton's counterpart with the Democratic National Committee, encouraged the formation of women's Democratic clubs. In Blair's view, these clubs could "attract women who might not otherwise be drawn into party work," be a "proving ground for the development of woman's leadership," and provide an opportunity to publicize party policies. Furthermore, in Blair's view, women's partisan clubs presented a "technique" for organizing that women already understood.[66]

Blair promoted the development of women's Democratic clubs from her position with the DNC. Republican women's clubs developed somewhat more sporadically and more independently, at least at first. Decades before 1920, Republican women had already begun organizing themselves into partisan women's clubs—Republican in name, but not necessarily connected to the official party. It was through this club movement that large numbers of women eventually became involved in Republican politics, often with goals, strategies, and sensibilities that diverged from those women officials whose Republican work was conducted primarily through the party's official organizations.

SO MANY JOAN OF ARCS

★ THE POLITICAL STYLE OF

INDEPENDENT CLUBWOMEN

Over the next decades, some women on the party commit-
tees would continue to call for greater influence, but only a small number of the country's women could ever become active Republicans this
way. Women's Republican clubs, by contrast, had enormous potential as
a grass-roots movement. Because these clubs were, for the most part,
established outside the official party, Republican clubwomen would be
much less restrained by concerns about party loyalty than women working on party committees. Organizing outside the party committees,
clubwomen were free to define partisanship and their political interests
on their own terms.

In their clubs, women fashioned a political style based on the ways
they defined female partisanship.[1] The political style of Republican clubwomen, unlike that of many other women activists of their time, was
explicitly connected to party politics. Although some clubs formed that
were tightly controlled by local party organizations, this chapter concerns itself with clubs that were more independent. The founders of
these clubs did not consider the advancement of the party their primary
purpose. Rather they explored how party politics could be used to advance their own political agenda. Often they understood this agenda to
be an explicitly female one. In the case of black clubwomen, this agenda
was tied firmly to advancing the interests of African Americans in politics. In either case, Republican clubwomen displayed no intention of
abandoning the values, separate organizations, or independence that
had characterized middle-class women's politics to that point.

★ In the fall of 1936, Iowa's *Jefferson Bee* printed a nostalgic recollec-
tion of the parades, banners, and bands of nineteenth-century political
campaigns. "While political campaigns are still waged with vigor, and
are often enlivened with spectacular oratory," the *Bee*'s writer noted,

"they do not compare in picturesqueness and enthusiasm with those of the old days." The piece inspired an irritated response from sixty-nine-year-old Ella Taylor of Traer, an organizer of Republican women in rural Tama County. Commenting on the *Bee*'s wistful reminiscences in her regular women's column in the *Traer Star-Clipper*, Taylor recalled old-time political parades in Traer complete with elaborate floats, headed by the Traer band, and followed by torchbearers. "Of course," Taylor wrote, with sarcasm typical for her writings on women's exclusion from politics, "there were no women because it was in the days when the women were classed with the Indians and the idiots." In those days, she recalled, every schoolhouse held a political meeting during the weeks before an election at which speakers and debaters addressed the issues of the campaign. Taylor had begged her husband to take her to one of these meetings, but women were not welcome. "Why should they [be]?" Taylor asked rhetorically. "They couldn't vote and they only took up room that ought to be given to a voter."[2]

For many years, most historians have echoed Taylor's depiction of nineteenth-century partisan politics as steeped in male rituals from which women generally were excluded. Party activity took place in male spaces—saloons, barbershops, and middle-class social clubs—from which women were barred either explicitly or by custom. Even when women were present at parades or rallies, they were usually spectators or employed symbolically as female embodiments of political principles or cultural icons.[3] More recently historians have begun to uncover a greater presence of women in nineteenth-century partisan political activity than had previously been appreciated.[4] Indeed, as historians have begun to emphasize, "[l]ong before national woman suffrage, [women] entered parties, worked in campaigns, and sometimes held political office."[5]

Republican women already were forming partisan clubs by the end of the nineteenth century.[6] At this time, other women's clubs were exploding in numbers. It was in these female voluntary organizations (most of which were nonpartisan), that American middle-class women in large numbers pursued their own political agendas and developed their own political style with accompanying values, rituals, spaces, and strategies. Michael McGerr describes this as a "voluntarist style," embraced by middle-class women before 1900 and again after 1920. This style was issue-driven, focused on gathering information and promoting education about public problems, and relied on connections between domestic responsibilities and public life to justify women's political engagement.[7] These mass organizations of women developed a "critical approach to male public life." Women helped reshape public life by combining the values associated with "women's sphere" (such as morality, purity, and education), newly created public institutions (women-only clubs, charity organizations, and single-issue lobbying groups), and new understandings of what fields were proper concerns for politics and government (family and social matters, for example).[8]

Certainly there was no monolithic women's politics. Women's particular interests varied, depending not only on race and class but on the region of the country in which they lived, on whether they were urban or rural dwellers, on the occupations of their husbands, and on their individual personal experiences. But the organized women who were active in various causes typically understood themselves to embody a set of values distinct from those of men, and they saw their political work as stemming from different impulses. Women's exclusion from formal politics and their underrepresentation in the economic sphere certainly contributed to this contrast. Whereas a man might be in politics quite openly to enrich himself or to gain power, women seemed to be in politics for loftier reasons.[9]

In reality, the division between male and female politics was not so absolute. In many ways, the idea of separate male and female political cultures and styles was a middle-class, urban one. In the Farmers' Alliance, a precursor to the Populist Party that emerged in Gilded Age Kansas, a notion of separate male and female politics was largely absent. The gender systems of the immigrant farm populations targeted by the Alliance were different from those of native-born urban dwellers who adhered more closely to the ideology of separate spheres. In rural communities, life and work were understood as family enterprises. Men and women performed different roles, and men had authority over women, but their lives were devoted toward common ends and were lived in common spaces. The Farmers' Alliance took its cue from these patterns of life and adopted a "mixed-gendered approach" to organizing farmers. Alcohol was banned at political meetings, and women and children were welcome. These meetings drew on the model of family churchgoing, more popular among isolated rural people than in urban areas where women had become the primary church attendees.[10]

Furthermore, even among the urban middle classes, strict divisions between male and female politics showed signs of erosion in the late nineteenth century. The Prohibition Party in the 1880s had adopted the language of Protestant moral reform and Christian mission into its political rhetoric. One of the most powerful symbols of all that was wrong with male politics—the urban political machine—had fallen under attack from upper-class male reformers as early as the 1870s. And by the 1910s, male and female Roosevelt Progressives were working together on many issues (temperance, social welfare legislation, and good government campaigns, for example) that appeared to reflect feminine concerns. A relationship between male reformers and female politics was certainly presumed by many male partisans. Tellingly, partisans attacked male reformers who advocated independent (nonpartisan) voting, electoral reform, and a merit system for civil service jobs in terms that questioned the reformers' masculinity.[11] During the Progressive Era, parties could overcome assumptions that political parties were inherently corrupt by including women as participants in party affairs. Women's support was important to the political parties during the Progressive Era because women "embodied nonpartisanship" symbolically, even when they behaved as partisans.[12] And women certainly did behave as partisans, providing necessary volunteer and participating in campaigns.[13]

By the time the women's suffrage amendment was ratified, the boundary between male and female politics in reality may have been more porous than it appeared, but it was still evoked in unambiguous imagery. During the 1922 Pennsylvania primary contest for the Republican nomination for governor, for example, a Philadelphia reporter for an antimachine newspaper contrasted in stark, gendered terms the supporters of the regular machine Republican, George E. Alter, with the supporters of the independent reform Republican, Gifford Pinchot. On election night, the reporter visited both the Alter headquarters and the clubhouse of the Pinchot-supporting Republican Women of Pennsylvania and wrote the following account: "Oratory, cigar stubs, red flares, red liquor and cuspidors, on one hand; conversation, cigarettes, orange punch, expensive perfume and broad A's on the other, represent, in brief, the extremes of atmosphere permeating the various campaign headquarters last night while the returns from the State-wide primary election were coming in." The reporter went on to describe the Republican Women of Pennsylvania setting as "cultured." The women are "well-dressed" and engaged in "much conversation." And although they smoke cigarettes, the atmosphere is not clouded by smoke. By contrast, the men consume liquor, which could only be acquired illegally. The Alter headquarters is impenetrable, filled with a "solid wall of backs" and obscured by "three layers" of cigar smoke. A party hack is giving an overblown, meaningless speech. Meanwhile, the "real business of the evening" is being conducted upstairs, in a different room.[14] Notably, these heavily gendered images functioned here as a metaphor for political differences that were heavily class-based. Allowing women to symbolize culture and civility in politics obscured the class elements of the contrasts reformers were attempting to draw.

In this particular case, so-called feminine politics prevailed. Pinchot, the reform candidate, triumphed in the primary and went on to win the governor's seat. Columnist Harriet Hubbs reported that there seemed to be a "unanimity of opinion" that women had been a large, and possibly decisive, factor in Pinchot's victory.[15] The images of obfuscated, corrupt male politics and cultured, unclouded female politics probably rang true for many of the newspaper's readers, even if they suspected that such characterizations were overly simplistic. Women also participated in the Alter campaign through a separate club movement affiliated with the machine Republicans; men (including, obviously, Pinchot himself) were involved with the independent reform campaign. But a gender-based contrast of political styles was what many had anticipated women's suffrage would bring. It was not simply that women supported "women's issues" but that they supposedly stood for a different kind of politics itself—one based on principle, civic duty, independent thinking, and honesty rather than pragmatics, personal ambition, unthinking party loyalty, and unsavory behavior. As Republican Lillian Feickert of New Jersey put it, "[w]omen are not looking for gain in politics . . . in that they differ from the men. . . . Women are in politics for what they can put in it, not what they can get out of it."[16]

As women attempted to develop their own notion of partisanship, encounters between "male" and "female" political styles were inevitable. Parties appeared to some female activists as the only institutions through which they could realize their political goals. They needed access. Women leaders recognized that women had much to learn. Most women were said to be ignorant of the political issues of the day and of such mysteries as polling places, voting booths, the marking of ballots, the structure of parties, and the running of campaigns. If women did not overcome this ignorance of electoral and party politics, they would perpetuate their exclusion. But political parties were also symbols of a distasteful male political style that many women rejected.

Mixing politics with women's clubs could overcome the negative images women associated with partisanship. Women's Republican clubs began emerging before national suffrage; the Nineteenth Amendment would provide new impetus for organizing. Mrs. Herman Blum of Philadelphia noted in 1925 that political clubs had initially been very unpopular among women. According to Blum, women thought that politics was "something you read about in the newspapers; polling places were dirty holes where men smoked." Then, she continued, small groups of women started "preaching" a new doctrine: "Politics was the science of good government; politics was a duty, a patriotic sacrament; the ballot was a weapon for supreme good; in the hands of feminine crusaders it would bring peace in place of war; . . . through it women could become so many Joan of Arcs fighting for the salvation of the land and the people they loved."[17] Blum was referring to women's political clubs of all stripes, although she was herself involved with the Republican club movement.

Activist women who wanted to enter formal politics somehow had to resolve the tension between their desire to be involved with partisan politics, and the negative connotations that partisanship held. Some, like Harriet Upton, entered the regular Republican organization and found opportunities to work within it. But far more women became involved in Republican Party politics thorough women's Republican clubs. These clubs did not emerge with a single vision. They differed by class, race, region, and degree of partisanship. Yet together they shared the broadly defined features of a similar political style, one that was inherited from decades of presuffrage activism but that was characterized by its practitioners' desire to wrestle with the possibilities of partisanship. The club alternative allowed women to explore partisan politics from the safety and familiarity of traditional women's organizations. In this way, women could approach partisan politics cautiously and attempt to redefine it on their own terms. It also gave some women reason to believe they could continue to pursue a "women's agenda"—by being in the world of politics, while remaining above it. The club alternative, with which women experimented in the twenties, would become the primary means for ordinary women to engage with party politics throughout much of the twentieth century.

★ Republican women's club leaders in the twenties began new local partisan organizations, marked by a distinctly women's partisan style, that sought to integrate partisanship into women's lives and thereby bring American women into party politics. These female organizers described their activities as a departure from the way men ran local official party organizations. Unlike local party organizations, which typically shut down during the interim periods between elections, women's partisan clubs aimed to maintain a year-round party presence. Women's partisan clubs served a different purpose than the existing party organizations. Targeting a population of citizens who had not yet developed the habit of voting, women's organizers knew that they had to find a way to make politics part of day-to-day life. Through their efforts to enter partisan politics, enfranchised women introduced new styles of local party organizing to twentieth-century partisan politics.[18] Women's partisan clubs hoped to provide the consistent political socialization largely abandoned by partisan men, while using methods reflecting what they understood to be their own distinct political values.[19]

Republican women's clubs in the 1920s took several different forms. The kinds of club activity women had been involved with previously informed the goals and strategies they brought to their party work. Different Republican club founders, of different backgrounds, operating within different political contexts, foresaw varying ways that clubs could resolve the tension between a preference for women's political style and the need to work with and within the parties. Although Henrietta Livermore of New York envisioned an elite, social club that would remain disengaged from party politics for the most part, Alma Lorimer of Philadelphia proposed independent clubs with a progressive agenda as a way to promote women's political values, to preserve women's political style, and thereby to reform party practice. African American women, led by Nannie Burroughs of Washington, D.C., tried to pursue traditional black clubwomen's goals of "racial uplift" and social work through the vehicle of partisanship. Because no one at the RNC was trying to organize women uniformly, the relationship of partisanship to women's political activism was open to a variety of interpretations in the 1920s. Although their efforts to transform the world of politics and women's place within it were rarely as successful as women hoped, many Republican women's clubs nonetheless began to reshape local political life in their communities.

★ THE WOMEN'S NATIONAL REPUBLICAN CLUB

Some women who formed Republican clubs did not really intend their clubs to be political. The membership of the exclusive Women's National Republican Club (WNRC) consisted of elite white socialites whose interest in the nuts and bolts of politics was minimal. Henrietta Livermore founded the club in 1920 with other members of the New York Republican Women's State Executive Committee. Livermore herself was a party regular who served in the New York and National Republican organizations. Yet she also saw a "vital need" for a women's Republican organization outside the party where less politically inclined women could develop an interest in politics and an understanding of the purpose of parties.[20]

The WNRC called itself a "national" organization and, by 1927, claimed a membership of 3,000, representing thirty-seven states.[21] Most of those members, however, were from New York and the surrounding states. Many states were represented by only a single member. The WNRC held parliamentary law classes, debates on current issues, and other educational programs targeting new voters, but it made no pretense of being a mass organization of women. The membership was made up of elite women (including the wives of former Republican presidents) and was deliberately exclusive. Eventually the club established an invitation-only membership policy and a requirement that prospective members be known personally by at least one state governor.[22] The WNRC maintained a clubhouse, conveniently located in the heart of New York's shopping and theater district, where members could pay to stay overnight while in the city. The clubhouse was decorated with Early American furniture, collected by members, to provide a feeling of "early American history."[23] This emphasis on American heritage suggests the connection of members to patriotic societies and their "old-stock" backgrounds.

The Republican Party, the party of business and property in the 1920s, was also "a status party."[24] The WNRC was an outlet for women whose Republicanism was already a part of their understanding of themselves as Americans and as social and economic elites. As Livermore described, the object of the club was to give women a chance to meet socially as "Republican women and not merely as part of a political organization." She believed a good Republican woman did not need to concern herself "principally with legislation."[25] Republicanism held broader meanings for WNRC members.

The WNRC offered elite women a means to learn something about political issues, to socialize with other Republican women of their standing, and to add "Republicanism" to their other prestigious activities. In this sense, it probably nurtured and reinforced preexisting identifications with the GOP. The WNRC did not set out to reform the party, to change the way politics worked, to fight for particular issues, to prepare women for larger roles in politics, or to generate mass support for the party among women (goals that other Republican women's clubs variously embraced). Thus the Women's National Republican Club posed little challenge to the dominance of male partisan culture or to male political power.

★ THE REPUBLICAN WOMEN OF PENNSYLVANIA

Meanwhile, Republican women more interested in political activity formed clubs, such as the Republican Women of Pennsylvania (RWP), with independent agendas that were associated with certain elements of the Progressive movement. Many of these women came to partisan politics because of their support for various aspects of white middle-class female reform. For women in these clubs, Republicanism was about particular principles, which were connected to specific policy positions. A responsible partisan voted for the candidates who best represented those principles and was less concerned with whether GOP leaders had endorsed the candidate or even whether the candidate was running on the Republican ticket. To independent Republican women, this was a form of partisanship in line with their own values of an educated citizenry, clean politics, and a politics driven by principles and issues.[26] To the Republican organization against which they sometimes battled, however, these women were promoting not partisanship but disorder.

The Republican Women of Pennsylvania shared some characteristics with the Women's National Republican Club. RWP members were also white socialites found regularly in the public eye. Throughout the 1920s, the RWP held high-profile events, such as Christmas charity sales and annual card parties organized around ethnic or historical themes that were publicized in the local society pages. But, unlike the WNRC, the RWP also had an explicit political agenda. The RWP operated in a political environment in which a Republican machine (controlled in the twenties by party boss Congressman William S. Vare) had dominated local politics for decades.[27] As opponents of that machine, the RWP concerned itself intensely with local (Philadelphia) and state politics.

The RWP's founder was Alma Lorimer, wife of the publisher of the *Saturday Evening Post*. In September 1920 leading Pennsylvania Republicans asked her to organize statewide women's activities for the Harding campaign. Toward this end, the middle-aged Lorimer gathered women with whom she had worked in the Red Cross Auxiliary during World War I and formed the Republican Women of Pennsylvania.[28] By 1926 the organization claimed 10,000 women in its network of clubs, mostly in Eastern Pennsylvania.[29] In contrast to other women who founded Republican clubs after 1920, Lorimer had not participated in the suffrage movement (she described herself as having been neither a suffragist nor an antisuffragist). She developed her administrative experience during her tenure as chairman of the Philadelphia Red Cross Auxiliary. Her sons grown and her family duties diminished, she now chose the political education of women over "bridge parties, teas, and receptions."[30]

Although the RWP originally formed to support Harding's presidential campaign, the club soon turned to politics at a more local level, establishing itself as an independent voice in Republican affairs. From the beginning, Lorimer declared her women's Republican organization to be nonfactional. It would not become part of the official state or city Republican machine and would oppose "objectionable" candidates, including those supported by the Republican organization.[31] When given the opportunity to have the RWP affiliate with a proposed state Republican Women's Council, Lorimer demurred, arguing that to associate with a statewide council would "impair [the RWP's] usefulness as a body of independent Republican women."[32] At the same time, Lorimer distinguished her club from nonpartisan ones, declaring that "if we are Republicans [we must] work inside the party. . . . We must be in one place or the other."[33] Lorimer insisted, at least initially, that women could embrace Republicanism without fully embracing the party.

Lorimer endorsed an independent kind of Republicanism that was indeed factional, despite her insistence to the contrary. By promoting voter education, Lorimer hoped that thoughtful, informed voters would defeat the machine candidates she opposed. In addition to supporting Pinchot's 1922 primary run for governor, the Philadelphia branch of the RWP routinely endorsed other Republicans who challenged the candidates handpicked by the party bosses in subsequent primaries.[34]

Lorimer and her fellow Republican Women of Pennsylvania were certainly not alone in their opposition to Philadelphia's Republican machine. The city had long had a reputation for being the worst-governed city in America, an observation immortalized by Lincoln Steffens in a series of articles written around the turn of the century. For decades, reformers, through ostensibly nonpartisan or third-party organizations, had tried to defeat the machine, with only occasional success.[35] Reformers were typically wealthy, native-born whites who wanted to see local governmental institutions purged of party politics and run efficiently according to their own values. The machine was supported at the polls by working-class immigrants and African Americans. But it was also succored by the inability of "nonpartisan" reformers (who remained allied with the national Republican Party) to form coalitions with local Democrats, by the fact that many Philadelphia business leaders were profiting from the machine's corrupt practices, and by the general apathy of the middle and upper classes.[36]

This apathy appalled Lorimer and her fellow clubwomen, and they took on the reform cause with a vengeance. The Republican Women of Pennsylvania objected to the machine for reasons similar to those of male reformers. In the RWP's rendering, however, the struggle against the organization was not a class struggle (although it undoubtedly was) or an abstract struggle between good and evil, but a struggle over political values and styles that was gender-based. Believing local Republican officeholders to be complicit with and profiting from the violations of Prohibition laws, Lorimer declared that women favoring law enforcement had to support those candidates opposed to the organization. She set up a contrast between women's political goals and those of the (male) political machine. "We want the spoils of office," Lorimer declared, "but our idea of what those spoils should be differs from those of the political machine. We want fewer job holders, no graft and lower taxes. We want the alliance between politics and crime abolished. We want the police to protect the home instead of the speak-easy."[37] The extreme party loyalty of organization Republicans was also disturbing to the Republican Women of Pennsylvania. Lorimer opposed strict party loyalty as well as the straight-ticket voting it demanded. "Why," Lorimer asked, "should men and women in politics degenerate into 'robots'? . . .—mechanisms dominated by a boss and subservient to his will!"[38]

The RWP promised women a means to affect local politics by studying current issues, carefully considering candidates and their qualifications, and supporting certain legislative measures (particularly those affecting the welfare of women and children and women's citizenship).[39] The RWP campaigned for cleaner streets, the enforcement of prohibition, "proper amusements," and maximum-hours laws for women workers and against measures to exempt women from jury duty.[40] In 1929 the RWP helped lead a successful movement urging the police department to establish a women's bureau, which would assign female police officers to the problems of juvenile girls and vice crimes.[41]

To achieve their political goals, the Republican Women of Pennsylvania took on tasks of political socialization and education. For example, its "Political Plattsburg," held in 1924, was a three-day course in practical politics where women voters, in preparation for the 1924 primaries, received instruction in the two-party system, the history of the Republican Party, American government, and the art of speechmaking. This event received favorable coverage in the local press, as well as the endorsement of the RNC.[42] The RWP also sponsored speakers (including vice presidential candidate Charles Dawes in October 1924) who regularly encountered audiences of thousands of women. During the 1924 fall presidential campaign, the RWP operated the "Keep Coolidge Inn" at midday, where supporters (men and women) could stop for wholesome political fun, campaign spirit, and lunch.[43] Ultimately, however, the RWP was more successful in its efforts to promote the national GOP ticket among women (goals that all local Republican factions shared) than in its efforts to break the grip of the local machine.

The RWP and other independent progressive clubs hoped that they had found, through the partisan club movement, a means of engaging with partisan politics without compromising their own political values. They tended to believe that women had to work within the parties rather than through nonpartisan organizations, but insisted on an independent stance vis-à-vis the official party. This stance had both strengths and weaknesses. By 1929 statewide networks of independent, quasi-partisan Republican women's clubs were well established in several eastern states and were developing in Indiana, Kentucky, Michigan, and Ohio.[44] Representatives of the WNRC, the RWP, and other East Coast clubs had begun meeting annually to share ideas. Participants viewed themselves as an indispensable new part of American politics. Their meetings, however, did not include representatives from another vital, highly organized movement of Republican women, the National League of Republican Colored Women (NLRCW).

★ THE NATIONAL LEAGUE OF REPUBLICAN COLORED WOMEN

In the early part of the twentieth century, virtually all women's clubs and organizations were racially segregated. Not welcome in white women's groups such as the General Federation of Women's Clubs and the PTA, African American women formed their own organizations, such as the NACW and the National Colored Parent-Teachers Association.[45] Thus it is hardly surprising that women's partisan organizations formed after 1920 did so along segregated lines. Even before national suffrage, black women began organizing Republican clubs across the country, particularly in northern urban areas that had attracted African American migrants from the southern states. As Evelyn Brooks Higginbotham notes, the "conflation of woman's suffrage and black urban migration made possible greater political opportunity and leverage for blacks as a group."[46] The women's political club movement in Chicago, which began in 1913 when Illinois women received limited suffrage, was particularly vital. There, African American clubwomen successfully pressured the Republican machine to back a black candidate, Oscar De-Priest, for city council, an indication of the strength of organized black women.[47] After 1920 black women built on this tradition.

Whereas white women's reform and suffrage organizations faced a potential division along party lines after women got the right to vote, black women's organizations did not. The vast majority of black voters, including black women, remained loyal to the Party of Lincoln in the 1920s. The party may not always have lived up to their expectations, and African American voters occasionally rallied around black independent candidates. However, most black voters continued to see the Republicans as the party with which they could work most productively. Black political clubwomen viewed their political participation as vital to the campaign for antilynching legislation, to the efforts to elect black officials, and otherwise to improving the status of African Americans. For the most part, black women do not seem to have experienced the deep ambivalence about partisanship so common among white women. Indeed, historian Patricia Schechter goes so far as to suggest that "disinterestedness" was a white female ideology.[48]

In 1924 black Republican clubwomen embarked on national coordination. That year, the National Association of Colored Women, although not a partisan organization, nevertheless devoted its energies to the Coolidge campaign. The RNC chose Hallie Q. Brown, the NACW president at that time, to head the black women's campaign for Coolidge. Brown was able to channel the NACW—a far-reaching, highly organized network of middle-class black women's clubs devoted to service and racial uplift—into more openly political work.[49] The NACW's newsletter, *National Notes*, was even temporarily transformed into a party organ. Black women enthusiastically formed Republican clubs and Coolidge-Dawes clubs. They participated locally in the Coolidge campaign by canvassing voters, sponsoring political speakers, and conducting get-out-the-vote campaigns, earning praise from Republican officials.[50]

The two African American Republican national committeewomen, Mary Booze (Mississippi) and Mamie Williams (Georgia), who were also members of the NACW, wanted to maintain black women's enthusiasm for the GOP beyond the Coolidge campaign itself. Immediately following the biennial meeting of the NACW in August, Williams and Booze assembled some of the attendees to form a new organization of black women that would be permanent, year-round, and explicitly partisan.

The leadership of the National League of Republican Colored Women included such prominent women as Nannie Burroughs (president) and Mary Church Terrell (treasurer).[51] Working through the connections its leaders had to the black women's club movement, the league established a national umbrella organization of black women's Republican clubs (something that white clubwomen would not succeed in doing until the late 1930s).

The NLRCW promised its members it would remain a vital force after the campaign was over. By 1926 it had representatives in thirty-seven states; twelve of those states by 1929 had sufficient club activity to merit a state director.[52] Organizers expected women in small clubs to study political issues and develop a partisan commitment that would mobilize them to work and vote for Republican candidates. League leaders wanted to ensure that African American women were not prevented from voting by their own husbands and that white employers were not attempting to influence the votes of their African American maids.[53] League leaders also hoped that the existence of the new Republican group would enable the NACW to return to its nonpartisan tradition.[54]

The clubs of the NLRCW shared with the RWP an independent spirit that meant they were willing to challenge official Republican organizations when they felt the party did not represent their interests. Black clubwomen, however, did not so readily frame their independence in terms of gender. Partisan work for black women was so strongly linked to overcoming racial discrimination that beliefs about women's "virtuous nature or moral superiority" were less central to club rhetoric than they were for many white clubs.[55] Still, NLRCW leaders did occasionally suggest privately that women could bring an honesty and noble purpose to party politics from which too many current black male leaders, in their view, had strayed.[56] Some African American men drew similar conclusions about the integrity of black women's political activities compared with those of men. Speaking to a black Republican women's group in Minnesota, George Woodson of Des Moines recalled his belief that the Nineteenth Amendment would mean a change from the dishonest voting practices in which some African American men had engaged. Woodson stated that he had thought in 1920 that "colored women [would] stand up longer without pay for principles that are right, than a colored man [would]." For that reason, Woodson suggested that black women use the Nineteenth Amendment to test the nullification of the Fifteenth Amendment in the southern states by voting in those states and taking their cases to the Supreme Court if denied the right to vote.[57]

Woodson's comments indicate that the use of women as symbols of political purity crossed racial lines, even if those symbols were not used in precisely the same ways.

League women saw working for the GOP as a means of helping all African Americans. In this sense the black organization, like many white women's Republican clubs, brought an existing women's political agenda to partisan politics. The guiding concerns of the nonpartisan NACW became the concerns of the NLRCW as well; indeed, there was a great deal of overlap between the two organizations.[58] Black Republican club leaders, Burroughs wrote, needed to be women who were unselfish enough to work "not for the benefit of themselves—and their friends—but for the advancement of the millions that are looking to them to use their new political power wisely, rightly, and righteously."[59] By proving that black women voters could act intelligently and honestly, Nannie Burroughs and her associate Daisy Lampkin hoped to repair the standing of African Americans in the GOP. And by helping to ensure victories for the "party that wrote our rights into the constitution," perhaps the circumstances faced by African Americans in the country as a whole, including the South, could be improved.[60] The NLRCW decided it would promote a slogan for the 1928 presidential campaign that revealed what for them was at stake in the election: "Oppose in State and National Campaigns any Candidates Who Will Not Committ [sic] Him or Herself on the Enforcement of the 13th, 14th, and 15th Amendments."[61]

Black women's hard work for the national ticket in 1924 and again in 1928 led Nannie Burroughs to make demands on the party for recognition: that the RNC establish a permanent headquarters for black women and that a black woman be appointed to the Women's Bureau and the Children's Bureau.[62] Burroughs demanded what she felt black women had earned. After all, director of the RNC's Women's Division Sallie Hert had commended the part of African American women in mobilizing votes for the national ticket during the 1928 campaign.[63]

That the RNC did not fully accommodate black women's demands was not due entirely to racism; white clubwomen also found the party at all levels to be less responsive than they felt was deserved. Yet because independent clubs did not always cooperate with their local party organizations, they were not in a position to ask for much in return. Independent women's clubs such as the Republican Women of Pennsylvania were able to maintain their own voices and to promote and preserve their own political values. But with independence came isolation. As Felice Gordon notes in her work on an independent Republican women's organization in New Jersey, in pursuing independence the club's members "isolated themselves from the male politicians and were not . . . exposed to the arguments and concerns of the real power structure."[64] Yet independent clubwomen placed great value on their autonomy.

★ A variety of women's Republican clubs flourished in the 1920s and even into the early 1930s. In 1932, despite the ongoing Depression, which undermined support for the GOP, national director of women's activities for the RNC Lenna Yost reported on the various kinds of women's clubs that existed at that time. She indicated that thirty-three states had statewide organizations of clubs.[65] These clubs differed in terms of class, race, and region, as well as their reasons for supporting the Republicans, their relationship to the party structure, and their vision of women's politics (Yost acknowledged some, though not all, of these divisions). But most Republican clubwomen, due to their perceptions of inherent differences between the sexes as well as to their newness to formal politics, understood their own connection to partisan politics to be different from men's. Despite the many dissimilarities among them, women's Republican clubs in the 1920s exhibited several features generally shared in common that would shape the Republican club movement during the next decades.[66]

In the decade after gaining the right to vote, many women whose political leanings were Republican remained skeptical of the act of voting; many more considered sustained partisan activities to be neither appropriate nor compelling. Convincing Republican women to become politically active involved more than educating them about voting procedures and about Republican principles. Republican club leaders, although responding to different goals and different local circumstances, generally focused on three broad themes in their appeals to women that served to create a partisan Republican culture welcoming to women. First, they linked partisanship to social networks and activities that were already familiar to the women they targeted; second, they emphasized that Republican politics was the natural outlet for a pressing crusade that women needed to lead; and, third, they contrasted female virtue (selflessness, courage, honesty, or success) with male failings (cowardice, corruption, or ineffectiveness).

Women's Republican clubs, not surprisingly, all made links between partisan politics and the female social world to which members already belonged. The leaders of the National League of Republican Colored Women, the Republican Women of Pennsylvania, and the Women's Na-

tional Republican Club drew the core of their very different memberships from existing club and social networks. During these early years,
clubwomen made little effort to persuade non-Republicans to join the
cause. Instead they focused on making active those women whom they
already knew and whom they believed to be Republicans. These might
be wives of prominent Republicans or businessmen or women known
through other club work or religious activities. Republican clubwomen
(black and white) developed and reinforced partisan identification as
part of their understanding of who they were as women and as citizens.
In this way GOP clubwomen sometimes reinforced narrow definitions
of "women" and "women's interests" that conformed to their own social status and political identity. In organizing through social networks,
Republican women's clubs effectively confined their membership to
women who were comfortable socializing with each other.

Within these recruitment limits, the strategy for building membership combined familiar social activities with partisan politics. Meetings
were held in women- and family-friendly locales, such as parks, libraries,
clubhouses, and churches, in contrast to the proverbial "smoke-filled
rooms" associated with party politics in the past. Most women's clubs
promised informal, unthreatening discussions of issues (with a partisan
tilt) where women could freely ask questions without fear of embarrassment. It was important to have regular meetings where something
noteworthy took place that could be reported in the local newspaper.
This might involve bringing a speaker or a candidate, conducting a
charity sale or fashion event where women dressed in historic or ethnic
costume, staging a political debate, or having a local musical group
perform. For some clubs, such as Ida B. Wells-Barnett's Third Ward
Women's Political Club in Chicago, it might involve running and supporting female candidates, although this was not the focus of most
clubs.[67] To compete with other women's groups (including bridge clubs
and civic organizations), club programs needed to be interesting, politically informative, and, as Iowa club leader Ella Taylor put it, "inter-
spersed with fun and play."[68]

By emphasizing education and women's moral role in reforming society, most Republican club activity in the 1920s and 1930s fit into a long
tradition of women's voluntarism and associationalism. Livermore and
Lorimer were happy to have their political clubs participate in the well-
publicized charity social events with which their members were familiar. Ella Taylor, on the other hand, did not place partisan club work in
the same category as other contemporary women's voluntary associa-

tions. After the clubwomen she led had worked hard in the 1936 elections, Taylor asked them, "Are we [now] going to turn back to our club work, our social life, and forget all about our high resolves as pertains to our duties of citizenship?"[69] Taylor insisted on a rhetorical separation between "political" and "social" activities while recognizing that social elements were important to attracting women to political activity. Many potentially Republican women also belonged, variously, to patriotic, reform, social work, or charity organizations that were nonpartisan such as the American Legion Auxiliary, Daughters of the American Revolution, the Red Cross Auxiliary, or the National Association of Colored Women. Clubs tended to view partisanship in terms that were compatible with its members' other civic activities. Defining Republican partisanship as a patriotic act, a civic responsibility, or an exercise in racial solidarity was an important means of persuading individual women to take the partisan plunge.

A second feature common to women's Republican clubs was their tendency to frame politics as an urgent crusade of good against evil. This crusading style of politics was partly a method of mobilizing women voters. Many women political leaders saw a need to conceive all political issues as urgent, often morally animated, crises in order to appeal to and engage women voters. An underlying assumption of many of the various Republican women's clubs of the 1920s was that women in general did not understand politics to be their business. Therefore, it was believed, women would not mobilize unless they could be convinced that an urgent crisis was at hand, the solution to which demanded the political activism of women (like "so many Joan of Arcs fighting for the salvation of the land and the people they loved," in the words of Philadelphia's Mrs. Blum). As Alma Lorimer put it, in discussing women's enthusiasm for Hoover's 1928 presidential bid, "women want to feel that they are fighting more than a political battle. . . . They must be actuated by a crusading spirit if they are to give their best efforts to a campaign."[70] In 1928 that crusade was, for many Republican women, the fight to prevent Prohibition's repeal or reform.

The crusading political style, in fact, had its origins in the nineteenth-century Woman's Christian Temperance Union's (WCTU) battle to stamp out liquor. Frances Willard's genius had been an ability to mobilize into the WCTU women who believed it was not their God-given place to engage in politics. Women fighting for temperance, Willard argued, were embarking on a mission ordained by God to restore civilization. Women had to lead this religious crusade because men were the cause of alcohol abuse and its problems.[71] The crusading language of Protestant women's reform movements often carried over into post-suffrage middle-class Republican women's politics, either through direct links among older Republican women leaders to the WCTU or through a more general canonization of its rhetoric. Well after Prohibition was no longer a going concern, some women would continue to invoke political arguments, language, and style that had been refined by its female proponents.

Black women, although concerned about alcohol abuse in their communities, had additional reasons to view protecting Prohibition as an issue of greatest urgency demanding a women's crusade. For African Americans, the idea that a constitutional amendment could be repealed had ominous implications. As Nannie Burroughs put it, "If the 18th amendment is not strong enough to stand—if we vote men into office who sanction its modification or annulment—we might as well sign the death certificate of the 13th, 14th, and 15th amendments. . . . They are our most sacred heritage, and we should wade through blood to safeguard them."[72] For African American women, religion, politics, community work, and the fight for racial justice were inextricably linked. The close ties between black women's political clubs and black churches meant that "Christianity shaped the vocabulary, ritual, organizational base, and identity" of black clubwomen, providing a rhetoric of politics as an urgent, religious, crusade.[73] Black clubwomen emphasized the grave importance of keeping the Democrats (with their links to institutionalized southern racism) out of power. "The race is doomed," the NLRCW argued, "unless Negro Women take an active part in local, state and national politics."[74]

The "crusades" that Republican women embarked on in the twenties—for Prohibition, against political machines, or (in the case of black women) against white supremacy—were often at least loosely connected to aspects of progressivism. In later political contexts, the crusade that "actuated" Republican women would be variously reconfigured as a crusade against the New Deal in the thirties, against international socialism in the fifties, or for Barry Goldwater in the sixties. What united these female political movements over the decades was less their political substance than the rhetoric of the female political crusade employed by leaders and participants.

A third feature Republican women's clubs shared in the 1920s was their assumptions about the superiority of women, variously defined. The centrality of racial discrimination meant that black clubs exhibited less overt gender consciousness (and less "sex antagonism") than white clubs, but assumptions of female superiority were not entirely absent from black women's political organizing. Although the world of partisan politics might appear complicated and unseemly, women would have to enter it because, as so many club leaders made clear, women could not rely on men to protect the home, the community, the race, or the country. There were different reasons for their doubts. Lorimer thought men were driven by selfish motives to political practices that did not benefit society. Burroughs despaired that black men, weakened by a political system that denied them real influence, were enticed into corrupt arrangements that undermined the position of all African Americans within the party. In the 1930s Iowa's Ella Taylor would come to argue that New Deal attacks on business and fear of the stigma of the Republican label crippled Republican men to the point where women were becoming more devoted and courageous partisans than were men.[75]

These three features of independent Republican clubwomen's politics were common to many of the Republican women's clubs in the 1920s that tried to bring newly enfranchised women into politics. In the 1920s these features were often associated with progressive-leaning clubs. Some future Republican leaders would try to downplay or eradicate these features—particularly the construction of politics as a moral crusade and notions of female superiority, less so the emphasis on existing social networks—because they saw them as harmful to women or harmful to the party. Yet these features of Republican clubwomen's politics would persist within parts of the GOP club movement well into the 1960s. As the decades wore on, however, and the political zeitgeist and the Republican Party itself changed, these features would no longer be associated with the party's progressive wing but increasingly with its conservative one.

★ In the late 1920s, a period of GOP dominance, Republican women's clubs thrived. Hoover's 1928 campaign played a role. The RNC Women's Division that year organized several fifteen-minute radio broadcasts targeted toward women, encouraging them to hold radio parties where they would gather with friends in their homes to listen to and discuss radio broadcasts of speeches by GOP leaders. The radio talks were to be "in the nature of 'Political Gossip'" and of "especial interest to women."[76] These efforts further stimulated the growth of dispersed and varied women's Republican clubs, notably in the rural areas of the Middle West, where women's clubs had been slower to form. Journalists cited the use of radio broadcasts in the 1928 campaign as one of the factors leading to an increase in women's voting that year due to radio's effectiveness in bringing politics into remote homes.[77] It was at this time that Ella Taylor of Tama County, Iowa, already a member of her local Republican Party Committee, was asked to organize Republican women in her county for the Hoover campaign. In organizing for the 1928 election, Taylor convened meetings in libraries, theaters, and homes throughout the county. She held rallies and covered-dish suppers where Iowa Republican leaders spoke to crowds about the general issues of the campaign in language designed to appeal particularly to women. After Hoover's election, the Tama County Republican Women's Club would not disband as campaign clubs usually did, but remained active. One year later, the county club claimed 1,200 members.[78]

The Tama County Republican Women's Club (as well as the Women's National Republican Club, the Republican Women of Pennsylvania, and the National League of Republican Colored Women) formed while the Republican Party dominated national politics. In the 1930s, as the country entered a new period of Democratic ascendancy, clubs faced new challenges. Unfortunately, there are few records that make it possible to follow these particular Republican women's organizations deep into the 1930s.

The WNRC continued holding its exclusive events throughout the period, endorsed Hoover's run for a second term, and in 1935 hosted an anti–New Deal women's conference.[79] The RWP scrapbooks end in 1934 and do not resume until the 1950s, leaving the precise fate of the club during the thirties unclear. Nannie Burroughs found it increasingly difficult to enlist RNC support for her efforts with the NLRCW, and the organization seems to have disbanded in the early thirties.[80] Individual black women's Republican clubs, however, remained active, notably the Virginia White Speel Women's Republican Club in Washington, D.C., the Colored Women's Republican League of Chicago, and the Women's Political Study Club of California.

Mobilizing Republican women in the 1930s was considerably more difficult than it had been in the 1920s. But some clubs nonetheless thrived. Before anything else, leaders first had to identify women who were even willing to "creep out of the debris" and "wear a Republican label."[81] One way that successful club leaders kept their membership intact and engaged was to call for a new women's crusade, this time configuring the New Deal as the urgent crisis. Iowa's Ella Taylor made regular use of this strategy. If more women only knew the truth about the "perils

"Roused to the danger." Ella Taylor (fourth from right) with board and committee members of the Third District Federation of Republican Women's Clubs, May 1937. Taylor believed that if women truly understood the perils of the New Deal, they would be activated to defeat it. (Photo courtesy of Joyce Weise.)

that threaten America," Taylor stressed to a female audience in the late thirties, they would be "roused to the danger" and called to action.[82] These dangers included what Taylor described as Roosevelt's socialistic economic policies, exorbitant taxes, the threat of communism, the immorality of young people, and the neglect of the nation's crime problems, issues that Taylor spoke about at length. Taylor garnished her speeches generously with quotations from prominent men who believed women possessed special qualities that would save the nation (if they could be convinced to embark on a women's crusade). J. Edgar Hoover, for example, declared that women were crucial to crime prevention and William Hard claimed that "the salvation" of the United States from communism and dictatorship rested "in the hands of its women."[83]

In attacking the New Deal at a time when many hard-hit Iowans supported Roosevelt's policies, Ella Taylor was fighting an uphill battle.[84] Activating the apolitical was especially difficult when the GOP was unpopular. This may be why Taylor employed such apocalyptic attacks on the New Deal in her appeals to women and suggests that the most successful women's organizations in the thirties may have been those that used the most dire rhetoric. Taylor's club was one of those successes. Despite grim times for the GOP in Iowa, Ella Taylor was able to form a districtwide association of Republican women's clubs in 1936. The Third District Federation of Republican Women's Clubs' efforts on behalf of Republican candidates in 1936 earned the attention of state political leaders, who subsequently supported Taylor's efforts to organize Republican women in other districts.[85]

The New Deal would also activate new groups of women whose intense opposition to Roosevelt and his policies would motivate them to join Republican or quasi-Republican women's organizations. The early thirties saw the birth of a new Republican women's organization, Pro America. Pro America formed in Seattle in 1933 as a women's group dedicated to clean government and to preserving the American form of government (code phrases for New Deal opposition). Pro America grew out of a local garden club, whose members became alarmed over the apparent strength of the Unemployed Citizens' League of Seattle in 1932.[86] While it clearly had an affinity with the Republican Party (indeed, many members were actually on the party's right), Pro America was unwilling to declare its partisanship too loudly.[87] Although most of its members were Republicans, Pro America also aspired to recruit so-called Constitutional Democrats, who identified with the Democratic Party but who objected to many of President Roosevelt's New Deal measures. In this sense, Pro America was more an anti–New Deal women's group than it was an explicitly Republican one. In many of the western states where Pro America was most active, however, it was the only organization for Republican women and would be an important consideration of any future effort to organize Republican women nationally.

At the end of 1931, while Hoover was still in office, Sallie Hert spoke to the Republican National Committee on the merits of women's Republican clubs. It was important to have these year-round organizations, she argued, where women could develop a "sustaining interest" in the "literary and cultural side" of the party so that they would maintain their interest and feel that they were "a going part of this concern." Hert believed the party should be doing more to encourage this kind of activity. Such encouragement was cost effective and could reduce the "great overhead and expense" of creating "campaign machinery" for each election.[88] No response to Hert's suggestions was recorded. Certainly Republican women's clubs muddled along during the 1930s, but they were hardly a potent force for the party (nor were they an influential outlet for women's independent political voices as they had been in some cases during the twenties). Not until 1937 would the RNC finally look seriously at the political possibilities presented by these women's clubs.

Republicans were slow to understand many aspects of the New Deal's success with American voters, including women voters. Syndicated political columnist Doris Fleeson later recollected that in the early thirties GOP national recognition of women consisted primarily of "putting the more photogenic and silver-foxed national committeewomen . . . on the front row at important meetings."[89] Democrats were much more effective in reaching out to women than were the Republicans. Beginning in 1932, the Women's Division of the Democratic National Committee, under Molly Dewson, began building an organized, nationwide network of female party activists. Dewson worked through the regular Democratic organizations, seeking to install a woman vice chair on all state, district, county, and precinct committees. To sustain women's interest in the party year-round, Dewson developed what she dubbed the "Reporter Plan." By 1936, 15,000 women were serving as "Reporters," bringing information about the New Deal to their communities and developing an active sense that they belonged to the party. Dewson also began a Democratic newsletter for women and launched a women's grass-roots fundraising campaign.[90]

Also important was the Democratic administration's record of bringing women into government in unprecedented numbers. The New Deal's response to the Great Depression entailed an expanded government bureaucracy of programs targeting the traditional concerns of social workers. Because women made up the majority of trained social workers, they were often leading candidates to staff these new agencies.[91] Some women, most notably Secretary of Labor Frances Perkins, achieved high positions and received prominent attention. The activist role of First Lady Eleanor Roosevelt further strengthened the perception that the Democrats were doing an outstanding job of offering leadership roles and opportunities to women. The representation of women in party leadership probably was not the most important concern of women voters at the time, but the Democrats clearly were doing better in this area than Republicans.

★ In 1937 RNC chairman John Hamilton wanted to help the deeply troubled and divided GOP. Hamilton was intimately familiar with the party's weaknesses, having served as Republican presidential candidate

Alfred Landon's campaign manager in 1936. In 1936 Roosevelt had defeated Landon triumphantly, winning 60.4 percent of the popular vote and losing only the diehard Republican states of Vermont and Maine. In Congress, the Democrats increased their representation in both Houses to record totals.[92]

At the level of the Republican National Committee, the party seemed to consist of a few wealthy national committeemen and committeewomen who met only occasionally and who had little understanding of the American electorate. The more vocal national committeewomen of the early 1920s largely had been replaced by women who viewed their seats as positions of honor rather than influence, who tended not to speak at meetings, and who voted with the committeemen from their states. Old Guard Republicans continued to dominate the RNC after 1932; the party's response to its defeat reflected that control. RNC chairman Henry Fletcher had promoted a strategy for the 1934 congressional elections of directly attacking the New Deal. This approach showed Fletcher to be out of touch with the vast majority of American people who, regardless of class or region, generally believed they were benefiting from the New Deal. After the 1934 election debacle, when Democrats made additional gains in Congress, some party insurgents began arguing that the party needed to redefine itself and end the Old Guard's control. Conservatives, however, had continued to believe that holding the line would pay off once the abnormal electoral conditions resulting from the immediate impact of the Depression were over.[93]

Republicans were bewildered after their crushing defeat in 1936. By selecting a Westerner, Alf Landon, to head the presidential ticket, they had believed they could reunite the regional factions of the party. As Clyde Weed argues, party leaders' preoccupation with winning back western insurgents had blinded them to the fact that Republican losses in the East were long-term rather than merely temporary. After 1936, according to Weed, Republicans at last considered the possibility that the New Deal had not only deprived them permanently of their Western base but had formed a powerful coalition in the Northeast of organized labor, recent immigrants, blacks, women, intellectuals, and young voters.[94]

This was the political reality facing John Hamilton when he became RNC chairman. Although Hamilton was considered a conservative, he sympathized with those Republicans who now wanted to modernize the party and make a more sincere attempt to reach people at the grass roots.[95] Hamilton hoped to begin to reestablish the GOP as a unified political party with a national message, a strong year-round presence, and a loyal grass-roots constituency. He successfully advocated the creation of a year-round RNC headquarters and a full-time salaried chairman with a staff.[96] In November 1937 he formed a committee made up of state Republican workers from across the country whose task was to develop a statement of principles for the party.[97] Also integral to Hamilton's reform plans was finally to begin translating the potential of the women's vote into a constructive force for the GOP.

By the late 1930s the thousands of Republican women's clubs, scattered across the country, composed a substantial part of the GOP's limited grass-roots presence. These clubs had no unified or coordinated purpose, however. Elite clubs, independent clubs, clubs organized by the party, African American women's clubs, and Pro America all claimed to speak for some constituency of Republican women and each had very different ideas about what women's political involvement entailed. Even some of those clubs that had originally formed to cooperate with the party (as in Tama County, Iowa) became independent by default because the party in the thirties, in a state of disarray, seemed to have had no use for them. Clubs in the thirties followed no uniform program. Some clubs stuck to social or educational activities. Others were performing extensive volunteer work for the party. Because many localities were already organized in some fashion, it would not be possible to build a new, top-down organization of Republican women. Rather, a national leader of Republican women somehow would have to bring the diverging interests, concerns, philosophies, agendas, and rivalries of existing clubwomen under one banner.

Wanting to correct past mistakes, RNC chairman John Hamilton looked to women's Republican organizations in the late thirties as a place to nurture a Republican presence at the grass roots as well as to build the women's vote. These efforts did not entail going after the women's vote by proposing policies of interest to women—the RNC after all was not a policy-making body. Hamilton instead focused on turning local GOP women into loyal Republican voters who would support, rather than criticize, the party. To lead those efforts, Hamilton turned to the Republican national committeewoman from Maine, thirty-seven-year-old Marion Martin. In September 1937 Hamilton chose Martin to serve in the newly created position of RNC assistant chairman in charge of women's activities.[98]

Marion Martin would become instrumental in mobilizing women on behalf of the Republican Party in the late 1930s and 1940s. In creating the National Federation of Women's Republican Clubs, Martin tried to purge the movement of many of the practices and assumptions clubwomen in the 1920s had embraced proudly: independence, separatism, the crusading political style, and a belief in women's moral superiority.

PLAYING THE MAN'S GAME

★ MARION MARTIN AND THE CREATION OF THE NATIONAL FEDERATION OF WOMEN'S REPUBLICAN CLUBS

Marion Martin was part of a younger, post-suffrage generation who brought to her party work an understanding of women's relationship to political life that differed considerably from earlier club leaders. Martin fought against many aspects of Republican women's political style in the belief that both women and the party would benefit in the end. For Marion Martin, a disciplined women's political organization had clear advantages both for the party and for women. She believed that a nationwide army of organized Republican women, committed to the success of the party, truly could help the ailing GOP. Equally important, she believed that if women gathered themselves into a disciplined, loyal organization, male party leaders finally would take them seriously. A party loyalist, Martin also was a consistent advocate of women's advancement in public life. Her struggles to balance those two considerations marked her leadership and reflected her particular women's agenda. That agenda was a thorny one, for while it was intended to be empowering, it often conflicted with the aspirations of Martin's own followers.

★ Martin was born in 1900 in Kingman, Maine, to a father who operated a wholesale potato business and a mother who was a civic activist. William and Florence Martin were prosperous and supportive enough to nourish their daughter's dreams of becoming a research chemist by sending her in 1913 to study at Bradford Academy in Massachusetts, a private secondary school for girls.[1] Following her graduation in 1917, Martin attended Wellesley College. After her second year at Wellesley, however, she contracted tuberculosis and was forced to leave school. Returning to her parents' home in Maine, she sank into a lethargy from which she did not emerge until the late 1920s. A trip around the world appears to have energized her. Clearly Martin enjoyed a privileged background, yet she saw herself as someone who had overcome serious obstacles through her struggle with ill health. Central to Martin's philosophy as a Republican and as a women's advocate was her belief that through persistent hard work one could surmount whatever hardships life presented.

Hard work and persistence paid off for Martin herself. After returning home from her travels, Martin was "eager to participate in things again." No longer willing to be sidelined by her illness, Martin eagerly pursued both an education and a career. She resumed her college education at the University of Maine, graduating in 1935 with a B.A. in economics. She was thirty-five. Meanwhile, she had also entered politics, serving two terms each in Maine's house and senate (from 1931 to 1938).

As one of only a handful of women in the state legislature, Martin was initially a novelty in Maine. Yet she quickly earned a reputation as an influential political figure in her own right—a woman who had successfully assimilated to male politics. Attempting to explain Martin's achievements, Portland's *Evening Express* editorialized in 1936 that "it is more probable that her agreeable experience in political life has been due to the fact that she has met all of the tests of a man's game with flying colors than to the fact that men are going out of their way to be nice to women in politics."[2]

The advantages of Martin's ability to play the "man's game" seemed clear in 1936 when she was selected to replace Maine's retiring Republican national committeewoman. Her challenger was known for her aggressive work organizing Republican women across the state, but the leading state party faction supported Martin. That year she also played a key role in mobilizing Maine voters for the Republican ticket, helping to organize what she claimed was the first statewide house-to-house canvass in Maine.[3] Maine was one of only two states that went for GOP presidential candidate Alf Landon in 1936 and one of the few to claim statewide success for the party that year, electing a Republican governor and securing the state's three congressional seats.[4]

Although new to the RNC in 1936, Martin stood out from many of her female colleagues. Martin had earned her place among the Republican elite not through the reputation of a husband or father, but through her own work as a legislator and a Republican campaigner. Also, in contrast to most Republican national committeewomen, the thirty-six-year-old Martin was young and unmarried. Martin further distinguished herself by speaking her mind at RNC meetings. From the onset of her tenure, Martin consistently advocated increased representation and power for women in party affairs. Martin framed these demands in the language of helping the party, suggesting to the RNC in 1938, for example, that the Republicans were "handicapped" in their efforts to attract women to the party by the Democrats' reputation for "favoring women." Quite simply, Martin noted, Democrats had given jobs to women, whereas Republicans had not.[5] The Republicans, of course, were not in power, and there were fewer opportunities to recognize women's work.[6] Yet, in Martin's view, Republicans in the thirties had not used what opportunities they did have to reward women adequately for their contributions. Women particularly resented it, according to Martin, when Republicans "pick[ed] a dummy to represent them." Women did not want "rubber stamps" but "women qualified to carry out the work and women that the women themselves favor."[7]

Men in the party were happy to sing the praises of women, to declare that a certain campaign could not have succeeded without women's efforts, or to assert that women had done "90% of the work" in a given campaign or would do "75% of the work" in another.[8] But such praise did not necessarily translate into real rewards. Marion Martin challenged party leaders to live up to their rhetoric.[9] She urged that women be appointed to committees where real decisions were made, and she encouraged party leaders to select qualified women as political appointees and as candidates for elected office. Under her leadership, the National Federation of Women's Republican Clubs lobbied for the passage of 50-50 policies (a longtime goal of women in both parties) that would require all party committees (national and state) to be composed of equal numbers of men and women. The Republican Convention did pass such a rule applying to the National Convention committees in 1940; all appointed committees were to consist of a chairman and an equal number of men and women. To the frustration of Martin and other women leaders, however, this reform was ignored in the case of the important Resolutions Committee, which drafted the party platform. Not a single woman sat on this committee at the 1940 convention.[10]

When Hamilton named Martin assistant chairman in 1937, she also became the head of the RNC's Women's Division and the most important mobilizer of Republican women to date.[11] Marion Martin began organizing Republican women about four years after Molly Dewson launched her work with the Women's Division of the DNC. Both Dewson and Martin had attended Wellesley and as adults lived outside of heterosexual marriage (Dewson lived in long-term partnership with another woman, whereas there is no evidence that Martin had a similar relationship). There were also important differences between the two women that shaped their political organizing. Before entering party politics in 1928, Dewson had acquired years of experience in social reform work through female reform organizations such as the National Consumers League. By 1912 she had become a nationally recognized expert on minimum-wage legislation. Dewson also became actively involved in the women's suffrage campaign in Massachusetts. Martin, almost thirty years Dewson's junior, was too young to have participated directly in the suffrage campaign. And although she too was involved with issues affecting working women, Martin obtained her primary political experience not through women's organizations but through the male-dominated world of the Maine state legislature and senate.[12] When Dewson began organizing Democratic women, she was informed by an earlier tradition of female activism, separatism, and progressivism. Martin, of a younger generation, was not.

★ Martin's first activity as assistant chairman of the RNC was to tour the United States in the fall of 1937 assessing the state of women's Republican organizations. It worried Martin that female party regulars (such as the national committeewomen) were not the ones conducting the principal women's activities in most states. Instead, many of these women's clubs operated as "single units" without ties to each other or to the party organization. To Martin's dismay, these clubs often engaged in practices she and John Hamilton found unacceptable, but which were in keeping with the political style developed by partisan clubwomen in the 1920s. Martin observed Republican women's clubs trying to change party policy, endorsing candidates in primaries, and even occasionally working for Democrats. Indeed, some clubs had actually developed as a means to protest the way the Republican Party was operating locally.[13]

The latter group particularly concerned Martin. These independent, autonomous organizations had been a popular form of women's political organizing in the 1920s, representing an attempt to redefine partisanship in the wake of women's suffrage. As a party official, Martin criticized these groups, because they "were not working very hard for the Party but were working for themselves."[14] Many were "frequently misguided and utterly ineffectual." They were, therefore, no asset to the GOP.[15] And yet because these clubs often constituted the only women's Republican organizations, they were the Republican Party to many rank-and-file women voters.

From her position as head of the RNC Women's Division, Martin

*Party Loyalist. Marion Martin, founder of the National
Federation of Women's Republican Clubs, sometime after her
departure from the Republican National Committee. Undated.
(Photo courtesy of William Martin.)*

hoped to reign in and discipline these clubs. She recommended the
formation of a national umbrella organization, linked to the RNC, that
would have jurisdiction over state federations of individual clubs. Martin and her supporters hoped to create political machinery out of the
existing clubs that would reach into local communities across the country. As executive director, Martin would steer this machinery from
Washington. Under her direction, the clubs would continue to combine
political education with social activities, but would now use standard-
ized study materials prepared by Martin's office. According to her vision,
women would discuss the materials in their club meetings, learn both
sides of an issue, become acquainted with the Republican position, and
thus become competent spokeswomen for the party. Most important
for the party, clubs would work in tandem with a uniform message and
purpose.

Not all prominent Republican women agreed on the desirability of
forming a national organization of women's clubs. Some committee-

women feared that a new organization would be built in opposition to the party structure.[16] Others, however, resented the implication that they themselves were not currently doing an effective job organizing women in their states. Resistance from certain national committeewomen would plague Martin throughout her ten years of work with the Federation.

Martin's intention to enforce her own version of partisanship also made other Republican women, outside the National Committee, wary of the Federation idea. A California leader wondered how the Federation could include the many different degrees of partisanship exhibited across the spectrum of Republican women's clubs. Should the Federation be composed only of clubs that were "Republican in the strictest political sense"? Or should the Federation be a "loose" one including better-government clubs, study clubs, and anti–New Deal clubs that generally supported the GOP but did not explicitly restrict their membership to Republicans?[17]

In California, these concerns focused on the role that the right-leaning Pro America would play in any federation of Republican women. Agnes Cleveland of Berkeley saw value in Pro America as a mechanism for recruiting women who were "afraid" of party machinery. She did not want any new Republican women's organization to develop an antagonistic relationship with Pro America. But Pro America was not the "straight-line Republican movement" Cleveland believed was also needed.[18] Other women, including many in Pro America, feared that the Federation would promote intense partisanship at a time when women perhaps could be mobilized more effectively against the New Deal across party lines. Being emphatically partisan when the party was in such disrepute might create unnecessary obstacles. Furthermore, strict partisanship had been resisted even by a number of clubs calling themselves "Republican."

Martin, however, was intent on creating a women's political machine. Under the plan she ultimately proposed to the national committeewomen in December 1937, only strictly partisan clubs could affiliate. Pro America was asked to be a charter member but declined, presumably deciding it did not want to become purely partisan.[19] The bylaws of the National Federation of Women's Republican Clubs defined the Federation as an auxiliary to the RNC, whose duty was to promote political education, loyalty to the party, uniformity of purpose, and "a national approach to the problems facing the Republican Party."[20] Through the Federation, the RNC hoped to create some semblance of a national message. Matters of party policy, the bylaws made clear, were the province of elected party officials and not the Federation. Party loyalty for women required them to remain neutral in intraparty conflicts.[21]

Although not unanimous in their support, the national committee-women voted in December 1937 to form the National Federation of Women's Republican Clubs and accept its bylaws.[22] The following September, the National Federation held its first meeting in Chicago. By that time, eleven states (none in the South) and the District of Columbia had formed statewide federations that subsequently joined the National Federation. Seventy-five individual clubs from twelve additional states had also joined. In total, eighty-five clubs had affiliated with the Federation, including four "colored women's clubs." Together these clubs represented 95,000 women, according to Martin's estimates. By comparison, the League of Women Voters reported its 1938 membership as 43,116, or about half the membership claimed by the fledgling Federation.[23]

Martin, now executive director of the Federation, set out to expand the organization with the assistance of Joyce Arneill, Martin's hand-picked choice for Federation president.[24] The unsalaried president, who remained based in her home state of Colorado, was the ostensible leader of the Federation. But the day-to-day direction remained in Martin's powerful hands. With Martin, based in D.C., serving as both head of the RNC Women's Division and the Federation, the two Republican women's organizations were essentially one and the same, because the single most important project of the Women's Division was the Federation itself.

During the next several years, Martin and her assistants embarked on regional organizing trips in order to promote the Federation and encourage clubs to affiliate. Federation leaders repeatedly complained to each other that men were uninformed about women's activities and often did not seem to want women working in party politics at all. Men reportedly refused to give women anything meaningful to do or to accept their help. Furthermore, national committeewomen and state vice chairmen often had an antagonistic relationship to the Federation that inhibited organization and effectiveness. Several of the national committeewomen also apparently suspected Martin was building up the Federation as her own personal political machine in order to keep herself in office.[25]

Creating women's political machinery out of the disparate independent women's club movement was no easy task. Federation leaders had to enter different states, be aware of all potential areas of local fric-

Building a National Federation. Uniting the disperse women's club movement into one national organization required travel and diplomatic skill. Here Marion Martin's assistant, Jane Macauley (on stairs) is shown deplaning in Seattle with several women leaders from Washington State, 10 May 1946. (Photo courtesy of Jane Hamilton Macauley.)

tion, and keep peace without alienating any person or group. And they needed to convince the hundreds of disparate local clubs across the country to give up their often-cherished independence, form state federations, and affiliate with the national organization. The difficulties in doing so suggests the many different definitions of women's Republicanism in circulation. Furthermore, racial divisions, snobbery, and personal rivalries contradicted any sense that these organizations represented a unified movement. But a unified movement was what Martin was determined to build.

★ Martin's vision of the Federation as a tightly run "educational arm of the Republican Party" had a dual meaning. First, women would educate their communities about current issues and Republican philosophy. Subjects of study programs in the early 1940s included general histories of the American party system, labor relations, reciprocal trade agreements, taxation, and the various proposals for establishing and enforcing the peace once the war was over.[26] The Federation encouraged clubwomen to develop and express informed opinions on political issues through letters to the editor and other public forums. In 1940, for example, the Federation organized a project through which local clubs would carefully read newspapers and listen to the radio in order to monitor what New Deal advocates were saying. Members would then respond to "every statement that can be answered, every charge that can be refuted," through the public forums of those media.[27] The idea, however, was not widely implemented. Martin speculated that the women perhaps lacked confidence in their ability to carry out the project and noted that this was further proof of the dire need for the Federation's educational program.[28]

Central to Martin's tenure as head of the Federation was the promotion of the rights and interests of women in party politics. Training women for participation in all aspects of the political process and convincing men they had to share power with women were as much on Martin's agenda as advancing the GOP. Republican women serving as elected officials were regular speakers at meetings and conventions, and the Federation encouraged competent clubwomen to run for political office.[29] The other meaning of the Federation's educational agenda, then, entailed women educating and training *themselves* in the skills necessary for their own political advancement, a process that included not only education about current political issues but also the practice of party discipline.

Martin's commitment to the twin goals of the Federation (promoting both women and the party) meant that neither could ever be understood in isolation from the other. Helping the party required increasing opportunities for women. In this sense the two goals reinforced each other. At the same time, party loyalty and the party's own traditions inhibited Martin's public criticisms of the GOP's failures to enable women's advancement. To criticize too forcefully or too openly could lead Republican women to question their party and could play into the hands of the Democrats. Open criticism could also undermine Martin's attempts to see women earn legitimacy within the terms of Republican Party politics.

One of the first tasks of preparing women for leading roles in political life, in Martin's view, involved ridding "politics" and "partisanship" of their lingering associations with corruption and unwomanly behavior. Instead Martin wanted to substitute the notion that partisanship was respectable, feminine, and patriotic—as critical an aspect of a woman's civic identity as her nation. "We should stress at all times," Martin wrote, "to make politics a polite subject of conversation."[30] By "politics" she meant *partisan* politics. In this regard, the Federation had to do battle against the popularity of nonpartisan groups such as the League of Women Voters. Although it encouraged its members to join political parties, the LWV itself eschewed partisan politics, arguing that its members should consider issues only in terms of the "public interest."[31] Martin criticized the LWV for indoctrinating women with a philosophy that presented nonpartisanship as the highest ideal of citizenship. She resented what she saw as the self-righteousness of nonpartisan women and stressed her view that women had a civic responsibility to work within the parties.[32] This approach meant developing party discipline.

While emphasizing that individuals should act according to their own convictions, Martin urged clubs neither to endorse candidates in primaries nor to take official positions on issues controversial within the party. Yet those clubs that historically had prided themselves on their independence understandably were reluctant to embrace a National Federation to which party loyalty and discipline would be central. Sarah Pell, president of the Essex County [New York] Women's Republican Club, expressed the lingering appeal of the independent notions of partisanship Martin hoped to overcome. In local elections, Pell insisted, she sometimes found reasons to support non-Republicans. "[F]rankly," Pell stated, "I feel that loyalty to the Nation must come before loyalty to the Party." Similarly, Margaret Sawyer of Berkeley, California, pressed the Federation leaders to clarify their definition of party loyalty. Did party loyalty entail "dumb subservience" or did it include women committed to good government?[33] The notion that partisanship was unpatriotic or that it required women to sacrifice their civic virtue was strongly held by many Republican clubwomen. Martin would consistently try to dismantle these views by preaching an alternative definition of women's partisanship and civic responsibility that stressed partisan loyalty and preservation of the two-party system.

The question of partisanship was a major obstacle to federation. So too were local power struggles and a certain class snobbery that prevented some "society women" from working with less-elite Republican women. Racial difference, not surprisingly, also prevented women from joining together with their fellow Republicans. Despite black women's persistent loyalty to the GOP, organizing them was never a real concern for the Federation leadership. In 1940 a group of African American women led by Jeanette Carter and Lethia Fleming organized the National Association of Republican Women (NARW) for the purpose of integrating African Americans into full citizenship by organizing black women into Republican clubs.[34] Some of the clubs that affiliated with the new organization, such as the League of Republican Women of Chicago, had also been members of the National League of Republican Colored Women of the 1920s. Its national director was Fleming (who had organized black women for the Harding campaign). The NARW was not sponsored by the RNC (as the Federation was) but did publish a monthly journal of Republican opinion, *Women's Voice*, during 1939 and 1940, which was edited by Carter. Articles in its pages espoused standard Republican arguments about government and the economy, as well as criticisms of the Democrats' treatment of African Americans and attacks on the cowardice of the current black Republican leadership. The NARW had optimistic aspirations of enlisting 100,000 women in member clubs and planned a large conference for the fall of 1940. The Federation took little notice of its activities, apparently not viewing this parallel black women's organization as a competitor for the affiliation of black women's clubs; the NARW seems to have evaporated after the 1940 campaign.[35]

Although black women's clubs were told they were welcome in the Federation, no special attempts were made to recruit them. According to Martin, the Federation was "working on the assumption that they [African Americans] are citizens like all of us and can be appealed to by a general appeal."[36] Some state federations allowed black women's Republican clubs to affiliate with the state organizations of mainly white clubs. A survey from September 1939 suggests that about seventy-one black clubs were affiliated with state federations.[37] Aware of the sensitivity of racial issues, Martin tried to ascertain the relationship between white women's and black women's Republican clubs in the various states. A questionnaire sent to various state organizations during the early days of the National Federation revealed an assortment of provisions for "colored women or clubs of colored women." Some states, like Pennsylvania and Michigan, admitted black women and black women's clubs into the state organization on the same terms as white women and white women's clubs. Connecticut leaders said they included African American women in white groups. They had "tried separate organizations," the Connecticut respondent stated, "but they work much better under our direction." The Federation of Republican Women of Maryland respondent, on the other hand, reported that black women had their own organizations. "If you'll pardon me," she replied testily to what was apparently a sensitive subject, "we know best about this question."[38]

Ultimately, the Federation's Advisory Committee chose a policy of ostensibly welcoming black women's clubs into the national organization but allowing racially exclusionary policies to exist at the state level. Where state organizations "still observe a color line in membership," an exception would be made for black women's groups so they could affiliate directly with the National Federation. As Martin advised one club, if it did "exclude colored members, that is entirely your right and prerogative; but we do hope you will encourage the colored clubs to realize that there is a place for them and that they are welcome members of the national group."[39] This compromise reflected Martin's sympathy with the discomfort many women of her time (not only Republican women) felt concerning mixed-race organizations. Certainly Martin's insistence that black women were citizens like other women in the eyes of the Federation was unconvincing.

The Federation leadership declared that it embraced all Republican women but never backed up that claim by giving a hearing to the issues black women found most salient. Like other Republicans, Martin viewed the "Party of Lincoln" as the logical political home of African Americans. If a majority of black voters were currently supporting the Democrats, Republicans often viewed this as a temporary situation created by the Democrats' buying black votes with relief money, not because of a true African American disenchantment with the GOP. The Federation promoted a policy of "tolerance" with respect to minority groups and called for "further appreciation" of their "outstanding contributions."[40] But these words were not accompanied by efforts to include black women in substantive ways. When given the opportunity to write a piece for the black women's Republican magazine, the *Women's Voice*, Marion Martin stuck to safe themes. She compared women (as a minority in politics) with other minority groups, like African Americans, and extolled the progress all minorities had made under the American system of government. On the relationship between black and white women politically or socially, Martin was silent.[41]

United States entry into World War II presented additional challenges to Martin's efforts to build her partisan organization. Practically speaking, wartime fuel rationing inhibited the travel necessary for organization, particularly in rural areas. And the Federation canceled its scheduled 1942 biennial convention "in the interest of needed wartime

Twenty-Nine Days to Go. Although for the most part clubs organized along segregated lines, white Republican women did occasionally work with African American women, as in this photograph from the New York Dewey Headquarters in 1948. From left to right are Mrs. Norton Pearl, Jane Macauley, Judy Weis (past president of the Federation and associate campaign manager for the Dewey-Warren ticket), Peg Green (president of the Federation), and Mame Mason Higgins, probably of the RNC Women's Division. (Photo courtesy of Jane Hamilton Macauley.)

conservation."[42] But the problems caused by the war were not limited to logistics. The war presented many new opportunities for civic-minded, patriotic women to volunteer their time on behalf of the war effort. About one-fourth of American women as a whole participated in officially sanctioned wartime voluntary activities. Middle- and upper-class women in particular embraced such enterprises for they were already experienced with organized activities outside the home through their other club and civic work. This volunteer work probably did little to help win the war, but it did contribute to overall morale by giving financially comfortable women an outlet for their patriotism and by demonstrating that the "rich were doing their share."[43] Federation leaders understandably feared their fledgling partisan movement would dissolve if its members embraced patriotic volunteer activities at the expense of holding Republican club meetings.

Martin and other Federation leaders addressed this problem in two ways. First, they encouraged Republican clubs to do Red Cross and other war work as a body, thus fusing patriotism with Republican partisanship.[44] Other middle-class women's organizations, such the League of Women Voters, similarly encouraged local chapters to do war work as a club, which probably helped keep local chapters alive and provided good public relations for the organization. League women could talk about the important political issues created by the war while they wrapped bandages. As one league pamphlet put it, "[i]deas were equally as important as the bandages to the fate of democracy."[45] Like the LWV, the Federation insisted the war only made the traditional work of its members more important.

A second way Federation leaders tried to hold the organization together during the war was by insisting on the need for women to preserve a "virile two-party system." Many American women considered it unpatriotic to engage in partisan politics in wartime. The widespread desire to unite behind the country's leaders during a time of crisis undermined the appeal of women's organizations affiliated with the opposition (Republican) party.[46] In her organizing efforts, Martin had stressed political engagement as a civic duty, the dignity of partisanship, patriotism, the value of volunteer activity, and the dangers to the country posed by the New Deal. Nonpartisanship, already appealing to many American women, proved during wartime to be a particular obstacle to Republican organizing among women. In response, Federation leaders presented the tyranny of a one-party system as a real danger at a time when Americans not only desired a unified nation but also had a three-term president who seemed uninterested in stepping down. Martin challenged nonpartisan calls for "unity" and "patriotism" by arguing that it "will profit us nothing to win a war against autocracy and totalitarianism if we become totalitarian in order to do it." Women, Martin urged, needed to participate in politics to preserve American institutions for men while they were away at war. One of those important institutions was the two-party system.[47]

★ Convincing a large, dispersed, and diverse group of Republican women to practice the kind of party discipline the Federation preached was unrealistic. Divisions within the Republican Party itself in this period were so great that it was unreasonable to think women would somehow transcend those divisions. What was the Federation to advise when the positions stated in the Republican Party's platform were either not to Martin's liking or controversial among party women? Different Republican women and women's clubs felt strongly about various issues, and they were not always on the same side. And many clubs valued their independence from the party. Martin's strategy for achieving women's power depended on women proving themselves to be party loyalists. This meant avoiding controversy and thus avoiding public discussion of many significant yet divisive issues. A look at the Federation's response to some of the party's 1940 platform planks illuminates the difficult dynamics of this strategy.

★ THE EQUAL RIGHTS AMENDMENT

In 1940 the GOP became the first major party to endorse in its platform the Equal Rights Amendment to the constitution. The ERA was first proposed by Alice Paul in the early 1920s, and the National Woman's Party remained its strongest supporter throughout the thirties, forties, and fifties. Many prominent women and women's organizations, such as the League of Women Voters, opposed the ERA because of fears that it would eliminate labor laws granting special protections to working women. The amendment's supporters typically were well-educated, professional women.[48] Organizations in favor of the ERA lobbied both parties to support the amendment. As Cynthia Harrison suggests, arguments that the ERA would dismantle protective labor legislation provoked little concern among probusiness Republicans, which probably explains why the GOP endorsed the amendment in 1940, four years before the Democrats.[49]

Those Republicans who supported the ERA plank undoubtedly believed it would increase the party's appeal to women. Yet while most NWP members were Republican, the ERA did not have the broad endorsement of women, not even of Republican women. Both the leadership and the rank and file of the Federation were divided on the issue. Some Republican women of the progressive tradition may have had reservations based on concerns about protective legislation. But other Republican women opponents had reasons that had little to do with the fate of women workers. One of Martin's colleagues believed the amendment had "all the dangerous aspects of class legislation," while Marion Martin explained her own opposition as discomfort with the drastic step of a constitutional amendment.[50] While head of the Federation, she did not take a public stand on the issue, however. Her primary concern, she claimed, was for the good of the party, and she presented her opposition to the party's ERA plank in those terms. She knew the ERA did not have wide support and argued that if the GOP campaigned too vigorously on the issue it would stir up controversy and alienate many women.[51]

The National Woman's Party, assuming that the Federation was supporting the ERA once the plank was in the party platform, continually approached Martin about coordinating activities between the two organizations. The Federation did distribute ERA materials provided by the NWP to the national committeewomen and state vice chairmen. The Federation, however, did not send the material to the club presidents because, as Martin put it, "there is no need to stir up sleeping dogs." Martin knew that the Federation was not actively working to support the ERA plank, but did not want to admit this to the NWP, whose members she described as "pains in the neck."[52] Yet the Federation's objective of "promoting [the party's] ideals" seemed to require that it support the planks of the party platform.[53] Martin usually adhered strictly to this kind of discipline. But because she herself opposed ERA and also had reasons to believe the issue to be potentially explosive in the Federation, her support was not forthcoming. It seemed that the Federation could neither support nor oppose the ERA plank.[54]

The Executive Board of the Federation addressed its dilemma in 1943 by sending a confidential letter to the RNC chairman and the Republican minority leaders expressing the board's opposition to the ERA plank as "premature, unwise, and unnecessary." The letter also stated strongly that members of the Federation board resented the RNC's failure to consult with them. The board went on to suggest that had there been women on the Resolutions Committee, as the Federation had repeatedly urged, this potentially disastrous situation would not have occurred.[55] By 1944 women were, in fact, serving on the Resolutions Committee, under a new move by the RNC.[56] This reform, however, did not lead to removal of the ERA plank as Martin had predicted—the Republican platform continued to contain support for the ERA through the next several conventions.[57] By the 1950s, the Federation itself was endorsing the amendment.

★ CIVIL RIGHTS

The 1940 Republican platform also contained a strong statement against racial discrimination and disenfranchisement and included some programmatic proposals to address these problems.[58] Although they never succeeded in getting a real hearing for their concerns, some

African American women did try to make the Federation actively support the party's official endorsement of racial equality. One of the more vocal clubs was Betty Hill's Woman's Political Study Club of California. Hill was an unflagging advocate of the Republican Party and black civil rights. An active member of her local NAACP, Hill had been involved with efforts in Los Angeles to eradicate segregation of black nurses and discrimination against black interns working at General Hospital.[59] Hill was a member of the California Republican State Central Committee and the founder of the Woman's Political Study Club.

Hill's commitment to the Republican Party in the 1940s did not stem merely from a rote association of the party with Abraham Lincoln. Like many white club leaders, Hill opposed the "creeping collectivism" of the New Deal. She also held criticisms of the New Deal particular to its effect on African Americans. These criticisms were consistent with standard conservative Republican appeals to black voters of that time. The New Deal, Hill argued, had "fooled" African Americans by "setting up twenty-five percent bureaucrats among them with the other seventy-five percent on the dole." By giving relief to blacks, Hill argued, the New Deal was denying them the one thing that she believed had enabled them to persevere and progress in the past—the ability to work. Hill maintained that "the dole" had "set the colored American back one hundred and fifty years."[60]

While condemning the New Deal's impact on African Americans, Hill also urged her own party to take constructive action. In 1944 Hill's club passed a resolution calling on Congress to enact legislation to prohibit racial discrimination in the District of Columbia. Two years later, Hill sent a copy of the resolution to the president of the California Council of Republican Women, Barbara Whittiker, requesting that the resolution be taken up at the Federation's biannual meeting. Not knowing how to proceed, Whittiker wrote to Marion Martin about the matter. "Leave it to Betty Hill to bring up some headache," Martin replied. She advised Whittiker to deal with Hill through invoking bureaucratic procedures.[61] It is apparent from the tone of Martin and Whittiker's correspondence that they did not intend to push Hill's resolution, however. Whether the resolution was ever considered by Federation delegates is unclear, but it was certainly never endorsed. What African American Republican women like Betty Hill thought of or realistically expected from the Federation is not clear from this exchange. In any case, the Federation had no intention of going out on a limb on behalf of a controversial issue to which the GOP itself gave only token support.

Civil rights and the Equal Rights Amendment were relatively minor issues for the party in the early 1940s. Isolationism, by contrast, was at the forefront of intraparty conflict. After France and Britain declared war on Germany in 1939, Republican women were bitterly divided (as was the party as a whole), over the proper response of the United States. Should the United States aid the forces fighting Hitler? Should the United States begin preparing for the possibility of war? Or should the United States maintain its isolationist posture as embodied in the Neutrality Acts of the late 1930s? In 1940 the GOP nominated internationalist Wendell Willkie as its presidential candidate, despite the strength of isolationism within the party. The party platform that year declared that the Republicans would keep the United States out of war but would aid those countries fighting for liberty, a plank that was certainly not satisfactory to all Republicans.[62] In the spring of 1941, after weeks of contentious debate, Congress passed Roosevelt's controversial "Lend-Lease" proposal to lend arms to the Allies. Some Republican women, convinced that the defense of European allies was vital to U.S. security, wanted the party to endorse the president's proposal. Others were emphatically opposed.

Martin did her best to keep such issues out of the Federation, but the task became increasingly difficult. After a western organizing trip in the autumn months before the December attack on Pearl Harbor, President Judy Weis reported that the Federation rank and file represented the entire spectrum of thought on the war, from "outright intervention to blackest isolationism."[63] The majority, however, seemed to Weis to be emphatically against American engagement. To crowds of women demanding to know what the Republican Party was doing to keep "the boys" out of the war, Weis could reply only with unsatisfactory words about bipartisan foreign policy while trying to turn attention back to domestic issues.[64] When one club called on the Federation to take a stand on aiding the allies, the Federation Executive Committee decided the subject was too contentious and restated its opposition to the Federation or its member clubs taking positions on controversial issues. "[W]e should concentrate our activities," the resolution read, "in providing a fair, objective educational program in order that honest information may be available to all the members and that they in turn with this information can act according to their best judgment."[65]

This was a precarious balance for the Federation to maintain. When faced with an issue as divisive as the war, the best the Federation could do and still maintain its mandate of supporting the Republican Party was to encourage women to study the issues and be informed. Meanwhile other women's organizations that had Republican (or anti-Democratic) leanings but lacked the partisan imperative to avoid the war issue had taken clear stands. The isolationist, anti–New Deal mothers' groups that had proliferated in 1939–41 were organizing against Lend-Lease and military preparedness.[66] And the National Board of Pro America, in October 1941, declared the organization in favor of aid to nations fighting Axis aggression.[67] Many Republican-leaning women who wanted to be politically involved had the choice of joining a women's organization that, unlike the Federation, had declared itself on the most pressing issue facing the country.

After the United States entered the war, most prominent isolationists publicly declared their support for the war effort. Yet among the rank and file, the old divisions were not immediately healed. Such divisions persisted among women as well. Martin alerted her colleague Wilma Bishop, who was preparing for an organizing trip in August 1942, that she would still encounter intense feelings surrounding the isolation-intervention debate, even though the issue supposedly had been moot since Pearl Harbor. Martin advised that it was best to avoid the subject. But if Bishop should be "cornered" by those who wanted to attack the party or any Federation members for their pre–Pearl Harbor position, she should give the answer Martin herself had "found effective"—namely, that Republican isolationists had voted their convictions and that it was necessary to have had different opinions about what would keep the United States out of war. Martin adopted the standard argument of moderate Republicans who had opposed FDR's pre–Pearl Harbor foreign policy. Although it was important to support the war effort now, Martin encouraged Bishop to point out that it would never be known whether war might have been avoided without Roosevelt's policies. All that was certain was that Roosevelt's policies had not prevented U.S. involvement. Martin's carefully worded statements were designed to show support for the war effort while still allowing room to criticize the president.[68]

Because her chief goals were to advance the Republican Party and to achieve inclusion for women in party affairs, Martin stifled debate on issues that she thought would encourage dissension, such as the ERA, civil rights, and aid to the Allies. Women had to overcome the reputation, she argued, that they were unable to work harmoniously with each other or with the men of the party. This is somewhat ironic, given the divisions within the party as a whole over the New Deal and the nation's role in the world that had erupted in the fight over the 1940 presidential nomination.[69] Although men in the party also divided on many issues and disagreed with elements of the party's platform, they were not similarly stigmatized as disloyal when they did so. Engaging with the pressing issues facing one's party could be viewed as a responsible form of partisanship and citizenship. Yet women's partisanship was not understood in the same ways as men's.

Martin sought to present the women's organization as united for the good of the party. She wanted the party to consider seriously women's input. But her strategy for convincing men that women could be trusted with such important responsibilities was to shun arguments that women were independent thinkers with their own agenda and to avoid any sense that women might rebel if not given proper consideration. This was a paradoxical strategy for empowerment that Martin arrived at based on the constraints of party politics and the hierarchical culture of the GOP, as well as on her own brand of feminism.

★ Like a broad spectrum of women political leaders of her time, including Eleanor Roosevelt and Margaret Chase Smith, Marion Martin did not consider herself to be a feminist. In the late thirties and early forties, "feminism" connoted the small group of women in the NWP who continued the campaign for the ERA. Yet like Roosevelt and Smith, Martin advocated women's advancement. While emphasizing that Martin's own self-definition never included "feminist," it is useful to explore Martin's activism as part of a very broadly defined tradition of women's rights activism.[70] Doing so reminds us that a gender critique of power relations does not necessarily predict one's other political beliefs and helps explain why advocates of women's rights have not always supported other components of a liberal or leftist agenda. Marion Martin held a set of political principles that led her to develop a specific analysis of women's subordination and strategies for addressing that condition. These same principles also gave her a home in the Republican Party.

To Martin, the ideal world was one in which various segments of society were not divided into competing interest groups but instead recognized their common interests and duties as citizens. She was suspicious of the idea that an activist federal government could mediate conflicts between groups. In Martin's ideal world, conflicts were resolved calmly and rationally by knowledgeable people with a commitment to promoting what was best for the community or country as a whole. She felt that the country faced a "depressing future" because "one per cent of our people . . . think and the other 99 per cent emote."[71] Martin believed an educated citizenry to be fundamental to the health of society and that all citizens should take responsibility for becoming informed in order to contribute to the nation's political conversations. Martin found it proper that educated, qualified people should be in leadership roles. She believed anyone who was committed to hard work and patience could play such a role. Those who were not willing to work should not expect to be listened to or to reap political rewards.

Martin's worldview was compatible with the anti–New Deal politics of moderate Republicans in the 1930s and 1940s. Like other Republicans, Martin described the New Deal government as wasteful and corrupt. In her view, New Dealers exploited their political positions by using ostensibly nonpartisan offices to promote the New Deal and by using relief funds to buy the votes of vulnerable segments of the electorate, such as the unemployed and African Americans. Martin saw the New Deal as the antithesis of a principled, rational politics based on the careful weighing of competing arguments. She was not optimistic that the federal government could right wrongs or solve social problems. Rather, she feared that it would use its authority to perpetuate or exacerbate such problems, including the subordination of women.

Looking toward the end of World War II, for example, Martin became concerned that an all-powerful Democratic administration would give preference to men for postwar government jobs and that the private sector would imitate such a policy. Her concerns centered on the Economy Act of 1932, which had made the federally employed wife of a federally employed man a priority for layoffs.[72] The Economy Act was not a New Deal measure, but it was an example of the federal government's efforts to respond to unusual economic conditions. In 1943 Martin read in the newspaper that women "would be returning to the home, thereby creating a lot of jobs for the men as soon as the fighting was over." For Martin, this report raised concerns that the federal government would force women out of their jobs after the war. "If the Government, having a life and death hold on industry as it does at the present time, did adopt such a policy in the future," Martin warned, "the result as far as women's employment is concerned would be chaotic."[73] Martin's wariness of big government, in this case, stemmed from a justified suspicion that the state was not free of sexism and from a concern that a government as powerful and influential as FDR's would have the power to institutionalize discrimination through its far-reaching sway.

Martin further objected to the New Deal because it seemed to set certain groups of society against others. As Martin told a gathering of Republican women in 1940, what drove her personally in speaking out against the New Deal was that she sensed a "breakdown in American morale, the result of class hatreds fomented by the New Deal."[74] Although not wholly indifferent to the grievances of workers, Martin rejected the idea that society was divided into different classes with competing interests. She was hostile to most strikes but allowed that they were sometimes necessary to redress "justifiable grievances." She confessed in 1941 that she herself sometimes became so carried away when speaking on the subject that she would feel compelled to call for an outlawing of all strikes. As a pragmatic politician, however, Martin was more cautious than that and recognized that it would do "a great deal of harm to the Party" if Federation leaders were to give ammunition to charges that the GOP was "an anti-labor party."[75]

Besides being compatible with moderate Republicanism, Martin's worldview also led to a particular analysis of women's inequality. Her analysis focused almost exclusively on discrimination against women in political life. In addressing the problem of women's low representation in politics, Marion Martin believed she had to do battle on two fronts. One battle was against men and the irrational, outdated, yet persistent prejudices that many men held against the very idea of women's substantive participation in politics. From her position on the RNC, Martin tirelessly challenged men's resistance by providing party leaders with names of qualified women and by lobbying for reforms that she thought would give women more voice in party affairs.

The second battle Martin thought she had to fight was against women themselves. Martin believed the majority of women had failed to accept the responsibilities and duties of full citizenship (as she defined it). Although she did not explicitly describe it this way, Martin saw herself, and the women she handpicked to serve as Federation officers, as a kind of vanguard that would help prepare women for fuller participation in politics. Martin wanted to help other women become successful in politics. She hoped that serious women's study clubs could address some of the deficiencies from which she believed women suffered. She allowed that most women would best receive their political training in women-only organizations, because that was where they were most comfortable. Yet she worried about many of the social aspects of women's organizing. Martin held that women, or at least the women her clubs targeted, generally were less informed and more apathetic about political issues than men, that they were often snobbish and petty, and that they had a tendency toward extremism and silliness. Martin had only contempt for "starry-eyed dowagers" who were bored by political work but who joined Republican clubs because they were interested in their own social advancement.[76] "A woman's Republican club," Martin emphasized, "is not designed as a social medium whereby a woman with social aspirations may achieve her objective; but it is for the purpose of making votes for the Republican Party. If we are primarily social rather than political in our attitudes, we are more apt to antagonize than to win votes."[77] Martin attacked those women who reinforced the stereotypes of women's political clubs popularized by the cartoonist Helen E. Hokinson. Hokinson's cartoons depicted stout, expensively dressed, middle-aged club ladies, consumed by trivial concerns, their own self-interest, and an overblown sense of their own importance.

Martin had definite ideas about what Republican women should be doing during their club meetings. She worried that women did not use the program suggestions and study materials sent to them by the National Federation, and particularly disapproved of clubwomen putting on programs that discouraged active learning. Bringing in outside speakers attracted a passive membership and did nothing to develop "informed and articulate Republican women." Attending rallies did not provide women with arguments to use later. And when club meetings centered on introducing and passing resolutions, women tended to vote automatically rather than to discuss issues, ask questions, and mull over the matter later. Some clubwomen, such as Helen Shorey of Maine, found that as a result of club activities their newspaper reading habits were changing to concentrate on political writers at the expense of the society and sports pages.[78] Yet despite the carefully prepared study materials that Federation leaders sent to club presidents, Martin continued to receive reports that some clubs viewed themselves as social clubs whose purpose was to talk politics over card games.[79] Martin also despaired at the preference of women's clubs for activities she thought silly. She and Judy Weis shared with each other their exasperation at, for example, the practice of clubs presenting guest speakers with stuffed or carved elephants, or asking prominent Republican women for pictures of their everyday shoes.[80] It was no wonder, in Martin's view, that men were reluctant to take women seriously as political actors.

Marion Martin put a negative spin on another feature of women's politics that others before her had viewed more favorably—the tendency to frame political involvement as a women's crusade. Martin saw women as having a weakness for emotional oratory that made them susceptible to appeals by fringe organizations. In 1939 Martin cautioned against encouraging Republican women to work with an organization called the Clearing House for National Interests. The Clearing House was calling for mass rallies in support of congressional investigations of subversion. Although she recognized that antisubversion was an issue that resonated with many Republican women, Martin urged that "great care" had to be exercised in "stirring [them] up" to work on such issues. She was suspicious of organizations like the Clearing House, which she characterized as an "alarmist group." One of the only things enabling such organizations to expand, Martin believed, was "the fact that women like to be alarmed and these groups, with little regard for accuracy or objectivity, set their women to work and the lid's blown off."[81] Here Martin offered an analysis of why many women were attracted to fringe political movements. Because women "like[d] to be alarmed," they were vulnerable to the appeals of extremists who used simplistic, emotional, "alarmist" rhetoric to gain support. Martin had reason to be concerned about women joining extremist organizations. In the late thirties, women's organizations opposed to U.S. involvement in the European conflict were attracting members in numbers much higher than her moderate, Republican organization. Many of the leaders of these organizations were women whose antiwar views were connected to anticommunist and anti-Semitic conspiracy theories and who relied on dire rhetoric to recruit female members.[82]

"Alarmism" was Martin's interpretation of the crusading political style and was something she associated with financially comfortable older clubwoman who clung to a politics Martin believed was no longer appropriate for a post-suffrage generation. While Martin saw this tendency of women as a weakness, earlier Republican women leaders had emphasized women's need to be motivated by crusading language that expressed issues in stark, moral terms. Crusading language was problematic for Martin, because it seemed to lead to uncompromising, ideological positions. Martin sought to temper extremism among women. She tried to dissuade women from turning what she saw as reasonable objections to the New Deal (that it was creating a corrupt and wasteful bureaucracy, for example) into an equation of the New Deal with socialism. Such irresponsible rhetoric, Martin feared, might cause people to "question our whole system of government."[83]

Although she believed women could best be mobilized through separate organizations, Martin made clear that her modern Federation did not support the separatism (or sex antagonism) of previous women's organizations. Many partisan women leaders in the 1920s had claimed to reject sex antagonism but clung to vestiges of it. The idea of a unique women's politics was still embraced fairly widely by the women Martin was organizing, however. A statement in the Federation's 1940 handbook concerning "political etiquette" reflected Martin's view. The work of the women's Federation should be, according to Martin, "so effective that there is no necessity for a 'war between the sexes.' . . . In order to gain recognition by the men officials of the Party women must so organize and so conduct themselves as to gain the respect of Party leaders by becoming indispensable to Party success. Recognition cannot be gained merely by continual warfare demanding rights, privileges, recognition and by petty bickering over these matters."[84] Martin was not committed to the view that women had a unique perspective or a unique morality. In contrast to women like Alma Lorimer in the twenties, Marion Martin did not think Republican women should be out to reform or transform male politics. They were merely seeking a way in.

Although some Federation leaders did applaud women's hardworking crusade for the party in contrast to the weak, fearful, and ineffective efforts of men, Martin sought to avoid having such spirited talk develop into militant attacks on the persistent relegation of Republican women to secondary, decorative roles in the party. This was a delicate balance and difficult to maintain. While expressing frustration with men in her private letters, Martin tried to be careful, in speaking publicly, not to create the impression that she was building, through the Federation, an uncooperative faction. To do so, she wrote, "would scare the men and arouse them to active opposition."[85] It also, of course, might have cost Martin her job. Martin tactfully introduced criticisms of the male leadership as strategic warnings. In 1945 she told the RNC that there was "seething and boiling on the part of women because they feel they have been given the doorbell ringing jobs to do, but are never given a voice." She assured those present that this was not true at the national level, but that it was true in many states and needed to be corrected.[86]

The Federation could only be justified, in Martin's view, so long as it was contributing to the success of the party as a whole. This was a view entirely different from that of earlier Republican club leaders such as Alma Lorimer for whom being "uncooperative" was a hallmark of their independence. Martin's view also differed from Democratic organizer Molly Dewson's. In embarking on her work of organizing Democratic women in the 1930s, Dewson had stated that her "main duty [was] to build up the organization of the women, not to speak in behalf of the Party."[87] Martin saw the relationship of the women's organization to the party differently. Martin's understanding brought her sensitivity to the ways in which her party operated together with her own views of how a political party should function. Her attempts to avoid factionalism was a pragmatic strategy for gaining the trust of men, which she considered crucial to women's advancement, a logical strategy given the traditions of the GOP. Having male allies was, and would continue to be, essential for female Republican leaders. Furthermore, the very idea of a women's faction contradicted Martin's own view that problems could be solved in a harmonious manner or that a transcendent civic identity should trump other differences among citizens. Here she distinguished herself from leaders of women's organizations such as the National Woman's Party and the Woman's Christian Temperance Union, whose members she referred to disparagingly as "dogmatic old harpies."[88]

Martin's reluctance to view women as a separate interest group within the party was matched by a difficulty in comprehending differences among women themselves. Although as a practical politician she recognized that her movement had to embrace all kinds of women for it to grow, Martin was not able to develop real strategies for appealing to diverse groups of women. Martin had, for example, no racial analysis of power relations or of political interest. She rejected what she labeled "factionalism" for all groups.

One way Martin thought women's clubs could avoid being perceived as a faction was to maintain neutrality with respect to intraparty conflicts. She encouraged nationally directed projects such as a 1939 letter-writing campaign in support of Republican-endorsed amendments to the Wagner Act.[89] She objected, however, when individual clubs took official stands on controversial issues such as whether the United States should enter the war in Europe while party leaders remained bitterly divided on this issue. Martin believed her approach would be the best for women who had to overcome their reputation as undisciplined, uninformed, and emotional troublemakers. However, the Federation's emphasis on women's responsibility to be politically informed and active was a message of empowerment that was at odds with Martin's own insistence on party discipline.

Illinois clubwoman Mrs. E. G. Goddard challenged Martin on this contradiction in 1944. Goddard was a staunch opponent of the proposed United Nations and wanted the Federation to take a strong stand against such "entangling alliances." Consequently, she was exasperated

by a Federation statement urging clubs to refrain from passing resolutions dealing with national policy. Goddard pointed to the irony of
Martin's strategy for giving women a voice in party affairs. "After we
voluntarily agree to be silent on the paramount issue, which is foreign
policy," Goddard noted, "we turn around and crusade for 50-50 laws—
equal representation of women on major political committees." Goddard complained that the fight for such reforms made women feel like
they were doing something, but "what good will 50-50 laws do us if we
continue in the way we have started—saying 'Aye, aye sir,' and merely
rubber-stamping every policy the men propose and promote. Why do
we want more rights when we are deliberately stifling and refusing to
exercise those rights which we already have?"[90] In Goddard's view, the
demands of partisan politics were an obstacle to women ever becoming
a real political force.

Martin undoubtedly cringed when she read Goddard's next statement that the "INTERNATIONALIST PROGRAM" (as Goddard called the UN)
was the "communist-fascist-socialist program" of the New Deal and that
this program would take over the Republican Party just as it had taken
over the Democrats "unless the women speak and speak now."[91] Martin
despaired when this kind of "alarmist" language came from women in
the Federation. Yet club members like Goddard, trained through the
Federation to believe in women's important role in politics and to have
confidence in their own views, would not remain content with the restrained, cooperative, approach that Martin advocated.

Certainly Marion Martin's women's agenda was conservative. It was
assimilationist, arguing that women needed to conform more or less
to the world of male politics as a precondition to achieving political
equality. It was unable to recognize race as a serious issue affecting
women. It was elitist in its underlying implication that most women
needed to be directed by leaders like Martin who had already successfully entered men's world.[92] And it created a predilection against independent activism among women. Yet it offered a clear strategy for
gradually dismantling the persistent obstacles to women's equality that
women's suffrage had not eradicated—a strategy that is understandable
within the context of Martin's own support for the Republican Party
and her corresponding conviction that acceptance into the party was a
worthwhile goal for women. There were many ironies in Martin's efforts
to promote both women's political advancement and the GOP. Yet there
was also a coherent logic to those efforts. During the decade in which
she led the National Federation of Women's Republican Clubs, Marion

Martin articulated a women's agenda that was akin to those Republican principles that she also advocated.

In the 1946 midterm elections, the Republican Party at last experienced significant victories, winning both houses of Congress and a majority of the nation's governorships. The conservative turn that enabled these victories was partly a reaction against organized labor's successes in winning wage increases through strikes—the costs of which business leaders passed on to consumers, undermining support for labor and the Democratic Party. Yet Republican leaders also recognized the important contribution of women's work to party successes. Marion Martin took this opportunity to step up her regular demands that the party reward women's competence and contributions. Fresh from the November victories, Martin called on those present at the December 1946 RNC meeting to live up to Republican rhetoric about the importance of women's party work. She implored members to urge the newly elected Republican governors to appoint qualified women to state office and to start listening to women's input. "We need it not because we are feminists," she insisted, "but because there are a great many non-partisan women's organizations that do wield an influence in this country, and they have been spreading the word . . . [that] the Democrats recognized women better than the Republicans did."[93]

★ Martin always tried to present her women's organization as a training ground of cooperative party workers. Yet she still managed to make enemies on the Republican National Committee. Five days after her December 1946 speech to the RNC, Marion Martin was asked by then chairman Carroll Reece to resign. Reece's firing of Martin was controversial, and his precise motivation remains unclear. Years later, Martin herself would insist publicly that she had left the RNC because she disagreed with Reece's desire to involve the RNC more directly in setting policy for the party.[94] Although this disagreement did occur, it was not the major issue between Reece and Martin, and other nonofficial accounts, including some of Reece's own correspondence, clearly indicate that Martin did not resign voluntarily.[95]

Martin's departure drew press coverage across the country. Many women leaders, in and out of the party, saw Reece's move as a direct affront to GOP women. Political columnist Doris Fleeson implied a direct link between Martin's outspoken efforts on behalf of women in the party and her termination. The new chairman, Fleeson said, was provoking "widespread fear" that he intended to "minimize the women's part [in the party] and turn it back to the kind of amateur window-dressing it formerly was."[96] Senator Margaret Chase Smith (R.-Maine) accused the RNC publicly of giving the impression that it was "slamming the door on women" and demanded that Reece offer an explanation for the "questionable circumstances" of Martin's departure that would satisfy women voters.[97]

Although it is tempting to see Martin as a victim of a party that was hostile to women, the story is more complicated. Martin was most likely a casualty of existing divisions within the party. Over the years Martin had successfully worked with several different RNC chairmen, representing different wings of the party. During campaigns, the GOP presidential candidate usually selected the chairman; at other times the selection reflected the faction of the party that dominated the RNC. Martin, who was up for reappointment as assistant chairman each time a new chairman was selected, had remained in her position through the tenures of several different chairmen.[98] Martin's role as an advocate for Republican women was always vulnerable because she depended on male allies for her position. In 1946 she lost that crucial support. The new chairman, Reece, was a supporter of Robert Taft's wing of the party, and the Taft forces sought at that time to purge the Dewey forces from the committee's leadership. Although Martin had tried to remain neutral in such conflicts, she was seen as having favored Dewey in 1944.[99]

Furthermore, many national committeewomen simply did not like Martin. Martin's most prominent opponents among the committeewomen were Taft-ites, such as the formidable Katharine Kennedy Brown. But the reasons some committeewomen opposed Martin also derived from a feeling that Martin did not allow them enough input into directing women's activities for the party. One of Martin's most outspoken enemies was Irene Gerlinger, national committeewoman from Oregon. Gerlinger's long battle with Martin stemmed from one of Martin's failures to overcome local rivalries in forming the Federation. Gerlinger had been involved in a long dispute with Federation board member Wilma Bishop over leadership of Republican women in Oregon. Gerlinger accused Martin of using underhanded tactics to favor Bishop and let other prominent Republicans, including Reece, know of her complaints. When Reece asked Martin to resign, Gerlinger "rejoice[d]" and later proudly took credit for Martin's dismissal.[100] Although there were surely other factors at play, the insistence of Gerlinger, Brown, and others that Martin lacked rapport with the committeewomen and was unable to bring harmony to the women's organization certainly would have helped Reece to conclude that Martin was dispensable.

After Martin's resignation, the fate of the Federation was unclear. Several of Martin's enemies were mentioned as possible successors to the position of RNC assistant chairman.[101] There was even talk that the Federation would be eliminated altogether. In the end, Reece appointed Martin's assistant, thirty-year-old Jane Hamilton Macauley, to replace Martin. Macauley had links to both the Taft and the Dewey camps, so was considered nonaligned.[102] She was also younger than Martin, and Reece perhaps considered her more pliable. The Marion Martin era in the Federation's history came to a close. Martin returned to Maine where she became the first woman appointed state commissioner of labor, a position she would hold for twenty-five years. A series of both Republican and Democratic governors reappointed Martin seven times to that position.[103] She retired in 1972 and died 8 January 1987.[104] In 1972, in a new climate of female activism, Martin wrote "I'm not for the Women's Lib Movement because I think that if women would work as hard and steadily in their chosen fields as men do they can achieve as much. Nothing is handed to you on a silver platter."[105] This vision of the plucky individual overcoming obstacles and achieving success was how Martin saw herself. Yet it denied the real battles she had found it necessary to wage against men's deeply embedded resistance to women in public life.

It is impossible to assess the growth of the Federation in the early 1940s with any precision. By the end of 1940, membership records indicate that Federation membership ranged from 120,000 to 160,000 in about eighteen to twenty-one statewide federations (including the District of Columbia) plus membership in individual clubs in about twelve additional states.[106] In a report to the RNC, however, Martin stated that by June 1940 membership was at 250,000.[107] Because membership totals were estimates, the Federation seems to have measured its growth in terms of whether new clubs were being organized. In this regard, the Federation showed slow but steady growth during the war years. By the end of 1944, statewide federations were organized in twenty-eight states plus the District of Columbia. Fourteen additional states, many of them in the South, had at least one individual club affiliated directly with the Federation.[108]

In whatever way growth is assessed, the Republican Party certainly had a stronger women's organization in place during the 1940 and 1944 presidential campaigns than it had in the past. During these campaigns, Martin encouraged the regular party women to make use of the army of volunteers available through the Republican clubs. In 1940 Martin urged the national committeewomen and state vice chairmen to enlist clubs to help conduct voter polls; in 1944 Federation president Marie Suthers encouraged clubs to organize absentee-ballot drives for soldiers.[109] In later years, volunteer work for the party would become among the most important activities of Federation clubs. Under Martin, however, the long-term educational aspects of the clubs remained most important. To overcome their political weaknesses, Martin felt Republican women needed to be trained as informed and loyal party spokespersons. Martin intended Republican women's clubs to socialize women into her vision of women's party politics to the long-term benefit of the Republican Party and of women themselves.

The Federation would change substantially in the postwar era. It expanded its reach, grew in size and sophistication, and, in many ways, moved away from Martin's vision. Martin had never succeeded in fully eradicating the independent women's political style she had found so detrimental to both women and the party. After World War II, the "alarmist" rhetoric of moral politics and skepticism about party loyalty to which many Republican clubwoman still adhered would help foster a hardening right-wing politics among a significant number of Federation women.

THE RETURN OF
THE FEMALE POLITICAL
CRUSADE

In the aftermath of World War II, American society changed in ways that would offer new opportunities to the Republican Party and to the National Federation of Republican Women. The country confronted inevitable postwar demobilization, resulting in economic restructuring, massive labor unrest, shortages of goods and housing, and inflation. A new wave of black migration northward continued to change the face of northern cities. Many white families relocated to new areas of economic growth in the southern and Sunbelt metropolitan areas. Black Americans, hoping to capitalize on the antiracist rhetoric used to rally support for the war against Germany, called for an end to the second-class citizenship they were offered at home. In doing so, they unleashed forces that would eventually lead to political realignment as the Democratic and Republican Parties gradually reconfigured their positions on civil rights and states' rights.

On the international front, Americans confronted a very different world than that of the 1930s. Alone among the Allies, the United States had emerged from the war with a strong economy and a strong military. The United States also held the secrets of the atom bomb. Together with other world leaders, U.S. policy experts negotiated a new global order, anchored by international bodies such as the United Nations and the World Bank, which were designed to promote economic development, human rights, and peaceful resolution of conflicts. United States relations with its former ally, the Soviet Union, deteriorated as each country sought to expand its own sphere of influence around the globe. The USSR became America's new enemy. President Truman and Congress initiated the Loyalty Program (1947) and the McCarran Act (1950) to weed alleged communist sympathizers out of government. The Cold War had begun.

Republicans were poised to take advantage of the political opportunities offered by the end of World War II. Roosevelt was dead, and Truman lacked the popularity of his predecessor. As a result of midterm elections in 1946, Republicans took control of the House and Senate. By 1947 public opinion was turning against Truman and the Democrats, who many Americans believed were too closely aligned with an increasingly powerful labor movement. Feeling invincible, Republicans renominated Thomas Dewey as their standard-bearer. Dewey's second defeat in 1948, along with the loss of Republican majorities in Congress, was a major blow for the GOP, which tried to analyze its mistakes and plan for the future. Meanwhile Truman, supported by a Democratic Congress, set out to serve the country a "Fair Deal," including public housing, expanded social security, a higher minimum wage, and civil rights legislation.

In the postwar period, the National Federation of Republican Women positioned itself to help the GOP take advantage of its new potential. The Federation, looking to expand, sought a membership broader than its previous core of longtime loyal Republican clubwomen and party activists. When Marion Martin first organized the Federation, she had faced the challenge of uniting groups of clubs that, while diverse in important ways, already identified with the Republican Party. Martin had seen her immediate task as one of damage control—to stop independent-minded Republican women's clubs from undermining attempts to build a unified party. She stressed partisan loyalty and encouraged women to cooperate with men by giving up their idea that they represented a separate, purer alternative to male politics. In 1948 Elizabeth Farrington became president of the Federation. Under Farrington's leadership, the Federation moved beyond the goal of merely holding itself together. It was able to begin expanding its base by appealing to new constituencies of women ranging from moderate civic activists to women at the fringes of mainstream politics.

Farrington's strategy for uniting these diverse elements differed in key ways from Martin's. Farrington resurrected the themes of a separate female politics and of women's moral superiority that Martin had sought to relegate to the past. Yet Farrington was not simply returning to the nineteenth-century women's political style that had influenced women like Alma Lorimer in the 1920s. Like Marion Martin, Betty Farrington was a party loyalist. She used the language of women's difference and moral superiority not to promote an independent female political agenda but to unite American women on behalf of the GOP. In doing so, she unintentionally nourished a right-wing constituency within the Federation that would prove to be at odds with the Federation's mission to promote party loyalty. Once Federation leaders reinvoked the language of the women's crusade, they were unable to control the enthusiasm it unleashed. As the Federation's membership began to surge, so too did the membership's impatience with the moderate (or "modern") Republicanism that became ascendant in the 1950s. Federation leaders rejoiced at Eisenhower's victory in 1952 and positioned the Federation to support him. Many rank-and-file women, however, retained their attraction to a "purer" politics and had no patience with those who tried to control or censor them.

★ After the exit of Marion Martin in 1946, the Federation eventually moved away from many aspects of Martin's Federation, both in terms of its structure and its model for women's participation in politics. It was not immediately clear that this would be the case. Jane Hamilton Macauley, Martin's immediate successor, shared much of her predecessor's vision for the Federation.[1] When she took over as assistant chair, Macauley initially assumed that she would be only an interim figure while the Taft and Dewey forces battled for control of the party. But when Dewey received the nomination in 1948, his choice for RNC chairman (Hugh Scott) retained Macauley as assistant chairman. A devoted supporter of Marion Martin, Macauley continued her predecessor's emphasis on party loyalty and voter education in her work with the Federation while also encouraging women's political advancement.

Not everyone at the Federation appreciated Macauley's leadership. Some influential Federation women in the late 1940s were increasingly dissatisfied with the Federation's relationship to the RNC and to the Women's Division. Reformers focused on the 1948 Federation convention in St. Paul—where the membership would select a new president—as an opportunity to initiate change. The biennial convention that year proved a bitter one due to ongoing disputes about the structure of the Federation. The relationship of the Federation to the RNC had been controversial from the Federation's inception.

The election of forty-seven-year-old Betty Farrington to the Federation presidency was a triumph for those, such as Wilma Bishop and Marie Suthers, who had long sought greater autonomy for the women's Federation.[2] Particularly objectionable was that the RNC assistant chair-

Vote Republican. Thirty-year-old Jane Hamilton Macauley succeeded Marion Martin as assistant chairman of the Republican National Committee and head of the National Federation of Republican Women. Undated. (Photo courtesy of Jane Hamilton Macauley.)

man (a salaried woman appointed by the RNC chairman) served as executive director of the Federation. Those who supported restructuring —like Farrington, Suthers, and Bishop—wanted the volunteer Federation to be run by its own president elected by its members, rather than by the Women's Division's paid staff.[3] By the end of Farrington's two-term presidency, this change had been enacted. The position of Federation executive director was eliminated altogether and the Federation and the Women's Division officially separated.[4] The Federation changed its name from the National Federation of Women's Republican Clubs to the National Federation of Republican Women. The Federation also began making efforts to raise more of its own funds. By 1953 the RNC still carried a little more than half of the Federation's budget, however, helping cover costs of rent, staff, materials, and postage.[5]

The Federation's desire to free itself from the yoke of the RNC might appear to have been a feminist call for greater female political power.

Republican Rivalries. Under the leadership of Elizabeth Farrington (front row, second from left), the Federation would loosen its ties to Jane Macauley (front row, second from right) and the Republican National Committee. Undated, probably 1948. (Photo courtesy of Jane Hamilton Macauley.)

This was hardly the case. Those demanding more autonomy resented above all that the RNC assigned salaried career women to lead the Federation (an organization of middle-aged, volunteer housewives), rather than allowing the Federation to choose its leadership, a subject that is taken up in the next chapter.

Most of the changes to the Federation's bylaws sought by Farrington and her supporters would not go into effect until the end of her term. Yet from the very beginning Farrington was in a better position than any of her predecessors had been to take over the day-to-day mechanics of running the Federation. As a D.C. resident she could be physically present and in charge. Farrington negotiated for the Federation to have its own offices, separate from the Women's Division. She hired her own staff and arranged to sit in on the meetings where Macauley and members of the RNC Research Committee drew up the study materials that were sent to the clubs.[6] While Farrington was successful in gaining somewhat more autonomy for the Federation, her leadership was also significant for its style of outreach and the kind of politics it engendered.

★ Betty Farrington was born Mary Elizabeth Pruett in 1898 while her parents, missionaries from Tennessee, were serving in Japan.[7] She spent much of her childhood in Hollywood, California, and was educated at the University of Wisconsin. After graduating in 1918 with a degree in journalism, she worked in Washington, D.C., as a correspondent for a Wisconsin news syndicate. In 1920 she married fellow Wisconsin graduate Joseph Farrington, whose family was among the white elite of the Territory of Hawaii. The Farringtons, who first came to the islands in the 1890s, ran Honolulu's *Star-Bulletin*. Joseph and Elizabeth lived in Washington, D.C., after their marriage, where both worked as newspaper reporters. After three years in Washington, the couple returned to Hawaii when Joe's father was appointed governor of the territory. Joseph became publisher of the *Star-Bulletin*, and Elizabeth wrote for the paper and studied Oriental culture at the University of Hawaii. During their time in Hawaii, the couple began raising a family.

In 1942 Joseph Farrington was elected as Hawaii's nonvoting representative to Congress, and the couple moved back to Washington. It was at this time that Elizabeth became involved with Republican club work. She joined the D.C. League of Republican Women (an elite group of Washington socialites and congressional wives), became its president in 1947, and revived the slumping club. Throughout her life, Elizabeth Farrington retained an interest in Asian culture and, along with her husband, championed the cause of Hawaii statehood. Interested in the people, philosophy, and culture of Asia, Elizabeth Farrington and her husband were known to be "liberal and tolerant" with little patience for bigotry and prejudice.[8] While president of the D.C. League, Farrington served as chairman of the National Federation's Program Committee and became a prominent figure in the Federation.

Farrington brought more than a desire for Federation autonomy to her presidency. Wanting to avoid the "sin of talking to ourselves," Farrington set out to expand the reach of the women's organization, and thereby the reach of the party.[9] The end of the war presented the Federation with several new categories of potential clubwomen that it had previously done little to attract. These included civic workers, right-wing activists, and southerners. Some of these constituencies Farrington deliberately courted, whereas she merely tried to be tolerant of others. In her efforts to make all women believe the Republican Party had something to offer them, Farrington chose to focus on women's unique qualities—supposedly shared by all women—rather than on women's equality with men, as Martin had done.

One group Farrington targeted were nonpartisan, civic-minded women. The war had brought many previously uninvolved middle-class women into civic activism through their patriotic work in organizations like the Red Cross. Many of these women were presumably now eager for further activity but might drift away from public affairs unless encouraged to remain active. The postwar tendency of middle-class women to concentrate on homemaking rather than careers would have also contributed to the growth of the Federation; many educated, talented women in the late 1940s were looking for something to do. Marion Martin had hoped to channel their desire for civic activism into support for the Republican Party. Farrington shared that aspiration.[10]

Yet Farrington feared that the civic impulse was not benefiting Republicans. These fears were exacerbated by the release of a study in 1949 accusing many of the nation's ostensibly nonpartisan women's organizations of disseminating the policies of the Democratic administration. Entitled "Packaged Thinking for Women," this study charged that the Women's Joint Congressional Committee (WJCC), a clearinghouse for the lobbying activities of around twenty women's organizations, was distributing "packaged" materials of predigested study material to its member organizations. The WJCC was criticized for discouraging women from thinking independently. But the authors of "Packaged Thinking for Women" accused the WJCC of having a more sinister agenda. They claimed the WJCC was a tool of the State Department in an effort to create a pressure group of ten million women that would influence Congress to support Democratic (or even "socialistic") policies.[11] At a time when fears about domestic subversion were mounting, such charges carried real weight. The WJCC denied any impropriety and accused its critics of wanting to discourage the participation of citizen's groups in civic affairs.[12]

Betty Farrington seized on the opportunity this controversy offered. Farrington wanted to ensure that ostensibly nonpartisan women's organizations were not receiving materials explaining only one side of the issues. Her approach was to counter Democratic propaganda with propaganda of her own. To this end, she launched a drive to get the Republican message into the hands of nonpartisan women's clubs. A major weapon of this campaign was the Federation's new *Washington Newsletter*. The *Washington Newsletter* was a twice-monthly magazine of Republican opinion and witticisms, featuring columns by wives of conservative Republican senators and congressmen. Farrington sent the *Washington Newsletter* to the Federation club presidents, for use by the

Federation's own clubs. But Farrington especially wanted to distribute this literature to nonpartisan women's leaders (along with a letter outlining the merits of the two-party system). Farrington compiled a directory of 285 national women's organizations with legislative programs. She also called on her army of local club leaders to provide her with the names of women active in civic affairs in their communities so she could add them to her mailing list. Farrington was proud of her record in promoting Republicanism among new audiences, noting that when she took office, 6,000 Federation bulletins were being sent out once a month to Republicans only. By 1950, Farrington reported, 18,000 monthly bulletins and an equal number of twice-monthly *Newsletters* were sent out—not only to Republican leaders but to 12,000 leaders of nonpartisan women's groups as well.[13]

Although its precise impact cannot be measured, this effort marked a departure. The Federation had avoided nonpartisan women's organizations in the past. Marion Martin had viewed nonpartisan groups as dangerous because they threatened to siphon away active Republican women. Moreover, she believed many of these groups—particularly the LWV—"indoctrinated" women with the notion that nonpartisanship was the most responsible form of citizenship. Martin further suspected that many of these organizations were secretly more sympathetic to the Democratic Party.

Farrington, by contrast, saw nonpartisan women's organizations as a resource the Federation could exploit. Because the Democrats were the majority party, Republican victories required the party reach voters who did not identify as Republicans.[14] Civic-minded women, Farrington assumed, could become Republican voters, if properly influenced. In addition to sending the *Washington Newsletter* to such groups, Farrington also encouraged Republican clubwomen to "infiltrate" local chapters of the League of Women Voters, church councils, and PTAs.[15] Farrington's appreciation for community outreach was influenced by the Congress of Industrial Organizations (CIO), which sought to improve its standing in local communities during the immediate postwar years by establishing labor representation in the leadership of local community organizations (such as welfare departments, the Red Cross, and the YMCA).[16] Farrington personally had made a careful study of the CIO's organizing strategies, and she encouraged other Republican women to do the same.[17]

As the Federation grew after the war, it also drew a second group of women—those who were attracted to right-wing politics. The influence of this group was felt particularly in California and Illinois.

In the late 1930s isolationist mothers' groups hoping to prevent U.S. involvement in the European conflict had successfully activated large numbers of American women. Much as war work mobilized previously apathetic but politically moderate women into heightened civic duty, antiwar work encouraged an interest in politics among other women who held more-extreme views. The leaders of the isolationist mothers groups were typically eccentric extremists who mixed mother-centered arguments for nonintervention with virulent anti-Semitism and anti-communism. The groups they formed in the late thirties and early forties had opposed U.S. aid to the Allies, and any preparation for wars on foreign soil. Although these mothers' organizations were nonpartisan, many leaders and members also passionately opposed the New Deal and occasionally worked for Republican candidates.[18]

In the late thirties and early forties, isolationist mothers' groups grew in numbers far exceeding the reach of the Federation. While the Federation claimed a few hundred thousand members, the various mothers' organizations together had membership possibly in the millions.[19] The isolationist mothers' movement was really several different movements based in different cities, under different leadership. Some groups were led by fascist sympathizers, while others tried to retain a more respectable reputation. Many of the groups worked together with right-wing, isolationist demagogue Gerald L. K. Smith. Primarily middle-class and white, the different mothers' organizations shared similar ideas and rhetoric. They based their isolationism on arguments derived from members' positions as mothers or wives of draft-age men. Yet, as Laura McEnaney describes, the women in the mothers' movement also believed that "New Deal Democrats (financed by Jewish international bankers) were steering the United States into an internationalist foreign policy that would lead inevitably to permanent cycles of global war." This policy would take men from their families and would "accelerate what they believed were New Deal trends toward intrusive, centralized government and concentrated executive branch power."[20] In the logic of the mothers' movement, isolationism was linked to anti-Semitism, antistatism, and anticommunism. This is not to suggest that all of the women attracted to the mothers' cause were anti-Semites. Yet those millions of women who remained in the movement, attended meetings, signed petitions, marched for peace, and read the movement's literature were influenced by leaders who did hold extreme views.

After the war, many in the movement reframed their isolationism as opposition to the United Nations and other components of the new internationalism. Some Republican senators who had opposed inter-vention before Pearl Harbor, such as Robert Taft and Gerald P. Nye, expressed similar reservations about what they saw as the utopian ex-pectations of many early supporters of a postwar international body.[21] More-extreme critics, including many of the leaders of the isolationist mothers' groups, viewed the new internationalism as a step toward a Jewish- or communist-controlled world government. By that time, how-ever, the mothers' groups had been largely discredited, due to their iso-lationist stance, the postwar taboo against anti-Semitism, and the inves-tigation of several leaders on charges of subversion and collaboration with Nazi Germany (no one was ever convicted). Millions of the women whom the mothers' movement had mobilized found themselves with-out an outlet for their political ardor.

It is likely that many of these mothers' movement members and fellow travelers moved into the more respectable Republican women's clubs after the war. This seems to have been the case in California, particularly southern California.[22] There, clubs of "housewife activists" were "important incubators of McCarthyism."[23] Not all of those clubs were explicitly partisan, but the Republican club movement was a logi-cal place for such activists to gravitate. After the war, several Republi-can women's clubs in the Los Angeles area became increasingly mili-tant. These clubs disagreed vehemently with the state and local party, attacked Jewish leaders in the state, spoke out against the alleged communist-inspired plot for world government, and drew a battle line against all "Collective-Socialist" legislation.[24] President of the Califor-nia Council of Republican Women Jean Fuller complained that the way-ward clubs were "full of those wild eyed women who are extremely 'anti-everything.'" Later she suggested that many of the "most troublesome" women were "closely affiliated" with mothers' movement hero Gerald L. K. Smith. The California Council, she bemoaned, was having "con-siderable trouble over the state" due to Smith's "great emotional appeal" among "neurotic women." Smith's followers, Fuller claimed, had been infiltrating the council with their "venomous poison."[25]

Farrington was no isolationist or bigot, and she sympathized with Fuller's difficulties in building a harmonious organization. Farrington nonetheless sought points of common ground with the more militant clubs that brought Fuller so much angst. In her letters to members of these clubs, Farrington tried to focus on those aspects of their ideas with which she agreed. One agitated member of Southern California Republican Women complained to Farrington in 1949 about what she viewed as the constitutional violations, socialist policies, and desire for world government advocated by some Republicans. Farrington ignored the woman's attacks on fellow Republicans. Instead, Farrington offered her compliments on the fine work the club was doing in emphasizing that the Republican Party was "definitely opposed to any trend that is opposed to constitutional government."[26] That latter point may have been the only one with which Farrington agreed, but she chose to highlight that agreement. Marion Martin, by contrast, had often written long detailed letters to women whom she considered off base in their politics or partisanship, detailing her points of objection and the importance of supporting the party.

Farrington's efforts were not enough to keep some of the more militant clubs invested in the Federation. In 1951 several of the most outspoken California clubs, led by women in Los Angeles, briefly seceded from the California Council. These clubs accused the council of helping to destroy constitutional government and the Republican Party, as well as of endorsing totalitarianism because of the council's support for Governor Earl Warren and other "Hyphenated Republicans."[27] However, Farrington's tolerance enabled other right-wing clubs to find a home in the Federation. Working within the Federation rather than seceding, these clubs would continue to push for a more militant Federation.

For a third new constituency of women, Farrington turned southward. Seeking to capitalize on the demographic trends of the postwar period, she encouraged the expansion of the Federation into the southern states. When Farrington began her presidency, no southern states had statewide representation in the Federation. Marion Martin had welcomed southern clubs wanting to join on an individual basis, but white southern interest in the GOP had not seemed great enough to merit concerted organizing efforts. Southern disillusionment with the New Deal had been growing since the late 1930s, but not until 1948 did the Republican Party appear to have real opportunities to make gradual inroads into the one-party South. That year Truman had desegregated the military and had run on a Democratic platform that contained a civil rights plank. Truman's decision to court black voters led Strom Thurmond's Dixiecrats to bolt and opened up the possibility of southerners voting against the national Democratic Party. Furthermore, ongoing demographic and economic changes in the peripheral South were creating a constituency increasingly sympathetic to Republican appeals.[28]

Southern Republican club activity remained scattered and of dubious value in the late thirties and early forties. Certainly indigenous disillusionment with the Democrats had grown during the course of Roosevelt's presidency. Yet the sensibilities of some white southern women who hoped to organize Republican clubs provoked Martin's distaste for extremism. For example, Nettie Stewart of Atlanta—a lifelong southerner and white Republican whose grandfathers had both fought for the Union during the Civil War—energetically pursued Republican club work. Yet moderate leaders like Martin and Macauley found it necessary to correct and reprimand Stewart for her conspiratorial worldview and her reliance on anti-Semitic literature for her information about politics. As Martin politely pointed out, Stewart's club was "out of step with the majority."[29]

By the late forties, there was a new, more appealing, potential for a GOP women's club movement in the southern states: northern women who had relocated to southern metropolitan areas after the war, often because their husbands found professional opportunities there. Since 1945 the migration into the South had been largely white and middle class. These newcomers tended to settle in new communities, such as suburbs or rapidly expanding cities, where the pressures to adapt to local culture (including patterns of partisanship) were not great. In such communities, where residents were "more concerned about taxes . . . than about race," as one scholar of southern politics describes, Republicanism had the potential to take hold.[30] Women in these families sought to reestablish in their new neighborhoods the community institutions they had left behind. Some, who had been involved previously in Republican clubs before they moved, tried to establish new clubs in their adopted communities. These northern ambassadors to the South were easier for National Federation leaders to work with than women like Nettie Stewart.

Although their primary work was with white women, some of these transplanted northern clubwomen did attempt to organize southern black women as well. Through the course of their efforts to organize, they often ran into an open racism to which they were unaccustomed. Although most northern Republican clubs were segregated in practice, few Federation leaders challenged the desirability of having black women organize their own clubs. In some southern states, however, women organizers from the North found that segregation laws presented obstacles to organizing black clubs at all. Although not champions of integration, nor prone to analyzing their own prejudices against African Americans and Jews, the national leaders of the Federation were not overt racists or anti-Semites. Federation leaders may have had their discomforts with racial and religious minorities, but above all they understood that overt racism and anti-Semitism were not respectable. Anti-Semitism was the province of Nazis; racial prejudice the province of unsophisticated southern Democrats. Respectable, responsible Republicans eschewed such views. Thus Federation leaders and RNC officials remained puzzled over how to advise new club leaders in the South to adapt to the open racism and segregation they encountered. While willing to accept the idea that segregation might evolve for "practical purposes," northern leaders tended to be uncomfortable with policies that made racial discrimination explicit.[31]

Another obvious difficulty in building the GOP club movement in the South was the challenge of overcoming the traditions of Democratic loyalty among southern white women. It was one thing to agree quietly with the Republican Party or perhaps even to vote for its presidential candidate—between roughly 20 and 40 percent of voters in states of the "rim" South voted for GOP presidential candidates in 1940 and 1944.[32] It was quite another thing to join a Republican club and begin building a local Republican Party. At the local level, Republican candidates had virtually no chance of winning. Whatever obstacles prevented southerners from switching parties, those obstacles appear to have been greater among men than women. In 1952, for example, Eisenhower earned 59 percent of southern white women's votes, but only 41 percent of those of southern white men. Political scientists Earl and Merle Black have speculated that this dramatic difference may have been due to women's higher levels of education and the fact that Eisenhower's opponent Stevenson was a divorced man. They also point to the possibility that women, in the "privacy of the voting booth," may have been more willing to vote independently than were men (who presumably had a deeper investment in the tradition of straight-ticket voting).[33] Southerners who agreed with Republicans on many issues still needed to feel comfortable joining a partisan organization. Republican women's clubs, in the ways they combined social activities with partisan messages, could have been just the thing to help ease traditionally Democratic voters into the other party.

Farrington made an important gesture toward encouraging club development in the South when she invited those states to appoint representatives to the Federation Advisory Board. She met with the national committeewomen from southern states and listened to their analyses of the problems particular to organizing southern Republican women's clubs. She also advocated changes in the Federation bylaws (which went

into effect in 1953 after Farrington had left office) to redefine the requirements for statewide federation. These changes made it more feasible for
the fledgling organizations in the South to join the Federation. By 1951
there were 113 clubs in the South with a membership of 6,600, and club
activity was evident in all southern States except Mississippi and South
Carolina. "I think that is pretty good," Farrington boasted, "when the
Party itself has not really done the work."[34]

There were men in the party who took notice. When the Republican
Party began mobilizing in the South in earnest in 1953, organizer Jim
McKillips remarked that "[o]ne of the highlights" of a recent southern
organizing tour had been the "enthusiasm" of the women's organizations he encountered.[35] Farrington's successor, Nora Kearns, would go
on to increase outreach into the South, assigning regional organizers
there. In 1954 the Federation held the first national Republican meeting in the South, when the Federation Board of Directors met in New
Orleans that fall. By the end of that year, Florida, Louisiana, North Carolina, Tennessee, and Virginia had established statewide federations. By
1956 Texas and Arkansas had been added.[36] Georgia would soon follow. Spreading the Republican Party and the Federation into the South
meant focusing on those issues which united indigenous southern Republicans, Yankee transplants, and anti–New Deal southern Democrats.
Anticommunism, with its widespread appeal, seems to have been such
an issue.

✷ Farrington expanded the organization to include new geographical
and political constituencies of women. In her efforts to reach out to a
more varied population, Farrington also changed the tone and emphasis of the Federation. She was more overtly religious than her predecessors had been, and during her term the Federation began integrating
religious symbols and practices into the Federation. The Federation appointed a chaplain, began publishing monthly prayers in its newsletter,
opened its own meeting with prayers, and encouraged local clubs to
do the same.[37] (The religious messages of the Federation were largely
Christian, although leaders seemed to believe that they were being more
inclusive.) Farrington also invoked religious imagery in her descriptions
of politics, and of women's politics in particular. Accompanying Farrington's religious devotion was a hatred of communism and socialism. Beginning with her presidency of the D.C. League of Republican Women
in 1946, Farrington had begun focusing on the theme of "Liberty versus

Socialism," a theme that she also brought to her Federation work.[38] For Farrington, Christianity and anticommunism were inseparable issues. They were also, she believed, particularly pressing issues for women.

Farrington's construction of women's politics as moral and religious —as a crusade against evil—was by no means new. Earlier Republican women's clubs had celebrated women as principled, independent thinkers whose political activities were motivated by a desire to rise above practical politics and pursue principled crusades for unselfish reasons. Marion Martin, in forming the Federation, had tried to eradicate those features of women's politics from the Federation. Under Farrington, however, the Federation began to rethink its tactics. Rather than try to overcome women's attraction to politics formulated as female crusades, Farrington encouraged this association.

In the late 1940s and early 1950s the Federation leadership presented politics in catastrophic, gendered terms believed to resonate broadly with the women it targeted—white, middle-class, civic minded, patriotic, Protestant women who otherwise differed in their commitment to Republicanism and their positions along the political spectrum. In its efforts to build the Republican women's movement, the Federation returned to the idea that women had a unique and crucial role to play in politics. Focusing on simple (yet vague) moral themes gave a wide spectrum of women a means of identifying with the party. Although Farrington's strategies were different, like Martin she saw the Federation as an instrument to help the party. Yet Farrington was not an RNC employee as Martin was. And Farrington's turn to the language of the female political crusade lacked the obsession with partisan loyalty of the Martin years. Farrington did not try to define or control the Republicanism of her followers. Instead, she tried to be flexible and allow club members to understand women's moral mission in their own way.

Farrington's reintroduction of religious, morally charged political language coincided with the Republican Party's discovery of redbaiting as an issue with partisan advantages. The Federation in the early postwar years defined current political issues in moral and religious terms that embraced attacks on supposed subversive infiltration of American institutions, and openly equated the Democratic Party with socialism. It is hardly surprising that organized Republican women responded positively to campaigns against subversion. By early 1950 there were plenty of reasons for Americans in general to be prepared to accept charges of subversive infiltration of the government. The Soviet atom bomb test in August 1949 led many who were invested in a belief in American scientific superiority to conclude that the Soviets must have had help. The victory of Mao's communist forces in China, without apparent resistance from the United States, suggested communist sympathizers were directing the State Department. New Dealer Alger Hiss had just been convicted of perjury for lying about his activities as a Soviet spy.

That charges of subversion could be used as ammunition against a Democratic administration and against the entire New Deal made them particularly appealing to many committed Republicans. The Federation, too, was prepared to exploit the partisan advantages of anticommunism. In 1949 and 1950 the Federation's *Washington Newsletter* fed readers a steady diet of articles devoted to such topics as communist control of the General Agreement on Tariffs and Trade (GATT), "creeping" socialism, Reds in the Democratic government, domestic communism, and communism in the education system.[39] Federation women found exposing alleged subversion to be an issue of particular appeal to women.

Indeed, it was a Republican women's club that initiated the event that would provide the post–World War II Red Scare with its name— McCarthyism. When Joseph McCarthy gave his famous Wheeling, West Virginia, speech in 1950, it was at the invitation of the Ohio County [West Virginia] Republican Women's Club, which had brought the Wisconsin senator as its principal Lincoln Day speaker. During his speech, McCarthy claimed to have a list of subversives employed by the State Department. Some historians have questioned why McCarthy chose to give what would prove to be such a significant speech at a seemingly unimportant occasion—a Republican women's club event. Yet this venue was a logical one for the particular speech McCarthy gave. He seems to have understood his hostesses well. In his speech, he hit not only on the themes of communist subversion in the State Department, but also on communism's threat to religion and morality. "The great difference between our western Christian world and the atheistic Communist world," McCarthy explained, "is not political—it is moral." He went on to call for a "showdown" between the "Democratic Christian world" and the "Communistic atheistic world." McCarthy found a sympathetic audience in the capacity crowd of more than 275 clubwomen and other local Republican leaders.[40]

Anticommunism proved to be an effective message in attracting new members to the Federation. Most Federation leaders, however, were not willing to give their organization over exclusively to hunting Reds.[41] Farrington herself favored formulating anticommunism as a crusade in favor of Americanism, morality, and spirituality, rather than against communism per se. When one southern club decided to require all members to take an anticommunist oath, Farrington suggested that they instead adopt a more "positive position" by opening all meetings with an oath of allegiance to the flag or to the Republican Party. This would serve the same purpose of keeping subversives out of the club, she explained, while encouraging women in more-positive directions.[42] Farrington was not a zealot but did want to channel whatever political enthusiasm women might express to the benefit of the GOP.

Cold War anticommunism among Republican women was more than a response to current events or to current partisan politics. Anticommunist politics was in keeping with old traditions within the Republican women's club movement that had prevailed before the formation of the Federation. In order to recruit women in the past, Republican women leaders had framed political issues in the language of Protestant reform as urgent, moral crises, which demanded a strong female response. This strategy assumed that women were not interested in subtle political arguments and would only become involved if leaders framed politics as urgent female crusades against the forces of evil. Such assumptions had informed progressive Republican women's crusade for honest government, prohibitionist Republican women's crusade for the sanctity of the Eighteenth Amendment, and the antistatist, anti–New Deal crusade that had rallied diehard Republican women in the thirties. A great danger appeared to threaten important American institutions (such as the government, the Constitution, the church, or the family). Fighting that danger was the single most important issue of politics. Women, with their ties to the family and the church and their general moral superiority, were the best ones to fight this danger because men could not do it. In the early Cold War years, it was logical to mobilize women on behalf of a crusade against communism.

★ Farrington herself believed in her conception of politics as a moral and religious mission. She was also convinced that it would help mobilize large numbers of American women. Moreover, Farrington brought her moral conception of politics to bear on her contributions to general Republican Party strategy. Farrington's own vision of how the party as a whole should appeal to the American people was awash in moral absolutism. In 1949, after the GOP's surprising defeat the previous fall, the RNC created a national Committee on Program to help formulate a political message with broad appeal that would clearly distinguish the Republicans from the Democrats.[43] As Federation president, Farrington was named a member. Many Program Committee members deplored Democratic Party politics, which, they charged, looked not to the common good but to the loudest pressure group. Yet the realities of the current political situation forced many to equivocate. After the war, as politicians clamored to win the votes of veterans, farmers, blacks, and immigrants from central and eastern Europe, many in the GOP believed the party needed to articulate specific policies targeted toward these different groups in order to win them away from the Democrats.[44]

Farrington was not a reactionary, and she believed that party principles had to be brought into line with "present-day developments."[45] However, she did not believe the party could achieve unity by outlining a program with individual policies designed to appeal to particular constituencies. Such an approach, she feared, would inevitably lead to state, local, and sectional conflicts, compromise, and disappointment. She agreed with those who believed the party would fail if it supported a set of different measures, "each designated to attract the vote of an organized minority at the expense of the people as a whole." Instead, she supported establishing a "single fundamental moral issue" to use as the "test by which all other issues will be weighted." Campaigners could present this principle to the voters as emblematic of what the party stood for. It would then be up to the Republican members of Congress to interpret how different pieces of legislation measured up to that one simple truth.[46] Simplifying politics to a single moral principle could appeal to more ideological voters who wanted the party to stand behind solid moral principles. For Farrington the moral test by which legislation should be measured concerned whether it increased Washington's power. She equated this "yardstick" with each person's fight for "life, liberty, and the pursuit of happiness."[47]

Many Program Committee members agreed with Farrington's call for a single moral principle to lead the party. One member, Harold Mitchell, noted that this simplified presentation of politics might be particularly useful in reaching a segment of the population the party had missed up until that point: the wives of working-class men. Mitchell assumed working-class women to be incapable of understanding politics unless campaigners could stir their emotions. "They simply don't have the time to understand reasoned arguments," Mitchell declared. "They can understand and they can appreciate the moral and the emotional talk, but they can't understand a lot of reasoning."[48]

Other National Committee members agreed it was important that the party's statement of principles contain language that would appeal particularly to women. As the committeewoman from New Hampshire, Mrs. Dickinson, argued, the party needed a principle that women would work for because women usually were neither Democrats nor Republicans. "They will vote for what they think is the right thing," she noted.[49] Katharine Kennedy Brown of Ohio also urged that the party make special appeals to women. She proposed that the party's statement of principles include an acknowledgment that a "Christian civilization is the foundation upon which our country was founded and has grown great." This fact, Brown's proposal continued, separated the United States from communist Russia. The Democrats had ignored that difference and thus entered into foreign policy commitments at odds with the spiritual philosophy of Americans. The party statement of principles, then, should urge that Americans commit to a renewed emphasis on God. Brown was convinced the inclusion of such a statement would hold special appeal to women.[50]

The final statement of Republican Party principles approved by the RNC and the House and Senate Republican Committees was, in fact, more programmatic and less inspiring than Farrington and her allies had advised. It contained positions on specific policy proposals and advocated special programs for veterans, farmers, and other groups. Moreover, it did not contain Brown's language about Christianity.[51] The RNC Strategy Committee, however, did go on to recommend packaging all of the issues of the 1950 election under one larger theme: liberty versus socialism, a slogan that was "pure conservative Republicanism." Framing the campaign in this way supposedly would cover all issues of concern to Americans including taxes, deficit spending, the high cost of government, inflation, regulation, Godless materialism, and a decline in moral standards. In presenting the report of the Strategy Committee, Arthur Summerfield advocated a three-part strategy for 1950 that, although he did not say so directly, would rely heavily on women: a focus on the issue of liberty versus socialism, a move toward large numbers of small contributions, and a house-to-house effort toward precinct organization. "The Republican Party," Summerfield concluded, "down to the lowest precinct worker, is like a giant shaking itself wide awake for battle."[52] The Women's Federation, under Betty Farrington, would play a critical role in waking that sleeping giant.

While the RNC only partially accepted Farrington's idea that a simple moral truth should guide the 1950 campaign, Farrington herself dedicated the Federation program (through its newsletters and bulletins) and her own speeches to that idea. She encouraged Federation women to present Republican policies to the public in terms of one fundamental principle—the "moral issue of a free America." The "moral issue of a free America" was a vague battle cry that could mean fighting everything from communism to big government. In Farrington's rendering, "freedom" was the issue separating the United States from the communist world. Freedom had also defined the other great moral struggle that "gave birth to the Republican Party."[53] Farrington, whose favorite president was Lincoln, drew a direct line from the moral struggle to end southern slavery to the moral struggle to end communist slavery. Invoking the heritage of abolitionists who had fought to end the enslavement of blacks in the American South, Farrington urged Republican women to stop the current "march to federal dictatorship" and prevent Americans from falling victim to communism, which currently "enslaved" one-third of the world's people. Farrington cleverly tapped general, nonpartisan fears about communism, framed them as a women's moral crusade for freedom against big government in order to preserve "the integrity of the Republic," and linked that crusade to the history and heritage of the Republican Party.[54]

Farrington was equally concerned about communism's threat to Christianity. She linked the moral themes of Federation politics directly to efforts to "safeguard our Christian civilization." In Farrington's descriptions of politics and women's political work, other religious metaphors abounded. For example, in seasonally inspired language that evoked the Christian yearning for the coming of Jesus, Farrington expressed the need for a strong man to head the Republican Party after Dewey's defeat in December 1948: "How thankful we would have been if a leader had appeared to show us the path to the promised land of our hope. The world needs such a man today. He is certain to come sooner or later. But we cannot sit idly by in the hope of his coming. Besides his advent depends partly on us. The mere fact that a leader is needed does not guarantee his appearance. People must be ready for him, and we, as Republican women, in our clubs, prepare for him."[55] Farrington compared her nationwide campaigning during the 1950 midterm election to spiritual revivals where clubwomen experienced a "sort of contagious exaltation." And she likened Republican women workers to "Billy Sundays of the GOP," in reference to the evangelist's method of calling on his followers to bring unconverted friends to revival meetings.[56] Men also made use of religious metaphors in describing women's political activities, at least when facing a female audience. The chairman of the Republican Senatorial Campaign Committee, Senator Owen Brewster, for example, asserted in an article for the *Washington Newsletter* that due to the "Communist effort to destroy our Christian institutions, the women of this nation are becoming more and more conscious that the next step is the destruction of the home." He went on to insist that women were "determined" to take part in the upcoming election "to a greater degree than ever before."[57]

Farrington certainly did not invent the formulation of communism as a moral and religious issue. The Cold War could be viewed, in the simplest terms, as a conflict between economic systems (socialism versus capitalism) or political systems (totalitarianism versus democracy). It could also be viewed as a struggle between atheism and religious faith. Twenty-four percent of a cross-section of Americans who were asked in 1954 what things communists believed in replied that communists were "against religion." Americans offered this response more frequently than they did political dictatorship (18 percent), government ownership of property (18 percent), or the domination of the world by Russia (17 percent). Responses were clearly gendered. Women were more likely than men to describe communism as hostile to religion, whereas men were more likely to point to government ownership of property as characteristic. These gender differences held even when controlling for religious observance, indicating that women's higher church attendance alone was not responsible for this result.[58] When Farrington and others elected to mobilize women behind the Republican Party by linking religious faith to the battle against communism, there were good reasons to do so.

Farrington's method of political mobilization included traditional elements of women's politics. She emphasized women's difference from men in their unique concerns about morality, religion, and the family. She also defined political campaigns as crusades around a single issue that, if not acted upon, posed a grave danger. This attempt to establish a litmus test for all political action was a form of ideological thinking that was anathema to Marion Martin. Marion Martin had been wary of such rhetoric. She disliked the language of the women's political crusade for its uncompromising, separatist tenor, which she believed hurt the party and women themselves. Martin ascribed women's tendencies toward extremism to the fact that they "liked to be alarmed." Alarming voters, however, proved to be exactly what the GOP needed to do in 1950 and 1952 to knock the Democrats out of power. Appealing to women's role as religious crusaders and moral purifiers was a generic message that could be interpreted by the diverse constituencies of American women to which the Federation tried to appeal. But what would unite Republican clubwomen once the party was finally in power?

★ In 1952 Americans elected a Republican President for the first time since before the New Deal. The Federation found itself in an altogether new role: supporting the party in power. This required promoting loyalty to the new administration, a task that incoming Federation president Nora Kearns set out to fulfill. Partisan loyalty would become difficult to define in a political world in which the Republican president had broad appeal to independents and even Democrats and was more popular than his party. When the president disagreed with Republicans in Congress, it was unclear who represented the party's standard-bearer. Eisenhower had run on a platform that pledged to turn back elements of the New Deal, to balance the federal budget, to decrease federal power, to fight communism at home and abroad, and to replace the policy of communist containment with a foreign policy that did not accept the existence of a postwar Soviet sphere of influence.[59]

As president, however, Eisenhower supported a moderate political creed that, by his second term, came to be known as "modern" Republicanism. Modern Republicanism reflected Eisenhower's idea that traditional Republican tenets of individualism and self-reliance could be reconciled with mid-twentieth century realities that called for a government role in promoting a healthy economy, the well-being of the people, and international cooperation.[60] Eisenhower supported social security, massive public expenditures including the Interstate Highway Act, and international cooperation through the United Nations. He also, albeit reluctantly, sent federal troops into Little Rock, Arkansas, during 1957 to enforce the Supreme Court's ruling on school desegregation. The Federation officially sided with Eisenhower, lending its support to the United Nations, celebrating the administration's economic and social policies, and standing behind the decision to send troops to Little Rock. But Federation membership had grown to about 500,000 while the emphasis on female crusades for righteous causes dominated the Federation's messages to women. Not all of these clubwomen would now be willing to settle into a role of loyal, partisan cheerleaders.

Modern Republicanism was an attempt by Eisenhower to find a theme that would appeal to all Americans, rather than trying to build a complex coalition of interests. Many Republican clubwomen, however, found this theme wrongheaded and even treasonous. The right-wing constituencies that the Federation had brought into its ranks in the postwar years disagreed with the president on significant issues. While many women settled readily into the Federation's new role of supporting the president, others who had been mobilized by the Federation's appeal to their unique role in fighting communism and big government were not prepared to stop their crusade. The more militant members began to suspect that communist inspiration lay behind the new Republican administration's actions as well. Such women were dismayed when they could not enlist Federation support for their attacks on the president. Although their particular political concerns were different, these right-wing clubwomen agreed with earlier independent progressive Republicans like Alma Lorimer on the purpose of women's partisan clubs. That purpose was not to support the party blindly but to be vocal in one's disagreement when necessary. Whereas Lorimer had linked her independence to progressive causes, Republican women's independence in the 1950s proved a right-wing force in the party.

The Federation's refusal to endorse the Bricker Amendment provoked the most organized challenge to Federation loyalty in the 1950s. This proposed constitutional amendment, introduced in September 1951 by Senator John Bricker, addressed the concerns of those who feared that international agreements such as the United Nations Charter, the Universal Declaration on Human Rights, and the Convention on the Prevention of Genocide threatened U.S. sovereignty. The Bricker Amendment would have required that all treaties be reviewed for their compatibility with the U.S. Constitution and that Congress enact legislation before the treaty became law. It earned the support in the Senate of almost all Republicans and conservative Democrats, as well as such organizations as the American Bar Association, the American Medical Association, the National Association of Manufacturers, and the Daughters of the American Revolution.[61]

The campaign for the Bricker Amendment also produced a new conservative women's organization, the Vigilant Women for the Bricker Amendment. The Vigilant Women, founded in Milwaukee in 1953, was active throughout the country, though particularly in the Midwest. Its members wrote their senators urging support of the amendment and circulated petitions on the amendment's behalf. In 1954 Vigilant Women sent more than 600 members to Washington to lobby for the amendment and presented Senator Bricker with 300,000 petition signatures.[62]

Some Federation women were involved with the Vigilant Women and wanted the Federation to join the cause. This the Federation was unwilling to do. While a majority of Republicans in the Senate supported the Bricker Amendment, President Eisenhower did not. Eisenhower and his advisers feared the amendment would undermine the president's ability to be a leader in international affairs. Although Eisenhower originally tried to avoid an open conflict with the Republican right, his delaying tactics ultimately failed, and he was forced to take a public stance against the amendment.[63] In such a case, where Senate Republicans and the Republican president were on opposing sides of an important issue, the Federation leadership pursued the course established by Marion Martin. It took no official position on the amendment and urged member clubs to follow its lead.[64]

Republican clubwomen who supported the amendment were frustrated. The Federation was refusing to offer a platform for Republican women to use the power of their numbers to influence their party. They wanted the Federation's convention to endorse the amendment but were rebuffed by the chairman of the Resolutions Committee, Katharine Kennedy Brown. Brown, although herself a conservative, was convinced that Federation support for the amendment would be harmful to the party.

Vigilant Woman and Republican clubmember Ruth Murray of Wisconsin rejected this reasoning. Murray was unsympathetic to arguments about the need for political harmony in order to win elections. She distinguished her own activism from Brown's: "[W]here we perhaps differ fundamentally is that I am not a politician—I am a crusader—and the Bricker Amendment will never be accomplished through 'politics' per se." Murray challenged Brown's claim that raising such a controversial issue would go against the purpose of the Federation. "[I]sn't bringing this matter before a National Convention educational?" Murray asked.[65] At the convention, held in Los Angeles in September, Bricker Amendment supporters failed to pass a resolution that openly endorsed the amendment. However, Brown also failed to keep the issue out of the convention altogether. Delegates passed a resolution calling for treaty legislation to be considered in ways such that the Constitution "may forever be protected and preserved," a veiled reference to the Bricker Amendment.[66]

Like Ruth Murray, Vere de Vere Adams Hutchins, president of the San Francisco Council of Republican Women, also criticized the Federation's mission in 1957 when she attacked the Federation's refusal to take a position on the "Girard case." On 30 January 1957, a U.S. serviceman, specialist third class William S. Girard, was accused of manslaughter in the death of an elderly Japanese woman. After months of negotiating with the Japanese, the United States turned Girard over to a Japanese civilian court for trial. Eisenhower's secretary of state, John Foster Dulles, supported this decision. Girard's lawyers, however, argued that the soldier's constitutional rights would be violated if he were turned over to the Japanese. The case ultimately went to the U.S. Supreme Court, which, in July 1957, upheld the decision to grant Japanese jurisdiction in the case. Girard was tried and, that November, handed a three-year suspended sentence, allowing him to return to the United States.[67]

At issue in this particular case was Article XVII of the postwar administrative agreement between Japan and the United States, in effect since October 1953. Article XVII gave Japanese courts jurisdiction over crimes committed against the Japanese by U.S. troops stationed in Japan. Critics of the decision to turn Girard over to the Japanese, such as Hutchins, viewed the case as a challenge to national sovereignty and an example of the dangers of a too-powerful federal government.[68] Hutchins wrote to Federation president Catharine Gibson explaining her views explicitly in terms of the Federation's stated purpose. Hutchins argued that it would serve the cause of "political education" for the Federation to take a stand opposing the Supreme Court's decision in the Girard case, the Eisenhower administration's support for that decision, and the power of the federal government to enter into such agreements with foreign governments in the first place. Taking such a stand also "increas[ed] the effectiveness of women in the cause of good government" and "foster[ed] loyalty to the Republican party," all goals stated in the Federation's bylaws. Hutchins asked Gibson sarcastically whether the role of Republican women in the Federation was to lead the administration or to be at its command.[69]

This was an important question, Hutchins insisted, because it addressed the very heart of justifications for women's political participation. We should remember, Hutchins pointed out, that women were given the right to vote because "we would improve standards in our government." But were women really doing that? All women, Hutchins argued, whether mothers or not, were "used to keeping up standards, not only in our homes but in our own communities." It was natural, then, that Republican women should want to continue that work on the national scene as well as the local. Not to take stands on important questions like the Girard case would be to abdicate one's responsibility, to contribute to the denial of a citizen's (Girard's) rights, and to encourage the government to weaken the Constitution. Women must not be "lady

Gullivers," Hutchins was fond of saying, lying helpless with their hands and feet bound.[70]

Murray and Hutchins wanted the Federation to exercise its political clout by putting its weight behind particular issues. To do so would have gone against existing Federation bylaws, but a minority of National Federation leaders was coming to support precisely such a change in Federation policy. The Federation Board of Directors discussed the issue at some length during a meeting in 1957. The majority of Federation leaders still saw the Federation primarily as an auxiliary to the RNC, whose existence (and funding) could only be justified so long as it remained a constructive force, which included remaining ostensibly neutral in party conflicts. Yet three state presidents did speak in favor of the Federation adopting its own positions and agenda.[71] Clearly, there was a movement within the Federation in favor of greater autonomy. Supporters of autonomy tended to be those on the party's right who were unsympathetic to the dominant modern Republicanism.

Efforts to keep the Federation strictly neutral in party conflicts had never been entirely effective. Despite the leadership's emphasis on loyalty and its position of neutrality with respect to intraparty conflicts, the Federation by the late 1950s and early 1960s had acquired a reputation for being more conservative than the party as a whole.[72] The Federation, it is important to bear in mind, did not represent all women, not even all Republican women. Furthermore, the Federation membership represented a range of opinion within the Republican Party. Yet the Federation's reputation confirmed popular ideas about women's more conservative nature and the moral and religious basis of women's political activism.

Pundits, political strategists, and Republican women organizers noted this reputation. No one made much attempt to explain it, however. To many people, women's conservatism was simply a natural condition, not requiring analysis or explanation. Certainly notable exceptions to this link existed, not only within society as a whole but within the party itself. In one well-publicized party showdown between moderates and the right, for example, Republican senator Margaret Chase Smith earned attention for her courageous "Declaration of Conscience" against McCarthy's communist hunting.[73] Yet assumptions about women's alleged conservatism persisted.

★ Before exploring the perceived link between women and conservatism in postwar America, it is necessary to think first about what it meant to be conservative in the 1950s. Conservatism itself is a slippery concept, used to describe an intellectual tradition, positions on specific political positions and social views, and an individual's general temperament and deportment. Betty Farrington herself (again calling on the heritage of Lincoln) insisted that Republican conservatism contained the impulse for reform so long as that reform did not threaten individual liberty.[74] In the 1950s some self-identified "conservatives" were only beginning to claim the term as a description for a legitimate American political philosophy. Influential consensus historians of the period argued that the United States, founded in revolution with utopian aims, had no conservative tradition. Americans with different political interests may have argued fiercely at times over specific issues. Supporters of these factions, however, had held a set of "shared convictions" about private property, individualism, and competition that developed out of American economic and social experiences.[75] These shared convictions were fundamentally liberal.

Yet, the historians of the 1950s were writing during a time when the old political terms were changing. The Great Depression, advancing technology, World War II, and the onset of the Cold War had disrupted assumptions about the nature of society, the role of government, and the responsibility of the United States in international affairs. A majority of Americans may have accepted a shift to internationalism, greater government responsibility for the welfare of the people, and increased federal authority over the states as a logical extension of American political values. That acceptance, however, was never unanimous.

Those who spoke of the Federation's conservatism in the 1950s referred to its members' positions on political issues of the day and, more specifically, to their hostility toward all that, to them, smacked of communism, subversion, or immorality. An eagerness to denounce any alleged case of subversion and immorality may not seem to be expressions of the most sober conservatism. Indeed, many conservative writers would have preferred to write such expressions out of their movement altogether. Clinton Rossiter, one conservative writer who analyzed the subject in the 1950s, summed up the political right as the "anti-Roosevelt coalition." Conservatives, Rossiter argued, were only one part of that coalition, which also included authoritarians, "professional haters," and sheer opportunists who could not properly be called conservative.[76] In popular usage, however, to argue that the National Federation of Republican Women in the 1950s was more conservative than the party was to identify its members with the right wing of the party. This was also to suggest that Federation women, in contrast to the Eisenhower administration, tended to oppose the domestic New Deal–inspired programs, the United Nations, and Eisenhower's decision to send federal troops to the South and to support McCarthy and the Bricker Amendment. To employ the terms "right-wing" and "conservative" here as though they were synonymous is problematic but unavoidable given popular usage.

Testing the claim that Federation women indeed were more conservative (or more right-wing) overall than the rest of the party is impossible. There are no surveys or polls detailing the membership's positions on various key issues. Moreover, the Federation certainly never promoted itself as a conservative force per se. The Federation's right-wing sympathies were understood rather than explicitly cultivated. Such a reputation was self-perpetuating. But the Federation was never monolithic. In parts of the country where the party itself was more liberal (such as New York and New Jersey), moderates dominated the club movement.

Yet there is evidence that American women as a whole in general during in the 1950s were more conservative (or right-wing) than men on at least one issue: their intolerance of communists, socialists, and atheists.[77] Social scientist Samuel Stouffer found that American women were less willing than men to allow socialists, atheists, accused communists, and admitted communists to speak in their communities or to have their books available in local libraries.[78] The gender difference was not great, but it was consistent across subcategories, including education, occupation, region, and even church attendance.[79] It is unclear whether this gender difference also existed within the Republican Party since Stouffer did not break down his sample by party affiliation. Whatever gender gap may have existed in the party probably was not great, in any case. Moreover, it is important to bear in mind that the GOP claimed female moderates as well as male right-wing enthusiasts. There seems to have been a general impression, however, that the Republican women who joined the Federation (as opposed to joining other party organizations, holding Republican offices, or merely voting) were among the party's more conservative (or right-wing) women.

But why was that so? Stouffer merely reported his findings. He did not seek to explain them. One contemporary who did at least begin to explore the reasons for women's militancy was Seymour Martin Lipset. In a lengthy footnote to his now classic essay on the radical right, Lipset speculated about women's apparent enthusiasm for right-wing crusades. Lipset cited Stouffer's research and noted that women had been behind many local efforts to weed subversive ideas out of libraries and schools. Lipset offered an explanation that fit within his own paradigm for understanding the American Right. Lipset suggested that women were more subject to "status anxiety" than were men and therefore more prone to right-wing ideas.[80] Lipset made little headway, however, when he tried to use status anxiety to explain women's right-wing attitudes. To justify his claim that women were more susceptible to status anxiety, Lipset was able to offer little more than the observation that women, more than men, were involved with "organizations of old family Americans" (such as the DAR).[81] Wedded to the "status anxiety" thesis, Lipset did not pursue the interesting question of whether and why American women might have had greater affinity for movements of the radical right than American men had. Although he looked primarily to status concerns in his analysis, Lipset also relied on general assumptions about women's greater religiosity and greater concern with morality in politics to explain women's conservatism.[82]

Many Republicans in the 1950s probably would have agreed. Historian D'Ann Campbell has suggested that by 1940 the "special [nineteenth-century] link between morality and gender roles had largely dissolved."[83] Perhaps this was true among the U.S. population in general, but these associations within the Republican Party had never disappeared; during the 1950s they were revived energetically. Both women and men used the language of the moral or religious crusade in describing women's politics. They did so frequently enough to beg the question whether the speakers were sincere in their usage. When Senator Owen Brewster claimed that the "women of this nation" were being mobilized because of the "Communist effort to destroy our Christian institutions," did he really believe this, or was he saying what he thought his female audiences wanted to hear? When women employed similar language, what were their intentions?

It was not necessarily inherent religiosity or morality that led women to evoke such terms in their political work. Their vocabulary also reflected the ways in which the very nature of politics and citizenship has been gendered historically in the United States. The justification for women's political behavior had long rested on women's indirect citizenship, particularly through women's role in raising new citizens.[84] Historically, women political activists had sought other justifications for their politics than self-interest—justifications such as the selfless desire to protect their families or their nation. One reason some women have described their politics as a women's moral crusade was that this language offered them a form of political legitimacy. Moral, spiritual, and family matters traditionally have been among the few political arenas in which men grant women authority. Perhaps politics was a man's world. Yet women had something to contribute—in symbolic terms at the very least—when domestic issues, economic matters, and even foreign policy were phrased morally, religiously, or with reference to the home. This is not at all to suggest that women have been insincere in their attraction to moral political crusades. Most women who used that language probably did so out of a deeply felt response to the issues at stake. But certainly the political opportunities and discourses available to women have helped to nurture and shape that response.

At different times women have evoked motherhood, religion, or their special moral role in order to vest themselves with moral authority that could earn them access to political power or influence. Examples include the temperance movement, the suffrage movement, and women's peace organizations. And to encourage women to support certain right-wing movements, women have been told that the movement bolsters, honors, and fulfills their traditional roles as mothers and moral caretakers (this was certainly the case with many of the isolationist mothers' groups in the late 1930s).[85] Yet not all of these movements can be characterized as movements of the Right. This suggests that the link Lipset drew between women's concerns with morality and right-wing politics was a tenuous one. Women have used the politics of motherhood and the crusading political style in the name of issues across the political spectrum—including, in the case of Republican women, 1920s progressivism as well as 1950s McCarthyism.

This moral rhetoric gave women a political role, but it restrained the possibilities for articulating political demands and even limited the range of issues with which women engaged. To assure women that they possess a unique moral authority could also be to deny them any real political power. Women who are convinced that men respect their moral authority may not demand that men grant them any political authority. Republican men regularly gave speeches to women in which they praised women for upholding civilization and Christian virtues. This practice was typically condescending and indicated little real consideration of women's concerns. Some theorists have suggested that moral rhetoric actually hinders the possibilities for political discourse. To present one's political demands as "moral" suggests that one's demands are nonnegotiable. If women's demands are nonnegotiable, then there is no substantive place for women's concerns in mainstream political discourse.[86] To an extent, this is what troubled Marion Martin when she complained that women preferred being "alarmed" to the more mundane activities of political education and negotiation.

Although Martin and Farrington differed in their assessment of the merits of the crusading political style, they shared a belief that women had a unique inclination to frame politics in urgent, moral terms. But were they correct? Any given woman was not necessarily any more religious or more concerned with morality than a given man. But it seems to have been largely women who defined political issues in uncompromising, moral terms. The Republican Party in the 1950s counted among its numbers both moderate women and right-wing men. But the popular associations of conservatism, right-wing activism, and religious faith with women led some men on the right, who felt shut out of the Republican Party, to look to women to promote their cause.

One Illinois man wrote to the Federation president in 1957 about his unhappiness that the Republicans had endorsed the United Nations and had given no recognition to God in its 1956 platform. Given these facts, the man wrote, "one can only wonder just how long any remnants of our Constitution, set up under God, and our Christian country will survive." The answer to that question, he believed, was "squarely in the hands of the women of America." He decried the men who had been running Republican politics but took comfort in the fact that there were more women than men in America. It was time, he declared, that "the women wake up to the fact that they and they alone must emerge as the governing body of the party. The GOP women are notably more conservative than the men's organization, yet they meekly tag along, doing the work, sacrificing their principles, and thankful for the crumbs that the men hand out to them. . . . If our country is to be saved, you women must do it. . . . You must work to spread patriotic information at the grass roots to counteract all the propaganda being hurled at us."[87] This man called on conservative Republican women to take over the party. But his characterization of the party as divided between women who were righteous conservatives and men who were godless, liberal sellouts masked another division within the party that may be more important here: the division between insiders and outsiders. This distinction is important to understanding the political crusades of Federation women in the 1950s.

Federation women's attraction to the crusading political style and to the phenomenon of women who "like to be alarmed" was partly a function of clubwomen's status as outsiders in the Republican Party. The women's club movement had not done as much to bring women into the center of party affairs as Marion Martin had hoped. Federation women were, by and large, kept out of political decision making. The rewards that Federation women gained from working in politics were not the rewards of patronage, financial gain, or access to power. They were, rather, the rewards of fighting for a cause they believed in. Consequently, the National Federation of Republican Women attracted and retained women who were inclined to view political issues (like communism) in intractable religious and moral terms.

The Federation's theme of women's unique moral authority (rather than equality) and its emphasis on the religious nature of politics resonated deeply with women who were driven to politics by their passionate commitment to particular issues. These were women who had little reason to expect reward for compromise. Rather, they were committed to ideas on which they would not equivocate, earning them a reputation for being more conservative than the party as a whole. Thus the Federation's conservative reputation and the penchant of its more right-wing members for uncompromising political crusades is explained not merely by the fact that its members were women (as contemporary commentators assumed). Also important was the fact that its members were party outsiders (who happened to be women) at a time when moderates dominated the party. So long as Federation women continued to see themselves as party outsiders, they had little to lose by retaining their attachment to issues beyond compromise.

In 1920 women's newness to formal party work made them clearly outsiders, a situation that perhaps masked the extent to which many men also felt left out of party decision making. In the forties and fifties however, as some women moved into leadership positions in the party, gender no longer distinguished so neatly those inside the party leadership from those outside. In 1964 ideological grass-roots Republicans would gain prominence in their successful effort to nominate Barry Goldwater for president over the opposition of party insiders. This movement of party outsiders, who defined their politics in the language of moral crusades, included thousands of men and women. Yet gendered language would continue to be used to refer to the tendency of these Republicans at the margins to extol moral, religious, right-wing politics.

Right-wing Republican women took their moral role extremely seriously. For the most part, they did not field female candidates for political office. Nevertheless, they were convinced that their moral authority could and should be used to support causes to which they truly were committed—not merely to bolster a political figure (such as Eisenhower) who they felt undermined their beliefs. The Federation in the 1950s earned a reputation for being more conservative (or right-wing) than the rest of the party. Some women, such as Ruth Murray and Vere de Vere Hutchins, openly attacked the GOP. The vast majority of Federation women, however, continued to support their party even when they disagreed with it. Their support took the form of hundreds of hours of volunteer work that became increasingly crucial to the party's grassroots organization.

THE
HOUSEWORK OF
GOVERNMENT

In 1956 the president of the National Federation of Republican Women, Nora Kearns, insisted that hers was "not a militant organization demanding that women be elected to office. Rights do not
enter into the picture."[1] This characterization of one of the largest organizations of politically active American women—as uninterested in
women's rights—probably was not what many independent club leaders in the 1920s would have hoped two generations of women's voting
and party activism would bring. Yet it was a characterization Kearns
offered proudly. When Marion Martin created the National Federation
of Women's Republican Clubs, she had hoped that a national organization could help the Republican Party by curbing the independent—and
therefore intractable and unpredictable—women's clubs. But she also
expected the Federation to be a training ground for future women leaders, whom the party would tap to run for office, serve as political appointees, and play decision-making roles in the party. Martin had made
a tacit (and perhaps naive) bargain with party leaders, in which the party
loyalty of Republican clubwomen was offered in exchange for future access to leadership.

By the 1950s the Republican women's club movement had become
a network of supportive female auxiliaries steeped in domestic metaphors that reinforced postwar ideals of family and suburban life. The
Federation's goals had changed, as had expectations about women's
place in party politics. Marion Martin's goal of promoting political access for women for the most part had been replaced by service and boost-
erism. The National Federation of Republican Women offered women
primarily a supportive, auxiliary role in political life. And indeed, the
Federation had proved itself to be critical to party successes. But by defining women's political work during the Eisenhower years in the popu-

lar language of postwar domesticity, the Federation offered little challenge to male political authority. Federation members during the 1950s
earned a reputation for holding views more conservative than those
of the party as a whole; yet they were being trained by the Federation
leadership to subordinate those views to the good of the party.

The Federation had accepted for itself a place at the margins of the
party. Yet this was not the only role offered Republican women in the
1950s. Women in the 1920s had explored two ways of entering party
politics: forming separate clubs outside the regular party structures
and achieving positions for women in the regular party organization. A
new generation of women pursuing this latter goal offered a model of
achievement for women in politics in the fifties. What were two alternative strategies for increasing women's political influence in the twenties
had come to represent, thirty years later, competing models of womanhood as well.

★ By the 1950s few would have disagreed that women were an integral presence in partisan politics. That women had carved a niche
for themselves, however, did not mean that they were fully integrated
into the parties. Mary Louise Smith's recollections of Republican Party
work in Iowa during the fifties describe what were often extreme divisions between male and female partisan behavior: "I was going to campaign headquarters and answering the telephones and doing mailings
and going door-to-door canvassing and it was almost entirely female.
That piqued my curiosity. It seemed to me that surely it was not a
party of all women. I knew there were men someplace. The more you
began to inquire, what you found was that they were doing the policy-
making things. Many of them were down in Des Moines. That was what
gave rise to the concept of smoke-filled rooms."[2] While party regulars
ran for office, selected candidates, and planned strategy, Republican
clubwomen in the fifties performed the day-to-day, face-to-face political
work that was crucial to building the party locally. Women put together
voter lists, conducted precinct surveys, sponsored talks by candidates,
registered Republican voters, and drove them to the polls on election
day.

During the Eisenhower years, clubwomen increasingly took on responsibility for the party's grass-roots volunteer work. Indeed, a survey conducted in the 1950s indicated that among core Republican Party
activists, 56 percent were women. This was noticeably higher than in
the Democratic Party, where women were only 41 percent.[3] Republican

leaders talked about this kind of political activism in ways that indicate that they understood it to be "women's work." A 1954 set of Republican talking points on women and government noted that "we, as Republicans, [can] be proud of the women who work on the home front, ringing the doorbells, filling out registration cards, and generally doing the housework of government so that the principles of the Republican Party can be brought to every home."[4] A woman leader a few years later put it another way: Republican women volunteers were the "political hewers of wood and drawers of water."[5]

The "housework of government" was an apt metaphor to describe women's partisan work. Republican women's role within the party was to perform the day-to-day work that received little glory but was critical to sustaining and building the party. Men in the party understood that the jobs women did were tedious and assumed that most men simply would not perform them. But as RNC publicity director Robert Humphreys suggested, women would carry out such jobs because they derived a "sense of achievement" in taking on tasks that most men found "too boring or time-consuming." One could get women to do a lot of things, Humphreys continued, that a man would not find "up to his capacities."[6] Humphreys proposed a plan for improving party fortunes and countering Democratic efforts that relied on the Republican women conducting door-to-door or telephone polls of voters—tasks that were presumably "too boring or time-consuming" to ask of Republican men.

The idea that women's function in party politics was to perform "the housework of government" was different from the Progressive Era idea, famously promoted by Jane Addams, that women were "social housekeepers." Addams's notion of social housekeeping was an explicit argument for women's empowerment. She insisted that women's domestic responsibilities required their participation in public life.[7] Certainly organizers of Republican women in the fifties drew superficially on the main metaphor of "social housekeeping"—that women's political activism might help clean up government and society's ills. In the 1952 election, for example, women voters were encouraged to clean up the mess in Washington by voting Republican; they were given "Ike and Dick" brooms to drive the point home. And a senator speaking to the Federation's 1954 convention conveyed the idea that women voters brought cleanliness to politics by invoking that old Republican icon, the elephant. The elephant was an "appropriate symbol" for Republican women, the senator noted, for "[t]his noble creature has been described as one with a vacuum cleaner in front and a rug beater behind."[8] More cute than insurgent, these metaphors suggested none of the claims to female power that Addams's notion of social housekeeping implied.

The "housework of government," however, did effectively evoke the grass-roots organizing work that women in the 1950s performed for their party.[9] Robert Humphreys's concerns about grass-roots organization were inspired by the efforts of organized labor on behalf of the Democrats. GOP leaders in the fifties worried constantly that their forces were unable to counter the organizing done by the political committees of the AFL and the CIO (seen as even more formidable once the two organizations merged in 1955).[10] During the 1954 elections, those candidates supported by the CIO–Political Action Committee (CIO-PAC) won 126 House, 15 Senate, and 8 gubernatorial races, including some offices in traditionally Republican areas. Polls revealed a correlation between increased PAC activity and increased voting for Democratic candidates. This correlation was also evident among "union wives," a group that the CIO-PAC had specifically targeted in 1954.[11]

Labor historians have pointed out that labor's close alliance with the Democratic Party in the late 1940s and 1950s did not prevent a turn to the right in American politics. This alliance, in fact, stemmed from the failures of organized labor to build a labor party in the immediate post-war years. Organized labor's transformative visions of social unionism of the mid-1930s gave way to the more narrow goals of business unionism after the war. In electoral politics, although organized labor helped considerably in the election of Democratic candidates in the North, labor's political work was not rewarded with substantial influence in the setting of Democratic Party policy.[12]

The GOP did not see it that way, however. In Republican rhetoric, there existed a dangerous symbiosis between the Democratic Party and the unions. This connection was offered both as a description of a political injustice (suggesting that the unions and the Democratic Party held undue influence over the votes of working people) and as an analysis of Republican shortcomings. As Martha Whitehead of Indiana noted during a Federation strategy session in 1958, the Democratic Party's public relations work was "being done for them by the union. I think that is our big problem." In Whitehead's mind, the Federation could be to the Republican Party what the unions were to the Democrats, in terms of performing the work of outreach.[13] As the Republicans worked to build their party in the mid-1950s, they focused on two major strategies: media campaigns to promote Republicanism and building an organization at the grass roots. A grass-roots force required more than local

party officeholders. The GOP needed committed, informed forces willing to do hundreds of hours of volunteer work—that is, the "housework
of government"—and to take the GOP message to the people.

The party came to depend on women for improving its grass-roots
organizing. In the years following the end of World War II, the Federation grew in size and organizational sophistication. Postwar suburban homemakers, who had an automobile and whose children were
of school age, often had the flexibility in their schedules to allow for volunteer and civic work, including political work. The postwar years, in
fact, would prove to be a time in which all kinds of women's civic activism flourished.[14] Under the leadership of President Elizabeth Farrington, the National Federation of Republican Women grew in size, claim-
ing a membership of around a half million women. The Federation had
a consistent goal of doubling that number, although it never succeeded
in doing so. Clubs seem to have had a core of leaders and activists who
were supplemented by a more fluid membership at the periphery that
tended to increase during election seasons and slacken during interim
years. By 1956 Federation women were members of more than 3,000
local women's Republican clubs in forty-six states, plus Alaska, Hawaii,
and the District of Columbia.[15] The Federation also began to expand
into those areas that would later become key areas of GOP strength—the
South and the Sunbelt. Federation women became skilled in public relations, outreach, and mobilization.

Farrington initiated important new projects and new directions for
the Federation. For example, the Federation took the lead in precinct
organizing for the party. In the presidential election of 1948, 45 million eligible voters had not gone to the polls. The party needed Republican precinct workers at the grass roots to help mobilize more voters
in subsequent elections. Precinct organization, a Democratic strength,
was sorely lacking in the GOP. The Federation under Farrington began
reorganizing itself on a precinct basis. And Farrington launched the
School of Politics. This series of three-day training sessions, held in
Washington during May 1950, was designed to train Republican precinct workers across the country. Although initially intended to train
both a man and woman from each precinct, the overwhelming majority
of those who attended the School of Politics were women. Democratic
women, under DNC vice chairman India Edwards, set up similar meetings in different regions of the country. In contrast to the Republican
Schools of Politics, some Democratic schools reported that more men
attended than women.[16]

Republican School of Politics attendees were expected to come to Washington having first completed a couple of weeks of research on their precinct, gathering information about residents' economic conditions, the institutions and persons who were influential in the area, and the ethnic and religious background of residents. At the School of Politics, participants learned how to use that information to be effective precinct workers. At the end of the course, which featured sessions with party representatives such as RNC chairman Guy Gabrielson, Congressman Joseph Martin, and Senator Robert Taft, "graduates" were given a certificate signed by Republican leaders and were expected to conduct similar sessions in their home precincts.[17]

Party leaders were impressed by Farrington's efforts. The School of Politics was quickly adopted by the RNC itself, and state central committees were encouraged to hold similar schools. By September 1950 twelve states were conducting Schools of Politics with an average attendance of 1,200 county and precinct workers per session.[18] When Republicans gained twenty-eight House seats in 1950, the committeeman from New Mexico gave partial credit to the Schools of Politics for inspiring the Republican organization into believing that the party could win.[19]

Female volunteers also were highly visible during the 1952 presidential election. That year, the RNC launched a national campaign to attract women voters under the auspices of the RNC Women's Division (headed by Ivy Baker Priest of Utah) and the Women's Division of the Citizens for Eisenhower. Prominent Republican women went on speaking tours, while countless ordinary women addressed envelopes, went door to door registering voters, raised funds, and arranged cooperative childcare so that more women could be involved.[20] Although Priest clearly ran an effective campaign, this army of women volunteers did not emerge from nowhere. Republican women's clubs were critical to the effort; they were a significant source of committed partisans who had experience campaigning, who were willing to devote their volunteer time, and who already were responsive to the message that women's concerns were best addressed by the GOP.

Clubwomen took on other party-building tasks as well, including the Plan of Action, begun under Federation president Nora Kearns in 1954.[21] This effort was a series of initiatives intended to create an "army of volunteer women" to offer service to the local party officials during election time. These women would be trained to canvass precincts, ring doorbells, make speeches, fold literature, and "do the hundred and one odd jobs that a successful campaign requires." The "Marginal Districts" project, like a similar campaign undertaken by the CIO-PAC, targeted specifically those precincts in districts where either the Democratic or Republican majority in recent elections had been slim.[22] In 1957 Bernard Lamb, national director of field organization for the Republican National Congressional Committee, relied on women volunteers across the country to compile lists of voters "right down into the precinct level."[23] But women did more than go door to door. A representative of the Texas Federation reported that during a special election in 1957 for a U.S. senator, more than thirty county headquarters were staffed entirely by Republican clubwomen, and in almost half of those cases, the local club had opened and financed the headquarters.[24]

Notably, the serious tasks of fundraising, organizing speaking events, and assisting voters on election day were configured as distinctly feminine activities that apparently no man could be expected to perform. Indeed, Paula Baker suggests that as party work became "women's work" in the twentieth century, the work itself became less skilled and less likely to lead to advancement, similar to what occurred in many parts of the economic sector at the same time.[25] The association of women with the volunteer work of the party would become so complete by 1958 that the RNC director of campaign activities, Robert Humphreys, went so far as to refer to Republican *men* as a "great untapped source of party workers."[26] In 1962, when National Federation of Republican Woman president Ruth Parks requested that the men of the Republican National Committee wear small gold keys to promote the latest Federation project (the Seven Keys Plan), she promised them lightheartedly that wearing the keys would not condemn them to the feminized work of local party activism. "I want the boys to be assured," Parks emphasized, "that if they wear a gold key it doesn't mean that you [sic] are a member of a Republican ladies' club. They are not going to call on you to bake cakes, or to raise money, or make decorations for tables, or to take a handful of tickets, or be responsible for a Lincoln Day banquet, or baby sit on election day."[27]

As Republican women took on grass-roots organizing, they defined that work in ways that emphasized hospitality and neighborliness. The intense, local partisan politics of brotherhood, characteristic of the mid- to late nineteenth century, had largely disappeared by the mid-twentieth century. Although both parties had been making increasing use of the media as a means of getting their messages to voters, grass-roots organizing was not entirely moribund. Both parties in the fifties, but especially the Republicans, relied on middle-class housewives to connect partisan politics to the everyday lives of citizens in their communities. This meant emphasizing the home and the neighborhood as key sites of political organizing.

The middle-class, nuclear family, located in the new suburbs and presided over by full-time homemakers, seemed in the 1950s to offer a defense against the "hazards of the age."[28] Leaders of the club movement, trying to reach out to the new population of young women in the suburbs, designed many of their political projects especially for the young suburban housewife who felt a duty to be politically involved, but whose physical world supposedly did not extend much beyond her home and neighborhood. In 1955, for example, the Federation established what it called "Kitchen Kabinets." The Federation appointed a Republican woman to its national Kitchen Kabinet to be responsible for following the activities of each member of Eisenhower's cabinet. One of these members of the national Kitchen Kabinet was a young Phyllis Schlafly, who later become president of the Illinois Federation and a candidate for the Federation presidency. Kitchen Kabinet members would share "political recipes on GOP accomplishments with the housewives of the nation." This was done by sending monthly bulletins on "What's Cooking in Washington" to local clubs. Individual clubs were encouraged to establish their own Kitchen Kabinets of women who would take responsibility for exchanging "recipes" with other club members.[29]

The "Kitchen Kabinet" associated women's political activities with the home metaphorically, but other such associations were literal. In previous decades, Republican clubwomen had held their meetings in public spaces, such as libraries, theaters, and fairgrounds. As the social lives of middle-class families came to center more and more on the private dwelling in the postwar years, so too did the political lives of middle-class Republican clubwomen. For example, a standard registration drive became, as a women's project, "Welcome Neighbor," a drive for women to register new residents and nonregistered voters.[30] The "Flag in Every Home" project promoted flag display and the association of the Republican Party with the American flag.[31] Democrats instituted similar programs linking women's political life and domesticity, including "Read and Sew for '56," a plan to encourage women to get together to discuss items in the Democratic Digest while sewing items featuring the donkey symbol to use for gifts or for future fundraising activities.[32]

Another project that brought political activity into Republican homes was "Operation Coffee Cup," initiated by the Federation in 1956. The

Federation publicized this carefully coordinated campaign effort as an approach that would "revolutioniz[e] campaigning." For their part in Operation Coffee Cup, clubwomen across the country held coffee klatches in their homes where Republican candidates met informally with a small number of guests over coffee and cookies. Operation Coffee Cup also brought national candidates into women's homes via televised events at which Eisenhower and Nixon drank coffee and engaged in carefully scripted conversation with a select group of women. Operation Coffee Cup set up meetings with politicians, even the president and vice president, in ways emphasizing that participants were just another group of housewives sharing a friendly cup of coffee in a neighbor's living room.[33] This association was furthered by the new era of television. As Federation membership chairman Mrs. Richard Simpson noted, television had removed politics from public spaces and transferred them to women's sphere (the home).[34]

Operation Coffee Cup, intended to show that the GOP was "the party of all people," brought politicians into women's homes, on women's terms.[35] In contrast to the candidate debates or speeches for the general public that women's clubs had sponsored in the twenties and thirties, Operation Coffee Cup relied on women sharing the intimacy of their households to bring candidates to the voters. Meetings were kept small and guests attended only at the hostess's invitation. This policy was intended to accommodate the hostess, but it also reveals a weakness of using neighborliness as an organizing strategy. Clubs were instructed to consider "racial, religious and social, etc., aspects" in choosing Coffee Cup hostesses in order to assure "a wide range of coverage."[36] Organizers apparently assumed that hostesses were likely to invite into their homes only those women who were of similar backgrounds. The Federation acknowledged diversity among women by always including among its goals the increased participation of African American, "ethnic," laboring, and professional women. But lacking real ideas for making such appeals (as well as any strong commitment to doing so), the Federation primarily attracted white, middle-class homemakers.

The Federation's outreach projects seemed particularly intended for young, earnest, yet uninformed suburban mothers. The Federation's "Republican Roundtables," for example, were suburban versions of traditional study clubs where women had gathered to report on various topics with the goal of self-improvement. Roundtable hostesses were encouraged to invite a small number of acquaintances over to form weekly study groups in which each member would report on topics like "the two-party system," "election laws," and "Republican accomplishments." The Federation also provided study materials and reference materials.

A skit demonstrating how the Roundtables should function, performed at a Federation Board of Directors Meeting in March 1956, suggests who the Federation expected this particular tactic to reach. In the skit, a woman named Ann invites several other women to her home to organize a Republican Roundtable. Only two of the women are Federation members, although by the end of the meeting the others decide to join. Being acquaintances rather than good friends, the women initially bond over topics related to gardening and children. The women repeatedly acknowledge in a lighthearted manner how uninformed they are regarding political and civic matters. When one woman is given source material on the role of political parties to help with a report she is to give at a later date, she is dismayed but undaunted. "You mean all that small type? . . . well, I'll get Herman [her husband] to explain it to me as I go along." A grocery delivery interrupts the meeting toward the end, inspiring a discussion of how low prices have been since Eisenhower was elected. The women end their meeting with enthusiastic plans to meet again the following week. One woman declares that the meeting was useful not only for its educational value but also because it was so pleasant to meet with the other women. "I've had a lovely morning!" she declares.[37]

This skit emphasizes the political ignorance of the female characters but also their enthusiasm to learn. Their discussion of the price of groceries was meant to show that even uninformed homemakers had a framework within which to understand (and be interested in) politics. The setting for political activity is clearly domestic, and one sees that the club functions as a social outlet as well, suggesting those who conceived of the Republican Roundtables understood how hungry some housewives were for adult company. Federation material, such as this Roundtable skit, instructed women in the 1950s that politics was about hospitality and friendliness, not about conflict over issues or interests. This was also the message of Eisenhower's "modern" Republicanism, which relied on the belief that Americans generally were united by their patriotism, prosperity, and security rather than divided by class, race, or political philosophy. But "modern" Republicanism was itself a divisive factor among Republicans, including Republican women.

Under the Federation model, politics became an extension of what suburban housewives supposedly did every day: talking on the telephone, watching television, cutting out invitations in the shapes of elephants or coffee cups, sharing "recipes" with friends, having coffee with a new neighbor. Politics could be made perfectly compatible with the domestic lives of suburban housewives, including a strong family life. Sylvia Hermann, chairman of the Federation's Campaign Activities Committee, warned that some husbands might "have to eat a cold supper once in a while" and that occasionally the dishes might "go unwashed." But this sacrifice would be worth it if women could help elect a Republican Congress in 1954.[38] There were other reports that Republican club work could actually be good for a marriage. A member from Reno, Nevada, claimed that the divorce rate in her state had dropped since the formation of women's Republican clubs. Political activity supposedly gave women something to talk to their husbands about besides "domestic crises."[39]

The political interests of women, although centered in the home, were also understood to extend beyond the home into the neighborhood. Again and again, men and women emphasized the crucial role that women in particular could play in selling the party through their daily contacts. The party had to appeal to a constituency far broader than hard-core Republican loyalists. Personal contact, then, was considered extremely important in swaying voters. As Nora Kearns told the Republican Women of Pennsylvania in 1955, "you have, within your organization, the power to shape political opinion—the power to mould and strengthen the political viewpoint of the people who belong to your country club, your bridge club, the neighbors up the street, the grocer, the laundry man, the garage mechanic—in fact anyone with whom you come in contact in your daily living." Kearns encouraged women to make it a point to say something favorable about the GOP to at least ten persons per day.[40]

Federation leaders hoped hospitality and friendliness could reach even presumably Democratic voters, such as "labor wives." Assumed to be the wives of union men rather than wage earners or union members themselves, "labor wives" could be reached "over the teacups and over the back fence," through conversations about "our children and all of those things"—in ways in which "they won't know what you are doing."[41] Going after "labor wives" was a logical strategy. The results of a study conducted by the CIO-PAC after the 1952 elections had indicated that the votes of CIO members' wives had helped swing the presidential election for Eisenhower. These results had led the CIO-PAC to launch new campaigns to target the wives of CIO members, including "family conferences," efforts to frame political problems as household problems, and the addition of women's columns to union newspapers.[42] These efforts proved partly successful in 1954 when Democrats made midterm election gains.

The potential to win these female voters back to the Republicans was not lost on Federation leaders. Republican club leaders saw value in reaching out to the wives of union men, believing they could appeal to them as housewives with common concerns. Differences in economic position, in social status, or in partisan affiliation presumably could be overcome through contact with a committed, commonsense Republican woman—a political campaigner in the guise of a friendly neighbor. In an increasingly suburbanized world, however, in which the majority of suburban residents were professionals, white-collar workers, and their families, it is doubtful that many GOP women actually lived next door to, or even shopped at, the same stores as "labor wives."[43]

Republican clubwomen helped give the Republican Party a local face in new and growing communities where residents lacked long-held institutional and social affiliations. Republicanism meant more than Eisenhower's tax proposals or foreign policy, although these were important. The Republican Party was also the kindly woman who offered neighbors refreshments, talked about her children, and offered to sell a flag to adorn one's new home. While some people surely found such behavior irritating (especially those of different political convictions), others no doubt welcomed such efforts, which offered a sense of community and common purpose.[44]

Efforts by Republican clubwomen to be clever and creative in their program proposals occasionally backfired, as when a 1958 fundraising booklet included among its suggested fundraisers a "striptease" auction. Such an auction would feature a well-dressed club member who would auction off her hat, jewelry, and clothing, removing each item as it was purchased and giving it to the buyer. In the end the model would be left on stage, wearing a bathing suit or bra and panties. Someone called the item to the attention of syndicated columnist George Dixon who wrote a piece professing shock at the idea. The column appears to have been written with a sense of humor (as when Dixon imagines with horror "some of the stalwart Republican ladies I know being a party to taking it off to put it on for the Grand Old Party"). Yet the column provoked genuinely outraged letters to the Federation, which ultimately chose to revise the pamphlet, limiting its fundraising suggestions to more traditional ideas, such as bake sales.[45]

Although Republican clubwomen did important work in boosting the party, they also created make-work for themselves. They invested enormous creative resources in planning parties, writing clever campaign scripts, and bestowing honors on each other. The Federation emphasized the importance of giving members something to do and honoring them for the work they did. Doing so made members feel a part of the cause and may have increased their commitment.[46] Meanwhile, interest in political issues among Republican clubwomen reportedly remained low. The Program Planning Committee chairman found it necessary in 1958 to encourage clubs to include a report on "at least one current and vital political topic" per meeting. The "primary reason" for having meetings, she reminded gently, was to "further political education." No meeting would be complete, then, "without some reference to it." Dorothy Christiansen, of the Iowa Council of Republican Women's Program Committee, urged women to read the Federation's objectives (the first of which was to "promote an informed electorate") at the beginning of every meeting. "[T]oo often," Christiansen lamented, "women's groups get side-tracked . . . from their real purpose simply because they either do not know or understand their real objectives."[47] Although the Federation claimed to encourage women's involvement with the issues, its function as a party auxiliary actually seems to have worked against such goals. Clubs that became too involved with issues (such as the Bricker Amendment) risked being labeled disloyal if their views were incompatible with those of the party leadership. It is understandable, then, that many clubwomen would have lacked enthusiasm for substantive political issues and, furthermore, that those who did hold strong political views would chafe at the Federation's definition of party loyalty.

Clearly the National Federation had an integral place in the Republican Party—one that was acknowledged by men as well as women. It was a distinct women's place, however, and one that did not challenge Republican men's position as the candidates and the decision makers. Through its public messages, the Federation defined clubwomen's relationship to the party in terms of support, encouragement, and loyalty—a relationship that would have been anathema to the independent Republican clubwomen in the twenties. Marion Martin, too, had emphasized loyalty and support as the ideal qualities for women in the party. Yet she had offered a vision of women in public service that the Federation largely abandoned in the 1950s. Clubwomen were not supposed to be interested in their own political advancement but in serving the party. This model for Republican women is illustrated by one 1956

Federation slogan in which Ike and the Republicans were the ones "For Whom the Belles Toil."[48]

Women's campaign work was praised precisely because its voluntary nature indicated that it was done for unselfish reasons. One candidate who emphasized women's selflessness on his behalf was Senator Gordon Allot of Colorado. Speaking before a Federation audience in 1955, Senator Allott recalled that he had twenty women working in his campaign headquarters, and "out of those women there was not a salary, not a dollar of a salary paid to a single woman." Senator Allott acknowledged that some critics might claim that this showed he was "a cheapskate." In fact, he argued, women worked willingly without pay because they were so dedicated to the campaign. At the same meeting, Senator Barry Goldwater of Arizona pronounced women the backbone of the party because they had a "driving spirit" that was critically lacking in the party's men. On another occasion, Ray Bliss, chairman of the Ohio State Central Committee, complained that he had to pay male campaign workers in his state, whereas women would work for free.[49]

In celebrating the role of clubwomen as unpaid volunteers, the Federation echoed long-held ideas that women entered politics for the public good, rather than for personal gain; for reasons of altruism rather than of self-interest.[50] Republican clubwomen justified their political activities in language that echoed long-standing constructions of female citizenship in the United States—the notion that women's civic responsibilities and identities rested on their role in raising new citizens.[51]

Republican clubwomen were encouraged to see themselves as working for the Republican Party on behalf of their families' futures. Their political work was crucial because clubwomen, without the obligations of full-time work outside the home, had the time to be involved and to work for the Republican cause. This work not only involved campaigning, registering voters, and generally spreading Republicanism among adults. Republican women also promoted American values and institutions (both political and moral) in their family life. Male Republican party leaders lauded GOP women for the important role they played in politics, not only as voters and workers but also by maintaining "orderly Christian homes" and teaching children principles of "decency and character." The Republicans did not have a monopoly on such rhetoric. In 1955 Democratic presidential contender Adlai Stevenson characterized women's role in politics in similar terms. Stevenson identified a woman's role in politics as stemming from her role as wife and mother. "Women," he suggested, "especially educated women, have a

Republican Roundtables

Mrs. Carroll D. Kearns, President
National Federation of Republican Women
1625 Eye Street, N. W.
Washington 6, D. C.

Republican Roundtables. (Convention forms— 1956—9th Biennial Convention, Chicago, Ill., box 101, NFRW records; used with permission from the National Federation of Republican Women.)

unique opportunity to influence us, man and boy." A woman, Stevenson continued, should "inspire in her home a vision of the meaning of life and freedom."[52]

Federation leaders in the 1950s embraced similar understandings of the relationship between women, the Republican Party, and home life. The "taproot of Republicanism" could extend into every American home, according to Nora Kearns, because women in those homes created "a political atmosphere through their determination to serve the spiritual and material needs of their family."[53] Kearns's successor Catharine Gibson echoed similar themes in a 1957 speech to female Young Republicans. Gibson told these young women that they were the ones to "gently mould the lives of tomorrow's citizens—both boys and girls. You will set the tenor of your home. By joint action together, you will have the kind of playgrounds, schools, churches and political parties that will shape the destiny of this nation."[54] The literature promoting the Federation's Republican Roundtables visually illustrates the multiple roles of ideal Federation women. While their children play nearby with a toy elephant and a children's GOP primer, a group of women sit around a table reading literature on American government, the Republican Party, and political campaigning.[55]

During a time when the family was presented as a safeguard of American institutions, values, and strength, the Republican Party was configured as a family as well, with roles for men, for women, and for young people (including not only Young Republicans, but also College Republicans and Teen-Age Republicans). The program from the 1952 Iowa Republican convention illustrates this construction: an idealized nuclear family is labeled as "the defenders," protecting the political (and partisan) traditions of the nation. Catharine Gibson used the metaphor of the family to explain why women should avoid taking sides in party controversies: "Woman . . . is the strong and binding force that holds her home together. . . . She does not pit one against the other, or battle with one against the other." Women's strength in defending their families was, according to Gibson, the greatest asset they brought when they assumed leadership positions in the party, "our *political* family." One of Gibson's pet projects as Federation president was her promotion of mother-daughter memberships as a means of recognizing "family responsibility toward the Republican party."[56]

Many women on the party's right continued to place devotion to a moral cause before devotion to the party. The role of family peacekeeper was not what Vere de Vere Hutchins emphasized in her own construction of Republican womanhood. Hutchins placed greater emphasis on women's role to "keep up standards" in homes, communities, and politics. For Hutchins, this meant challenging her party when she disagreed with it, rather than promoting harmony. The message emanating from Federation headquarters in the fifties, however, followed Gibson's model.

Most clubwomen in the 1950s were urging neither a policy-making role for the Federation nor the naming of substantial numbers of women as candidates or appointees for public office. Republican clubwomen claimed they were only interested in serving the party (and thereby their country and their families). This does not mean that they did not expect to be rewarded for their work. What the Federation wanted above all was appreciation for and recognition of the Federation's honored place in the Republican family. And Federation women, at least privately, expressed considerable dissatisfaction at what they felt was the party's failure to reward them adequately.

The Defenders.
1952 Iowa State
Republican Presidential
Convention program
(Iowa State Republican
Convention, 1952,
General, box 1, AL
papers).

President Eisenhower's victory, to which Federation women believed they had made important contributions, produced disappointments in this regard. The RNC Women's Division urged Eisenhower to offer more top women appointments than Truman had, and he did.[57] Federation women, however, were not pleased with Eisenhower's choices. To Federation leaders such as Nora Kearns and her colleagues, it appeared that Eisenhower was honoring the wrong kinds of women with appointments and thereby demeaning loyal Republican volunteers.

Of great concern was that outgoing Federation president Betty Farrington was overlooked entirely, despite a campaign by Federation clubwomen to secure an appointment for her.[58] Farrington's work in expanding the Federation and perfecting its usefulness had been key to Republican victory in 1952, and those who wrote letters on Farrington's behalf said as much. What supporters seem to have found most important in the proposed Farrington appointment was that the Fed-

*Republican Mothers. The National Federation of Republican Women
promoted women's role in passing Republicanism down through the
generations. Shown here is Indiana's representative to the Federation's
Mother-Daughter contest in 1960. From left to right, Sheri Malsbary,
Marilyn Malsbary, Mrs. Keith Malsbary, and Mrs. S. S. Walton.
(Mother-Daughter Award Winners, box 46, NFRW records. Reproduced
by permission from the* Journal and Courier, *Lafayette, Indiana.)*

eration itself be recognized. Federation loyalists were frustrated, then, when Ivy Baker Priest (who was affiliated with the RNC Women's Division) received an appointment (as U.S. treasurer) whereas Farrington did not.[59] This omission would fuel the already existing rivalry between the all-volunteer Federation and the Women's Division run by salaried employees.

Often the signs of appreciation and recognition that Federation women sought were symbolic rather than substantive. When in January 1957 the Federation found itself omitted from any role in planning Eisenhower's inaugural parade, Gertrude Detweiler of Idaho wrote that while she would be "the last one to do anything to antagonize the men," she felt strongly that the Federation "must insist" on being recognized or "we will find it harder each year to get the women to work." The Federation sent a resolution to the Republican National Committee in protest.[60] This emphasis on recognition and appreciation now eclipsed earlier Federation goals of moving women into positions of power and decision making. Clubwomen knew they had an important place in party politics. As long as men acknowledged and honored that place, most women seemed willing to leave the business of writing platforms, choosing candidates, and running for office to men and go about their own party activities—political housework and hospitality.

Yet not every one was satisfied with this division of political labor. Women on the right wanted the Federation to take a stand against "modern" Republicanism, as discussed in Chapter 4. And leaders of the Iowa Council of Republican Women expressed frustration with the entire club strategy for entering partisan politics. In a 1953 bulletin to its members, ICRW leaders complained that the party had relegated women to ancillary positions in the party. The ICRW charged that Iowa men, and the state's Republican leadership in particular, had kept women out of politics and thus forced them into club activity as their only arena of civic service. Women, the ICRW argued, had failed in their duties as citizens by accepting this marginal role. But men had also failed in their own civic duties by focusing exclusively on politics and business and not "integrating themselves into fields of other interests."[61] Iowa GOP club movement leaders in the 1950s correctly observed that there were limitations in dividing party politics into men's and women's spheres.

★ In her groundbreaking book, Betty Friedan described housewives in the 1950s as afflicted with a "feminine mystique," trying to fill their days with bridge, club meetings, children, and housework that didn't really need to be done.[62] Republican club leaders defined their movement in terms that resonated with that domestic ideal. In many respects, they made political work compatible with postwar domestic ideals by transforming Republican club activity in the 1950s into something that closely resembled other forms of suburban socializing and housework. When done under the auspices of the Republican women's club, these activities were imbued with a purpose that many housewives allegedly found lacking in their lives. Club leaders departed from the "feminine mystique" by insisting that women's duties extended beyond responsibility for their families to include a civic responsibility to be involved in politics.

This was true for women involved in other civic organizations as well. Groups like the LWV and the PTA, according to Susan Ware, "created public roles for women denied access to the usual sources of power."[63] Women's partisan clubs played a similar role, which helps account for their popularity in the fifties. One Maryland woman described her participation in the Federation's School of Politics as a life-changing experience. Arnilla Myhre had been a lifelong Republican, but that identity had meant little to her other than to dictate the way she voted. After attending the School of Politics training sessions, she explained in a letter to the men who had conducted them that, "*having been asked* by you to take an active part, my life has changed. For me the Republican Party has come alive. It is no longer something vague, shadowy, outside, you. Today it is me, too. Mine, something I must work for, also. . . . It's like 'getting religion.'" Myhre went on to credit Elizabeth Farrington for having known how to strike such a resonant chord with American women. "Mrs. Farrington realized what you may not have known—that for years the intelligent non-employed women of this country have been hungry for something concrete and compelling to do for their country —thirsty for action worth taking."[64] Myhre anticipates Friedan in her description of the frustration of educated middle-class housewives. But Myhre also reinforces Ware's point that through political clubs, some housewives were able to define public roles for themselves and thus find a sense of purpose. The auxiliary relationship of Republican women's clubs to the party meant that partisan clubs did not really offer women an arena of power or influence, but it did offer them the opportunity to feel necessary—to their country, their party, and male leaders.

Friedan blamed popular magazines for creating a picture of domestic bliss that stifled women's ambitions and expectations and left them bored, frustrated, and deeply dissatisfied. Others who have reexamined women's activism and popular culture during the period have found that the postwar popular ideals of womanhood were more complicated and ambiguous that Friedan allowed. Magazines in the fifties typically profiled women who were successful public figures alongside women who found fulfillment through making sandwiches. That an "ethos of individual achievement" was promoted in postwar magazines along with the feminine mystique indicates that mass culture was filled with contradictions.[65] The Republican Party in the fifties offered models for women's political behavior that were similarly ambiguous and contradictory. The National Federation of Republican Women in the 1950s promoted women's political activism in terms that defined women principally as wives, mothers, and suburbanites. Yet there was a competing discourse from within the Republican Party that celebrated and promoted women's political achievement. That discourse emanated primarily from the Women's Division of the Republican Party, headed by Bertha Adkins.

While Federation leaders during the Eisenhower years publicly downplayed women's political ambitions and concentrated on service to the party, Bertha Adkins encouraged women to become leaders. Adkins prided herself on her success in promoting the names of specific women for presidential appointments. She gave speeches encouraging women to pursue political careers and publicized the activities of women political leaders. And she instituted regular occasions for Eisenhower to meet with women leaders from a variety of organizations and occupations in order that he develop a sense of women's capabilities.

Adkins's background differed from that of most postwar Federation leaders.[66] Whereas Farrington and Kearns were the wives of congressmen, Adkins was a single woman with a paid career. Indeed, she had more in common with Marion Martin than with the leaders of the Federation. After receiving her B.A. from Wellesley College in 1928, Adkins began a career in education, teaching at a private school in her home state of Maryland. She had looked forward to a leisurely life in which she would work part-time as a teacher, with time off for golf in the afternoons, and would eventually marry. Her life plans were interrupted by the Depression, when financial circumstances forced her to find fulltime work as a college administrator. She took a job as dean of women at Western Maryland College and later as dean of residence at Bradford Junior College (formerly Bradford Academy, where Marion Martin had received her girlhood education). When her mother died in 1946, Adkins left her job at Bradford, returning home to Salisbury to keep house for her father.

There she became involved with politics. In 1946 she worked on the campaign of a successful Republican congressional candidate and in 1948 joined his reelection campaign. That year, according to Adkins, when the post of Maryland National committeewoman became vacant, the men from her district successfully lobbied to secure her the position as a means of recognizing the district's electoral successes. Adkins chose to be a particularly active national committeewoman and worked hard to involve women in the local party committees. She was identified with the moderate wing of the party, expressing her opposition to socialism while recognizing that society had an obligation to meet certain minimum standards for social needs, such as housing, health, and education.

In 1950 RNC chairman Guy Gabrielson asked Adkins to come to Washington to work as executive director of the RNC Women's Division. Her moderate brand of Republicanism was apparently not an issue for the more conservative Gabrielson (who is today perhaps best remembered for his denunciation of sexual deviants as security risks).[67] At the Women's Division, Adkins did much to reach out to nonpartisan women's organizations at the national level, attending their meetings and making contacts. In 1953, after Ivy Baker Priest accepted the appointment as secretary of the treasury, Adkins succeeded her in the renamed position of assistant to the RNC chairman. That year, under Chairman Leonard Hall, the RNC was reorganized and all special divisions, including the Women's Division, were placed with a "special activities group" of which Adkins was named assistant to the chairman.[68]

Adkins prodded Eisenhower to make female appointments by developing a roster of women with qualifications that would enable them to work "in a variety of places."[69] Adkins encouraged women to develop the qualifications necessary for a career in politics, always emphasizing that only the very best women be appointed. Women had to be better than men, she frequently said, because if one woman were to be difficult, or to perform poorly, men would use her as a reason never to hire another.[70] By 1957 approximately 130 women were serving in the Eisenhower administration. As one woman argued, most were there "because of the persuasion and fight put up by Bertha Adkins."[71] In 1957 Adkins herself was appointed undersecretary of the Department of Health, Education, and Welfare (HEW), where she served until the end of Eisenhower's term.

Party Professional. While most Republican women remained at the margins of their party, some achieved positions of influence. Here Bertha Adkins is shown with President Eisenhower and Len Hall, RNC chairman in Washington, D.C., 17 February 1954. (Bertha Adkins Photographs, no. 80-23-14, Dwight D. Eisenhower Presidential Library, Abilene, Kansas; photo by Abbie Rowe, courtesy of National Park Service [79-AR-2980-A].)

Adkins publicized women's political successes and activities through means such as the Women's Division's monthly bulletin *Women in Politics*, which tracked and celebrated the achievements of women holding elected or appointed office.[72] Adkins designed *Women in Politics* to be sent to women leaders in nonpartisan organizations as a means of promoting good relations between women's organizations and the Eisenhower administration. Adkins also facilitated direct contacts between Eisenhower and national women's leaders, organizing a series of breakfast sessions with the president for prominent women—Republicans, Democrats, and nonpartisans—in 1955. These sessions, which were eventually suspended after Eisenhower suffered a heart attack, were significant, Adkins maintained, because they gave the president genuine insight into the effectiveness of women's organizations, which he otherwise lacked.[73]

While promoting exceptional women for public office, Adkins also saw the potential for other women to serve the party as volunteers. In this sense, her vision of grass-roots women's involvement was similar to the Federation's. Adkins believed that women were especially suited for the kind of politics that was increasingly a matter of casual, unofficial contact between candidates and the public. In 1955–56 she directed a national women's fundraising project, called "Thank You, Mr. President," that relied on women volunteers going door-to-door collecting small contributions for state and national Republican finance committees from other women.[74] Through such projects, Adkins promoted precisely the kind of women's political activity for which the Federation trained its members. Women, Adkins suggested to a Virginia Republican club, had "time for such things as registration checks and door-to-door visits" and were the most willing to go person-to-person.[75] Like Federation leaders, Adkins here depicted "women" as middle-class housewives with a great deal of free time. This was not her own situation, however. Adkins was an unmarried professional woman who valued her career and who supported herself financially. And although she had worked the polls on election day, Adkins admitted that she personally had never done "actual doorbell ringing."[76]

The National Federation of Republican Women and the Women's Division of the RNC were rivals during the 1950s. Several women leaders in the Federation privately identified their enemies not only as the Democrats, the liberals, and the communists but also as the women in the Women's Division. Federation leaders celebrated their own position as volunteers in contrast to Bertha Adkins and her assistant, Anne Wheaton. Adkins and Wheaton were not volunteers, but professionals paid by the RNC. Federation leaders viewed Bertha Adkins and the Women's Division as competitors for status and funds from the party and believed that the Women's Division wrongly received greater consideration.[77] This was despite the fact that the Women's Division was essentially eliminated in 1953.

Adkins, however, saw herself as the leader of all Republican women. This included not only women in the Federation but also the women members of the national, state, and local party committees, other women's volunteer groups, and women who had been involved with the nonpartisan Citizens for Eisenhower. She also understood the need to promote the party and its candidates to audiences beyond hard-core GOP activists. Adkins tried to create electoral victories by nurturing Eisenhower's broad appeal and by selling "modern" Republicanism. Some Federation leaders, however, believed Adkins's efforts to reach out to other groups amounted to a strategy of purposefully undermining the Federation.[78]

Adkins's efforts at outreach disturbed clubwomen's more-conservative sensibilities; but they also seemed to insult Federation women's devotion to Republicanism. Federation women approved of outreach when it meant distributing Republican materials to nonpartisan women's organizations. But they felt that "real" Republicans should be the ones rewarded and honored by the party. For Federation women— invested as they were in a model of Republican womanhood that claimed to reward selfless devotion to the party—it was frustrating when the party rewarded and publicized professional party women who seemed to view politics as a paid career rather than an act of love and whose Republican credentials were sometimes suspect.

In 1956 Federation leaders brought their complaints about Adkins and the Women's Division to RNC chairman Len Hall in two face-to-face meetings. Their list of grievances included inadequate attention to the Federation's part in party affairs and failure of the Women's Division to acknowledge the Federation's role in projects implemented largely by Federation women.[79] When Wilma Bishop of Oregon suggested "very innocently?" to Hall that the Federation could easily raise its own funds and go its own way, she reported that Hall was emphatic that they not do that. "THAT was the ONLY TIME the old boy really quickly rose to my bait," Bishop reported triumphantly. "AT ONCE, and with MUCH VEHEMENCE he said, 'Oh no, Mrs. Bishop, *that* would only makes [sic] matters MUCH worse—we do not wish you to do that.'" Bishop felt she had touched a nerve and believed she had found proof that the RNC did know how much it depended on the Federation.[80]

Hall, for his part, reportedly insisted that the dispute between the Federation and the Women's Division was merely a "conflict of personalities."[81] Other observers saw the rivalry between the Women's Division and the Federation as one based on political philosophy. The Federation was more conservative, and the Women's Division tried to prevent the Federation from making potentially damaging statements on policy.[82] Although Adkins's papers do not indicate that she was similarly antagonistic toward the Federation, other accounts do suggest that the rivalry was mutual.[83] It is, in any case, plausible that Adkins would not have accorded the volunteer group the consideration it desired. Federation members generally were politically more conservative, led lives very different from hers, and did not value professional accomplishment in the same way that Adkins did.

★ Perhaps Federation leaders' frustration with the status of the Women's Division stemmed partly from recognition of its own failure. The favor granted the Women's Division was evidence that the party did not truly value the Federation's model of Republican womanhood. Although it gave lip service to the value of female volunteers, when seeking women's input or leadership, the party preferred full-time, trained professionals like Bertha Adkins. But Adkins's own position as a paid organizer of women depended on the existence of a mass organization of volunteers. The Women's Division may have offered support for women's political ambitions, but it was not a grass-roots organization in the way the Federation was. It could not by itself generate an interest in partisan politics among the masses of apolitical women. For its women's fundraising campaigns and conferences, Bertha Adkins's Women's Division drew heavily on women who had already been activated through the club movement. Through their activities, Republican clubwomen challenged popular notions that homemakers in the fifties were not interested in politics. Yet the Federation had done little to bring more women into the center of party decision making or to provide a forum for women to express group concerns.

The conflict between the Women's Division and the Federation was more than a conflict over resources, honors, prestige, or even political philosophy. It was also a conflict between two models for Republican womanhood: one that nurtured personal ambition and one that often maligned it; one that viewed career as a valuable part of a woman's life and one that located women primarily in their homes; one that found it acceptable for women to be single and one that had difficulty conceiving of women outside marriage and motherhood; one that could imagine women expressing political self-interest and one that limited women's political concerns largely to acts of family devotion or altruism. This conflict mirrored broader contradictions about womanhood in American culture, conflicts that would begin to find expression during the next decade, when a new generation of feminists began raising them. Not surprisingly, the political parties were among the first institutions that mainstream feminists would target for reform in the early seventies. Those women who wanted a role in politics beyond performing the housework of government would demand a more substantive part in shaping their parties.

Republican women's clubs nurtured in many ordinary women an interest in politics and public life, which they might not otherwise have had. Most women remained at the club level. Some ambitious and talented women, however, found party politics to their liking and looked for opportunities to play a larger role. Some became leaders within the club movement itself. They were obvious candidates to serve as delegates to the party's presidential nominating conventions in those states that sought to include women in their delegations. In fact, more than 90 percent of the female delegates and alternates to the 1956 presidential convention were Federation members, according to a Federation survey. Federation president Nora Kearns claimed that the survey results demonstrated that the Federation was the most important source of party leadership.[84] This claim is undoubtedly overstated, because the survey did not reveal how many of the delegates were also members of their state and local party committees. Involvement with party committees would probably have been a more likely path to delegate selection because women with those ties had closer access to networks of influential men through work in the regular organization. As it had been for Martin and Adkins, having male allies in key places was critical to women's advancement in the party.

The survey's sample is not representative of Federation women in general, for it describes only those women who took on additional roles in party affairs (as delegates) and not those women who merely joined a club and remained at that level. The profile of the Federation suggested by this survey needs to be assessed with care, yet it does provide some rare demographic data on Republican clubwomen. The picture that emerges from the survey is of churchgoing, civic-minded women who, in addition to politics, were involved in a host of other volunteer activities. Of the 303 women who answered the survey, 91 percent reported that they were Federation members. Twenty-four percent had held elected or appointed public office. Of the female delegates and alternates, a slight majority (57 percent) listed their principal occupation as housewife; 43 percent listed another occupation. The jobs most often cited were newspaper-related, secretarial, educational, and entrepreneurial. Each respondent was involved in an average of ten community or civic activities, the most common being those that were church-related. Others included a dizzying array of organizations involving hospitals, children and youth, history, patriotism, music, professions, and the United Nations, among others. The Federation also asked the delegates why they had originally entered politics. Women gave multiple responses, the most frequently cited being an identification with the principles of the Republican Party and a belief that it was one's duty as a citizen (20 percent each). Fifteen percent mentioned family influence or a view that politics was interesting. Tellingly, only three women (or less than 1 percent) responded that they became involved with politics because they wanted to have a voice in party policies, a figure that surely would have dismayed independent Republican clubwomen from the 1920s.[85]

Some clubwomen, of course, did use experiences, reputations, and networks gained through their political volunteer work to move into the regular party organization. Mary Louise Smith, for example, was elected national committeewoman from Iowa in 1963, went on to be named to the RNC Executive Committee, and later served as the first woman chairman of the RNC from 1974 to 1977. Some local clubs produced and supported women candidates for local and state office. On the national level, former Federation president Marie Suthers unsuccessfully sought a congressional seat in Illinois. Her successors at the Federation, Judy Weis and Betty Farrington, were both elected to Congress (Farrington after first being appointed to fill her husband's seat when he died in office in 1954).[86] The Federation may have served as a stepping stone for women who were already ambitious and were looking for an outlet for their talents. Whether it developed individual talent and ambition among the majority of its women is less apparent.

Even granting Kearns her claim that the Federation was "the chief source through which the Republican Party can recruit qualified women for top assignments," it does not follow that the Federation necessarily encouraged women to *want* those top assignments.[87] In building the powerful model of political women as housewives who just wanted to help, the Federation also constructed ideological obstacles for those women who ultimately desired to do more. A model of women's political work as an extension of suburban social life, of housework and hospitality, offered little room to picture women in seats of political power.

Republican clubwomen presented themselves in the 1950s as helpful housewives. But many also defined themselves as a moral force that could and should be more influential in politics, even if that role was not at the traditional centers of power. The frustration that many clubwomen felt with the moderate direction of the party in the fifties had the potential to be channeled into something mighty. Cecil Kenyon, president of the California Council of Republican Women in the late 1950s, spoke to that potential when she suggested that a morally charged Federation could affect more directly the philosophy of the party and the course of American politics. If every Republican woman joined a club, Kenyon suggested, "we can determine many policies for the moral and spiritual benefit of our party." Women saw mistakes being made at the precinct level that Kenyon believed could have been prevented if women had more say. And, Kenyon lamented, women had been forced much too often to work for candidates they didn't believe could win. We need, she argued, "a Billy Graham in our Party."[88]

Soon thousands of Federation women would indeed find a Billy Graham.

TO BE NEUTRAL OR NEUTRALIZED?

★ REPUBLICAN WOMEN AND THE GOLDWATER CAMPAIGN

During the 1950s the National Federation of Republican Women continued to bolster its position as the major supplier of grassroots workers for the GOP. The party had come to rely on the work of its political housekeepers. It also depended on them to be loyal to the Republican Party rather than to any specific issue, candidate, or faction. Meanwhile, the Federation's members had also developed a reputation for being more conservative than the rest of the GOP. Clubwomen had rendered hundreds of hours of volunteer work for the party, even when they were lukewarm about its candidates. The club movement had at least the potential to push the party in the direction of conservative, morally charged politics, as Cecil Kenyon's plea suggests. Yet, party loyalists among the Federation leadership had been generally successful in tempering this potential by emphasizing to clubwomen the merits of party loyalty and discipline. Responsible partisanship, the Federation had instructed Republican women for years, was about compromise.

In the mid-1960s, the perils of taking the reliability of women's loyal volunteerism for granted would become clear to many in the party's inner circle. The party's dependence on female volunteers would prove problematic once those volunteers in large numbers abandoned their traditional adherence to loyalty and neutrality. During Barry Goldwater's presidential bid, Republican women's clubs moved to the center of party concerns as party renegades and regulars alike battled for the Federation's allegiance. Barry Goldwater's operatives seem to have been among the first to realize the power that could come with controlling the organization that did so much of the grass-roots work for the party. After Goldwater's defeat, RNC officials concluded that they needed to reassert the auxiliary relationship of the volunteer women's organization to the RNC. Through the ensuing struggle over definitions of political womanhood, Phyllis Schlafly would emerge as a new women's leader who would successfully blend political conservatism with arguments that elites were denying ordinary women a political voice.

★ When Barry Goldwater spoke in 1958 at a Federation regional conference, he gave the best talk Federation member Gladys Penland of California had ever heard anyone deliver. "He was magnificent," she pronounced.[1] Indeed, Goldwater was one of the more popular speakers at national and regional Federation events during the 1950s. At that time, Goldwater was emerging as a leader of the party's right wing, whose adherents' frustrations with Eisenhower's domestic, foreign, and economic policy agendas had been swelling. While Republican conservatives associated with Robert Taft were generally willing to compromise with party liberals to win elections, those who would come to identify with the Goldwater movement (both men and women) were far less committed to party loyalty. Goldwater himself "publicly broke" with the Eisenhower administration in 1957.[2] Insisting that any growth in government threatened freedom, Goldwater objected in principle to many programs supported by "modern" Republicans, including federal aid to education, federal housing programs, and federal enforcement of desegregation orders in the South. In the area of foreign policy, Goldwater represented a new brand of GOP conservatism. Soundly rejecting the isolationism associated with Taft conservatives, Goldwater insisted that the threats of communism around the world required the United States to take more-decisive action.[3]

Goldwater often presented his views couched in rhetoric that was particularly appealing to conservative Federation women in the fifties. In his speeches, he frequently emphasized the relationship of morality and religious faith to politics. In 1955, for example, Goldwater told a Federation Board of Directors meeting that "politics is pretty much like a religion, you have to practice it with fervor, you have got to believe in the thing. When we talk about Republican principles we are talking about God, we are talking about the Constitution, we are talking about the sacred things in this country."[4] Goldwater discussed politics and Republican principles as "sacred things" requiring passionate and uncompromising commitment. This rhetoric was in line with those on the Federation's right wing who viewed political principles as absolute and morally charged, and who had chafed at the demands of party loyalty and political compromise.

Goldwater proved in the 1950s that he could inspire women to dedicate themselves to his political campaigns. In 1955, as described by one

"Without the National Federation of Republican Women there would be no Republican Party." Among members of the National Federation of Republican Women, Barry Goldwater was a popular and sought after speaker, partly because he had a long history of giving credit to their work. Here he is shown with fellow Arizonans Mrs. Marian Sundt, Ruth Gaddis Jeffries (Federation officer,) and Mary Jane Phillippi in 1954. (8th Biennial Conv. 1954, box 143, NFRW records. Used with permission from the National Federation of Republican Women.)

activist, women volunteers began building an organization in Arizona to counter the efforts of the AFL-CIO's Committee on Political Education (COPE), which had targeted Senator Goldwater for defeat in 1958. For three years, as many as 9,000 Arizona women worked to ensure Goldwater's reelection. Women's efforts did not go unnoticed. Goldwater was one Republican leader who regularly pointed out that the party could not "do without the women" when it came to the "tough political chores" of campaigning.[5] And he insisted that "if it were not for the National Federation of Republican Women, there would not be a Republican Party."[6] For several reasons, Goldwater seemed to be the kind of politician sought by those on the Federation's right who were disappointed in current party leadership.

By the late 1950s conservative Federation women across the country were eager to channel their energies on behalf of a presidential candidate they could support unequivocally. They were not alone. Enthusiasm for Republican conservatism was evident in the spring of 1960. Supporters formed Goldwater for President and many Young Republican and College Republican chapters endorsed Goldwater for vice president.[7] That year, conservative Republicans launched a serious movement to capture control of the party when they sought to win the presidential nomination for Goldwater.

The conservative renegades failed in 1960. The party nominated Richard Nixon, who dashed the hopes of conservatives by choosing a liberal (Henry Cabot Lodge) to be his running mate. And Nixon, more concerned about the party's left wing than its right, made concessions to GOP moderate Nelson Rockefeller regarding the party's platform. This capitulation to Rockefeller left many conservatives in the party feeling betrayed.[8] Shortly after the convention, Clifton White, John Ashbrook, and William Rusher, who had known each other through their work with the Young Republicans, began plans to draft Goldwater to make a serious run for the GOP nomination in 1964.[9] To convince Goldwater to consider a presidential bid, they hoped to generate an outpouring of support outside the traditional party leadership. Women—as party workers, delegates, and potential voters—were a significant part of this drive to win the nomination for the Arizona senator.

Goldwater organizers were running a renegade campaign without the support of party insiders. Party regulars viewed Goldwater as an extremist whose reputation as a hawk and as an opponent of federal civil rights legislation was a liability. For Goldwater to win the nomination in 1964, he would need a momentum of support from the grass roots. His campaigners, then, worked on generating that groundswell. Key to this effort was having Goldwater enthusiasts take over the party's auxiliaries. If Goldwater backers could get themselves elected to leadership positions in those auxiliaries, the campaign would have valuable access to the party's grass-roots activists. Historians have demonstrated the importance of the Young Republicans and the California Republican Assembly to the Goldwater movement in this regard.[10] Yet White and his colleagues also considered the National Federation of Republican Women essential to their plans. If they were going to build a grass-roots movement to support Goldwater's nomination, capturing the party auxiliary that typically did much of the work of local presidential campaigns would be crucial.

In his memoir of the Draft Goldwater movement, Clifton White himself described women and the Federation as being of central importance. Early on, White established contacts among a group of Federation conservatives that included Katharine Kennedy Brown, California Federation of Republican Women president Lucille Hosmer, and Ione Harrington of Indiana. They set their sights on the September 1962 convention in Phoenix, where the Federation would elect its new set of officers. Normally there would have been little opposition to the Nominating Committee's proposed slate of officers. In 1962, however, White and his Federation allies secretly drew up an alternative slate of officers. At the convention, these Goldwater women surprised delegates with a list of nominations from the floor. Their list included the Nominating Committee's own choice for president, Dorothy Elston of Delaware (a Goldwater supporter), but submitted the names of four strongly pro-Goldwater alternatives for the other offices.[11]

These maneuverings by Goldwater supporters were successful. Federation delegates elected the four insurgent candidates over the Nominating Committee's choices and went on to adopt a series of decidedly conservative resolutions. These included statements in support of school prayer and opposing federal aid to education, Medicare, the Kennedy administration's arms control policies, and its alleged softness on communism.[12] The efforts of Goldwater backers in Phoenix resulted in "significant gains" in the women's auxiliary.[13] As one conservative later suggested, the 1962 Federation convention was the first time that "ideology" had played an open role in the choice of Federation leadership.[14] The Federation's enthusiasm for Goldwaterism was never unanimous. Yet, conservatives in the Federation, aided by the support of Clif White's group, were beginning to flex their muscles.

The National Draft Goldwater Committee was officially formed in April 1963. Three weeks later, the senator's candidacy got its "first big test" at the Republican Women's Spring Conference in Washington.[15] Goldwater forces had by this point been successful in getting supporters into top positions at both the Federation and the Women's Division. The Spring Conference, attended by women from across the country, would show the extent to which that support extended to the grass roots. Many conference attendees, according to White, were women who were active not only in the party but as community and state civic leaders as well.[16] Selling Goldwater's candidacy to these women, therefore, could have a broader ripple effect beyond the conference itself.

The results of the Spring Women's Conference were even better than

Goldwater drafters had hoped. Draft Goldwater leaders Ione Harrington, Judy Fernald, and Rita Bree ran a Goldwater Hospitality room at the conference, where prominent Republican women served coffee and distributed petitions, buttons, and other Goldwater literature to the more than one thousand women who visited the suite.[17] The response was "overwhelming," Clifton White wrote to Goldwater. "I would not have believed it if I had not seen it. The ladies started coming into the Suite at 9 o'clock in the morning and we had difficulty closing at midnight." The Goldwater Hospitality Suite was the most popular at the event, according to White. He estimated that 95 percent of the women who visited the suite were "enthusiastic supporters."[18] In contrast, White described Nelson Rockefeller's suite as "deserted and forlorn."[19]

In White's view, the 1963 Spring Women's Conference was a significant moment in tipping the balance in favor of the Goldwater nomination. Until that point, White recalled, Rockefeller had been far ahead in the polls. White and his fellow Goldwater backers had been confident that Goldwater enjoyed great support among grass-roots party workers but conceded that the wariness of Americans toward the label "conservative" kept many in the party from publicly supporting him. The enthusiasm generated by the Women's Conference, where Goldwater was a featured speaker, helped overcome that reticence. According to White, the Republican Women's Conference "marked a vital change in the party workers' attitude. The women were leading the way in the shift from covert approval of Goldwater to overt endorsement."[20] Inspired by the Arizona senator, Republican women carried their Goldwaterism back to their communities where they energetically embarked on petition drives in support of his candidacy. White described the enthusiasm of the Republican women as contagious. "We knew," wrote White in retrospect, "they would carry the message of Goldwater's obvious popularity back with them to thwart the shallow soundings of the professional pundits."[21]

Goldwater's supporters were also able to dominate subsequent Republican women's meetings. The Federation's Twenty-fifth Anniversary celebration, held in Chicago in September 1963, was "another smash performance for Goldwater." The event, hosted by the Illinois Federation of Republican Women, was dominated by members of Goldwater's "fan club," a Des Moines reporter observed. Phyllis Schlafly, as president of the Illinois Federation, played a crucial role in setting the tone of the event. Given the opportunity to choose a speaker, the conservative Schlafly selected Barry Goldwater. Six months later, Schlafly would publish her pro-Goldwater political tract, *A Choice Not an Echo*, which would go on to become an important piece of unofficial Goldwater campaign literature.

At the Chicago meeting, the local Cook County Republican women's club conducted a straw poll on delegates' choice for the 1964 nomination. Results indicated that Goldwater was the first choice of 262 out of 293 Federation delegates who voted.[22] On first glance, this appears to have been a ringing endorsement. There were 700 delegates at the convention, however. The majority of Federation delegates (who probably supported a variety of candidates) refrained from stating a candidate preference at this early date. In doing so, they adhered to the Federation's tradition of official neutrality in internal party issues. The Federation was not supposed to take sides in primaries because its role was to support whomever the nominee might prove to be. Goldwater backers, on the other hand, were already committed to their candidate and were willing to say so regardless of the departure from Federation policy. This suggests that the division of Goldwater supporters from the rest of the party regulars already was evident—not only in terms of issues but in style as well.

Although Goldwater backers were able to dominate Federation events, their control of the Federation was never secure. Expecting a major battle at the Federation's 1964 convention to keep Dottie Elston and other Goldwater supporters at the helm of the Federation, White's committee began preparing early for this fight. It is "[i]mportant," Ione Harrington stressed, "that we keep control as women are strong arm for B[arry] G[oldwater]." Goldwater forces focused on the April meeting of the Federation's Nominating Committee, which would select the next slate of candidates for Federation office.[23] Their success in influencing the Federation's Nominating Committee in 1964 translated into another pro-Goldwater Board of Directors, one that now included Phyllis Schlafly as first vice president.

Maneuvering Goldwater backers into positions of Federation leadership did not ensure that the Federation would devote itself to working on behalf of the senator's nomination. After all, the Federation and its officers were supposed to be officially neutral. Yet significantly, many of Goldwater's supporters were those in the Federation who were already frustrated with arguments for neutrality and party loyalty. Goldwater strategists saw it as a definite boon that they had allies controlling many of the state Federations as well as the national.[24] Support early on from the national and state Federations helped generate the necessary momentum at the grass roots that ultimately would help earn Goldwater the nomination. The strategy of controlling the Women's Federation as a means of generating and demonstrating "grass-roots support" also illustrated one way in which, during the Goldwater campaign, women themselves came to serve as important symbols of grass-roots moral outrage.

★ Although Barry Goldwater would ultimately fare poorly with female voters, he appeared initially to be a candidate with particular appeal to women. Even before he won the Republican nomination, Goldwater looked to be more popular with women than his chief rival, Governor Nelson Rockefeller of New York. In May 1963 the divorced Rockefeller announced his marriage to Margaretta "Happy" Murphy, who herself had divorced her husband a mere one month earlier. This news hurt Rockefeller with the voters. According to Gallup polls conducted before and after this news, women in particular reacted negatively to the governor's remarriage. Rockefeller's support fell ten points among women, while his support among men remained largely unchanged.[25]

Like presidential candidates in the past, Goldwater made special attempts to appeal to women that included elaborate praise for their service, skills, and character. In Goldwater's experience, women had "keener insight," and were "more informed about domestic and political affairs" than were their husbands. Hitting on a well-established theme of Republican Party politics, Goldwater noted in 1964 that more women than men were working at the grass roots. "[F]rankly," he added, "the men ought to be ashamed of themselves. . . . They seem to be only interested in their business, the club, gin rummy, . . . and I think they should spend some of that time worrying about the situation that we find ourselves in in America and that America finds herself in around the world."[26] These were not new themes for Goldwater. He had been emphasizing women's contribution to politics for at least ten years.

Goldwater's appeal to conservative women went beyond his image as a faithful husband and his recognition of women's contributions to party work, however. In his campaigning, Goldwater repeatedly touched on themes that fit comfortably into one important tradition of women's Republicanism—the presentation of politics as an urgent, often morally charged, crusade against evil. To a mixed-gender audience of military graduates and their parents, Goldwater argued, for example, that the ideological rift dividing the world was much deeper than a political one between "so-called liberals" and "totalitarians." Instead, this divide was a spiritual one between all those who "believe in a transcendent order and an enduring human nature" and all who "would treat man as an animal, as a creature of appetite—to be dealt with according to the rigid blue-prints of the social planners."[27]

Goldwater's view of the struggle against communism was in line with those who understood the primary problem with communism to be its rejection of spirituality—a view Samuel Stouffer's 1955 study had revealed women were especially likely to hold. Some female supporters in 1964 looked to Goldwater as an almost religious leader. "I fully believe," wrote one woman, "that you were sent by God to take over and help our states, cities, towns and so forth to straighten things out and help them to become brave where they have become weak and fear to speak out Christ [sic] principles." According to another, "Barry will build a shining world out of the dust."[28]

The Goldwater movement is well known for having brought political neophytes into activism. Goldwater's candidacy inspired women who had not done campaign work before, but who suddenly were inspired to devote "all of our time" to his cause. One sixty-five-year-old woman wrote that she was spending her grocery money each week for Goldwater and had seventy votes promised for the senator.[29] Yet Goldwater's campaign also drew in many Federation stalwarts, including Katharine Kennedy Brown. Barry Goldwater was the candidate many on the Federation's right had hoped for in the 1950s. Significantly, however, the rhetoric of male Goldwater supporters at the grass roots was not so different from that of their female counterparts. Goldwater's ideological, uncompromising politics alienated him from many Americans but resonated with conservative grass-roots activists. His political crusade tapped general frustrations with the compromise that was apparently expected in mainstream politics.

Given the liberal leanings of the RNC, mobilizing support for Goldwater's candidacy required forming an alliance of "pragmatic, right-leaning politicians," "intellectual right wingers," and "ideological grass-roots conservatives," as historian Mary Brennan has detailed. Each was important to the movement. The members of this coalition did not always agree on strategy. Conflict developed between those willing to compromise their conservative principles in order to win the presidency, and those who were unwilling to sacrifice ideological purity for that purpose.[30]

The distinction Brennan describes was one that had long been used to describe (however simplistically) the differences between male and

*"The women are strong arm for B. G." At their 1964 Presidential
Convention, Republicans chose Barry Goldwater as their nominee,
due in no small part to the groundswell of support generated by women
at the grass roots. ("Woman in Several Reds, Hilton Hotel," 14 July 1964,
Charles Cushman Collection, Indiana University Archives, Bloomington,
Indiana. Used with permission from the Indiana University Archives.)*

female politics. Women voters supposedly had a particular propensity to
see political issues in intransigent, ideological terms, to be uncompromising about such issues, and to be thereby unwilling or unable to engage in the compromise and give-and-take demanded by practical politics. It was these features of women's political style that Marion Martin
and her allies had hoped to purge from the Federation's membership,
but which Betty Farrington had revived in the postwar period.

During the Goldwater campaign, "grass-roots" supporters in general
developed a reputation for being ideological and uncompromising in
their political views and naive in their sense of how politics worked.
Party leaders had traditionally associated these qualities with women.
Of course, the grass-roots right did not consist entirely of women. The
increasingly visible right-wing grass-roots movement outside the party,
including the John Birch Society, had many male adherents. And mixed-
gender suburban organizing in some locales facilitated the emergence
of the grass-roots Right in the early 1960s. In Orange County Califor-

nia, for example, right-wing politics served as an important basis for socializing, friendship, and community; married couples often became involved together.[31]

Both men and women formed parts of all three segments of the Goldwater coalition. Goldwater and his campaign organizers, however, seem to have particularly (if implicitly) identified the "ideological grass-roots conservatives" with women (and "women" with the grass roots). This did not mean that strategists believed the grass roots to be predominantly female. More likely, it indicated that Goldwater strategists so firmly associated the crusading political style of grass-roots conservatism with women that such connections were automatic and unexamined. Looking closely at the nature of the Goldwater campaign's efforts to appeal both specifically to women and, more generally, to "ordinary Americans" at the grass roots often reveals a slippage between the two.

The campaign's "Crusade for Law and Morality" illustrated one way in which "women" came to stand in for "the grass roots." The Goldwater forces sought to make morality a central issue of the campaign, comparable to what the missile gap had been in 1960. Strategists hoped to channel what it believed was a "latent concern" among American voters with the "moral decline of America" into a major campaign advantage.[32] When Goldwater strategists sought to emphasize these issues, they must have imagined that voters would follow a link between concern about social morality, a sympathy with moral conceptions of public issues (such as the role of the state), and a preference for a candidate (such as Barry Goldwater) who would be unwavering on those issues.

After Goldwater received the nomination and named Dean Burch as head of the RNC, the grass-roots campaign continued to be run by Clif White, through Citizens for Goldwater-Miller. Citizens' purpose was to mobilize those who did not normally participate in elections. It intended its "Crusade for Law and Morality" to appeal to those voters by stirring up general concern about morality. These efforts were meant to appear to the public as unconnected to Goldwater himself. Once this concern emerged, according to strategy, Goldwater might step in and offer response and solutions. At the beginning, however, he was not to have any connection "with this manipulation" apart from reintroducing themes of spirituality and of morality in government into his speeches. These themes had long been part of Goldwater's repertoire and had endeared him to Federation women back in the fifties. In 1964 his campaign managers tried to create a broader public response to such themes that would extend well beyond militant Republican clubwomen. Although they spoke of arousing moral concerns among the general public, when Goldwater campaign leaders discussed specifics, much of the morality campaign they concocted seemed to target a female audience particularly.

One way Citizens for Goldwater-Miller embarked on its "Crusade for Law and Morality" was by creating and publicizing Mothers for a Moral America, a pseudo-grass-roots organization, ostensibly concerned with morality, not politics.[33] Mothers for a Moral America was supposedly founded in the fall of 1964 by a group of women in Nashville, outraged by the moral decay of America. Goldwater forces, however, were involved with Mothers possibly from the group's inception. According to a Citizens strategy document, the Mothers group was "a spontaneous, public movement—carefully coordinated with and through the Citizens [for Goldwater] committee."[34] Within a matter of weeks of the first Mothers meeting in Nashville, Citizens was sending blueprints for the formation of Mothers organizations across the country.[35] By October 1964 Citizens for Goldwater-Miller reported that there were units of Moral Mothers in every major city. Citizens for Goldwater-Miller also recruited several high-profile women to serve on the executive board of Mothers, including Dale Evans, Nancy Reagan, Hedda Hopper, and Ivy Baker Priest Stevens (former assistant chairman of the RNC).[36]

The "moral America" that the Mothers were "for" was one that they believed to be threatened by the big government promoted by liberals and Democrats. In a statement attributed to the original Nashville Mothers and publicized in a Goldwater campaign newsletter, it is clear that the seemingly apolitical "morality" was a code word for a conservative political agenda that matched Goldwater's own. "Thirty years of government paternalism," read the Mothers' statement, "has produced an attitude of irresponsibility which is deeply reflected in our citizens today." "Cradle-to-the-grave" security, the statement continued, robbed society of its initiative, thus leading to moral decay. "America, today," according to the Mothers, "is reaping the result in the actions of its youth as well as its adults." The Mothers also targeted teenage drug use, alcoholism, and the lack of respect showed by citizens to police officers. The Mothers insisted that it was their concern for good government, rather than partisan politics, that led them to endorse Barry Goldwater for president.[37]

Through the Moral Mothers, Citizens for Goldwater tried to create in a matter of months a broad network of women's clubs—nonpartisan, yet pro-Goldwater. Mothers was also a public relations gimmick that sought to associate moral outrage at the grass roots with the Goldwater campaign and to link that grass-roots moral outrage to a decidedly female brand of public involvement. In this way, the support of a morally outraged female public would serve as a symbol to attract all voters. By equating assumptions about the emotional, ideological nature of women's politics with the "grass roots," Goldwater campaigners "feminized" the grass roots itself.

An inescapable irony of the Goldwater campaign's feminization of the grass roots was that Goldwater's appeal to men was greater than his appeal to women. The picture of Goldwater's campaign as a moral crusade may have inspired the GOP's more conservative women, but women as a whole did not much like Goldwater. Even Republican women did not support him overwhelmingly. After Goldwater received the GOP nomination at the Republican convention in July, his candidacy remained controversial within the party and many Republican voters expressed uncertainty about who they would support in November. Fifty-seven percent of undecided Republican voters were women. And a larger proportion of Republican men than women preferred Goldwater to Johnson than the ratio of men to women in the party would have indicated.[38] After the election, polls revealed that women had voted more overwhelmingly against Goldwater than had men: 40 percent of men and 38 percent of women had cast their ballots for the Arizona senator. This difference was more significant than it might appear. Since 1952, women had been voting in higher numbers for Republican presidential candidates than men.[39]

The RNC Research Committee, in its postelection analysis, duly noted Goldwater's failure to maintain high levels of support among women.[40] The Ripon Society, an organization of liberal and moderate Republicans founded in the early 1960s, explained that women had turned from the GOP because women were "ordinarily more sensitive than men" to candidates identified with stability and security.[41] American women had not responded well to Goldwater's candidacy. Yet Goldwater supporters now controlled the National Federation of Republican Women. The party's leading women's organization seemed to be grossly out of step with American women as a whole. This situation was potentially problematic, and the RNC would seek to address it.

★ After the Goldwater debacle, Republican leaders tried to recoup and rebuild the party. Early in 1965 the Ripon Society issued a 124-page report analyzing the mistakes of the 1964 campaign. The Ripon Society called on the party to reverse its "weird and frightening" 1964 Southern

Strategy, which had sought to capitalize on white resentment against the 1964 Civil Rights Act. The Ripon Society instead urged the GOP to embrace the cause of civil rights, conduct voter registration drives among African Americans, and reach out to black civil rights leaders. African American support for the Republican presidential nominee had, after all, dropped noticeably: Nixon had won 32 percent of the black vote in 1960 whereas Goldwater won only 6 percent.[42] The Ripon Society argued that the GOP should hold a policy conference, and it recommended the "unequivocal dissociation" of the GOP from "irrational and irresponsible extremist elements" and the recruitment of "qualified, vigorous, articulate, and moderate candidates" to run for Congress in 1966.[43]

Moderates wanting to distance the party from Goldwater launched a "frontal assault" for control of the party at all levels.[44] One of the first moves in this direction was the controversial effort to oust Dean Burch, RNC chairman under Goldwater. In early 1965 Burch resigned in the interests of the party. The RNC replaced him with Ray Bliss of Ohio, but without the blessing of many of the RNC's more conservative members.[45] To Bliss's supporters, the Ohio Republican was a nonideological leader who could restore harmony among the bitterly divided factions. Goldwater loyalists, however, considered Bliss a hatchet man determined to purge all conservatives from party leadership. Certainly there was some truth to that charge. Yet Bliss seemed mostly to have been concerned with encouraging those forces in the party willing to promote unity. That ruled out many Goldwater supporters who were not interested in harmony and unity when it meant compromising their own beliefs. Conservatives labeled Bliss's efforts a liberal "plot to steal the GOP."[46]

In retaking the leadership of the party, moderates believed that the Goldwater debacle had repudiated conservatives' explanations of party misfortunes. Conservatives had long argued that if the GOP would only nominate a truly conservative candidate, the party would be victorious. The party, according to this analysis, had erred repeatedly in choosing candidates like Willkie, Dewey, and Eisenhower who did not offer a real alternative to the Democrats. In 1964 observers (including Republican strategists) believed conservatives had finally been proved wrong in their assumptions about the American electorate.[47] Recent scholarship, however, interprets the Goldwater campaign differently. Goldwater's supporters may have lost the election but they had won the war. The Goldwater campaign had made significant Republican inroads in the South and Southwest and among Catholic voters in the Northeast. The campaign also launched the political careers of conservatives who would

later become important figures in the New Right, including Paul Weyrich, Lee Edwards, Patrick Buchanan, and Ronald Reagan. The 1964
campaign, in other words, nurtured the conservative forces that would
eventually elect Reagan president in 1980.[48]

An additional significant outcome of the Goldwater movement was
that it launched the career of Phyllis Schlafly. Phyllis Stewart was born
August 15, 1924, in St. Louis. Her Catholic parents, who valued education for their daughters, scrimped in order to send Phyllis and her
sister to a Catholic girls' school. Having faced economic difficulties during the Depression, however, the Stewarts were not in a financial position to send Phyllis to the prestigious college she desired. Undeterred,
she left the small Catholic women's college that had given her a scholarship and resolved to attend St. Louis's Washington University. To pay
her way, she worked a forty-eight-hour-a-week night job in a munitions
factory, while attending college during the day. In 1944, having gradu-
ated in three years, she won a scholarship for graduate work at Radcliffe.
After receiving her master's degree in government, Schlafly worked for
a year in Washington, D.C., before returning to St. Louis and eventually
taking a job with a bank. As part of her job, Stewart took charge of the
bank's newsletter, which she filled with her own political commentary.
Her columns attracted the attention of thirty-nine-year-old lawyer Fred
Schlafly. The two found commonalities in their passionate interest in
conservative politics. In 1949 they were married.[49]

Although the Schlaflys eventually had six children, motherhood did
not prevent Phyllis Schlafly from pursuing her political interests. In
1952, having already begun raising her family, Schlafly ran for Congress
against an incumbent Democrat. Following a campaign in which the
press and her opponent made much of Schlafly's sex, she was defeated.
She did not attribute her loss to any prejudice against female candidates,
however. She was running as a Republican in a Democratic district,
Schlafly later explained. Any opponent would have had a tough time.[50]
Yet clearly it was due to the fact that this was a "doomed" campaign that
local Republicans had selected a female candidate in the first place.[51]
After her defeat, Schlafly continued her political activity in Illinois in
the manner of thousands of other women of the period—as a Republican Party volunteer and clubwoman. In 1960 she was elected president
of the Illinois Federation of Republican Women and four years later was
named first vice president of the National Federation.

Schlafly was ushered onto the national political stage in 1964 by her
small, self-published, book, *A Choice Not an Echo*. Written in a simple,

polemical style, Schlafly purported to document a plot by a cabal of "kingmakers" to control the selection of presidential candidates. Beginning with the choice of Wendell Willkie to head the party's ticket in 1940, these "kingmakers," Schlafly alleged, had manipulated the Republican national conventions through use of "hidden persuaders and psychological warfare techniques." The "kingmakers" had convinced convention delegates to nominate candidates who would avoid what Schlafly considered the hard issues (generally issues of domestic subversion, political corruption, and internationalism).[52] The "kingmakers," according to Schlafly, were a group of financial, political, and media elites with a personal stake in internationalist foreign policy. Schlafly charged that this group periodically met in secret to "make important plans they do not reveal to the public." One of the goals of the "kingmakers" supposedly was the eventual melding of the two parties, demonstrated, in Schlafly's view, by the fact that many, including Nelson Rockefeller, had accepted political appointments in both parties.[53] This cynical behavior, Schlafly complained, was destructive of the two-party system. In language that foreshadowed one of her future complaints about the blurring of rigid gender roles, Schlafly noted that "voters expect Republicans to be Republicans and Democrats to be Democrats. Trading in and out of both parties confuses the issues and especially the responsibility."[54] In her book, Schlafly concluded that Goldwater was the obvious choice for conservatives. Goldwater, Schlafly argued, was the one candidate who would "not pull his punches to please the kingmakers."[55] Schlafly's book had none of the careful, reasoned tone promoted by party moderates. But many men and women at the grass roots were sympathetic to Schlafly's charges that the party was ruled by a secret, elite group.

Although never officially endorsed by Goldwater or his campaign staff, Schlafly's book would become an important piece of campaign literature, along with Goldwater's ghostwritten books *Conscience of a Conservative* and *Why Not Victory?* The first edition of *A Choice Not an Echo*, printed in May 1964, sold 600,000 copies. A second edition printed in June sold another million, requiring a third printing in August. Distribution was entirely through word of mouth, as Schlafly did no advertising. Readers ordered the seventy-five-cent paperback in bulk and distributed it to friends and relatives. Its actual influence is difficult to gauge. Schlafly offers anecdotes suggesting that delegates to the 1964 convention received many copies of *Choice* from constituents wanting to persuade the delegate to vote for Goldwater.[56] When Goldwater opera-tive Stephen Shadegg later questioned delegates, 93 percent said they had read the book, and 26 percent believed reading the book had led them to support Goldwater.[57]

Through the popularity of her book, Schlafly built a name for herself among alienated grass-roots conservatives in general—both men and women. Her previous political experience, however, had been primarily in organizing Republican women. Schlafly characterized her early political activities in Illinois as those of a Republican loyalist. She had been volunteering for the party since 1945, she later reported, promoting good government and trying to persuade women to work for the party. Schlafly insisted that throughout the 1950s she remained a steadfast partisan. When a candidate she supported was not nominated, she nonetheless campaigned in her state for the party's choice "just as energetically and enthusiastically" as if her candidate had been on the ballot. As Schlafly described in *A Choice Not an Echo*, however, she finally grew disenchanted with the arguments for party loyalty. "I can look back on campaigns in which I saw Republicans of the local level working their hearts out for a cause they believe to be just," Schlafly wrote, "only to realize, after it was all over, that the kingmakers had given them a candidate who would not campaign on the issues. . . . In the interest of Party unity, I have kept silent as we sustained each tragic defeat. But as we go into the crucial campaign of 1964, I believe that my loyalty to the thousands of Republicans who labor in the precincts compels me to speak out."[58] Although she used gender-neutral language, the grass-roots workers for whom Schlafly felt compelled to speak were, for the most part, the women she had led as Illinois Federation president. During the 1964 presidential campaign, Schlafly developed a vast and loyal following among grass-roots women. Many were members of the National Federation of Republican Women.[59] And Schlafly believed she was the logical choice to be the next head of that organization.

★ As part of its efforts to repudiate the 1964 campaign, party regulars tried to reestablish control of the Young Republicans and the Women's Federation. *National Review* publisher William Rusher noted that it was "no accident" that these two organizations were the "bulwarks of conservative sentiment" within the party. Rusher's explanation for the conservatism of these groups was that the Federation and the Young Republicans were the only branches of party apparatus that elected their national officers in grass-roots conventions. In 1965 Rusher believed the grass roots of the GOP were "as solidly conservative as they ever were."[60] Conservatives retained control of the Young Republicans, decisively electing a new conservative leader at its 1967 convention. Convention delegates also registered a preference for future conservative standard-bearer Ronald Reagan as the Republicans' next presidential candidate, according to a poll conducted during the convention. "What made the victory especially satisfying to conservatives," according to one sympathetic observer, "was that it was achieved without rancor."[61]

By contrast, "rancor" quite aptly describes the struggle for control of the National Federation of Republican Women. After Goldwater's defeat in 1964, the Federation suffered a decline in membership, presumably in response to the party's misfortunes. Those remaining in the Federation were divided over their assessment of how the party should deal with its conservative members. Although she herself had been a Goldwater supporter, Federation president Dottie Elston now threw her weight behind party unity. She worked hard to rebuild the Federation and the party, emphasizing the need to overcome factions and disagreements. As a leader of GOP women, Elston emphasized the necessity that "we remain a united party, that we submerge any thoughts or acts which would divide our Party." Elston also said she made a point of not criticizing fellow Republicans when speaking to the press.[62] In terms of the post-1964 goals of party regulars, Elston was an ideal leader.

Elston's second term as Federation president expired in September 1966, however. A major contender to succeed Elston was the Federation's first vice president, Phyllis Schlafly. Schlafly was well known nationally and commanded a large and devoted following of Republican women, many of whom were Federation members. Schlafly, a staunch conservative and an unrepentant Goldwater supporter, was not impressed by arguments supporting compromise for the sake of party unity. As columnists Rowland Evans and Robert Novak editorialized, many in the party foresaw "disaster" if "nature [took] its course" and Schlafly was elected Federation president.[63] Party strategists could no longer take Republican women's clubs for granted; they would soon move to the forefront of party considerations, as party leaders—first women but eventually men as well—tried to involve themselves in steering the Federation's decision making. Perhaps for the first time, it now mattered to the RNC who was president of the National Federation of Republican Women.

As early as 1965, a loose group of Republican women, mostly affiliated with the party's official bodies, were discussing ways to ensure that control of the Federation would remain in moderate hands. Party offi-cial Elly Peterson would play a key role. As current Republican state chairman of Michigan and a former RNC assistant chairman, Peterson was a prominent and influential Republican who was also a close ally of Goldwater rival Governor George Romney of Michigan. In 1965 Peterson took sides in the contest for president of the Michigan Republi-can Women's Federation when she openly backed Ruth Hobbs, a fellow member of the state's moderate faction associated with Governor Romney, over a pro-Goldwater candidate. Hobbs pledged in her campaign that she would return the Michigan Federation to a closer working relationship with the State Central Committee. Hobbs's eventual win was viewed as an "important victory for Romney-style moderates" over the state's right-wing faction. It was also a victory for those support-ing the Federation mission of promoting cooperation with the official party.[64]

Elly Peterson's apprehension about the direction of the Michigan Fed-eration was not limited to the direction of the women's organization in her own state. It was instead part of a broader concern for the fate of the national Federation, about which she was "extremely disturbed." Al-though not affiliated with the Federation herself, Peterson recognized its importance and by 1965 was already working with her allies to try to keep moderates in control.[65] Returning moderates to leadership of the Michigan Federation was only one part of that project.

The future direction of the national Federation was clearly at stake in the upcoming election for its leadership. As first vice president of the National Federation who enjoyed an impressive following among Republican women, Phyllis Schlafly expected to succeed Dottie Elston as president when the next elections were held during the Federation's 1966 Biennial Convention. This possibility was certainly chief among Elly Peterson's concerns regarding the Federation, a concern shared by Republican women in other states as well. But in late 1965 Peterson learned the good news that Elston had spoken against Schlafly and was, at least unofficially, supporting Californian Gladys O'Donnell as her suc-cessor.[66]

Dottie Elston's tacit support for O'Donnell was a crucial boost for those trying to keep Schlafly from the Federation helm. O'Donnell, who was a pioneer aviator in the 1930s, had served as president of the California Council of Republican Women (by now called the California Federation of Republican Women) from 1954 to 1955 and had been a delegate to the Republican National Convention on several occasions.[67]

During Elston's term as president, O'Donnell served as program chairman of the National Federation. O'Donnell's conservative credentials were long-standing. She had supported Taft in 1952 and Goldwater in 1964. Yet during a split within the California Federation in 1965, O'Donnell was among the pro-Nixon forces who had been attacked by more-conservative women in the California Federation.[68] Clearly O'Donnell supported those in the party who wanted to restore harmony and to distance itself from the party's Right. If the "extremists" took over in California, O'Donnell warned, "it will be a dark day for the Federation, and . . . the national situation is almost beyond hope."[69]

Despite her past support for conservatives, O'Donnell (like Elston) now seemed committed to bringing harmony to the party and to returning the Federation to its role as a neutral, educational arm of the party, loyally performing the housework of party politics. O'Donnell made this stance clear from her position as the Federation's program chairman, using her monthly mailing, *Build!*, to endorse party loyalty. In a 1966 missive on the destructiveness of discontent channeled in the wrong direction, O'Donnell wrote "[t]he Republican Party is the one instrument which can save our nation. Surely we can find the tolerance and accommodation in our thinking to make its survival our common cause."[70] Later, as a candidate for Federation president, she pledged to make the Federation an organization that would "accommodate everyone—conservative, moderate, and liberal."[71]

For O'Donnell, winning the Federation presidency would be no easy task; Schlafly commanded an imposing following. As Elly Peterson put it, she and her allies would have "real problems electing Gladys. The nut fringe is beautifully organized."[72] Schlafly's opponents focused on three strategies for improving O'Donnell's chances: delaying the Federation's presidential election scheduled for 1966 to give time for Schlafly's support to dwindle; moving the planned convention out of California (a Schlafly stronghold) and into the East (where moderates controlled key states); and ensuring that moderates retained control of state Federations (which would send delegates to the national).[73]

Those wanting to stymie the "nut fringe" were successful on several fronts. In September 1965 the Federation Board of Directors initiated a rule change that moved the Federation conventions to odd numbered years (election off-years), thus postponing the selection of Elston's replacement until 1967. The Federation's Executive Committee in 1966 voted to move the 1967 convention site from Los Angeles to Washington, D.C., a move seen as less favorable to Schlafly. And in March 1967 the Federation's Nominating Committee announced O'Donnell as its official candidate.

Previously, the Federation presidency generally had been an uncontested office. The Federation's Nominating Committee drew up a slate of candidates for all offices; delegates to the Federation's convention then essentially ratified the Nominating Committee's choice. At times, dissenting voices grumbled about the official slate, but such dissent was handled quietly. In 1967, for the first time in its history, the Federation presidency was bitterly and openly contested. What ensued was an acrimonious battle between party regulars and Schlafly insurgents for control of the Women's Federation.

Schlafly did not accept the Nominating Committee's decision to offer O'Donnell as its candidate. On 5 April 1967, she announced her own candidacy and set out to discredit O'Donnell as well as the process that had selected her.[74] Depending on whose perspective one takes, the battle over the Federation presidency was either an attempt to purge conservatives from the Federation and squelch women's independent voices or an attempt to return the Federation to its traditional role as a noncontroversial auxiliary that would help the party rather than be a divisive force. Complicating this conflict was the fact that it was simultaneously one between moderates and conservatives *and* one between party regulars and party outsiders. In either case party regulars clearly did not want Schlafly to become leader of the Women's Federation.

Schlafly herself was aware that she was being targeted and denounced what she viewed as a conspiracy by Elston and RNC chairman Ray Bliss to keep her out of Federation leadership. These two, Schlafly maintained, were steering the Federation's leadership to make decisions harmful to Schlafly's candidacy. In arguing her case, Schlafly made much of the fact that she had served as a Federation officer while O'Donnell had not. Schlafly stated publicly that "custom and courtesy" dictated that she, as Federation first vice president, be "invite[d] . . . to serve as president."[75] In fact, Schlafly exaggerated the strength of this tradition; in the past, the candidate for the presidency usually, but not always, had been a previous Federation officer.[76] Gladys O'Donnell had not been a Federation officer, but she had served as president of the California Council of Republican Women as well as Federation program chairman. Schlafly saw it as an act of desperation that the Nominating Committee had found it necessary to overlook all of the current Federation officers in choosing a candidate. This point had validity, although O'Donnell was not the Federation neophyte that Schlafly suggested.

Supporters of shifting elections to odd-numbered years argued publicly that it would free Federation women during election years to remain in their communities campaigning rather than be distracted by planning and attending a national convention.[77] Schlafly interpreted the rule change differently. She correctly viewed it as a stalling tactic by her opponents who hoped her popularity would subside or that they could find their own candidate if the Federation convention (and election) were postponed by a year. Moving the convention out of California also worked against Schlafly, as she emphasized bitterly. Although O'Donnell was from California, that state was one of Schlafly's (and Goldwater's) strongest centers of support. California clubwomen generally favored Schlafly for Federation president.[78]

Accusations flew back and forth. Schlafly's opponents did stoop to some low tactics in their fight against her. Elston sent Federation members excerpts from a Goldwater letter praising O'Donnell's political credentials. The mailing omitted the full text of the senator's remarks, which included equally supportive statements about Schlafly, and which contained Goldwater's declaration of neutrality in the contest.[79] Schlafly supporters countered with their own questionable strategies. California national committeewoman Ann Bowler mailed charges to Federation delegates that O'Donnell had fabricated her conservative credentials. Twenty-eight national committeewomen and three previous RNC assistant chairmen (including Elly Peterson) rebuked Bowler publicly, calling her charges unfair and unfounded.[80] The sixty-three-year-old O'Donnell further accused Schlafly supporters of doctoring a photograph of O'Donnell to make her look older than she was in order to support their argument that Schlafly, at forty-two, represented youth.[81]

Over 3,000 women attended the Federation convention in May 1967, where the election took place. Tears were shed, contentious memos circulated, and insults traded in the press. The final vote of the 1967 Federation convention delegates was 1,910 (56 percent) for Gladys O'Donnell and 1,494 (44 percent) for Phyllis Schlafly. Schlafly held her performance to be remarkable considering the forces mobilized against her. Despite the RNC's efforts to diminish Schlafly's support at the convention and the Federation leadership's obvious bias in favor of O'Donnell, Schlafly had lost by only slightly more that 400 votes.[82] She did not accept defeat. Convinced that she was the choice of a majority of Federation members, Schlafly publicly accused the RNC and Dottie Elston of election irregularities. She charged that O'Donnell's supporters had bused uncredentialed delegates from New York and New Jersey to weight the convention in their candidate's favor. And Schlafly and her supporters also made allegations of voting machine tampering. The Federation's Executive Board dismissed Schlafly's charges by a vote of 58–2.[83]

O'Donnell herself denied Schlafly's accusations of wrongdoing, though she acknowledged that the fight had been a difficult one. In describing her victory, O'Donnell remarked on her experience as a candidate and as Schlafly's opponent. "It's much easier to work for a candidate than to be one and I especially learned about women in politics. And I can tell you, as a result of that, I am very much inclined to agree with Margaret Mead the anthropologist, women should not be drafte[d] for combat. They are too fierce."[84]

The press seemed to agree. The acrimony surrounding the Federation convention briefly earned national attention. *Time* magazine commented on the tenor of the Federation convention, suggesting that female opponents lacked the decorum and sportsmanship of men. "[T]he dame game," *Time* reported, "is not the same as the masculine variety. Nor is it very ladylike." A *Washington Post* reporter described the convention as "near pandemonium" with uniformed private police being employed to remove "raucous alternates" from the floor.[85] Women, as characterized in these reports, hardly appeared as the civilizing influence on politics that suffragists had once predicted.

Her failed bid for the Federation presidency left Schlafly further disillusioned with her party and with traditional Federation strategies for integrating women into the GOP. In December 1967, Schlafly published a new book, *Safe—Not Sorry*, in which she devoted an entire chapter (entitled "The Purge") to exposing the scheme (as she saw it) to deny her the Federation presidency. The discussion of behind-the-scenes chicanery and Schlafly's hyperbolic, hard-hitting tone were similar in style to her other self-published books, including *A Choice Not an Echo*.[86] In her discussion of her fight for the Federation presidency (which she characteristically writes in the third person), however, Schlafly did not limit her charges to accusations that liberals were plotting to keep conservatives out of power:

> They [the liberals] were joined by all those who feel it is to their own interests to keep Republican women neutralized. The Republican Party is carried on the shoulders of the women who do the work in the precincts, ringing doorbells, distributing literature, and doing all the tiresome, repetitious campaign tasks. Many men in the Party frankly

want to keep the women doing the menial work, while the selection of candidates and the policy decisions are taken care of by the men in the smoke-filled rooms. All those building their own political machine want only machine-people who can be controlled. In Phyllis, they recognized one who could not be neutralized or silenced, and who would fight for women to express their ideals in matters of policies and candidates commensurate with the work the women do for the Party.[87]

Many Republican men, Schlafly argued, preferred to keep women performing the housework of government and were determined not to let women choose their own leaders, express their own opinions, or exercise political power. Although Schlafly emphasized men's desire to keep women out of power, importantly, it was actually fellow Republican women like Peterson who had initially worked to prevent Schlafly's election. Certainly there were men in the party who allied themselves with Schlafly's opponents. And many in the press credited Ray Bliss with the underground campaign against Schlafly. Yet the movement had originated among national committeewomen and other female party leaders. Whether Schlafly knew this or not is unclear. In any case, she blamed the conspiracy primarily on Republican men.

Schlafly's use of the word "neutralized" cleverly exposed the weaknesses of Federation strategies for integrating women into the party. Since the Marion Martin years, the Federation had presented itself as a division of the RNC that would remain "neutral" in intraparty conflicts. This neutrality was the essence of the bargain that party women made with male leaders: the "neutrality" of Republican clubwomen was offered in exchange for the hope that women would eventually move into leadership positions. In 1967 Schlafly suggested that, far from a strategy for empowerment, promises of "neutrality" (or impartiality) effectively "neutralized" (or obliterated) Republican women's voices.

Schlafly boldly proclaimed what many other Federation women had been suggesting—albeit more timidly, diplomatically, or privately—for years. Women were carrying a critical share of the work of political organizing for the party, yet male political leaders, intent on holding on to their own power, were unwilling to grant women a real voice. For Schlafly, the RNC campaign against her belittled all Republican women because the RNC implied that it would not permit Federation women to choose their own leaders.

Schlafly also implied in her book that male leaders preferred women who did not represent the values of ordinary American women. She was particularly incensed about attacks against her that targeted her position as a mother of young children. She complained that Dottie Elston had suggested to the press that Schlafly would not be able to perform the job of Federation president because her role as mother of six would prevent her from moving to Washington as recent Federation presidents had done.[88] Schlafly bristled at the suggestion that motherhood was an obstacle to serving as Federation president. There was no rule, she pointed out, requiring the Federation president to reside in Washington.[89] Although many Federation presidents, beginning with Betty Farrington, had chosen to do so, Schlafly was correct that there was no rule to this effect. Before Farrington's term, Federation presidents had continued to reside in their home states (although this was also during the period when the Federation was run primarily by the RNC assistant chairman, who did reside in D.C.).

One effect of Elston's words, Schlafly complained, was to "discourage the mothers of young children by telling them bluntly they could be the peons in the precincts, but were barred from the highest office in the Federation."[90] Schlafly echoed Federation volunteers' long-standing resentments against professional women's leadership and argued that the party was rewarding the wrong model of Republican womanhood. Schlafly's depiction of women's political conservatism suffering rejection by a more liberal party included the dubious implication that different models of women's social roles necessarily corresponded to specific positions on the traditional political spectrum. The relationship of gender roles to political ideology was more complicated than Schlafly implied, but her message was a powerful one.

Schlafly's defeat was not a simple case of sexism, as her version might suggest. One cannot say definitively whether GOP regulars (including both men and women) sought to silence Schlafly's supporters because they were conservatives, because they were ideologues, because they were outsiders, or because they were women. Among Schlafly's supporters at the Federation, all of these identities came together. An illustration from Schlafly's book, *Safe — Not Sorry*, in which a woman stands before a door labeled "Republican Party Headquarters," depicts the convergence of her supporters' multiple identities within the party. Tacked to the door is a sign reading "Conservatives and Women Please Use Servants' Entrance." The woman, who has an angry look on her face, appears determined to try the knob of the front door anyway.

Schlafly's personal resentment had serious implications for the Republican Party, as the *Los Angeles Times* political editor suggested a month after the Federation convention. If Schlafly were able to convince a large number of her female supporters that eastern liberals had stolen the Federation presidency from her, "the women might keep their purses tightly shut and might not be as ready to ring doorbells, volunteer to stuff envelopes and do all the other chores they do during campaigns."[91] The departure of Schlafly's followers from the Federation not only threatened to disrupt the base of party support. Schlafly's showdown at the Federation also prompted the development of a new network of grass-roots conservative women that would prove significant to the unfolding debates over feminism in the 1970s.

★ The controversies surrounding the Schlafly-O'Donnell election are best understood within the context of the long disagreement among Republican women, dating back to 1920, over how women best could achieve power within the party. Should women try to prove themselves to be neutral party loyalists, not allied with any party faction, and thereby hope to win the trust of male party leaders? Or should they mobilize and articulate an independent agenda within the party? In 1967, on the eve of the eruption of second-wave feminism, these two viewpoints conflicted in the most open way to date.

The conflict between Schlafly and the RNC was one that had surfaced throughout the Federation's history. What was the proper relationship of the volunteer organization of Republican women to the RNC? The Federation was an auxiliary to the RNC, received financial support from it, and was governed by bylaws defining its mission clearly as one of support for party positions. While some individual women had always wanted the Federation and its member clubs to articulate a more independent voice, the leadership, beginning with Marion Martin, had supported the auxiliary role. Certainly many past leaders had complained that men took women's work for granted. But they had usually expressed that frustration as requests for recognition and representation, rather than as calls for Federation women to articulate their own agenda. Previous leaders had urged the party to give women a voice on the platform committee, to appoint more women to public office, to support women candidates, to give women a role in planning Eisenhower's inauguration, or to increase the number of women delegates at party conventions.

Few Federation leaders had argued that the Federation should be used to pursue an autonomous agenda, despite the fact that many individual clubwomen had called on the Federation to do just that. At times, clubwomen had argued that the Federation should use the strength of its numbers to weigh in against World War II, oppose racial segregation, support the Equal Rights Amendment, or support the Bricker Amendment. Wilma Bishop in 1956 had startled Len Hall by pointing out that the Federation easily could raise its own funds and become an independent organization if it wanted. But even Bishop, while wanting the Federation to receive greater autonomy and respect from party leaders, had never anticipated the Federation becoming a separate political organization with its own agenda. In 1967 Schlafly directed her complaints toward the very purpose of the Federation itself. Schlafly did not see the point of a large women's political organization whose actions were circumscribed and manipulated by the imperatives of male politicians —especially when those male politicians endorsed political positions she believed many women opposed. In her critique of male dominance in politics and in her assertion that motherhood should not preclude a woman from pursuing her ambitions, Schlafly sounds almost like a feminist in the making. Yet feminists' broader critique of fixed gender roles and their calls for constitutional solutions to problems of discrimination would prove anathema to Schlafly, and there would be no common ground.

With O'Donnell's victory, leadership of the Federation remained in the hands of women committed to moderation in political rhetoric. In an article appearing in the Federation's newsletter during 1969, research chairman Katherine Wright criticized the uncompromising, morally charged brand of politics that Schlafly, Goldwater, and other political crusaders had embarked on over the years: "Candidates have used the term 'crusade' so often in campaigns that many newcomers tend to confuse politics with a religion—to think in terms of 'conversion' to a 'true faith.'" This was a mistake, according to Wright. Politics was not a religion. It was "the means for translating ideals and aspirations into programs acceptable to a majority of citizens affected by them."[92]

Immediately after her defeat in 1967, Schlafly took 1,000 of her supporters into another room and threatened to form a "grass-roots organization made up of just plain old American women and mothers who believe in the cause of constitutional government and freedom." Ruth Bateman of Warrenville, Illinois, produced a charter for a proposed new organization, the American Federation of Republican Women. Mrs. George Thackeray, president of the southern division of the California Federation, which represented 40,000 women, vowed to leave the Federation when her term expired at the end of the year and urged other clubwomen to do the same. Twenty-six-year-old Maureen Reagan Sills, daughter of California governor Ronald Reagan and one of a Schlafly's original supporters, urged caution, however.[93]

In the end, according to press reports, Schlafly told her supporters to "go home and think about it, pray about it and then write me what you want to do." A week later Schlafly sent a letter to her backers in the Federation across the country suggesting that they remain in the Federation but withhold some of their dues. She went on to announce plans to set up her own program of monthly educational mailings which would reflect her personal political philosophy. Dorothy Elston believed that Schlafly's purpose was to undermine the Federation and charged Schlafly with "subversion."[94]

Schlafly did succeed in building a new grass-roots women's organization from the ruins of her defeat in 1967. Beginning in August 1967, three months after the Federation's convention, Schlafly began a monthly newsletter of her opinions on current events, the *Phyllis Schlafly Report*, which she sent to 3,000 of her Federation supporters. Schlafly also set up the Eagle Trust Fund (a precursor of Eagle Forum) as a means of collecting donations sent to her in support of the issues she publicized through her newsletter. As Schlafly's biographer notes, donors previously might have sent these funds to Republican clubs or other party organizations. In October 1968, Schlafly began holding yearly national political training conferences for women in St. Louis. There Schlafly's followers, the core of whom had been those women who had followed her out of the National Federation of Republican Women the previous year, learned strategies for defeating liberal candidates for local political and party offices. Schlafly focused her attention on the conservative issues she traditionally had pursued, such as national defense. Not until 1972 would Schlafly hit on the issue that would propel her and her followers into the political limelight. The *Phyllis Schlafly Report* in February 1972 was devoted entirely to challenging conventional wisdom that the Equal Rights Amendment was a logical reform whose time had come.

7

THE RISE
OF REPUBLICAN
FEMINISM

Phyllis Schlafly's 1967 battle with the Republican Party came at a time when other women in the United States were also growing frustrated with their auxiliary roles in male-dominated political organizations. Responding to the sexism of the New Left that had awakened them politically, white college-aged women began demanding their own voices and articulating their own interests, ultimately launching the women's liberation movement. Meanwhile a group of older women had been mobilizing since at least the early 1960s around issues of women's legal equality. President Kennedy's Commission on the Status of Women gave voice to the concerns of a large group of professional and working-class women — concerns that included job discrimination, inadequate childcare, and other persisting legal inequities.[1] Out of these two feminist impulses, a vigorous women's movement emerged that would transform the ways Americans thought about family, work, culture, and politics. Known collectively as second-wave feminism, this "movement" was a multifaceted one in terms of goals, strategies, and style. Feminists challenged the traditions of a variety of American institutions, including family, religion, education, and politics. Although feminists worked on a host of issues, ratification of the Equal Rights Amendment quickly became central to the agenda of most feminist organizations.

The emergence of second-wave feminism presented a new political context in which the National Federation of Republican Women was no longer the most important means for Republican women to participate in politics. The women's movement opened up new avenues for political participation. Women who once might have joined clubs and volunteered for the party began running for office themselves, leading autonomous women's organizations, or otherwise participating in political life on their own terms. The Federation in the seventies continued to be circumscribed by its mandate to support the party's platform and provide loyal partisan workers; as in the past, this provoked conflict among the rank and file. Under Gladys O'Donnell's leadership, the Federation would briefly swing its weight behind the ERA, although neither the leadership nor the membership unanimously supported the amendment. Meanwhile, other women who had begun their activism through the club movement found new avenues for organizing. The renegade women who followed Phyllis Schlafly out of the Federation did not go on to support ERA or second-wave feminism. They would, however, come to play an important part in defining that movement, leading the fight against ERA, and denouncing feminism.

Other women who, like Schlafly, had at one time been leaders in the Republican club movement, such as Rosemary Ginn and Mary Louise Smith, came to embrace feminism. Indeed, many Republican women responded positively to the feminist movement and pressed for a Republican feminist policy agenda. They fought as well for party reforms that would increase the participation of women in the business of party conventions.[2] Smith and Ginn, as well as Schlafly, had political goals that went far beyond performing the "housework of government" for the Republican Party. But they came to different conclusions about where, how, and on behalf of what issues their political energies should now be focused.

For Republican feminists, reforming their own party would be one of their chief concerns, as demonstrated at the 1972 Republican Presidential Convention. By 1975 GOP feminists had formed an official organization, the Republican Women's Task Force (RWTF), which was committed to fostering feminism in the party and maintaining an identification of the party with women's rights. During the mid-1970s there was an ideological space in the party for Republican feminists, and it appeared briefly that Republican feminism might be a real political force.

By the end of the 1970s, Republican feminists would find themselves marginalized and the political component of the feminist movement largely conceded to the Democrats. Throughout most of the decade, however, Republican feminists were optimistic that they could build on party traditions and forge a workable alliance between feminists and the GOP. A core group of Republican activists worked in the 1970s to promote a bipartisan feminism. They did this as members and leaders of both partisan and feminist organizations. These Republican women seized on many of the insights and objectives of the emerging women's movement and pressed the GOP to embrace a particular feminist agenda.

This agenda included support not only for the ERA (which the Republican Party platform had first endorsed in 1940) but also for reproductive rights, affirmative action, federally funded childcare, reform of discriminations in the tax code and Social Security system, extension of the Equal Pay Act, and job training and other assistance for "displaced homemakers." Although they saw this agenda as a forward-looking one, Republican feminists often described their feminism in terms of party traditions. A feminist agenda, they argued, was in line with the party's history of support for the principles of equal opportunity, individualism, and women's rights.

By the mid-1970s the American public was coming to broadly accept feminism—at least a particular kind of feminism that emphasized equal treatment for women by America's laws and institutions. After 1974, when the GOP was floundering in the wake of the Watergate scandal, important Republican Party leaders were ready to adopt those feminist issues that seemed to enjoy broad public support as part of a larger rebuilding strategy. Organized Republican feminists seized on the advantages this moment offered to consistently remind the party and the public of the compatibility of feminist politics with Republican principles and traditions.

★ It was at the 1972 convention that a feminist coalition within the GOP first emerged. That year, the party would consider a set of feminist platform planks promoted by the National Women's Political Caucus (NWPC), as well as a series of reforms intended to broaden the party's base. Although they would have important implications for women, these party reforms did not originate as feminist programs. They were instead part of a wider effort to make the party more appealing to minority and youth voters. Responding to the social upheavals of the late 1960s and recognizing the need for the party to expand its base, a group of reformers was hoping to change party rules in ways it believed would help make the GOP the "Party of the Open Door." The internal struggles over these reforms and the resistance women encountered, as well as the involvement of the National Women's Political Caucus, helped forge an alliance of Republican women sympathetic to the goals of organized feminism. At the 1972 convention, party women's decades-old concerns about representation fused with a more explicitly feminist agenda, creating a new constituency of Republican feminists.

In 1972 party reformers, including feminists, elected officials, and party strategists, took their case to Miami where the party held days of contentious hearings before and during its convention. It was not the first time Republican women, spurred on by a vital women's movement, had tried to remake their party. In 1920, shortly before the ratification of the Nineteenth Amendment, Ruth McCormick and Mary Hay had lobbied the Republican Convention on behalf of reforms they believed would best open the GOP to women. Fifty-two years later, Republicans were once more in the midst of revising their party's rules. Again, women would play a central role in the debates as both activists and as targets of reform. In 1972, however, in contrast to 1920, women also participated in these proceedings as party insiders. The Delegates and Organization (DO) Committee, which initially drew up recommendations for changes, was headed by sixty-one-year-old Rosemary Ginn, the national committeewoman from Missouri.[3] Women made up almost half the members of the convention's Rules Committee, which would evaluate reform proposals. And they were 30 percent of the entire convention delegation.

The immediate origins of the Rules Committee hearings dated back to the party's previous convention in 1968. That year, during a summer marked by nationwide minority and youth unrest, the convention adopted changes to the party's nondiscrimination clause (Rule 32) instructing state Republican parties to "take positive action to achieve the broadest possible participation in party affairs." According to the *Miami Herald*, adoption of this language indicated that the GOP "had become sensitive to the charge that there were too few Negroes and other minority groups represented at its conventions."[4] Indeed, African Americans had been about 3 percent of Republican delegates in 1968; persons under thirty less than 1 percent. As one newspaper account observed, in 1968 there were more African Americans serving on the Democratic Party's Michigan delegation alone than there were from all fifty states at the Republican Convention.[5] Furthermore, during the fall presidential elections, Richard Nixon would win only 12 percent of black voters. While this was a slight improvement over Goldwater's dismal performance in 1964, it marked a decline from Nixon's own results of 1960.[6]

This increasing weakness with black voters was one many in the party hoped to overcome. Elly Peterson, for example, while serving as RNC assistant chairman, was given a mandate to remake the party's image, to reach out to minorities, and to increase the interest of women voters. To move the GOP to more direct involvement with the problems of urban areas, Peterson began a program in 1969 called Action Now, modeled on efforts enacted by the Michigan GOP in Detroit. The idea was to set up centers in inner-city areas where residents could come for community life as well as assistance with their problems. This effort, it was hoped, would help the GOP with urban and minority voters and would also bring the GOP into closer contact with the day-to-day problems of those constituents. Insisting that the Action Centers were not a "campaign gimmick," Peterson referred to them instead as "the best kind of Republicanism." Peterson described the Action Centers as a deliberate counter to those championing a "Southern Strategy" for the GOP. Rather than abandon black voters and the industrial northeast, Peterson argued for a broader party.[7]

In response to criticisms that the party was neglecting important parts of the American electorate, the party had also begun pursuing internal reforms. The Republican Convention in 1968 established the sixteen-member Delegates and Organization Committee and charged it with drafting proposals for reorganizing and broadening the party. The Democrats, in the wake of their own highly contentious 1968 Chicago convention, had appointed its own commission to study Democratic Party rules. The McGovern-Fraser Commission had written new rules governing delegate selection for the 1972 convention requiring that state Democratic parties include youth, minorities, and women as delegates "in reasonable relationship to their presence in the population of the state."[8]

Although not compelled by a "convention debacle" as were the Democrats in 1968, Republicans began a similar process.[9] Led by Rosemary Ginn, the Republican DO Committee, after months of work, issued its preliminary report at the RNC's July 1971 meeting in Denver. Many of its proposals for "opening the door" were welcomed by the RNC as sensible and necessary. These included recommendations that party officials no longer be given "automatic" delegate positions and that delegate fees be eliminated. Such reforms promised to democratize the process of delegate selection. But controversy centered on those recommendations— what would come to be known as DO 7, 8, and 9—that sought explicitly to increase the participation of specific groups.[10] DO 7, 8, and 9, along with similar proposals from the McGovern-Fraser Commission, occurred in the broader context of what John Skrentny has labeled the "minority rights revolution," in which members of the Nixon administration designated the nation's "official minorities" and hammered out policies for explicitly increasing their opportunities in education, business, and employment.[11] Thus the proposals for Republican Party reform would borrow some of the language and logic of the minority rights discourse in combination with an understanding of the party's own history.

The first of the DO Committee's controversial proposals, DO 7, built on a reform dating from the 1940s. In 1944 Marion Martin and other Republican women had convinced the RNC to recommend that the Resolutions (Platform) Committee consist of a man *and* a woman from every state. That recommendation was generally followed at subsequent conventions. In 1960 the Republican Convention itself enacted a rule change providing for equal representation of men and women on all four major convention committees (Resolutions, Rules, Credentials, and Permanent Organizations), beginning in 1964.[12] DO 7 proposed that the size of the convention committees be again increased to add a member of a "minority ethnic group" and a person under the age of twenty-five from each state. DO 9 further spoke to the problem of low youth participation, recommending that states send a number of delegates under age twenty-five proportional to the population of young voters in the state. The DO Committee initially offered a parallel proposal pertaining to minority voters (that they be given delegates in proportion to their voting strength in each state), which the RNC dropped.[13] Women's participation in the party was addressed by DO 8, which confronted the persistently low number of women serving as convention delegates, an issue the party had not really explored since the first years following suffrage. DO 8 recommended that the states "endeavor to have" an equal number of male and female delegates at the conventions.[14]

Despite the inclusion of DO 8 among its recommendations, the DO Committee seems to have been primarily interested in broadening the party based on age and race. Concern about women's representation appears to have been almost an afterthought, at least in the beginning. Surveys sent to party leaders indicated little concern about women's representation in the party.[15] Yet DO 8 would ultimately fare better than those recommendations, DO 7 and 9, specifically dealing with youth and minority participation, the initial target of the DO Committee's reforms.

In Denver, conservative members of the RNC, led by Clark Reed of Mississippi, were reportedly "horrified" by the DO Committee's more controversial proposals.[16] Opponents attacked the "quotas" for young voters included in DO 7 and DO 9 and for minority delegates in DO 7. This line of objection was somewhat disingenuous, as "quotas" for women had been party policy for decades. Republicans had doubled the RNC in 1924 to add a committeewoman from each state. And they had voted in the forties and again in the sixties to expand the party's convention committees to include equal numbers of men and women. Although additional quotas for female delegates were suggested in DO 8, they seem to have generated little controversy, at least initially. Some in the media indeed joked about the subject. The *Washington Daily News*, under the headline "Gabby Delegates," noted dismissively that Republicans should not expect a quiet national convention in 1972 now that party leaders were recommending that half the delegates be women.[17]

Some Republican women objected to the DO Committee's proposals for increasing women's presence at party conventions. The Cheshire [New Hampshire] Republican Women's Club, for example, declared itself opposed to DO 8, calling it "sex discrimination in reverse." To these women, the issue rested on the right of New Hampshire citizens to chose their own delegation. "We are all women who will defend strongly our right to participate and to be heard," the club's secretary stated, "but we will defend with equal vigor the right of any well-qualified man, elected by his fellow citizens, to represent his state on a national committee."[18]

While some Republicans denounced the DO report, others endorsed it heartily. These included the (all-female) Southern Association of Vice Chairmen, led by Beryl Milburn, state vice chair from Texas. Milburn acknowledged that the real intent of the DO Committee was to increase minority and youth participation in party affairs. She urged party leaders, however, to remember that women voters tended to favor Republican candidates and warned the party not to jeopardize that advantage. Failure to increase significantly the number of women serving as delegates, she predicted, would have a "deleterious effect" on the party's image. Furthermore, it could alienate women already supporting the party. Echoing decades of similar comments by Republican women in the past, Milburn warned that Republican leaders simply did not recognize "the extent of the resentment of Republican women in this regard."[19] Wilma Rogalin, a former delegate from New York, concurred, noting that recognition of women at the conventions and in the platform was typically mere "tokenism."[20] Milburn and Rogalin's concerns had a long history in the party, but they would achieve new importance in 1972.

The DO Committee's report in 1971 was only an initial step in what would be a contentious and drawn-out process. Unlike the proposals of the McGovern-Fraser Commission, the DO recommendations were not binding (indeed journalists tended to dismiss the DO Committee as less ambitious and more secretive than its Democratic counterpart). Therefore, Republicans would have to vote on the recommendations at their 1972 convention. Anything the convention passed would not take effect until 1976. The first step in this process was a hearing by the RNC Rules Committee, a week before the 1972 convention.

Because the head of this committee, Florida national committeeman Bill Cramer, was opposed to the reforms addressing representation, it seemed quite possible that the DO Committee's recommendations would be quietly set aside. But interest in reform was revived shortly before the convention by feminists working with the National Women's Political Caucus and by a group of Republican congressmen, led by Tom Railsback of Illinois. Railsback's Ad Hoc Committee, which included John Anderson (Ill.), Jack Kemp (N.Y.), Margaret Heckler (Mass.), and Bob Packwood (Ore.) among others, did not—as a group—support all of the DO recommendations. What the Ad Hoc Committee did endorse was an expansion of the party's nondiscrimination clause to include age and sex, a commitment by the party to "take positive action" to be more inclusive, as well as the adoption of DO 8 (the provision addressing women's representation as delegates).[21]

While Railsback was organizing support for reform, a group of eighty congressional opponents, including Philip Crane of Illinois, formed Republicans for an Open Party to fight those DO recommendations they believed were intended "to 'quota-ize' the Party."[22] Reforms aimed at broadening the party by assigning future delegate positions to "identifiable minorities" would, in the words of one opponent, "fragment Republicans."[23] In a letter sent to convention delegates, the conservative Crane insisted that proposed reforms would close, rather than open, the party by preventing dedicated, seasoned party workers from serving as delegates. Choosing his examples carefully, Crane asked his audience to imagine the injustice done to a "50-year-old woman who has labored for the Republican ticket in a dozen or more elections" whose rightful seat might have to go to a young person who had never even voted before.[24] Crane's choice of a "50-year-old woman" as an example of who would be harmed by the proposed reforms surely raised a few eyebrows among the many dedicated female party workers who had been overlooked in the past. Women, widely praised for their loyalty and service to the party, had, after all, been only 17 percent of the delegates at the 1968 convention.[25] In his example, Crane comfortably assumed that his listeners held images of Republican women as loyal female stalwarts who compared favorably to politically problematic young voters or black voters (an assumption belied, it should be noted, by the tremendous concern about

Republican women's loyalty demonstrated just a few years earlier in the efforts to prevent Phyllis Schlafly and her followers from controlling the National Federation of Republican Women).

Notably, Railsback's Ad Hoc group—although it clearly supported "opening the door"—also explicitly rejected "arbitrary and imposed quotas" and opposed DO 7 and DO 9 on those grounds. Railsback's group argued that "to single out any group or groups would discriminate against those groups which are not singled out."[26] One of the Ad Hoc group's members, Senator Bill Brock of Tennessee, held up the Democratic Party's McGovern-Fraser Commission as a foil for Republicans. The GOP had an "obligation and an opportunity," Brock declared, to give all Americans a political voice. But it should not follow the path of the Democratic Party, which, in 1972, had been "subverted by radicals who play blacks against whites, minorities against majorities, men against women and old against young."[27] (Brock's affiliation with the Ad Hoc Committee is interesting, as he himself is an illustration of how racial issues were transforming the political landscape. A former Democratic congressman from Tennessee who voted against the Civil Rights Act of 1964, he was elected to the Senate in 1970 as a Republican. By the 1980s he was considered a moderate on issues of affirmative action.)[28]

Despite its rejection of "quotas," Railsback's group supported requiring states to "endeavor to have" equal numbers of men and women in their delegations (DO 8), arguing that "women deserve special attention." The explanation for this contradiction rested first of all on tradition and precedent: for a number of years, Railsback pointed out, Republican Convention rules had required that there be a man and a woman from each state on the convention committees. Railsback also noted that women played a major role in getting out Republican votes and were "the backbone of the Republican effort at the grassroots." Moreover, Railsback insisted that DO 8 was not a quota, as it merely required states to make a "good-faith effort."[29] Basically, Republican women had, decades earlier, institutionalized a prescribed presence both on the RNC and at the conventions. Women had normalized their "quota" so that an extension of it in 1972 was acceptable to some, like Railsback, who were otherwise dubious of "singl[ing] out any group."

Equally important, however, was the fact that many Republican insiders seem not to have feared that an increase in female delegates would disrupt the status quo as an increase in youth and minority delegates might. As Republican feminist Bobbie Kilberg noted, opponents of reform feared a left-wing takeover of the party. Thus they fought proportional representation for youth and minorities. Yet some found such representation more acceptable for women.[30] Women were a familiar presence in the party, they were loyal workers, and they were certainly not viewed as a potentially disruptive left-wing force. Women were safe; or at least they seemed to be.

The feminist movement was hardly on the minds of the DO Committee when it was first appointed after the 1968 convention. Yet by the time Republicans would debate the committee's proposals in Miami, second-wave feminism had exploded. The feminist movement had shown women to be intent on organizing around gender issues in ways that had not been seen for decades. As Republican feminist Jill Ruckelshaus put it, both Democratic and Republican women "had tired of nothing but fashion shows and luncheons" at conventions and now wanted to talk about issues.[31] This development, together with the civil rights movement, the onset of affirmative action programs, and the newly ratified Twenty-sixth Amendment enfranchising eighteen-year-olds, meant attempts to affect the racial, gender, and age makeup of the party were at the heart of current political concern and controversy. Previously acceptable efforts to increase women's representation in party proceedings were now linked, in many minds, to militant, gender-based political activism, to affirmative action for minorities, and to radical politics in general.

The debates over reform in 1972 would galvanize a nascent group of Republican feminists. Yet by the time Rosemary Ginn presented the DO recommendations to the Rules Committee in Miami, several who would go on to become prominent Republican feminists had already begun their involvement with women's issues. Among them was Margaret Heckler, member of Congress from Massachusetts. Heckler, first elected to her seat in 1966, proved to be an ardent supporter of day care, the ERA, and women's rights legislation during Nixon's first term.[32] A Roman Catholic, she differed from most other Republican feminists in her opposition to abortion; yet in the early seventies, this position did not prevent her from identifying with the feminist movement. RNC cochairman Anne Armstrong (of Texas) championed the ERA.[33] Even more outspoken than Armstrong was her assistant, thirty-five-year-old Jill Ruckelshaus, the wife of Nixon's Environmental Protection Agency head. The youthful and engaging Ruckelshaus would earn a reputation as the Nixon Administration's most vocal feminist.[34] In Miami, Ginn, Heckler, and Armstrong received support from Republican women working with the National Women's Political Caucus, including Ruckelshaus, Betsy Deardourff, Bobbie Kilberg, Tanya Melich, and Elly Peterson. The National Women's Political Caucus would play an important role in linking long-standing dissatisfaction over women's low representation in the party to a broader feminist agenda.

The NWPC had been founded in 1971 by feminists seeking to develop a political component to the new feminism. Its purpose was to promote a women's rights agenda and the advancement of women in the political system.[35] The NWPC targeted both party conventions in 1972. That year, the NWPC encouraged and assisted Democratic and Republican women in running for positions as delegates and then worked with female delegates at the conventions to lobby for the inclusion of a series of feminist planks. In 1972, as both parties were in the process of reform, the proportion of female delegates at both national party conventions jumped noticeably—up to 40 percent in the Democratic Party (from 13 percent) and up to 30 percent (from 17 percent) in the Republican Party.[36] (Eighty-nine percent of Republican women delegates were white.) Although the increase in female delegates was substantial, it did not come close to the goals of the DO Committee. Only three states (Arkansas, North Dakota, and South Dakota) met the goals of DO 8 in sending Republican delegations that were 50 percent women.[37]

During a week of hearings that began before the full delegation had arrived in Miami, Rules Committee members heard heated testimony regarding proposed reforms.[38] The battle supporters of women's equality would face was indicated to Betsy Deardourff by the condescending manner in which Chairman William Cramer insisted on referring to female delegates as "very un-ordinary housewi[ves]" or "gentle lad[ies]."[39] While many of the committee's proposals generated support, concern focused, not surprisingly, on DO 7, 8, and 9. The opposition was coordinated by Clarke Reed. Those testifying against the DO reforms included Conservative Party senator James Buckley of New York. "No matter how well they are disguised," Buckley declared, "no matter from what wellsprings of human compassion they may arise, these calls for quotas are the most reactionary proposals being made today." Buckley, who would go on to be a strong opponent of affirmative action policies in general, urged the Rules Committee to recognize "individual merit as the sole criterion for judging persons."[40] A representative of the Young Republicans also testified against DO 7, 8, and 9 because of the group's opposition to quotas.[41] Buckley and other critics achieved important victories. As one participant recalled, a proposal requiring "interest group participation based in [sic] demographic data" (which would have addressed some of the principles of DO 7, 8, and 9) was narrowly defeated at the initial Rules Committee meeting.[42] Yet the Rules Committee also heard from supporters of reform, including a coalition of Republican governors, members of Railsback's Ad Hoc group, and Republican women working with the National Women's Political Caucus.

The NWPC's Republican representatives prepared background briefings and testified in favor of DO 8 at the Rules Committee hearings. They received support from male allies sporting "Men for Women" buttons.[43] Jessie Sargent, wife of the Republican governor of Massachusetts, presented the NWPC's proposals. In supporting efforts to expand women's participation in the party, Sargent echoed what Republican women had expressed in every decade since the 1920s: "Women have long acted as an auxiliary branch of the Republican Party, forced to play a secondary role. We have performed the menial Party chores and we have sponsored the social events, but when something really important is involved, like the selection of a presidential candidate, women are excluded."[44]

DO 8, which addressed women's participation as convention delegates, made it through the Rules Committee hearings, despite opposition from Buckley and others. DO 7 and 9 did not. With DO 7 and 9 rejected, supporters of reform sought a compromise proposal to address their concerns, settling on clarifying the "take positive action" statement adopted by the 1968 convention. That statement had called on states to "take positive action to achieve the broadest representation in Party affairs." Reformers now supported including additional language, spelling out specifically that states were to "take positive action" to include "women, young people, minority and heritage groups, and senior citizens."[45]

Opponents on the Rules Committee attempted to substitute the words "strive to achieve" for "take positive action" in an effort to weaken the nondiscrimination measure. Supporters of the stronger language held firm, however, and eventually won out. Bobbie Kilberg noted that supporters considered the "take positive action" language to be critical because it was a "synonym for 'affirmative action'" with "a legal and legislative history" beyond party rules that would give the provision teeth it would otherwise lack. The NWPC seems to have pushed harder for DO 8 than for DO 7 and DO 9. Yet, as Kilberg observed, the fight over "take positive action" indicated that women in the party were among the "prime movers" behind rule changes that would serve to include not only more women but greater numbers of other underrepresented groups including racial minorities in party proceedings.[46]

The NWPC's work with the Rules and Resolutions Committees helped create a community of feminists in the party and helped introduce a feminist language into party affairs. At the 1972 convention, Republican feminists working with the NWPC, such as Heckler, Deardourff, Kilberg, and Ruckelshaus, lobbied female delegates, encouraging them to use their influence to support the NWPC planks and the changes to Rule 32. The Platform and Rules Committee hearings had taken place in the days before the full convention began. Once the rest of the convention arrived, the NWPC held a rally for female delegates to generate enthusiasm for promoting women's rights measures in the party.

At this rally, Republican feminists hoped to spread the word about what had occurred during the previous week and drum up support among those party women who would be voting on the convention floor. The Republican "rally" differed from comparable events held at the Democratic convention. While Democratic feminists had dressed casually and yelled feminist slogans, Republicans were more demure. Speakers at the Republican event were seen "comb[ing] their hair, powder[ing] their noses, freshen[ing] their lipstick, and adjust[ing] their bra straps" before they spoke. And they were not able to take for granted the enthusiasm of their audience—a relatively small one of fewer than one hundred women.[47] While the Republican women affiliated with the NWPC were already allied with the feminist movement, most female delegates at the convention were not. That many Republican women resented women's treatment by the party did not mean they were ready to come out as feminists.

In fact, most delegates were, according to Betsy Deardourff, hostile to "women's lib." Deardourff described the work Republican feminists from the NWPC did with the rest of the female delegation as "effective 'consciousness-raising.'" Relatively privileged women, who had personally experienced few of the conflicts and frustrations that led other women to feminism were, according to Deardourff, "able to broaden their own understanding of women's issues."[48] For example, the national committeewomen from Arizona and Iowa, Mary Dent Crisp and Mary Louise Smith (both in their fifties, married, and financially secure), hadn't yet identified with the new women's movement. At the convention, however, they were persuaded by younger party feminists that the women's issues endorsed by the NWPC were consistent with Republican principles and worth attaching their names to.[49] Each would go on to become self-identified feminists and active supporters the movement.

Republican feminists encouraged prominent female party insiders

Feminist in the Making. At the 1972 Republican National Convention, party stalwarts like Iowa delegate and national committeewoman Mary Louise Smith (right) had their "consciousness raised." Here Smith is shown with Ronald Reagan, future standard-bearer of Republican conservatives. (Photographs—Mary Louise Smith et al., 1968–72, miscellaneous, box 135, MLS papers.)

to go out on a limb and declare themselves in favor of the NWPC's proposals for the Rules and Platform Committees. To that end the NWPC drafted a statement detailing the GOP's record of support for women's rights. The statement called on the Rules Committee to adopt DO 8, the Platform Committee to support a "strong women's plank," and the convention as a whole to pass a resolution "urging immediate ratification" of the ERA.[50] Approximately seventy-five women signed the statement, including such Republican notables as Armstrong, Ruckelshaus, Heckler, Smith, and Gladys O'Donnell.[51] The support of these female leaders was significant in demonstrating that women's issues had the backing of prominent party players. Yet the majority of female delegates at the Republican Convention was not actively supporting those issues. Indeed, a far more popular women's happening than the NWPC rally was a fashion show brunch attended by more than two thousand women, revealing Ruckelshaus's claim that women had soured on such events to be somewhat exaggerated.[52]

It seemed to *Washington Post* reporter Sally Quinn that while the ideas of Jill Ruckelshaus, Anne Armstrong, and Margaret Heckler were similar to those of their Democratic counterparts, Republican feminists came across as less familiar with the ideas and terminology of the women's movement and more deferential to men in the party.[53] That deference may be partly explained by the very real differences between the reform efforts in the two parties. Democratic and Republican reformers, while on the surface supporting similar changes, had based their support on different kinds of arguments. Democratic reformers spoke often about justice—the need for the marginalized to have a political voice. As the McGovern-Fraser report put it, "[I]f we do not represent the demands of change, then the danger is not that people will go to the Republican Party; it is that there will no longer be a way for people committed to orderly change to fulfill their needs and desires within our traditional political system."[54] Republican reformers, however, argued far more in terms of party competitiveness. Reform was necessary to show Americans that the GOP was the Party of the Open Door and that it was responsive to new political realities. This difference in strategy reflected differences in party structure and tradition and also helps to explain why the style of Republican feminists was so different from that of their Democratic counterparts. Republican women, in pressing demands, needed to be clear that they remained committed to what was good for the GOP.

While the *style* of Republican women leaders did not strike Quinn as truly feminist, she admitted that several of them had been quite forceful and effective in their work on the Platform and Rules Committees.[55] Republican feminists succeeded in getting the convention to endorse much of their agenda. In the end, most of the NWPC's proposals made it into the platforms of both the Democratic and Republican parties. (Neither party embraced abortion rights, the most controversial of the proposals.) Yet Republican feminists were generally pleased about their successes with the Platform Committee. Indeed, Republicans in the NWPC were reportedly more satisfied with what they had accomplished at their convention than were their Democratic counterparts, who were perhaps less prepared for the resistance they encountered.[56] Feminists at the Republican convention claimed credit for "the only change that was made" in the Republican draft platform that year. Participant Betsy Deardourff described the women's plank as the "only section of the Party's Platform not drafted by conservative Nixon operatives."[57] The plank included a day-care provision opposed by Richard Nixon.[58] Nixon had previously vetoed childcare legislation when Congress presented it to him, so feminists considered the incorporation of the day-care language in the Republican platform a significant victory.[59] Skeptics pointed out, however, that this language in its final form was weakened by a "loophole" paragraph opposing any "ill-considered" day-care proposals that might heavily involve the federal government.[60]

The NWPC also succeeded in winning the Republican Convention's endorsement of the ERA. This was particularly important because the Republican Party, like the Democratic Party, had distanced itself from the amendment during the previous two conventions, dropping it altogether in 1968.[61] In 1972 the GOP restored its long endorsement of the ERA. However, that endorsement meant something quite different in 1972 from what it had meant in any previous year. Traditional opposition to the ERA had come from Democratic and trade-union advocates of so-called protective labor laws, which regulated the working conditions of female workers. Supporters of protective legislation believed such laws provided necessary protections to vulnerable female workers and they understood that an ERA would make such laws unconstitutional.[62] By the early 1970s protective labor laws had been essentially nullified by Title VII of the 1964 Civil Rights Act (forbidding certain forms of employment discrimination, including discrimination based on sex), leading most traditional opponents of ERA to join supporters of the amendment. When Congress debated ERA in the early 1970s, attempts were made to add riders establishing that the amendment would neither nullify protective labor laws nor force women to be drafted into the military. These efforts failed and, in March 1972, Congress approved the unrestricted ERA and sent it to the states for ratification. The following August, when Republican Convention delegates endorsed the ERA, they were throwing their weight behind an amendment whose ratification, for the first time, was widely believed to be imminent.

The Republican Convention also accepted the Rules Committee's proposals, which included DO 8, the expanded "take positive action" statement, and the addition of sex and age to the party's nondiscrimination statement. Although these seemed like significant victories for feminists at the time, the language lacked any provision for enforcement. The convention appointed the confusingly named Rule 29 Committee to establish enforcement procedures over the next few years, but those measures were mostly eliminated by the 1976 convention. Furthermore, the less-controversial reforms that resulted from the work of party reformers ended up shifting power away from party professionals. This was an outcome of reform that Bobbie Kilberg had predicted, noting in 1972 that if "the system were really opened up and the delegates were not hand picked, moderate delegations would be replaced by substantially more conservative ones."[63] And it was among the moderates who made up the bulk of party professionals that feminist allies were most likely to be found.

Beyond the activities of its Resolutions and Rules Committees, the Republican Convention had other important effects on the women's movement within the GOP. Out of the 1972 convention proceedings, the Platform and Rules Committee debates, and the consciousness-raising and coalition-building work of the NWPC, a core group of Republican feminists emerged. Some held elected office, such as Heckler. Others, such as Ginn, Crisp, Smith, and Peterson were past or current officials in the party's state and national organizations. Additional Republican feminists lobbied for women's issues from their positions as aides and appointees within the Nixon administration, including Anne Armstrong and Jill Ruckelshaus. This group would come to form a base of support for feminist issues within the GOP. In 1973 and 1974, as this loose group was developing and was introducing feminist issues and perspectives into some party circles, the party itself was encountering serious problems.

★ In 1974 Richard Nixon resigned in the wake of the Watergate scandal, leaving the Republican Party in shambles. The Republicans continued to hold the presidency while Gerald Ford finished Nixon's term, yet public support for the GOP had plummeted. In the 1974 midterm elections, the GOP lost a record number of seats in the House. A mere 18 percent of the American people dared admit they were Republicans.[64] Republican leaders such as Ford were eager to insulate the party from the scandals and from Nixon himself, in order to demonstrate that the Republican Party was capable of reform and that it was still relevant to the American political process. These efforts were not limited to distancing the party from political corruption. As Tom Railsback and Senator Pete Domenici put it the following February, in explaining their support for implementation of the Rule 32 recommendations, the "*continued decline of the Republican Party*" required the party to consider the "political advantage of the party reaching out to designated groups." Railsback, an Illinois moderate, and Domenici, a conservative Catholic from New Mexico, were ideologically far apart on most issues. They agreed, however, that failure to adopt even the most "modest proposals" for broadening the party could well be viewed as "one more, perhaps the fatal, sign of Republican indifference." The two went on to note that public perceptions of the GOP were so poor that *even Republicans view their Party as less open than the Democratic Party.*"[65]

One early gesture Ford made to demonstrate the party's commitment to "opening the door" was his appointment of Mary Louise Smith to chair the Republican National Committee. Some observers noted Smith's lack of leadership experience. Yet others viewed Smith, who began her party work with the Iowa Council of Republican Women in Eagle Grove, Iowa, during the late 1940s, as a trusted party person who had worked her way up through the party ranks over decades (a contrast to Nixon's reliance on party outsiders). Smith was also an eloquent and inspiring public speaker as well as an experienced grass-roots organizer, having pioneered a precinct-organizing campaign in Iowa. Thus she had the long-standing Republican credentials to appeal to the party faithful, along with the commitment, skills, and organizing experience to broaden the party's base. Smith had also served as vice chairman of the party's Rule 29 Committee, which the 1972 convention had charged with investigating ways to implement the changes to Rule 32. She was, according to one reporter, among those Republicans who "spen[t] a lot of time worrying about ways to attract blacks and other minorities" to the party. Another analyst referred to Smith as a "symbol" of "Ford's determination to pull the Republican party back to its feet after the Watergate debacle."[66]

Also noteworthy, of course, was that Ford had chosen a woman to chair the RNC (a Republican Party first). Smith was not just any woman. By the time of her appointment in 1974, she was viewed as one of the party's "most ardent feminists." She was a member of the National Women's Political Caucus, and an active supporter of ERA and reproductive rights. Republican consultant John Deardourff viewed Smith's feminism as an asset to the party. "The women's movement is an emerging force in politics," Deardourff argued, going on to note that Ford's intelligent choice had stolen something from the Democrats.[67] Deardourff, a political moderate, who was married to feminist Betsy Deardourff, was surely influenced by his own views on feminism, yet his arguments were also based on his pragmatic interests in promoting the party.

That Ford, Deardourff, and others considered the selection of an "ardent feminist" for Republican Party chair to be a politically savvy

Wielding power. In 1975, Mary Louise Smith became the first woman to serve as chairman of the RNC. Here she is shown presiding at the 1976 presidential convention. (1976 RNC, box 135, MLS papers.)

move indicates their perception that, in the mid-1970s, many aspects of feminism were broadly accepted by American voters. Although he disparaged the feminism he associated with "an Abzug or the bra-burners," Deardourff's consulting partner, Doug Bailey, argued that Republican campaigners should not "make the mistake of equating them with the women's movement. It is massive, reaches into every home, and is inexorable—because involved is an issue of simple justice."[68]

Indeed, polling data seemed to support the perception that feminism enjoyed broad support. A Gallup poll conducted in March 1975 revealed that not only a majority of the population, but 56 percent of Republican women as well, supported the ERA (the focus of second-wave feminism in the 1970s).[69] Yet Deardourff and Bailey may have overestimated the strength of American support for feminism. Political scientist Jane Mansbridge, who carefully studied polling data on women's issues from the 1970s, concluded that "[m]uch of the apparent support for the Equal Rights Amendment in surveys came from a sympathetic response to the concept of 'rights,' not from a commitment to actual changes in women's roles."[70] It was the *perception* of broad support for the women's movement, however, that guided Deardourff's and Bailey's pragmatic arguments.

While Smith was running the RNC, others were working behind the scenes to promote Republican feminism. In the spring of 1975, about thirty Republican feminists, mostly associated with the NWPC, met in Washington to form their own organization.[71] Two issues lay behind the decision to form a Republican feminist organization. First, Republican feminists were concerned about the dominance of the NWPC by Democrats.[72] The NWPC was intended to be multipartisan and, from the beginning, a number of Republican activists had been involved. Republicans were always a minority in the NWPC, but their presence made an important statement about political feminism—that feminists had an interest in promoting women's involvement in electoral and party politics that transcended party affiliation. Within the NWPC, Republicans achieved a kind of special-interest status (similar to that of African Americans), with representation among the NWPC's leadership that was disproportionate to the roughly 10 percent of the organization's total membership that was Republican.[73]

It is easy to imagine that Republican attendees of the NWPC's first organizing convention in 1971 may have balked during the keynote address when speaker Paula Page evoked Malcolm X and Karl Marx, and called on the NWPC to campaign for an immediate end to the war in Vietnam and for free health care for all.[74] Indeed some Republicans seem to have initially dismissed the fledgling organization as Democratic-controlled or, worse, run by "kooks."[75] Yet Republicans hoped their presence would have what they viewed as a moderating influence on shaping the direction of the organization. As Jill Ruckelshaus later put it to a skeptic in the Montana Federation of Republican Women, "It is imperative to the success of the Caucus that Republican women remain active and contributing members, otherwise the Caucus simply becomes one more organization of radical ideas."[76] A number of Republican women came to take leadership positions in the NWPC, and in 1975 the NWPC elected African American Republican Audrey Rowe to be the organization's president. Yet Republicans were still a minority in the NWPC, which seemed to instill in them a preference for a separate organization.

A more immediate catalyst for forming a Republican feminist organization was disappointment with the RNC's recent rejection, in March 1975, of what organizers of the Republican Women's Task Force considered to be "any effective monitoring" of the components of the 1972 changes to Rule 32.[77] The rule changes heralded as a major victory for feminists in 1972 were in danger of becoming essentially meaningless in the absence of any kind of enforcement. The Rule 29 Committee had initially proposed that states set up "positive action" committees to co-ordinate state efforts at implementing the new rules and review compliance. Questions arose as to how compliance would be enforced and what the role of the RNC in that enforcement would be. Under a compromise proposed by party moderate Margaret Heckler and supported by "staunch conservative" Pete Domenici, the RNC would have been able to encourage states to submit "positive action" plans for review and comment but could not have *compelled* states to do so. However, under Heckler's proposal, a state's failure to develop a plan and make a good-faith effort to comply with Rule 32 could have been used as grounds for a delegate challenge at subsequent conventions. Heckler's compromise was approved by the Rule 29 Committee in December 1974 but rejected by the RNC in March 1975, after a campaign against the plan led by Clarke Reed.[78] As the Rule 32 debates had galvanized the nascent GOP feminist movement in 1972, the RNC's rejection of what Republican feminists believed to be adequate enforcement led, in 1975, to the organization of a formal Republican feminist group within the NWPC.

At their initial meeting in 1975, Republican feminists formed the NWPC's Republican Women's Task Force, agreeing that Republican feminists needed their own "vehicle through which they could communicate and pressure the party to expand the role of women." This included encouraging and supporting women to seek delegate positions as well as monitoring "positive action" efforts of the state parties.[79] The RWTF, run from Washington by Pat Goldman, hoped to take advantage of a moment when the party was remaking itself and when feminism appeared to have broad appeal across the political spectrum. Although opposition to feminism was growing, Republican feminists viewed opponents as a vocal minority of extremists. Feminists insisted to GOP leaders that feminism's continued broad appeal meant that a Republican Party "which responds positively to [the feminist] movement *and* which takes the lead in fostering and supporting its goals can be the majority party in the future." Such a party would be aided by a progressive, national Republican women's organization (namely the RWTF) that would help reinforce the association of Republicanism and feminism for the "politically conscious woman."[80]

The founders of the RWTF shared several broad goals. They planned to use their organization to monitor the party's efforts to reach out to women. And they hoped to increase the participation of women in Republican Party politics by encouraging women to become convention delegates and candidates for public office.[81] Although Audrey Rowe spoke of the special needs of African American Republican women and declared the meeting to be important in "getting black women and Republican women working on the same goals," there is no evidence that the RWTF made race a special concern.[82]

Overall, the RWTF viewed working through the party as the means for achieving its ends and trained its members accordingly. The RWTF distributed a monthly newsletter with updates on policy concerns and state-by-state instructions on the procedures for becoming a delegate to the Republican Convention. In some states, including Arizona, California, Michigan, New Mexico, and Texas, women formed local task forces, in reaction to their frustrations when the local GOP did not respond to women's concerns, particularly the ERA.[83] The RWTF was never large; in 1975 it claimed a membership of around 1,500.[84] The bulk of the RWTF's work seems to have been carried out by a small number of committed women activists in Washington. Yet this core group also hoped to develop a national network of feminist, politically active, Republican women. Notably, among the founders of the Southern California Republican Women's Task Force was Maureen Reagan, who had, fewer than ten years earlier, supported Phyllis Schlafly in her fight with the NFRW. Reagan remained committed to her father's conservative views on government, taxes, and defense but now called herself a "women's liberationist" and championed the ERA.

RWTF members did not just target women inside the GOP. They also attempted outreach to the larger feminist movement. Indeed, they hoped their efforts could attract more women to the political process "through the Republican Party."[85] RWTF members believed that when they agreed to speak at feminist events they were playing a role in developing new Republicans by providing living proof that "Republican feminism" was a going concern. The RWTF reported that "[m]any of our members relate similar experiences: upon conclusion of their remarks at a non-partisan gathering, women come up to speak with them, beginning their remarks with a startled, 'I didn't know there were Republicans like you.'"[86] Members also noted on occasion that their involvement was helping to make feminism seem less radical.

Nurturing an association of Republicanism and feminism also involved reminding the public about the GOP's traditional support for women's rights. Republican feminists consistently presented a picture of their party as one with an activist tradition and a historic commitment to rights, to equality, and to women's rights in particular. And they had evidence with which to make their case. The GOP had been the Party of

Lincoln, after all. Much of the support for women's suffrage (although perhaps not as much as Republican feminists in the 1970s claimed) had been associated with the Republican Party in the early part of the twentieth century. The Republicans had been the first major party to endorse the ERA, and some of the fiercest opposition to the ERA and to the modern civil rights movement had traditionally come from Democrats. Indeed, as political scientist Jo Freeman notes, the GOP had, to that point, "provided a much warmer reception to women, and in particular those women actively working to promote women's rights, than did the Democratic Party."[87] In the 1970s Republican feminists touted the GOP's history of support for the ERA as evidence of the party's traditional links to women's rights. In truth, Republican platform support for the ERA (and Democratic platform support, which followed in 1944) had been of little consequence in the forties and fifties, as there was no broad movement supporting passage and little likelihood that the amendment would pass Congress. Yet to Republican feminists in the seventies, establishing this history of Republican support for women's rights was important to legitimating their own claims that they could be both Republicans and feminists. As Jill Ruckelshaus noted, the point of such historical references was "to reiterate our belief that activism and reform are a tradition within the Republican Party."[88]

Regardless of party histories, by the mid-1970s the new women's movement had acquired an association with the Democrats. This was not necessarily due to differences in how the Old Guard of either party viewed feminist concerns. Feminists in both parties encountered resistance, ridicule, and hostility from many of their partisan comrades. But the different traditions of the two parties made it easier for Democratic women to achieve influence. Jo Freeman has explored the contrasts in party cultures (contrasts that were seen in the parties' different approaches to reform) that led to these different strategies and results. Democrats, Freeman explains, were traditionally comfortable with the concept of politics as a coalition of competing interest groups and could therefore accommodate second-wave feminists in the party even when they did not agree with them wholly. The Democratic Party gave feminists a hearing in the 1970s because they could claim to represent American women.[89]

The culture of the Republican Party, however, was one that had historically discouraged expressions of group concerns, leaving little space for GOP feminists to make appeals to gender identity. In the GOP, political connections were more important than constituencies. Women earned the right to be heard not as representatives of women but as allies of those currently in power, which is why it was so important for NWPC feminists in 1972 to win the support of prominent party women. Needing to work within the system, Republican feminists had to have their allies in key positions.[90]

During the Ford years, they had those allies. Yet the hold Republican feminists had on the Grand Old Party was far more tenuous than they liked to believe, a fact that would become clear in 1976. That year, Ronald Reagan's strong challenge to President Ford revealed the strength of Republican conservatives and signaled a decline in the viability of Republican feminism.

GOING DOWN IN FLAMES

★ REPUBLICAN FEMINISM AND

THE RISE OF THE NEW RIGHT

While feminists may have briefly believed they could be a force in their party during the mid-1970s, their influence began to decline beginning around 1976. This was due partly to the rise of another Republican woman activist, Phyllis Schlafly, as well as to the general restructuring the party was undergoing. The rifts between Republican women were important aspects of the forces that were reshaping the party during the 1970s. The GOP's ideology and strategy were in flux during the heyday of Republican feminism. Those struggles initially had nothing to do with feminism or women's rights. But feminism (and the backlash against it) would soon complicate the battle lines drawn in the 1960s.

By 1972 the GOP already had undergone a decade of internal struggles between established party moderates and a new coalition on the party's right, with which Phyllis Schlafly identified. As the civil rights movement profoundly altered the American political landscape, the political parties refashioned themselves. Nixon had won the 1968 election in no small part due to his reliance on a "Southern Strategy" that sought to woo traditionally Democratic voters by suggesting he might slow the pace of black civil rights advancements.[1] Yet he also declared the GOP should be the Party of the Open Door, inspiring the movement to revise the party's Rule 32 in order to broaden and diversify the party's base. It was the Party of the Open Door that feminists believed would welcome them; it was the party of the Southern Strategy and the New Right, however, that ultimately carried the day.

★ When feminist concerns emerged as divisive issues within the Republican Party in the mid-1970s, the party was already factionalized. After Goldwater's defeat in 1964, party moderates believed they had been vindicated, and they successfully kept conservatives out of leadership positions in the RNC and in the House and Senate. However, Goldwater supporters did not disappear. Republican conservatives "roared back" in 1966, scoring important gubernatorial and congressional victories that year.[2] One of those victories went to California's new governor, Ronald Reagan, who had given a stirring address at the 1964 convention. The Goldwater wing of the party briefly threw itself behind Richard Nixon, but by the mid-1970s it had identified itself with Reagan. Although the Watergate scandal initially seemed to disproportionately hurt party conservatives, their forces remained well organized.[3] Those Reagan Republicans who would confront party moderates during the 1970s could trace their movement back to Goldwater's challenge to the dominance of eastern, Rockefeller Republicans in the early 1960s. Feminism and women's rights had not been among the issues that had separated Goldwater Republicans from the rest of their party in 1964. By the mid-1970s, however, these issues would be of critical importance.

Influential party strategists in the late sixties had concluded that the party could benefit by reaching out to certain traditionally Democratic voters (white southerners, Catholics, and working-class ethnics) who rejected many of the social transformations of the 1960s, particularly those associated with the civil rights movement and the anti–Vietnam War movement. This so-called "Southern Strategy" moved those in the party's Goldwater-Reagan wing to mix conservative positions on race, religion, family, and gender roles into the agenda of what came to be known as the "New Right." The New Right coalition was an attempt by a new generation of conservative leaders to merge supporters of conservative single-issue causes into a large political coalition. Although some leaders were active in the Republican Party, most of the New Right groups preferred to work independently of the GOP and its institutions.[4]

Social conservatives on the New Right, who promoted traditional roles for men and women as the foundation of a stable society and who viewed feminism as a threat to that foundation, rejected many of the feminist issues that struck Republican feminists as consistent with Republican principles. Concerns about gender among social conservatives were intensified after Congress sent the Equal Rights Amendment to the states for ratification in 1972 and after the Supreme Court handed down its 1973 *Roe v. Wade* decision legalizing most abortions. As the influence of social conservatives on the Republican right grew, opposition to feminism became one of its battle cries.[5] For antifeminists, *Roe* and the ERA were fundamentally linked, because they were both endorsed by feminists and seemed, to critics, to threaten their notions of family stability.

A key member of both the Goldwater movement of the sixties and the New Right of the seventies was Phyllis Schlafly. Indeed, Schlafly's political development illustrates how gender issues were incorporated into existing conservative politics in the 1970s. After her Federation defeat in 1967, Schlafly remained committed to mobilizing women on behalf of the issues that Goldwaterism had inspired—strong defense, anticommunism, and small government. In 1970 she ran for Congress a second time and was belittled by her opponent who intimated that she should be home with her children rather than meddling in political affairs.[6]

Although Schlafly had clearly experienced sexism while pursuing her political ambitions, she felt no affinity with feminism. Indeed, the newly emerging feminist movement seems not to have immediately registered on her political radar. She was dimly aware of the Equal Rights Amendment, initially believing that the ERA might be "mildly helpful."[7] Yet she had no particular interest in the amendment, preferring to focus on her work opposing détente and the Strategic Arms Limitation Treaty (SALT). In 1972, after a friend persuaded her to look into the issue, Schlafly concluded that the ERA was not innocuous, as she had initially assumed, but dangerous.[8] By October, she had founded STOP ERA, an organization that would play a critical role in halting the amendment's momentum. Schlafly's opposition to the ERA reflected her social conservatism. The ERA threatened to disrupt what she understood to be the proper functioning of families, in which men had authority over women. Schlafly was sincere in these arguments. But her opposition was also deeply rooted in the antistatist Goldwater movement. The ERA's second section, empowering the federal government to enforce the amendment's provisions, suggested an increase in federal power that was anathema to Schlafly's long-held antistatism. Fears that a powerful government, emboldened by an Equal Rights Amendment, would threaten traditional gender roles in families and make women sexually and economically vulnerable reflects what Kim Nielsen, in her work on antifeminists during the post–World War I Red Scare, has described as the "gendering of conservatism." In other words, ideological support for a "noninterventionist government" became conflated with the "preservation of private and social patriarchy."[9] Schlafly's hostility toward feminism also derived from the grass-roots resentment against political elites she had voiced so powerfully during the Goldwater campaign and in her own bid for the Federation presidency. In the seventies, organized feminists (which to Schlafly represented both the disruption of families and the enlargement of government) were prominent among the "elites" Schlafly targeted.

When Phyllis Schlafly organized the STOP ERA movement in 1972, she already had a following of trained female supporters on which to build. These were the women who had left the Federation to pursue Schlafly's agenda outside the constraints of the Republican Party.[10] Once she came out against the amendment, Schlafly's movement grew to include thousands of fundamentalist Protestant women who previously had not been involved in politics. After 1972 the number of people receiving the *Phyllis Schlafly Report* increased from 3,000 to 35,000. Schlafly's anti-ERA forces raised money, sent out mailings, held press conferences, and lobbied state legislatures against ratification of the ERA.[11] In her efforts, Schlafly was now clearly working outside the circle of the Republican Party (with which she continued to identify), forming an effective alliance with Democratic senator Sam Ervin of North Carolina, perhaps the ERA's best-known male opponent. Together Ervin and Schlafly helped build a powerful opposition movement that crossed party lines.[12]

According to Schlafly, Congress had only passed the ERA because a "noisy claque of women's lib agitators rammed" the amendment through. Women's liberationists, Schlafly argued elsewhere, supported the ERA because they "hate men, marriage, and children. They are out to destroy morality and the family."[13] Schlafly opposed the ERA on several grounds. From conservative legal scholar Paul Freund, Schlafly adopted the position that the ERA could eliminate separate public restrooms for men and women.[14] Schlafly further insisted that the ERA would mean women could be drafted for combat duty, that the ERA would eliminate laws protecting only women from sex crimes, and that the ERA, because it would require child support and alimony laws to be gender-neutral, would "wipe out the financial obligation of a husband and father to support his wife and children." Her arguments, like those of her ally Senator Ervin, were based on her own reading of an influential analysis of the ERA appearing in the *Yale Law Journal* in April 1971. According to Schlafly's interpretation, the ERA would mean that big government would take away women's special privileges and protections.[15] And Schlafly was quick to object to government moneys or Republican Party resources being used to endorse the amendment. She cried foul, for example, when Anne Armstrong, in early 1973, sent a letter on RNC letterhead to Republican state legislators urging them to vote for the amendment.[16]

While Phyllis Schlafly's independent organization took a clear position on the ERA, the National Federation of Republican Women's positions on feminism and the ERA remained more ambiguous. Divisions over strategy and political ideology between leadership and rank and file had long been a factor in the Federation. Tensions over those divisions were heightened during the 1967 battle for the Federation presidency between Schlafly and Gladys O'Donnell. Those tensions seem to have been further exacerbated by the ERA. Clearly there was overlap between some individual Republican women's clubs and Schlafly's followers. A December 1972 resolution passed by the Martha Washington Council of Republican Women, for example, stated its opposition to the ERA in language that closely mirrored Schlafly's own assessment of the *Yale Law Journal* article.[17]

On a Federation-wide level, it was another matter. Under Gladys O'Donnell, the Federation renewed its endorsement of the amendment.[18] But O'Donnell went further in her support than any Federation leader had in the past, personally campaigning for the ERA in the name of the Federation. O'Donnell kept club presidents updated on the Judiciary Committee hearings where she testified on behalf of the ERA, and encouraged them to contact their representatives in Congress on the matter. Along with the leaders of other women's organizations such as the General Federation of Women's Clubs, the Business and Professional Women, and the Women of the United Auto Workers, O'Donnell signed a petition in 1970 urging the House Rules Committee to order the ERA out of the Judiciary Committee.[19] Defining the ERA in the partisan terms likely to appeal to Federation members, O'Donnell warned Federation members that Democrats were scoring political points from Republican stonewalling and insisted that "[w]e cannot let the Democrats win the most powerful force in the electorate—the women!"[20] Her arguments were not merely about partisan advantage, however. In urging Federation members to campaign for the ERA, O'Donnell pointed out that "action for complete equality for women as a matter of simple justice is so urgent and reasonable, we hope you will be willing to go that last extra mile to complete . . . what was started by those [suffragists] over 100 years ago."[21]

O'Donnell's second term as Federation president ended in 1971. She went on to work briefly for the Environmental Protection Agency until her death in 1973. Although the Federation continued its official support for the ERA as long as the amendment remained in the party platform, O'Donnell's departure seems to have marked the end of the Federation's brief period of active support. This was partly because O'Donnell left

the Federation helm, yet it was also due to the fact that the ERA was itself becoming more contentious. O'Donnell's successor, Connie Armitage of South Carolina, had, at least by the time her term ended in late
1975, come out against the ERA and in favor of Ronald Reagan's bid to
wrest the 1976 Republican presidential nomination from the more moderate Gerald Ford.[22] While the Federation continued to endorse the ERA
officially, the issue was controversial. As early as 1972, clubs in Florida
were reportedly "adamantly opposed" to the ERA and were influencing
the state legislature on the matter.[23] And members of the Northern Division of the California Federation of Republican Women protested the
Federation's endorsement of the ERA in November 1975, saying they believed the Federation's official position conflicted with the views of the
general membership.[24]

When socially conservative Republicans like Schlafly and many Federation clubwomen attacked the ERA and the "women's lib agitators"
who supported it, they attacked a movement that included a number
of Republican women who were prominent in the party. Republican
women from a variety of backgrounds, who initially came together over
the desire to increase women's presence at party conventions, were galvanized by the resistance they encountered. Some Republican feminists
did have connections to the liberal, East Coast, Rockefeller wing of the
party that Schlafly had long denounced. Audrey Rowe Colom, Tanya
Melich, and Margaret Heckler, for example, did hail from the East Coast.
But this was not the case for all Republican feminists. Others had begun
their political work in the Midwest or Southwest, including Anne Armstrong (Texas), Mary Dent Crisp (Arizona), Rosemary Ginn (Missouri),
and Mary Louise Smith (Iowa). During Goldwater's 1964 campaign,
some future feminist leaders had indeed opposed the Arizona senator
in his bid to head the party's ticket. Tanya Melich had worked on Rockefeller's campaign and Elly Peterson had supported Michigan favorite
son George Romney. Mary Louise Smith, however, was unaligned during the primary race and, afterward, chaired the Arizona senator's Iowa
campaign. Mary Dent Crisp, like thousands of other political novices,
got her start in politics in 1964 when, at age thirty-seven, she was inspired by Barry Goldwater to volunteer for his campaign. And Maureen
Reagan supported Goldwater for president in 1964, her father, Ronald
Reagan, for governor of California in 1966, and Phyllis Schlafly for Federation president in 1967.

Indeed, Republican feminists represented a range of geographical
backgrounds, ideological factions, and ages within the party. The ranks

of Republican women committed to feminism would come to include women who were more politically and geographically diverse than Schlafly's characterizations would allow. Maureen Reagan, scion of the conservative governor of California, and Audrey Rowe, who had begun her political involvement in the voting rights movement in Mississippi and who worked for the National Welfare Rights Organization, were ideologically quite far apart. In the American two-party system, however, partisan identity did not mean ideological uniformity. Ruckelshaus and Rowe may have been liberals; Armstrong and Reagan certainly were not. For some Republican feminists, tradition, social networks, and family ties played a role in their partisan identity. Certainly this was the case for Jill Ruckelshaus, who married into a prominent Indiana Republican family, and for Mary Louise Smith, whose family and friends were mostly Republicans. For other GOP feminists, Republicanism came as part of a political conversion. Maureen Reagan described her attraction to the policies of Dwight Eisenhower as a child and her shock when she later learned that her father was a registered Democrat. In her autobiography, she took a certain delight in noting that she had converted to Republicanism before her father.[25] Anne Armstrong was also a former Democrat who switched to the GOP during Eisenhower's 1952 presidential campaign. Armstrong explained that when she was a Democrat she had believed that a "boost" from the government was the "best way to do good in the world." She later concluded, however, that the "best thing that government can do is to let people get on their own feet and make their own decisions."[26]

Republican feminists, then, were Republicans for different reasons. They also came to feminism via different paths. Audrey Rowe cited the gender discrimination she experienced in the civil rights and peace movements as having led her to feminism.[27] Elly Peterson pointed to the "many inequities" of her political career, including being asked by her party to run for a U.S. Senate seat in 1964 and then finding that the financial support she had been promised was not forthcoming.[28] Mary Louise Smith credited a librarian in Des Moines for recommending *The Feminine Mystique* to her in the early 1960s. Betty Friedan's book "exploded in [Smith's] consciousness." Not until 1972, however, would younger women in the party convince Smith that the new feminist movement was relevant to all women, even middle-aged, financially secure women such as herself.[29] Mary Dent Crisp described how her own commitment to feminism, which like Smith's began at the 1972 Republican convention, was intensified in 1977 after she and her husband divorced. Finding herself in the economically insecure position of displaced homemaker without work history, the issues of the women's movement became more personal and she became more intensely committed.[30] Maureen Reagan had an epiphany that occurred while she hosted a radio show in 1973. A liberal feminist who appeared as a guest on the program convinced Reagan that the positions she espoused were feminist ones and that she ought to join the movement. Reagan's earlier experiences as a battered wife may also have informed her feminism.[31] While the conservative Reagan proudly claimed the term "women's liberationist," the more liberal Jill Ruckelshaus insisted she wasn't a "women's libber," although she was disparagingly called so by critics. "I don't particularly like being called a women's libber or a radical activist," Ruckelshaus told one reporter, "because I don't feel like a radical anything."[32] In the eyes of her detractors, however, this Republican Party insider was exactly that.

The diverse ideological and geographic backgrounds of Republican feminists suggest an important point: debates about the new women's movement in the 1970s were not simply layered on to existing party factions. These debates were themselves, as Jo Freeman has proposed, an important part of what has led to realignment of the Republican and Democratic parties since the 1960s.[33] As Bobbie Kilberg noted during the 1972 fight over Rule 32, many of the supporters (male and female) of the "positive action" language were individuals who considered themselves to be conservatives in other policy areas.[34] The Rule 32 debates galvanized female supporters of an activist approach to opening the party from across the party's ideological spectrum and brought them in contact with committed feminists. The political activism of women on behalf of women's issues, and the resistance it engendered, were themselves profoundly disruptive.

If feminism brought together activists of diverse political backgrounds, a similar point can be made about antifeminism. Although Phyllis Schlafly had strong roots in the conservative Goldwater movement, STOP ERA national media chairman Elaine Donnelly did not. While still in her twenties, Donnelly worked on the national campaign's media coverage and did a considerable amount of public speaking and organizing as well. She also headed Michigan STOP ERA and directed its campaign to rescind Michigan's ratification. Donnelly, with her "soft brown eyes and cheerleader's smile," suggested that the ERA supporters did not recognize the breadth of the movement opposed to the ERA. "They seem to expect an older person," Donnelly noted, "unattractive, or square, a

STOP ERA. *Elaine Donnelly (center) believed she offered a picture of* ERA *opposition different from the stereotypes held by supporters. Here she is shown at the Republican National Convention, July 1980, with two unidentified allies. (Photos, box 1, Elaine Donnelly papers, Bentley Historical Library, University of Michigan. Photo by William Archie; used with permission from the* Detroit Free Press.)

Happier Times. Governor George Romney and Elly Peterson helped build a moderate GOP in Michigan in the 1960s. In 1980, Peterson would part ways with Romney over his public opposition to the ERA. Here the two are shown at a dinner in her honor, 1964. From left to right, Lenore Romney, George Romney, Elly Peterson, William "Pete" Peterson. (Republican Party, Michigan, box 21, EP papers. Reproduced by permission from the Bentley Historical Library, University of Michigan.)

religious fanatic, someone who bakes cookies all day. . . . I don't think I fit." Of a different generation than Schlafly, Donnelly was raised as a Democrat and had voted for Hubert Humphrey in 1968. According to Donnelly's own words, it was her first meeting with Schlafly in 1973 that solidified the younger woman's initial opposition to the ERA and eventually led her to shift many of her other political positions to the right. Donnelly was not a party person, however, and not until the 1980s would she serve in the Republican Party formally.[35]

George Romney provides another example of how debates over feminism complicated the process of political realignment. As governor of Michigan in the 1960s, Romney was the standard-bearer of the Michigan GOP's moderate wing. He was an important political mentor to Elly Peterson, who was also a close friend of the governor and his wife, Lenore. In the winter of 1979–80, however, Romney, an active member of the Mormon Church, spoke publicly against the ERA, insisting that the movement had attracted "moral perverts." These statements from her longtime political ally provoked profound distress for Peterson. Romney continued to identify strongly with Republican moderates, was highly critical of Ronald Reagan during the 1980 primaries, and appears to have been deeply hurt by the rift with Peterson resulting from his ERA statements. Peterson and her colleagues, meanwhile, found it painfully ironic that Romney now seemed to be allying himself with Phyllis Schlafly on the ERA issue (even quoting her favorably). After all, Romney had been among the "me-too" Republicans Schlafly had attacked in A Choice Not an Echo during the sixties.[36] In any case, Romney's position on the ERA now placed him at odds with fellow party moderates and further suggests the intricate ways in which gender issues intersected messily with the broader process of political realignment in the GOP.

★ That realignment, signaled by the shift in fortunes of the Republican Right, was firmly in the works by 1976. Conservative Republicans, who had backed Nixon only to be disenchanted by major aspects of both his domestic and foreign policy, were even less happy with Gerald Ford. Ford's sins were topped by his choice of Nelson Rockefeller to serve as his vice president, but also at issue were various policy positions, including his support for the ERA.[37] Mutterings about the formation of a third party seem to have convinced Ford that he could not take conservatives for granted in 1976, and he made gestures toward that wing of his party (dumping Rockefeller from the ticket, for example). Conservatives, meanwhile, began to line up behind Ronald Reagan, who decided to take advantage of Ford's vulnerability and seek the Republican presidential nomination. Promising to make major cuts to the federal budget, to roll back détente, and to replace Henry Kissinger, Reagan presented a serious enough challenge during the primaries that Ford was not assured of the nomination going into the convention in August.

As the 1976 presidential campaign season approached, there were also signs that feminists in the GOP were losing influence. Yet feminists hoped the party's right wing could at least be convinced by pragmatic arguments to reach out to feminists for the sake of the party. Polling data suggested, for example, that Betty Ford was an asset to her husband among a public that strongly endorsed her "consistent and unbending advocacy" of the ERA and the women's rights movement.[38] Yet Ford also received plenty of negative mail regarding her activism.

The Republican Women's Task Force geared up for the 1976 presidential convention, hoping to build on gains made in 1972. Instead it found itself battling to hold its ground as Reagan supporters mounted a serious challenge to the incumbent Ford's nomination. Republican feminists were generally pleased with Ford, despite his personal opposition to abortion. For feminists, Betty Ford's activism on behalf of their causes added to her husband's appeal. Most Republican feminists were allied with Ford's campaign (Maureen Reagan was an exception) and lent their names and their time to promoting his election. Ford tapped feminist Elly Peterson to organize special voter groups for the campaign. The sixty-two-year-old Peterson, who had twice served as RNC assistant chairman and had also headed the Michigan GOP, came out of retirement to take this position with the campaign.[39] The Ford camp, however, was backing away from feminist concerns in an effort to stave off the Reagan challenge. His managers concluded that in order to defeat Reagan for the party's nomination, Ford would have to take a strong position against abortion.[40]

Even before the convention, many Republican feminists were "angry" at the treatment they believed the party was according them.[41] Despite protests from the League of Women Voters and feminists within the GOP, the Republican National Committee chose to hold its nominating convention in Missouri, a state that had not ratified the ERA. And only after complaints from the RWTF did the RNC make efforts to ensure the number of women participating in the convention as delegates and speakers would be comparable with that of 1972.[42] Noting that, as of May, the proportion of women delegates selected for the convention was actually down from 1972, Pat Goldman of the RWTF remarked that this was a "sad commentary on the lack of commitment" by the party to the principles established in Rule 32.[43] Tellingly, these disappointments occurred while Mary Louise Smith was the helm of the RNC, indicating the difficulties Smith faced in serving both feminism and the party. The RWTF worked with Democratic feminists to publicize the failures of both parties to address the issue adequately. By the time the actual convention was held, the Republicans did manage to achieve a very modest increase (to 31.5 percent) in the number of female delegates over 1972.[44]

RWTF members, deliberately attired in heels and dresses, were an active presence at the 1976 convention and managed to maneuver important victories. While the party leadership still supported the ERA, opponents had begun mobilizing within the party. Reagan delegates (of whom Phyllis Schlafly was one) were a strong presence at the convention. Schlafly called on the Platform Committee to take a stand against President Ford's "intimate involvement with the radical women's lib movement" and oppose the ERA.[45] Republican feminists, meanwhile, testified in favor of the amendment and its compatibility with Republicanism. Maureen Reagan noted in her testimony before the Platform Committee that she had become a Republican because of its support for "individual liberty and responsibility." No one had ever told her, she continued, "that the individual was only male, and so I believed in equal opportunity and I still do, which brings no conflict between my political philosophy and my belief in women's rights."[46]

In the end, other delegates supporting Maureen Reagan's father led the Platform Committee's Subcommittee on Human Rights to take no position in the platform on the ERA. Republican feminists, however, were able to muster their allies on the full Platform Committee and narrowly retained wording in the platform that supported the ERA. Knowing they lacked the votes to win a fight on abortion, however, feminists did not openly fight the addition of an antiabortion plank.[47] RWTF members also asked the Rules Committee—in the spirit of Rule 32—to grant College Republicans and the Black Republican Council voting representation on the RNC, a measure that was not adopted.[48] Although Ford won the nomination, Reagan's challenge clearly demonstrated the president's weak position. Reagan delegates were able to rewrite significant parts of the GOP platform and to facilitate the nomination of conservative Bob Dole as vice presidential candidate.[49] Indeed, Reagan Republicans had achieved much in 1976 and would be prepared to capitalize on their advances in 1980.

Ford became the Republican nominee but lost the general election. His defeat meant that allies of feminists would lose influence in the party. Republican feminists held out hope that they could continue to affect party policy through pragmatic arguments about the danger of alienating women voters. And they had some successes. After Jimmy Carter defeated Ford in November, Mary Louise Smith resigned her position as RNC chairman according to custom. The RNC chose Bill Brock as Smith's replacement. To the satisfaction of the RWTF, Brock, who would use his office to reach out to black, urban, and female voters, named one of the RWTF's own members, Mary Dent Crisp, to serve as his cochair.[50] Brock likely viewed Crisp as an excellent choice for this position because she not only was supported by party feminists but also had historic ties to Goldwater conservatives. Crisp appeared to be a unifier, but she would raise the ire of the New Right. From her position as RNC cochair, Crisp was outspoken on behalf of women's rights and would help persuade the RNC to support a three-year extension for ERA ratification when it became apparent that the amendment was in trouble.[51]

Bipartisan Feminism. Former Republican Party official Elly Peterson (left) and Democrat Liz Carpenter (right) served as cochairs of ERAmerica. *Here they address the National Education Association annual meeting in 1978. (*ERA *Activities, box 21,* EP *papers. Reproduced by permission from the Bentley Historical Library, University of Michigan.)*

Having succeeded in keeping the ERA in the GOP platform and one of their own in the RNC leadership, RWTF feminists could retain at least the illusion that feminists were an influential voice in the GOP. They understood, however, that they were losing ground—not only in terms of support for their issues among party leaders but also in public perception of the GOP's relationship to feminism. Moderate Republicans (including ERA supporters like Charles Percy of Illinois) were defeated during the 1978 midterm elections. Organized grass-roots opposition to the ERA and to feminism was swelling and becoming firmly associated with the GOP due to the activism of Phyllis Schlafly and others on the party's right. It was increasingly difficult for Republican feminists to persuade the public that feminism and Republicanism were compatible. At the NWPC convention in September 1977, Mary Louise Smith did her best to counter perceptions that "Republican feminist" was a contradiction. Smith insisted that "Phyllis Schlafly is *not* a role model for Republican women. While it's true that some of us may be homemakers, or law students, or Midwesterners, or articulate, or even blond and bouffant, for most the resemblance ends there."[52] And Elly Peterson certainly did her part in promoting the fact that Republicans supported the feminist movement when she served, from 1976 to 1978, as cochair (along with Democrat Liz Carpenter) of ERAmerica, an organization founded to promote the ERA in states that had not yet ratified.

It was a blow for Republican feminists like Smith, then, whenever leaders of their party publicly maligned all feminists and allied themselves either openly or implicitly with Schlafly. One highly publicized occasion where the Republican Right denounced feminists was the National Women's Conference held in Houston in 1977. The National Women's Conference was a federally funded event intended to develop a national women's agenda as a follow-up to the United Nations International Women's Year in 1975. The National Women's Conference had originated with an executive order signed by President Ford, and Congress had approved funding for the event. Ford then named Jill Ruckelshaus to preside over the commission established to conduct the conference. Individual states held their own conventions to establish priorities and select delegates to Houston. Many Republican women, at the state and local level, devoted themselves to planning and carrying out the National Women's Conference. Although Jimmy Carter replaced Ruckelshaus with Democrat Bella Abzug after his election, Republicans remained heavily involved, giving the conference (and the women's movement itself) what Republican Tanya Melich believes was a "centrist cachet" and a "mainstream legitimacy" that it might have lacked had Republicans not been involved.[53]

The National Women's Conference proved controversial when right-wing critics began attacking both the use of public moneys to fund the event and its dominance by ERA supporters. Antifeminist women, organized by Phyllis Schlafly, came to Houston and held a "pro-family" counterrally. They claimed to represent ordinary housewives who did not want equal rights and who believed they had been ignored by conference organizers.[54] The media covered this battle between women extensively. But a battle for the image of the Republican Party was also being waged.

At the National Women's Conference, the American feminist movement showed itself to be broad and diverse enough to include the out lesbians, union members, and "bouffanted" Republicans who sat together in sisterhood, however uneasily. Betty Ford, Mary Louise Smith, and scores of other GOP feminists attended the conference in Houston. Despite high-level support from moderate Republicans, however, others on the party's right attacked the National Women's Conference and its participants. During the conference, Congressman Robert Dornan (R.-Calif.) denounced conference attendees in a highly publicized statement as "sick, anti-God, pro-lesbian, and unpatriotic." The chairman of the local Houston Republican Party, Jerry Smith, referred to the delegates as a "gaggle of outcasts, misfits, and rejects." Mary Louise Smith, knowing how such public statements could damage the cause of Republican feminism, tackled Dornan and Smith in the press. "[W]e have many, many women in the Republican Party," she insisted. "These kind of remarks are going to make it difficult for them to be Republicans, if they are to be seen as what the Republican Party thinks about these issues."[55]

Privately, Republican feminists had to acknowledge that the image they were promoting—of a Republican Party open to feminism—was losing its basis in reality. Increasingly, Phyllis Schlafly was coming to represent, in many people's minds, the Republican Woman. This image made Republican feminism seem more and more like an oxymoron.

★ In 1980, as the presidential nominating conventions approached, Republican feminists faced a dilemma. In 1976 they had been able to mobilize their forces against Reagan delegates and hold their ground on some critical issues. In 1980, when it was clear Reagan would be the Republican nominee, feminist allies among delegates would be in the minority. Feminists knew they would lose platform fights over the ERA and abortion.

Some considered staying home. Reagan had stated his positions clearly, and there seemed little room for compromise. Others, however, including Ronald Reagan's feminist daughter Maureen, hoped Reagan could at least be persuaded to set aside ideology and accept pragmatic arguments for retaining a platform palatable to feminists. In the end, a contingent of women affiliated with the RWTF went to the convention in Detroit, preferring to "go down in flames" rather than concede their party to people they considered extremists.[56]

It was a dramatic convention, at least as far as feminists and their foes were concerned. While the party had smoothed over many of its ideological divides in recent years and hoped for a harmonious convention, the battles over women's issues threatened to disrupt Republican unity. The National Organization for Women staged a march echoing the suffrage demonstrations at the Republican National Convention sixty years previously. Supporters of the march included representatives of a broad range of organizations, including the Republican Women's Task Force. Demonstrators carried purple and gold banners designed to "replicate those used in suffrage parades in the 1900s." Promotional material from NOW deliberately linked the 1980 march in Detroit to the National Woman's Party's demonstration in Chicago during August 1920, noting that one of the banners displayed in that earlier event read "No self-respecting woman should wish or work for the success of a party that ignores her sex—Susan B. Anthony 1872." The intended relevance for 1980 was clear.[57]

Despite the efforts of NOW and Republican feminists, Reagan delegates succeeded in dominating the proceedings, nominating their candidate for president, and approving a platform explicitly at odds with many of the goals of Republican feminists.[58] In a great blow to Republican feminists, the platform did not endorse the ERA. While the platform expressed support for the principal of "equal rights and equal opportunities for women," it declined to support the ERA, insisting that the amendment's fate was a state matter. The platform supported a constitutional ban on abortion, as well as the appointment of federal judges who would uphold such a ban. The platform also expressed opposition to affirmative action. Long unhappy with Mary Crisp, conservatives forced her out of her position as RNC cochair. At the convention, Crisp voiced strong criticisms of the convention's position on women's issues. "[W]e are reversing our position and are about to bury the rights of over 100 million American women under a heap of platitudes," she declared.[59] This seasoned Republican official walked out of the convention and did not campaign for Reagan that fall. Instead, she went to work for the third-party challenge of former Republican John Anderson, whose positions on feminist issues were more to her liking.[60]

Among her colleagues, Crisp stood out for her boldness in publicly breaking with the party. Other prominent Republican feminists chose party loyalty. Mary Louise Smith, in her remarks to the convention, acknowledged the disagreements within the GOP but insisted the party was like a family in that disagreements could make all members "stronger and more respectful of each other."[61] Although the press feasted upon their defeats, a group of prominent Republican feminists did what they believed was best for their party and put a positive spin on events in Detroit. Clearly they understood that a great setback had occurred, but publicly they focused on what they had been able, nonetheless, to accomplish. Their presence and their lobbying efforts in Detroit, they claimed, had averted a more disastrous plank explicitly opposing the ERA. Although they lost ERA support in the platform, they were able to win planks pledging support for individual women's issues, reform of gender inequities in the tax code, and social security reform. A group of Republican feminists met with Ronald Reagan in Detroit and, as they described it publicly, found him open to their concerns. They extracted promises that he would enforce federal antidiscrimination law and would consider appointing women to high office, including the Supreme Court.[62] (Indeed, the efforts of Republican feminists to elicit these pledges from Reagan in 1980 surely contributed to his decision to appoint Sandra Day O'Connor to the Court in 1983.)[63] Although NOW criticized as accommodationist those women who met with Ronald Reagan, his daughter Maureen described the gains of Republican feminists at Detroit as no less than a "major political coupe [sic]."[64] Privately, however, Mary Louise Smith admitted that feminists "hadn't gotten very far" in their discussions with the Republican nominee.[65]

Rather than abandon the party they had actively supported (some of them for decades), a group of Republican feminists agreed to help Reagan that fall. Anne Armstrong served as cochair of Reagan's campaign. And Mary Louise Smith agreed to the campaign's request that she head up a Republican Women's Policy Advisory Board (WPAB) to advise the campaign on women's issues. Other prominent feminists, including Bobbie Greene Kilberg, Margaret Heckler, Audrey Rowe, and Maureen Reagan followed Smith's lead and joined the WPAB. Yet not all were persuaded by those who advocated working within the Reagan campaign. Michigan feminist Helen Millikan was dismayed that Smith had accepted the position, suggesting that it would have been "magnificent" if Smith "somehow had turned it down." And although Smith asked Elly Peterson to serve on the WPAB, Peterson declined.[66]

Throughout the fall campaign, the WPAB made suggestions for policy statements regarding women's issues, advised the campaign on ways to eliminate sexist language from campaign materials and speeches, and encouraged the campaign to engage more female speakers. While the creation of the Women's Policy Advisory Board may have played a role in convincing the RWTF not to endorse John Anderson, the Reagan campaign seems to have embraced few of the board's substantive recommendations.[67]

Why did these Republican feminists remain in a party that seemed to reject not only issues they valued deeply but also a whole movement that was dear to their sense of who they were? One reason was practical. These women were party activists whose experience in politics was rooted in party work. As Mary Louise Smith was fond of saying, her contacts and her resources were all within the GOP. If she were to leave the party, she would have lost her access to the one institution she could best influence. All of her political training taught her that she should remain in her party and use what clout she had to fight for changes in party policy from within. And Maureen Reagan argued that if American women were to reap real political benefits, they would need to have savvy representatives "on both sides of the aisle."[68] The WPAB certainly hoped (wrongly, for the most part, it turned out) that its efforts to elect Reagan would secure positions of influence for its members after the election.

Not only were their practical experiences, their skills, and their resources grounded in the GOP; these feminists were also philosophically Republican. Their views on economics, defense, and the power and size of government placed them at odds with Democrats on many important issues. To say they were feminists is not to say they were liberals on other issues. As Bobbie Kilberg put it, "I'd be flabbergasted if any of the Republican friends I have would consider voting for Jimmy Carter."[69] Kilberg, Mary Louise Smith, and others repeatedly pointed out that they were not just feminists, but were also taxpayers, consumers, and businesswomen. In those capacities, they continued to find their interests best served by the GOP. "The economy is a woman's issue," Smith insisted. "The Republican Platform is interested in overregulation, the burdens that keep businesses from being successful."[70] Republican feminists articulated a feminist agenda that appeared dangerously radical to the party's right, but which they viewed as akin to those Republican principles they also advocated.

In 1980 those Republican feminists who continued to work for Reagan had to redefine Republican feminism. Almost all of the members of Reagan's Women's Policy Advisory Board were supporters of the ERA, affirmative action, and abortion rights (alternative views were represented by STOP ERA member Elaine Donnelly who was brought belatedly onto the WPAB because of complaints about its ideological makeup). Yet these issues couldn't be discussed in the campaign for Reagan. In crafting appeals to women voters, then, the WPAB repeatedly argued that Carter's economic policies had caused inflation and high interest rates, which were hurting women. In other words, the WPAB began redefining Republican feminism in terms of Republican positions on economic issues—taxation, interest rates, regulation, and economic growth.[71] Certainly Republican women had always addressed such issues, but they were moved to the foreground in 1980 because there was little else Republican feminist campaigners could discuss. The GOP had forfeited any claim to be in support of what were widely considered the most important feminist issues of the day—ERA and abortion rights. During their work for the Reagan campaign, these women diluted the feminist language they had used unapologetically in the 1970s.

★ The 1980 Republican National Convention may have "effectively marked the end of meaningful bipartisanship for the American women's movement."[72] Yet the dire warnings Republican feminists issued to their party—that failure to support feminist issues would spell doom for the party—proved unfounded in the 1980s. Certainly Reagan's nomination, the 1980 Republican platform, and the association of the GOP with Phyllis Schlafly alienated many women voters. Reagan beat the unpopular Carter 51 percent to 41 percent overall (Independent John Anderson earned 7 percent). Among women, however, Reagan won by a much narrower margin of 47 percent to 45 percent. A year later, polls showed this exodus of women voters to the Democrats to have persisted.[73] Republican Kathy Wilson, chair of the NWPC, commented in 1981 on the party's loss of support among women using the pragmatic logic that had guided Republican feminists in the seventies: "If Reagan doesn't wake up to women, I think the Republican Party's time in the sun is going to be brief."[74]

Wilson was wrong. She overlooked a simultaneous voter shift that made the GOP's loss of women's support seem almost inconsequential. At the same time the GOP was losing support among women, it was gaining among white men. Many traditionally Democratic men who felt alienated by their party's embrace of women and minority concerns were switching parties. Democrats hoped to capitalize on the Republican weaknesses with women voters in 1984 by nominating Geraldine Ferraro as vice president. Republican analysts argued that their opponents were missing the point. Democrats should focus their concern on their candidates' poor performance among men, said Susan Bryant, a GOP campaign consultant. "They do so badly among men that the fact that we don't do quite as well among women becomes irrelevant."[75]

Wilson also made the common mistake of assuming that a "gender gap" would benefit feminist candidates (or harm antifeminist candidates). During the 1980s, commentators (particularly those advocating women's rights) interpreted the gender gap as a reflection of women's dislike of Reagan's positions on the ERA and abortion. That was an inadequate picture, as has been demonstrated by those social scientists who have examined the gender gap more carefully. Indeed, Republican strategists in the 1980s were effective in analyzing women's voting with great precision in order to target those women who were most likely to support Ronald Reagan. In 1980, 1984, and 1988 a majority of American women voted for Republican presidential candidates, despite the party's rejection of feminism.[76]

By 1984 Republican feminists had become marginalized in their party. At the Republican National Convention that year, they were able to play little role in the proceedings and the platform's approach to women's issues was "dictated" largely by Schlafly and her followers.[77] Although the GOP had rejected feminism, the party was increasingly open to women in leadership positions. Over the next ten years, Republican women successfully worked their way into the higher ranks of the party. For the most part, these leading women did not identify themselves as feminists and certainly did not play the role of linking the party to the feminist movement that leaders such as Smith, Peterson, and Ruckelshaus had played in the 1970s. In 1988, when the *Washington Post* profiled women working for the Bush campaign, it found that while the party had made significant progress in moving large numbers of women (including the then thirty-four-year-old Mary Matalin) into the "upper-middle ranks" of the Bush campaign, these were women who espoused no connection to the feminist movement or even to gender identity. "Their job is to do the job, they say," according the *Post*'s reporter, "rejecting explicitly the idea that they should speak exclusively to women or about 'women's issues.'"[78] This new breed of female Republican operatives, it seemed, rejected not only the feminist consciousness of the RWTF but also the female consciousness of Schlafly's Eagle Forum.

Certainly the gender gap that commentators observed during the Reagan years persisted into the 1990s. In every presidential election since 1980, female voters have been more favorable to Democratic candidates than have men. What that gap means—and, consequently, how it translates into party strategy—is less clear. The so-called gender gap masks issues of race, class, marital status, social views, and religious identity. Low-income women and minority women, for example, vote so overwhelmingly Democratic as to give the impression that gender is far more important to American women's voting than it actually is.[79] In the extremely close 2000 presidential election, in which Republican George W. Bush lost the popular vote but won the Electoral College, the votes of white women were evenly split between the two candidates. (Democrat Al Gore, meanwhile, won the votes of almost 100 percent of black women, but only slightly more than a third of those of white men.)[80]

Making it all the more difficult to discern the meaning of the gender gap in voting behavior are the ways in which the parties themselves have become gendered in popular discourse. In 1995 Republican senator Trent Lott (Miss.) described the differences between the two parties in the gender metaphors of pop psychology. Lott noted that Republicans and Democrats think differently, "just like men and women . . . I like to think we are the party of Mars."[81] Many Americans apparently feel the same way. An important part of what has fueled the shift of men away from the Democratic Party in recent years has been, arguably, the tremendous success Republicans have had in *feminizing* liberalism and the Democratic Party. Although the war on terrorism has certainly fed this process, it is not simply the product of a post-9/11 world. Beginning during the Reagan years, Republicans undertook the rhetorical work of linking liberalism to "weakness, dependency, and helplessness."[82] According to this configuration, a feminized Democratic Party weakens America by coddling its citizens and advocating misguided international cooperation to solve global problems such as terrorism; the more manly Republicans encourage citizens to be self-reliant and defend America by being tough and unwavering. So successful has this caricature of American politics been that in 2004 even a war veteran like Senator John Kerry found it necessary to prove he was not a "girlie man" by, for example, embarking on a highly publicized hunting trip in a key swing state.[83]

★ Where do feminists now fit into the "Party of Mars"? Certainly the Republican Party and the American political landscape shifted considerably in the decades following the rise of second-wave feminism, rendering feminism increasingly incompatible with GOP politics. Republican women engaged with a wide range of feminist activities in the 1970s. Although many Republican women had their consciousness raised, challenged traditional family relations, and spoke out against rape and domestic violence, it was the goal of legal equality that caught their imaginations and to which they devoted their organizational energies. The movement for equal rights and equal opportunity, epitomized by focus on passage of the ERA, was the aspect of the new women's movement that Republican women responded to most positively in the 1970s and that they believed their party could accept as conforming to party traditions. Even if party leaders did not concur that there were philosophical connections between Republicanism and women's rights, feminists hoped that the GOP would accept pragmatic arguments for reaching out to the feminist movement. The locus of power within the GOP had shifted by the late 1970s, however, and such pragmatic appeals (long associated with party professionals) found fewer supporters.

Certain feminist issues of the seventies—especially those based on arguments about equal rights, equal treatment, and privacy in reproductive choices—could be comfortably formulated as Republican issues. Federally funded childcare and affirmative action were perhaps more problematic fits, but most Republican feminists supported these policies as well. This indicates their openness to arguments that new kinds of federal action were required in order to extend the Republican Party's traditional support for the principal of equal opportunity.[84]

In the 1980s party officials who adhered to such positions, like Mary Louse Smith, placed themselves in conflict with stated party policy. Smith was rewarded for her loyalty to Reagan by an appointment to the U.S. Commission on Civil Rights. But her support for affirmative action and school busing to achieve racial integration conflicted with the positions of the Reagan administration, and she was later removed from the commission.[85] The National Federation of Republican Women in the 1980s was more in line with party ideology on promoting the advancement of underrepresented groups than was Smith. In a 1987 pamphlet issued on the occasion of the organization's fiftieth anniversary, the NFRW noted proudly the recognition and success women had earned within the Republican Party in the years since women had achieved suffrage. There were lessons to be learned, the pamphlet declared, from those Republican women who fought for suffrage, "overcame obstacles" and "earned positions of authority" in party politics—all "without the help of quotas."[86]

This picture succeeded more as an endorsement of the Reagan-Bush administration's opposition to affirmative action (and as a denunciation of Democratic Party efforts to bring more women into party affairs) than as an accurate description of the historical process by which women had achieved "positions of authority" within the Republican Party. After ratification of the Nineteenth Amendment in 1920, prominent Republican women had, in fact, negotiated with men on the Republican National Committee to initiate rule changes explicitly intended to create positions on the RNC for women and to increase the presence of women at the party's nominating conventions. At times Republican women even worked to have similar rule changes at the state level mandated by law. Women quickly concluded that the equal opportunity created by suffrage would not translate into equal access to the decision-making bodies of the Republican Party without creating mandated female positions. Women in the party continued to press for such changes in the following decades, culminating in the fight over Rule 32 in 1972.

The NFRW statement may not have held up under historical scrutiny. But it was a sign of the direction in which marginalized Americans would need to go to claim a place within the radically individualist GOP of recent years. Women and minorities today are welcomed and even celebrated by the Republican Party so long as they adhere to an individualist ethos that makes no claims about group rights. The views and experiences of "multicultural conservatives" (as Angela Dillard calls female, minority, and gay conservatives) who insist they "want to speak only as Americans, as individuals," are touted as proof of the relevance of Republican individualist rhetoric.[87] The female Bush operatives interviewed by the *Washington Post* in 1988 illustrate this point. As one put it, "I don't believe in women's issues. I just don't believe in that term. I think it's patronizing and narrow."[88]

The Republican Party of the 1980s and 1990s has been one whose emphasis on individualism disputes what Republican feminists in the 1970s had accepted: that certain Americans face persistent, structural barriers because of group identity that politics must recognize and address. Republican feminists had usually come to this conclusion because of the difficulties they experienced as educated, middle-class women attempting to pursue political, or professional, goals. At the 1972 convention, they had observed with frustration the debates over Rule 32 in which witnesses stood before the "all-white, almost all middle-aged and almost all WASP" Rules Committee and testified that the Republican Party was not in need of reform.[89] Women's frustrations with their more intractable party comrades, as well as their contact with the broader feminist movement, drew them to support not only changes to Rule 32 but the principles behind affirmative action for women and minorities as well.

In this sense, the Republican feminists of the 1970s differ from what linguist George Lakoff has referred to as today's "conservative feminists." Conservative feminists, Lakoff argues, reject the traditional conservative worldview that placed men over women, that discouraged women from pursuing careers, or that restricted women's sexual expression. In this sense they are feminists. Yet, like other conservatives, they place great emphasis on personal moral strength and reject the notion that stereotypes have "social causal powers," or that government action may be required to address these alleged "social causes."[90] The support that Republican feminists in the seventies gave to the ERA, to reforms designed to broaden their party, and to affirmative action, clearly distinguishes them from this brand of conservative feminism, which, while not entirely new, appears now to be gaining ground.

When feminist influence diminished after 1980, the Republican Party lost not only the voices of those urging the GOP to embrace the new women's movement. Because Republican feminists insisted that fulfilling Republican traditions of equal opportunity required government in some cases to actively expand and protect group rights, they were also among those more likely to urge the party to reach out to racial minorities. The waning of Republican feminism, therefore, also signaled broader impediments to creating a diverse Republican Party.

One should not exaggerate the commitment of Republican feminists to the concerns of black Americans (nor equate those concerns exclusively with support for affirmative action). Republican feminists in the seventies, like most other second-wave feminists, privileged concern about gender discrimination over race and class issues. But their support for "positive action" to open up party politics, government, and economic life to previously excluded groups suggested the possibility of alliances between this core group of female Republican stalwarts and minority activists, creating the potential for a bloc within a broadening Republican Party. The silencing of these Republican feminists after 1980 is one reason why the GOP, nearly forty years after the civil rights achievements of the 1960s, continues to appear hostile to or out of touch not only with the concerns of feminist women but with many minority groups as well.

In the seventies, women across the political spectrum—from Bella Abzug to Maureen Reagan—could understand themselves to be part of one feminist movement, even when they were of different political parties, disagreed on many political issues, and even disagreed about the meaning of feminism itself. Twenty-five years after Reagan's election, feminism itself has ceased to be a broad social movement as it was during its seventies' heyday. Party politicians today tend to view organized feminists as one of a number of special interest groups that are securely within the Democratic camp. Democrats still must retain certain feminist platform planks, such as support for abortion rights, in order to secure key parts of the party's base. Yet even Democratic candidates seem reluctant to talk about women's issues with much force.

And in the wake of its 2004 losses there are signs that the Democratic Party is actually reevaluating its position on abortion. Republicans, on the other hand, have conceded organized feminism to the Democrats and regularly include platform planks intended to appease social and religious conservatives.

During the 1990s, moderate, feminist Republicans watched in dismay as their party shifted ever more to the right and ever further away from the concerns of Republican feminists. Many Republican feminists, including Smith, Melich, and Crisp, continued to work to change the party's positions on women's issues, particularly abortion. Mary Louise Smith spoke out until her death in 1997 against her party's positions on women's issues and civil rights, its general drift away from its moderate wing, and its embrace of the Christian Right. Smith, who remained a loyal Republican throughout those years and believed she was doing what was best for her party, was nonetheless shunned by key party leaders during the 1990s.

Elly Peterson, on the other hand, despite her long-standing party credentials, increasingly moved away from partisanship (although not from politics). In 1982, when the Michigan Republican Party placed ERA and abortion rights opponent Richard Headlee on the ticket for governor, Peterson and dozens of other "prominent Republican feminists" associated with the Michigan RWTF publicly endorsed Headlee's Democratic opponent, James Blanchard. Blanchard won the election, becoming the first Democratic governor of Michigan in twenty years. During the campaign, Peterson was careful to state that neither she nor any of her allies were leaving the GOP. "They just do not feel that Richard Headlee represents the Party," Peterson declared.[91] This statement echoed the definitions of partisanship that independent Republicans in the twenties like Alma Lorimer had espoused. (A year later, one of Peterson's colleagues on the Michigan Republican Women's Task Force described the position of Republican feminists more bluntly: "We have not left the Party—IT has left us. And it is our hope that one day soon, it will return.")[92]

Unlike the independent crusader Lorimer, Peterson's political background was that of a party professional. Her ties to the party organization were indisputable, having devoted years of her life to serving as a party official. Yet by the early 1980s, she was moving away from partisan loyalty and in 1984 was calling herself an "independent."[93] In recent years, other GOP feminists have loosened their ties to the GOP, sometimes through dramatic public gestures. Tanya Melich, for example, published a book in the 1990s about the "Republican War against Women" in which she described her party's efforts to win the allegiance of social conservatives as no less than a strategy of misogyny.[94]

In addition, moderate Republican women in 1992 established a fundraising organization, called Republican WISH List (Women in the Senate and House), to support Republican women running for elected office. In 2001–2 it raised more than $750,000 for female candidates, the majority of whom won their seats.[95] Because WISH List endorses only candidates who support abortion rights, it explicitly defies the Republican platform and presents a challenge to those on the party's right. It is a challenge that does not seem to be registering particularly loudly today. (Indeed, during the 2004 campaign season, WISH List contributions were only around $250,000.)[96] Yet even WISH List's moderate successes are evidence that there still exists within the Republican Party a space to espouse moderate feminist politics.

Republican feminists like Mary Louise Smith, Mary Dent Crisp, and Maureen Reagan may have been correct when they argued during the 1970s that there was an inherent compatibility between traditional Republican philosophy and rights-oriented feminism. But it took a particular confluence of events to give that argument force: during the heyday of Republican feminism, the Republican Party was weakened by scandal, the leadership of the party was in the hands of moderates, and feminists themselves had the political credibility of being linked to a mass social movement. None of those factors is in place today. Republican feminism is not entirely moribund. And the GOP will continue to have to confront that fact as it carefully balances its need to mobilize its base of Christian conservatives while also winning the support of suburban women who are often critical swing voters. Yet while its distance from feminist concerns may still create some problems for the GOP, it is doubtful that Republican feminists will enjoy a revitalization of influence any time soon.

Conclusion

As Republican Party women divided over feminism in the 1970s, they made individual choices about what form their work (either for or against the movement) would take and about what their ongoing relationship to the party would be. Phyllis Schlafly and Mary Louise Smith were but two of these women whose choices can help illuminate the history of women's relationship to the party. Although Schlafly and Smith positioned themselves at opposite ends of the feminist spectrum within the Republican Party, they had much in common. Both Smith and Schlafly were midwesterners, Smith hailing from rural Iowa and Schlafly from an Illinois suburb of St. Louis. Both were college-educated and had married professionals (Smith's husband was a doctor; Schlafly's a lawyer). Both raised large families, Smith having had four children and Schlafly six. And, significantly, each had channeled much of her partisan work in the 1950s through the Republican women's club movement. (Schlafly had also run for Congress, something Smith never did.) In the 1960s, their political activism moved along different paths, however. In 1960 Schlafly became president of the Illinois Federation of Republican Women and by 1964 was serving as an officer in the National Federation of Republican Women; Smith, in 1963, used the statewide contacts she had gained through her work with the Iowa Council of Republican Women to be elected Iowa national committeewoman and thereby became a member of the Republican National Committee, eventually serving as RNC chairman. Smith's leadership within the RNC distinguished her from Schlafly and surely bolstered her faith in working within the party for change.

The stories of Smith and of Schlafly are both part of the larger, sometimes paradoxical, process by which women achieved a place in American politics. In the seventies, the "sweetheart of the silent majority," Phyllis Schlafly, organized and led those women opposed to the Equal Rights Amendment and to feminism in general. Schlafly represented the tradition of independent-minded Republican clubwomen who were wary of blind partisanship, who were suspicious of the way party politics functioned and who resented their own powerlessness within that system. Although Schlafly disparaged the feminist movement, the movement's development was a crucial aspect of the political circumstances that had empowered her.

Mary Louise Smith, ten years older than Schlafly, served as the first woman chairman of the Republican National Committee and embraced second-wave feminism. Smith, in contrast to Schlafly, was in a long line of Republican women who had espoused party loyalty and who had faith that working from within the party would bring results. Once the party distanced itself from feminism, many of those feminists who remained staunch Republicans were those, like Smith, who were intensely committed to the logic of partisan loyalty. Phyllis Schlafly and Mary Louise Smith came to represent different models of Republican womanhood, different views on feminism, different conceptions of party loyalty, and different examples of how women could be politically effective. Each helped shape the way the party responded to the new women's movement.

Schlafly and Smith displayed tendencies that had competed within the Republican women's club movement over the decades since 1920. When women first won the right to vote, they were outsiders in a political system whose rules and values many did not understand or appreciate. As party outsiders in the 1920s, Republican women were believed both to embody and to lack certain political traits that distinguished them from men. Men argued that women did not comprehend the game of politics or the necessity of compromise and party loyalty. Women's political motivations appeared to many observers to arise primarily from moral and religious considerations, rather than the considerations of pragmatic politicking. Women (or so it seemed to those Republicans predisposed to distrust them) could be uncompromising about the issues they cared about, and therefore their support of the party's candidates was unpredictable.

Initially Republican women organizers described these traits as strengths. Many hoped women would maintain a high ground above the wheeling and dealing demanded by practical party politics that seemed not to serve the public interest. Yet male party leaders saw women's tendency to reject compromise and vote according to their ideals and conscience as a threat to the political status quo. Republican women were not promoting partisanship, as men in the party understood it, but were discouraging party loyalty. From the onset of women's suffrage, male party leaders established "party loyalty" as a test of women's political maturity (despite the fact that men themselves often disagreed bitterly over party matters). Even with the establishment of the RNC-funded National Federation of Women's Republican Clubs, some individual club-women would chafe at the restrictions on their activism proposed by advocates of party loyalty.

Phyllis Schlafly, although initially a committed party worker, eventually rejected the arguments for strict party allegiance, while retaining her Republican identity. In this way she was similar to "purists" in both parties, who had begun demonstrating increasing clout beginning in the 1960s.[1] For Schlafly, women's political power meant the ability to have women's distinct voice heard. This distinct voice was one that honored, validated, and protected women's traditional roles and their position in the family and society. Women's political power, furthermore, was properly exercised altruistically for the benefit of family, community, and country, rather than "selfishly" (as Schlafly understood feminists' calls for power).[2] In party renegade Schlafly one hears the echo of some suffragists, as well as certain Republican women activists of the 1920s. Schlafly may have been concerned with a very different set of issues than women like Alma Lorimer, but she embraced a similar political style. This style stressed women's political independence, their differences from men, and a notion of politics as a female crusade. Through the Republican women's club movement and individuals like Mrs. E. G. Goddard, Vere de Vere Adams Hutchins, the Vigilant Women for the Bricker Amendment, and Phyllis Schlafly, the political style of independent Republican women of the 1920s survived over the next decades. That style, developed by female progressives in the wake of suffrage, would come to be channeled on behalf of more-conservative political causes.[3]

While Schlafly's renegades organized outside the party to achieve their aims, Republican feminists like Mary Louise Smith in the seventies worked to reconcile their feminist goals with their commitment to a strategy of working within the party. They had a clear feminist agenda and intended to use their political skills, positions, and contacts to advance it. They did so, however, within the framework of the party itself. Like Marion Martin and Bertha Adkins in earlier decades, these women worked inside male-dominated organizations and sought respect and cultivated alliances within them. Like Martin and Adkins, they pushed for greater representation of women in political decision making. Unlike Martin and Adkins, they did so within the context of a revived women's movement.

In the late 1960s and early 1970s, most feminists were not enamored of party politics. Neither party's Old Guard was particularly receptive to handing over a share of power to women. Yet the Democratic Party quickly became associated with feminism, while the Republican Party did not. Democratic feminists were confrontational in their demands at the 1972 and 1976 conventions. Republican feminists, however, preferred to work behind the scenes, to avoid public stances that were too controversial, and to preserve party harmony.[4] This was particularly true during Reagan's 1980 campaign when Republican feminists on Reagan's Women's Policy Advisory Board agreed not to discuss ERA and abortion. While other GOP feminists, such as Elly Peterson and Mary Dent Crisp, found that strategy naive or otherwise unacceptable, those who adopted it hoped their allegiance would be rewarded.

The strategy of using loyalty as a way to gain influence for women in the party had been promoted in the past most explicitly by Marion Martin. Believing that both Republican women and the party would benefit from such an approach, Marion Martin in the late 1930s and early 1940s encouraged clubwomen to conform to male understandings of partisanship, to downplay the idea that women had unique contributions to make or interests to pursue, and to avoid suggestions of inherent antagonisms between men and women. Martin insisted that women did not seek status as a separate interest group in the party but merely wanted an equal chance in politics as individuals. Martin's strategy for empowerment emphasized the importance of women acquiring party loyalty and discipline in order to gain acceptance by men in the party. Although subsequent Federation leaders did more than Martin to stress women's uniqueness and their strong convictions, party loyalty continued to come first. The power of this imperative is suggested by clubwomen such as Dottie Elston and Gladys O'Donnell, who, while Goldwater conservatives, remained committed to party loyalty and harmony after many of the Goldwater backers were shunned from leadership. It was also embodied by Mary Louise Smith who spoke out until her death in 1997 against her party's positions on women's issues and civil rights, its general drift away from its moderate wing, and its embrace of the Christian conservatives. Smith remained a loyal Republican throughout those years and believed she was doing what was best for her party. For her efforts, she was essentially denied any influence in the party during the 1990s, most notably in 1992 when she was excluded from the Republican National Convention.

Although adhering to different agendas and different models of GOP womanhood, Schlafly and the Republican feminists shared one perspective on women in politics in the seventies. It was time for women to move beyond performing the "housework of government" as their main contribution to partisan politics. This housekeeper role had emerged out of efforts to socialize women into partisan politics following suffrage. Women in the 1920s had wanted to make party politics part of the day-to-day lives of new women voters. Women's Republican clubs combined political education with traditional social activities to make women comfortable with politics. To educate women in particular, clubs brought speakers and held meet-the-candidate events from which male voters could benefit as well.

Marion Martin noted in her efforts to organize a women's auxiliary that it was necessary to give women substantive tasks and projects in order that they would feel useful and therefore committed to the party. She did not want clubs to revert to holding card parties or fashion shows and instead encouraged the party to utilize clubwomen as party volunteers. Yet these efforts often met with resistance from party regulars and women themselves who feared women were unqualified or unreliable. This changed after the war, when Elizabeth Farrington developed the School of Politics and began seriously to train women as precinct workers. The party, finding that women volunteers could be useful, developed a strategy of grass-roots organizing that depended on women's "housework of government." Yet as the party began to rely on women's volunteer services, women found themselves stuck in the roles they had created for themselves. By the 1950s it was clear that political socialization had become an end in itself, rather than a means to political influence. Clubwomen were being socialized into political roles that defined them largely as the hostesses and housekeepers of partisan politics. Not surprisingly, some women soon grew frustrated with this arrangement.

While that frustration inspired Mary Louise Smith to work her way up through the RNC, Phyllis Schlafly formed her own organization outside the party to mobilize around the conservative issues she supported. Although Schlafly's followers still performed volunteer political work, this work was no longer on behalf of the party per se. Instead, these women's energies were devoted to campaigning only for candidates who supported their own agenda, an agenda that came to center on antifeminism but which also, especially for Phyllis Schlafly, included a broader spectrum of conservative positions. Republican feminists, for their part, sought greater, more substantive involvement with party leadership and decision making in their efforts to promote a feminist agenda within the party. Although often quite critical of their party, they generally believed working within it to be the best way to achieve their goals. They also participated in feminist organizations, notably the Republican feminist organization RWTF. For both Schlafly and the Republican feminists, the old model of political housework appeared to offer little reward by the 1970s.

By the early 1980s it certainly seemed that Phyllis Schlafly had won the battle over feminism in the party (even if she and her allies had not succeeded in convincing the party to pursue vigorously all aspects of their social conservative agenda).[5] As the party underwent realignment and moderates were marginalized, feminists lost the allies in positions of power that had been crucial to getting their issues addressed. Political feminism, which for a time had supporters in both parties, became, by the 1990s, one of a number of interest groups firmly within the Democratic Party. Antifeminists increased their influence in the party during the 1980s. Consequently, they were able to facilitate the end of the GOP's tolerance for feminist positions on ERA and abortion and were quite successful at "purg[ing] liberal feminist women from the Party."[6] While it is tempting to conclude that Schlafly and her followers now offered the dominant model of Republican womanhood, a third model was emerging, one that would prove increasingly powerful. By the late 1980s, the party was trumpeting those women who displayed little gender consciousness at all but who instead championed their ability to succeed as individuals. Although these women typically rejected the gender conservatism of Schlafly's antifeminists and supported some feminist goals in principal, they rejected appeals to gender solidarity as well as arguments that public policy could address inequality.

Between the social conservatives and the "laissez-faire" conservatives that Rebecca Klatch has analyzed, Republican feminists were simply squeezed out.[7] The Democrats became the party associated with feminism. The voices of Republican feminists—women who found their moderate feminism compatible with a commitment to traditional Republican stances based on limited government, individual freedom, and equal opportunity—faded from the national debate. The concession of feminist issues to the Democratic Party may go largely unquestioned today. Yet it is worth asking whether Republican dreams of a bipartisan feminism were ever realistic. Answering that question requires drawing attention to a noteworthy feature of both the Republican Party and feminism in America: that they are both linked to a liberal tradition. Indeed, GOP feminists' expectations about the viability of Republican feminism, as well as their ultimate failures, point to the unusual nature of American feminism and its relationship to American politics.

The Republican Party, although today the more conservative of the two major parties, has roots different from those of conservative parties in other Western democracies. The Republican Party in the United States has a historical connection to individual rights and to reform movements, unlike European conservatism, which is rooted in traditions of skepticism about popular sovereignty and of a desire to preserve social hierarchies.[8] Growing out of a commitment to the northern ideology of "free labor" before the Civil War and to the principles of African American citizenship in the postbellum period, Republican Party philosophy from the outset emphasized the rights of the individual, equal opportunity, and self-help. However unevenly applied, these aspects of party ideology mean that the GOP traditions have allowed for the inclusion of a critique of women's unequal access to public life and to institutions of power. More specifically, Republican ideology could support a women's rights agenda of the kind associated with the rights-based, liberal feminism that became the dominant form of feminism in the United States. The activism of Republican feminists in the seventies was an attempt to realize that possibility.

Comparing the form that second-wave feminism took in the United States with the women's movements that emerged in other countries around the same time helps to illuminate what it was about American feminism that made it compatible with America's "conservative" political party. When American feminism reemerged as a political force in the sixties, it came from several sources. Multiple groups created what scholars have usually identified as two fairly distinct sectors of the movement: a "liberal" (or "women's rights") sector and a "radical" (or "women's liberation") sector. Each presented profound departures from prevalent views of women but engaged in different strategies, analysis, and political style.[9]

The "rights-based" sector originated among professional women affiliated with President Kennedy's Commission on the Status of Women in the early 1960s. These women were intimately aware of the multitude of examples where American law discriminated against women, and they sought legislative solutions, in the public arena, to correct those problems. These activities were conducted against the backdrop of the black civil rights movement and the growing consensus among Americans that laws treating blacks and whites differently were inherently unequal. The model of the black civil rights movement—the idea that "separate" could never be "equal"—provided, as Myra Marx Ferree has argued, a context for the development of feminist analysis, goals, and strategies that was particularly American. In the United States, the feminism that became dominant in the seventies drew on analogies to the black civil rights movement.[10] It emphasized equal treatment of the sexes before the law and equal access to public institutions, including arguments that the courts should treat sex distinctions in the law with the same scrutiny applied to racial distinctions.[11] The black civil rights analogy, so important to American feminism, was absent in other countries where feminist movements were emerging at the same time.

The feminism that came to dominate in West Germany, for example, grew out of the student, peace, and environmental movements. It was permeated by claims that women were more peaceful and more centered in nature than men, and was relatively tolerant of laws that provided different treatment for women when those differences were presented as privileges (such as protective labor laws, maternity policies, and exemption from military service). West German feminism emphasized patriarchy as the primary form of oppression and viewed men and women as possessing inherently conflicting interests.[12]

Views akin to these were most certainly part of the full range of American feminism. What is sometimes called the "radical" sector of second-wave feminism (or "women's liberation") emerged out of the student civil rights, anti–Vietnam War, and New Left movements. For women's liberationists, feminism involved a commitment to transforming American economic and social systems and to a class analysis of women's oppression. For some women this led to a celebration of women's differences from men. Women's liberationists offered important new ways of understanding women's subordination. Indeed, the different strains of American feminism did not exist in isolation. Many of the techniques and analytical strategies invented by women's liberationists found their way into the broader feminist movement, including the practice of "consciousness-raising"; a focus on transforming the nature of marriage, sexual, and familial relationships; and an emphasis on the problem of male violence. By participating in the feminist movement and by attending feminist events like the National Women's Conference, Republican feminists were exposed to these arguments and ideas. And for some women, these issues had profound personal relevance. By and large, though, what most appealed to Republican women and what they believed were compatible with GOP traditions were the issues of equal treatment.

Some organizers of Republican women, such as Marion Martin, had always seen connections between women's rights and the equal opportunity and the individualist rhetoric of the Republican Party. Equally devoted to the interests of the GOP, Martin maintained that the best means for women to gain power and influence in the party was to emulate male political styles and prove their competence, usefulness, and party loyalty. Although Martin did not describe herself as a feminist, she represents a tradition of women's rights activism within the party from which Republican feminists in the seventies were descended.

The sense that the party had a tradition of supporting equal rights stemmed, to a large extent, from its history as the Party of Lincoln, which had abolished slavery and passed the Reconstruction Amendments, granting rights of citizenship to African Americans after the Civil War. That legacy created a powerful identification among African Americans with the Republican Party that lasted for seventy years. Indeed, in the 1920s, African American clubwomen were extraordinarily active on behalf of the Republican Party, seeking to use the political process to pursue full citizenship for African Americans. Decades before the largely white National Federation of Republican Women became known for the essential volunteer work it performed during campaigns, black clubwomen formed the National League of Republican Colored Women, a national organization that performed similar work. Unlike Federation women in the fifties, however, the NLRCW in the twenties had a clear political agenda and consciously sought to shape the party in terms of its vision. That this once-vital constituency of Republican voters no longer exists is due to the profound way that issues of racial empowerment have reshaped the political parties and American politics in the late twentieth century.

The women's movement of the 1970s has also remade American politics. It remade the GOP in particular, by empowering both feminists and antifeminists within its ranks, revealing significant conflicts over the meanings of Republicanism, of gender, and of power. Although many of the specific debates between women were new, the conflicts did have a long history that dated back to the specific choices newly enfranchised women made regarding the best way to participate in party politics.

Suffragist and National Woman's Party advocate Alva Belmont felt women should have avoided party politics altogether and continued to organize separately as women. Some women who embraced Republican Party politics in the twenties feared that if women organized separately within the party they would perpetuate their own exclusion. Others rejected the compromises required of efforts to enter the party's decision-making bodies. One can disagree with the choices Republican women made, yet still understand their reasoning and appreciate the particular dilemmas that stemmed from their choices. As Joan Scott argues, the history of feminism is not the history of women making correct or incorrect choices among available options. Rather, it is the history of women (and some men) "grappling repeatedly with the radical difficulty of resolving the dilemmas they confronted."[13]

If dividing into separate clubs limited women's role in party politics, that division was crucial in enabling women to enter party politics at all. Republican clubs allowed women to ease into the masculine world of party politics by embodying a political style that embraced women's organizational traditions, linked partisanship to popular understandings of women's civic and moral responsibilities, and confirmed women's importance to politics. In their clubs, Republican women nurtured an identification with the Republican Party that fused with their identity as women and as citizens. The movement's growth indicates that it was a success in developing partisanship among thousands of women and in turning them into lifetime voters who felt a personal responsibility to be involved with government. During a time when few women ran for or held public office and when few women had influence within the party, the Federation gave Republican women a means of political involvement, and a perception that their party and their government belonged to them.

In bringing more women into the center of party decision making or in providing a forum for women to express group concerns, however, the club movement had less of an impact. Articulating a women's voice in the party was not necessarily the movement's purpose, however. Certainly some early independent leaders, such as Alma Lorimer, intended women's Republican clubs to define and support women's concerns within the party. Yet when the RNC decided to form and fund a women's organization in 1937, it understandably chose a woman for the task who, while a champion of women's advancement, was also committed to party loyalty and to an understanding of equal opportunity that denied women had interests distinct from men's. As Jo Freeman notes, the Federation's status as a party auxiliary ensured that it would not be a vehicle for expressing group concerns to the party.[14] Whether Republican clubwomen would have found more influence if they had remained isolated and independent, however, is doubtful. Martin was correct that women in the thirties who wanted to engage with party politics would have to adapt to party rules and traditions. But doing so was not a panacea. Certainly women like Smith, Ginn, and Crisp were firmly integrated into party leadership by the seventies. But it was necessary for them, from those positions, to make considerable compromises.

In the end, neither clubwomen nor party women pursued a strategy that was without its problems. What was required for women finally to become a force in the party was the context of the social movements of the 1960s and 1970s (both on the left and the right) that brought women into public life in significant numbers, turned gender issues into matters of great political importance, and demonstrated that ordinary citizens working outside traditional political institutions could transform party politics. The Republican Party—and American politics as a whole—is still struggling with the implications.

NOTES

ABBREVIATIONS

In addition to the abbreviations used in the text,
the following source abbreviations are used in the notes.

AA papers
  Anne Armstrong Papers, Nixon Presidential Materials, White House Central
  Files: Staff Members and Office Files, National Archives, College Park,
  Maryland

AL papers
  Anna Cochrane Lomas Papers, Iowa Women's Archives, University of Iowa
  Libraries, Iowa City

BA interview
  Bertha Adkins Interview with John T. Mason Jr., 18 December 1967, Columbia
  University Oral History Project. Transcript at Dwight D. Eisenhower
  Presidential Library, Abilene, Kansas

BA papers
  Bertha S. Adkins Papers, Dwight D. Eisenhower Presidential Library, Abilene,
  Kansas

BCR papers
  B. Carroll Reece Papers, Archives of Appalachia, East Tennessee State
  University, Johnson City

BG papers
  Barry Goldwater Papers, Arizona Historical Foundation, Hayden Library,
  Arizona State University, Tempe

CF papers
  Carrie S. Jorgens Fosseen Papers, Minnesota Historical Society, St. Paul

DC scrapbooks
  League of Republican Women of the District of Columbia Scrapbooks,
  1944–49, Private Collection of the National Federation of Republican Women

DCP papers
  Don C. Pierson Papers, Special Collections Department, University of Iowa
  Libraries, Iowa City

ED papers
  Elaine Chenevert Donnelly Papers, Bentley Historical Library, University of
  Michigan, Ann Arbor

EP papers
  Elly Peterson Papers, Bentley Historical Library, University of Michigan, Ann
  Arbor

FCW papers
  F. Clifton White Papers, Rare and Manuscripts Divisions, Carl A. Kroch
  Library, Cornell University, Ithaca, New York

HH papers
  Herbert Hoover Papers, Herbert Hoover Presidential Library, West Branch, Iowa
ICRW records
  Iowa Council of Republican Women Records, State Historical Society of Iowa,
  Iowa City
JHM interview
  Jane Hamilton Macauley Interviews with Author, 15 October 1996, 12 August
  1997
JHM scrapbook
  Jane Hamilton Macauley Scrapbooks, Private Holdings of Jane Hamilton
  Macauley
JW papers
  Jessica Weis Papers. Women's Studies Manuscript Collections from the Schlesinger
  Library, Radcliffe College. Series 2: Women in National Politics, Part B:
  Republicans (Bethesda, Md.: University Publications of America, 1994)
L-H files
  Patricia Lindh and Jeanne Holme Files, Gerald R. Ford Presidential Library,
  Ann Arbor, Michigan
LHH papers
  Lou Henry Hoover Papers, Herbert Hoover Presidential Library, West Branch,
  Iowa
LWH papers
  Republican National Committee, Office of the Chairman (Leonard W. Hall)
  Records, Dwight D. Eisenhower Presidential Library, Abilene, Kansas
LWVI records
  League of Women Voters of Iowa Records, Iowa Women's Archives, University
  of Iowa Libraries, Iowa City
Martin alumni file
  Alumni Files (1935), Marion Martin, Fogler Library Special Collections,
  University of Maine, Orono
MCS papers
  Margaret Chase Smith Papers, Margaret Chase Smith Library, Norwood
  University, Skowhegan, Maine
MLS papers
  Mary Louise Smith Papers, Iowa Women's Archives, University of Iowa
  Libraries, Iowa City
MM scrapbooks
  Marion Martin Scrapbooks, 1931–70, Private Collection of the National
  Federation of Republican Women
NFRW records
  National Federation of Republican Women Records, Dwight D. Eisenhower
  Presidential Library, Abilene, Kansas
NFRW-PR
  National Federation of Republican Women Records, 1970–72, 1986–87,
  Private Collection of the National Federation of Republican Women

NHB papers
Nannie Helen Burroughs Papers, Library of Congress, Manuscripts Division, Washington, D.C.

RG papers
Rosemary Lucas Ginn Papers, Western Historical Manuscript Collection, University of Missouri, Columbia

RPP I-a, I-b
Papers of the Republican Party. Part I: Meetings of the Republican National Committee, 1911–1980. Series A: 1911–1960; Series B: 1960–1980 (Bethesda, Md.: University Publications of America, 1988)

RWP scrapbooks
Republican Women of Pennsylvania Scrapbooks, Historical Society of Pennsylvania, Philadelphia

SW files
Sheila Weidenfeld Files, Gerald R. Ford Presidential Library, Ann Arbor, Michigan

TCRW scrapbook
Tama County [Iowa] Republican Women Scrapbook, Private Collection of Joyce Wiese

TDRW scrapbook
Third District [Iowa] Republican Women Scrapbook, Private Collection of Joyce Wiese

WJCC records
Women's Joint Congressional Committee Records. (Washington, D.C.: Library of Congress Photoduplication Service, 1983.

INTRODUCTION

1 Reference to a political party can mean the formal party committees, the candidates who run as members of that party, citizens registered as belonging to the party, those who vote for the party's candidates in a given election, or those who identify generally with the principles or symbols of a particular party. For the women in this study, the meaning of "partisanship" was often disputed.

2 Jo Freeman argues that Democrats were more likely to pursue the party strategy, Republicans the club strategy. J. Freeman, *A Room at a Time*, 85. The party strategy may have attracted fewer Republican women than did the club strategy, but it remained important to the Republican story, providing an alternative model of women's partisanship that many clubwomen explicitly rejected.

3 Gustafson, Miller, and Perry, *We Have Come to Stay*, xiv.

4 On party professionals, see Ranney, *Curing the Mischiefs of Faction*, 140–41.

5 On party purists, see ibid., 139.

6 On the Woman's Christian Temperance Union, see Bordin, *Woman and Temperance*; Marilley, "Frances Willard and the Feminism of Fear."

7 Morone, *Hellfire Nation*.

8 The National Federation of Women's Republican Clubs was formed in 1938. In

1952, the name was changed to the National Federation of Republican Women. Throughout the book, I usually refer to the organization as the Federation.

9 See Gustafson, *Women and the Republican Party*; Edwards, *Angels in the Machinery*; Varon, *We Mean to Be Counted*; Gustafson, Miller, and Perry, *We Have Come to Stay*.

10 See F. Gordon, *After Winning*; Nichols, *Votes and More for Women*; Cott, *Grounding of Modern Feminism*, 106–14; Andersen, *After Suffrage*; J. Freeman, *A Room at a Time*; Harvey, *Votes without Leverage*; B. Cook, *Eleanor Roosevelt*, 338–80; Ware, *Partner and I*; Perry, *Belle Moskowitz*; Miller, *Ruth Hanna McCormick*; Tilly and Gurin, *Women, Politics, and Change*; Gustafson, Miller, and Perry, *We Have Come to Stay*; Brodkin, "For the Good of the Party."

11 Notable exceptions include J. Freeman, *A Room at a Time*; Harvey, *Votes without Leverage*; Baker, "'She Is the Best Man on the Ward Committee'"; Brodkin, "For the Good of the Party."

12 Works on these conflicts that I have found especially helpful include Brennan, *Turning Right in the Sixties*; Cole, *Roosevelt and the Isolationists*; Graham, *Encore for Reform*; Hicks, *Republican Ascendancy*; Himmelstein, *To the Right*; Reinhard, *Republican Right*; Scher, *Politics in the New South*; Sherman, *Republican Party and Black America*; Weed, *Nemesis of Reform*; Weiss, *Farewell to the Party of Lincoln*; Rae, *Decline and Fall of the Liberal Republicans*; Gould, *Grand Old Party*.

13 See, for example, Blee, *Women of the Klan*; McEnaney, "He-Men and Christian Mothers"; De Hart, "Gender on the Right"; Mathews and De Hart, *Sex, Gender and the Politics of ERA*; Jeansonne, *Women of the Far Right*; Nielsen, *Un-American Womanhood*; Benowitz, *Days of Discontent*; Klatch, *Women of the New Right*; Nickerson, "Domestic Threats"; Nickerson, "Moral Mothers and Goldwater Girls"; Nickerson, "Women, Domesticity, and Postwar Conservatism."

14 Nielsen, "Doing the 'Right' Right," 169.

15 See, for example, Rae, *Decline and Fall of the Liberal Republicans*; Reinhard, *Republican Right since 1945*; Gould, *Grand Old Party*; Weed, *Nemesis of Reform*.

16 Cott, "Across the Great Divide." Quotation is from p. 154.

17 Young, *Feminists and Party Politics*, 37.

18 Gould, *Grand Old Party*, 426.

CHAPTER I

1 "Suffragists Show Fight at Chicago," *New York Times*, 12 June 1920; NWPC, *Republican Women Are Wonderful*, 5–6. For recollections of the weather during the convention, see Laas, *Autobiography of Emily Newell Blair*, 201.

2 Kraditor, *Ideas of the Woman Suffrage Movement*, 235–38; Cott, *Grounding of Modern Feminism*, 58–59.

3 "Suffragists Show Fight at Chicago," *New York Times*, 12 June 1920. Soon it became clear that a Supreme Court ruling preempted Tennessee's state law that would have required an intervening election between ratification by Congress and ratification by the Tennessee legislature. Because Tennessee was a Democratic-controlled state, NWP leaders then threatened to take

action against Democrats as well until the thirty-sixth state ratified. "Women Threaten Third Party Bolt," *New York Times*, 22 June 1920. In August, Tennessee did become the thirty-sixth state to ratify. Subsequent Republican literature would point out that, of those thirty-six states ratifying the Nineteenth Amendment, twenty-nine were Republican controlled, while eight of the nine states rejecting ratification were Democratic controlled. Good, *History of Women in Republican National Conventions*, 5.

4 "Suffragists Jeer at Chairman Hays," *New York Times*, 19 May 1920; "Republicans Urge Suffrage Action," *New York Times*, 2 June 1920.

5 On the Women's National Republican Association, see J. Freeman, *A Room at a Time*, 35; Gustafson, *Women and the Republican Party*, 73–74, 142–45; Gustafson, "Partisan and Nonpartisan," 6–8.

6 J. Freeman, *A Room at a Time*, 81.

7 "Women Organize to Press Demands," *New York Times*, 7 June 1920.

8 On the formation of the Republican Women's Executive Committee, see Transcripts of Republican National Executive Committee meeting, 13 February 1918, frames 216–17, reel 1, RPP I-a. See also J. Freeman, *A Room at a Time*, 82.

9 James P. Louis, "Mary Garrett Hay," in James, *Notable American Women*, 2:163–65; Perry, "Mary Garrett Hay and the Republican Party."

10 Ralph A. Stone, "Ruth Hanna McCormick Simms," in James, *Notable American Women*, 3:293–95; Miller, *Ruth Hanna McCormick*.

11 Miller, *Ruth Hanna McCormick*, 125.

12 See Riley, *Am I That Name?*, 67–95, especially p. 68.

13 "Mrs. Belmont Begs Women Not to Vote," *New York Times*, 6 July 1920. Belmont, a wealthy socialite and outspoken feminist, became president of the NWP in 1921. For biographical material on Belmont, see Christopher Lasch, "Alva Belmont," in James, *Notable American Women*, 1:126–28; Kraditor, *Ideas of the Woman Suffrage Movement*, 267–68. Historian Estelle Freedman has agreed with those suffragists who were wary of entering the parties, arguing that the decline of separate female institutions after 1920 and women's increasing emphasis on attempts at integration into the world of men led to a decline in feminist consciousness and thus a decline in radicalism. Freedman, "Separatism as Strategy." See especially pp. 521–26.

14 "Opposes a Woman's Party," *New York Times*, 26 August 1920. Catt supported women's involvement with the League of Women Voters, which was founded in February 1920 as the successor organization to the National American Woman Suffrage Association. Initially the LWV had a vast agenda encompassing issues of women's legal status, various items of progressive legislation relating to women and children, and peace issues. See Cott, *Grounding of Modern Feminism*, 86.

15 Quoted in Lemons, *Woman Citizen*, 90. See also "Topics of the Times," editorial, *New York Times*, 21 September 1920.

16 NWPC, *Republican Women Are Wonderful*, 7; "Women Organize to Press Demands," *New York Times*, 7 June 1920; "Women Not Content but Remain Loyal," *New York Times*, 10 June 1920.

17 "Democratic Women Predict Victory," *New York Times*, 15 June 1920.

18 These advertisements are located in *Woman Citizen* 5 (11 September 1920): 399; 5 (9 October 1920): 513.

19 Harriet Upton to Ruth Hanna McCormick, 20 June 1922. Quoted in Miller, *Ruth Hanna McCormick*, 142.

20 Anna Harvey concludes that an important factor in explaining why political parties courted women voters in the 1920s (and not subsequent decades) was that other organizations, namely the LWV, appeared to be mobilizing women themselves. Harvey, *Votes without Leverage*, 104–54.

21 Little biographical work has been published about these women. On Edson, see Braitman, "Public Career of Katherine Philips Edson"; J. Greenberg, "Katherine Philips Edson." On Fosseen, see Howes, *American Women, 1935–1940*, 300. On Livermore, see Gustafson, *Women and the Republican Party*, 182–83. On McCormick, see Miller, *Ruth Hanna McCormick*. On Upton, see J. Freeman, *A Room at a Time*, 96–99.

22 Higginbotham, "In Politics to Stay," 204.

23 Perry, "Defying the Party Whip," 102.

24 "Mrs. Catt Renews Wadsworth Attack," *New York Times*, 24 September 1920. On different women's reactions to the Wadsworth campaign, see Lemons, *Woman Citizen*, 94–95.

25 Hay further revealed her resistance to Republican loyalty when she later endorsed James Cox, Harding's Democratic opponent, for president. "Wants All Women to Stand Together," *New York Times*, 30 October 1920.

26 "Women Not Content but Remain Loyal," *New York Times*, 10 June 1920.

27 "Harding Betting Odds Drop on News of Suffrage Victory," *New York Times*, 21 August 1920.

28 "Mrs. Bass Presents Democracy's Claims," *New York Times*, 21 September 1920; B. Cook, *Eleanor Roosevelt*, 274–75. For more on Harding's "Social Justice Day," see Harvey, *Votes without Leverage*, 118–19.

29 "Negro Women in South Rushing to Register," *New York Times*, 19 September 1920; Lebsock, "Woman Suffrage and White Supremacy," 77, 83–87.

30 Gould, *Grand Old Party*, 226; Lemons, *Woman Citizen*, 89; F. Gordon, "After Winning," 18. Kristi Andersen presents a slightly more complicated picture, citing studies indicating that women's electoral participation after suffrage was greatest in places where efforts were made to mobilize women. In working-class, urban neighborhoods, Democratic Party organizations performed that function; among wealthy, native-born women, women's political clubs did so. Andersen, *After Suffrage*, 57–60.

31 J. Freeman, *A Room at a Time*, 23.

32 The RNC's evidence for this was as follows. In 1920, 7,604,754 more people had voted than in 1916, due presumably to the addition of women voters. Yet Cox received only 13,170 more votes than Wilson had in 1916, whereas the increase for the Republican candidate was 7,591,586. Transcripts of Republican National Committee Executive Session, 3 March 1921, frames 338–42, reel 1, RPP I-a.

33 Remarks by Mrs. Harriet Taylor Upton, Transcripts of Republican National Committee Executive Session, 3 March 1921, frames 370–76, reel 1, RPP I-a.

34 Harriet Taylor Upton to Carrie Fosseen, 16 February 1921, Correspondence and Other Papers, 1920–51, CF papers.

35 Transcripts of Republican National Committee Executive Session, 8 June 1921, frames 465–66, reel 1, RPP I-a; NWPC, "Republican Women Are Wonderful."

36 Harriet Taylor Upton to Carrie Fosseen, 16 February 1921, Correspondence and Other Papers, 1920–51, CF papers.

37 Some women had attended the 1920 convention as delegates and alternates from states where women already had the vote. The number of Republican women delegates and alternates was 27 and 129 respectively. The Democratic convention (where the total number of delegates was larger when compared with the Republican case) seated 93 women delegates and 206 women alternates. Fisher and Whitehead, "Women and National Party Organizations," 896, 898.

38 Charles D. Hilles (N.Y.), Transcripts of Republican National Committee meeting, 16 December 1935, frame 487, reel 4, RPP I-a.

39 Ibid.

40 Sherman, *Republican Party and Black America*, 19, 119, 156–58.

41 This debate is found in Transcripts of Republican National Committee meeting, 16 December 1935, frames 408–62, reel 1, RPP I-a. Quotation is from frame 421.

42 Under the new formula for delegate allotment, each state that had cast a majority of votes for Harding in 1920 would send 3 additional at-large delegates to the 1924 convention. In 1920 Harding had won thirty-seven states. Thus the number of new delegate seats to the 1924 convention was 111. Charles D. Hilles (N.Y.), Transcripts of Republican National Committee meeting, 16 December 1935, frames 485–87, reel 4, RPP I-a. Fisher and Whitehead list the number of Republican women delegates in 1924 as 120 and the number of women alternates as 277. They suggest that, although the number of Democratic women serving as delegates was always higher than their Republican counterparts, the patterns (up until 1944 when their study was conducted) were similar, given that the Democratic conventions were larger than the Republican. In both parties, women served in larger numbers as alternates than as delegates. Fisher and Whitehead, "Women and National Party Organizations," 898–99.

43 "Political Progress by Women," *North American*, 11 February 1924, RWP scrapbooks, 1920–24.

44 Harriet Upton to Members of Committee, 19 August 1921 and 31 December 1921, quoted in Miller, *Ruth Hanna McCormick*, 128.

45 Link and McCormick, *Progressivism*, 50–51.

46 This figure comes from Emily Newell Blair, cited in Andersen, *After Suffrage*, 90.

47 Remarks by Patricia Hutar, Transcripts of Republican National Committee meeting, 23 January 1965, frame 673, reel 4, RPP I-b.

48 Mrs. A. Haines Lippincott, "Independence within the Party: From a Talk

before the Republican Women of Pennsylvania," *Republican Woman*, March 1924, RWP scrapbook, 1920–24. A similar charge that women on the state committee were "scenery . . . not in the picture but back stage" was echoed by Alma Lorimer of Pennsylvania in her criticism of the State Central Committee's refusal to consult with women in selecting the delegates-at-large for the 1924 Republican presidential convention. Alma Lorimer, "The Delegates-at-Large," *Republican Woman*, January 1924, RWP scrapbook, 1920–24. See also "Women Rap the Delegate Slate Makers," *Times-Herald* (Norristown), 17 January 1924, RWP scrapbook, 1920–24.

49 On women's lack of influence on the national committees of both parties, see J. Freeman, *A Room at a Time*, 109–21; Harvey, *Votes without Leverage*, 160–62; Cott, *Grounding of Modern Feminism*, 109–13; Lemons, *Woman Citizen*, 110–11; Andersen, *After Suffrage*, 105.

50 On the National Woman's Party in the 1920s, see Cott, *Grounding of Modern Feminism*, 53–81.

51 "Says Women Must Learn through Their Mistakes," *Philadelphia Public Ledger*, 5 October 1920, RWP scrapbook, 1920–24.

52 "Republican Women Here Urged to Fight against Sex Antagonism," *Evening Public Ledger* (Philadelphia), 20 November 1924, RWP scrapbook, 1920–24.

53 Harriet Hubbs, "New Light on Equal Representation," *Republican Woman*, April 1923, RWP scrapbook, 1920–24.

54 Ibid. One woman who came close to making this suggestion was Bertha Bauer, who succeeded Ruth McCormick as national committeewoman from Illinois and who was president of the Chicago Republican Women's Club. When asked in 1929 whether a woman could serve in the president's cabinet or as vice president, Bauer responded, "We women ask for equal suffrage and for equal rights; for equality as representation on national committees, on state committees, on county committees. Then why not equal representation in representative government? I say: Yes, women as Cabinet members! Yes, as Vice President!" It is not clear from Bauer's remarks, however, whether she actually endorsed designated women's representation in elected and appointed government or whether she was expressing merely her enthusiasm for women being considered. "Discusses Possibility of Women for Vice Presidency or Cabinet Posts," 19 May 1929, clipping in RWP scrapbook, 1929. On Bauer's election to replace McCormick, see Miller, *Ruth Hanna McCormick*, 194–95.

55 "Woman's Place Is in the Home, and Man's Too," *Woman's Opinion*, December 1923, RWP scrapbook, 1920–24.

56 Alma Lorimer, "Women and Better Politics," *Republican Woman*, December 1925, RWP scrapbook, 1925–27.

57 Nannie Burroughs, "The Negro Woman and Suffrage," 15 June 1923, box 46, Speeches and Writings, NHB papers.

58 On the role of the NACW in the 1924 Republican campaign, see Higginbotham, "In Politics to Stay," 205–8. See also Gustafson, *Women and the Republican Party*, 192–93.

59 Nannie Burroughs to Sallie Hert, 16 February 1929; Nannie Burroughs to

Sallie Hert, 14 January 1929, General Correspondence—Letters Received—Hert, Sallie (Mrs. Alvin T.), box 37, NHB papers.

60 William O'Neill established an influential paradigm for understanding the political divisions of former suffragists after 1920 when he characterized them as either "social" or "hard-core" feminists. In the latter category he placed women in the NWP because of their unequivocal commitment to women's equality. Social feminists, according to O'Neill's formulation, were those women who actively supported other reform issues, such as protection for women and children, which led them to oppose the ERA proposed by the NWP in the early 1920s. O'Neill, *Everyone Was Brave*. Nancy Cott has challenged O'Neill's paradigm for masking complexity and ignoring overlap among the two categories. Cott, "What's in a Name?"

61 The issues in which the Republican Women of Pennsylvania became involved reflected this ambivalence. The RWP opposed the Goehring Jury Service Bill, a proposed state law that would have automatically exempted older women and the mothers of young children from jury duty. The RWP objected to the bill on the grounds that women were now full citizens and desired "no favors or distinctions because of sex." Yet the RWP supported the Mathay forty-eight-hour-week-for-women bill, which would have limited women's work week. "Women Opposing Bill on Jury Duty," *Philadelphia Public Ledger*, 19 February 1925; "48-Hour Week Bill Is Women's Issue," clipping ca. April 1923, RWP scrapbook, 1920–24.

62 Denise Riley has discussed similar problems stemming from the British woman suffrage campaign. By gaining the right to vote, women were supposedly "melt[ed] back" into the larger category of humanity. But if that were the case, enfranchised women were left with no means of making claims for what they perceived to be their own needs without "losing the ground of generality" that they had gained. Furthermore, to make claims that did not presume to include all of womankind was to suggest classism. Riley views these tensions between understanding women as "sexed" or as "human" to be ultimately unresolvable. Riley, *Am I That Name?*, 68, 94–95.

63 Andersen, *After Suffrage*, 17, 115. I have found the concept of shifting "gender boundaries" to be useful in understanding women's entry into party politics. Andersen herself borrows the idea from Judith M. Gerson and Kathy Peiss, who argue that "gender boundaries" is a more useful conception than "separate spheres" for understanding how gender systems operate because "boundaries" imply permeability and reciprocal "processes of negotiation as well as domination," rather than rigid separation. Gerson and Peiss, "Boundaries, Negotiation, Consciousness." Quotation is from p. 316.

64 Address of Mrs. Henrietta L. Livermore, Transcripts of Republican National Committee meeting, 11 December 1923, frame 512, reel 1, RPP I-a.

65 Ibid.

66 Laas, *Autobiography of Emily Newell Blair*, 223–24. Blair further discusses her efforts to organize Democratic women on pp. 258–65. See also Anderson, "Emily Newell Blair and the Democratic Party," 113.

CHAPTER 2

1 Michael McGerr defines "political style" as the different manners, forms, and trappings through which people "perceive, discuss, and act politically." Political style is one aspect of political culture, a much broader term that includes the ideological, cultural, institutional, and social components of politics. McGerr, "Political Style and Women's Power," 865; McGerr, *Decline of Popular Politics*, 9–10.

2 Ella Taylor, "Old Time Campaigns," *Traer Star-Clipper*, 23 October 1936 (which quoted the earlier *Jefferson Bee* article), TCRW scrapbook. A significant amount of information for this chapter comes from scrapbooks like this one. Although they are not ideal sources, scrapbooks, which typically consist of newspaper clippings, photographs, and brochures, are often the only places where material on women's organizations is collected. Women's letters and the official records of women's organizations have not always been preserved and archived.

3 Baker, "Domestication of Politics," 628; Testi, "Gender of Reform Politics," 1510–11. See also Andersen, *After Suffrage*, 12–14, 28–30; M. Ryan, *Women in Public*.

4 Varon, "Tippecanoe and the Ladies, Too"; Varon, *We Mean to Be Counted*; M. Goldberg, *An Army of Women*; M. Goldberg, "Non-Partisan and All-Partisan"; Dinkin, *Before Equal Suffrage*; Gustafson, "Partisan Women in the Progressive Era"; Gustafson, *Women and the Republican Party*.

5 Gustafson, Miller, and Perry, *We Have Come to Stay*, x.

6 J. Freeman, *A Room at a Time*, 153–54; Gustafson, *Women and the Republican Party*, 60, 73.

7 McGerr, "Political Style and Women's Power," 864, 866–68. Women's "voluntarist style," was an alternative to male politics that middle-class women developed in the nineteenth century. During the suffrage campaign, however, women embraced aspects of demonstrative politics (such as parades and rallies) that were similar to the popular politics that was now out of fashion among men. American suffragists borrowed this style, according to McGerr, not from American partisan politics of the past but from the British suffragists. After gaining the right to vote, women generally returned to the voluntarist style that had characterized their presuffrage political work. Ibid., 879–81.

8 Testi, "Gender of Reform Politics," 1511.

9 Baker, *Moral Frameworks of Everyday Life*, 82; Andersen, *After Suffrage*, 25–26.

10 M. Goldberg, *An Army of Women*, 127–36. Quotation is from p. 133.

11 Testi, "Gender of Reform Politics," 1525–26.

12 Gustafson, "Partisan Women in the Progressive Era," 12.

13 J. Freeman, *A Room at a Time*, 67.

14 "Metaphor and Smoke Mix at Campaign Headquarters," *Evening Public Ledger* (Philadelphia), 17 May 1922, RWP scrapbook, 1920–24.

15 Harriet Hubbs, *Philadelphia Public Ledger*, 9 August 1922, RWP scrapbook, 1920–24. Even before they could vote, elite women in Philadelphia had turned

their energies against machine candidates and in favor of reformers. See VandeCreek, "Unseen Influence."

16 Lillian Feickert, 1924, quoted in F. Gordon, "After Winning," 20.

17 "Women's Organizations Multiplying in Nation," *Evening Public Ledger* (Philadelphia), 6 June 1925, in RWP scrapbook, 1925–27.

18 Few studies deal with how ordinary Americans have experienced partisan politics in the twentieth century. Studies that examine nineteenth-century political parties as cultural and social, as well as political, institutions include R. Jensen, *Winning of the Midwest*; Kleppner, *Third Electoral System*; Palermo, "Rules of the Game"; M. Ryan, *Women in Public*; Baker, *Moral Frameworks of Public Life*; M. Goldberg, *An Army of Women*; McGerr, *Decline of Popular Politics*.

19 On the demise of political socialization among partisan men by the 1920s, see Burnham, *Current Crisis in American Politics*, 93–94.

20 Mrs. Arthur Livermore to Lou Henry Hoover, 4 February 1921, Girl Scouts and Other Organizations, Miscellaneous, 1920–29, box 49, LHH papers. See also J. Freeman, *A Room at a Time*, 100.

21 Alice Hill Chittenden to Lou Henry Hoover, 17 March 1927, Girl Scouts and Other Organizations, Women's National Republican Club, 1921–28, box 49, LHH papers.

22 Women's National Republican Club membership form, Girl Scouts and Other Organizations, Women's National Republican Club, 1940–43 and undated, box 49, LHH papers; Harriet Upton to Alma Lorimer, 5 February 1923, RWP scrapbook, 1920–24; "Interstate Conference of Republican Women," *Republican Woman*, June 1927, RWP scrapbook, 1925–27.

23 "A National Club for Republican Women," *Republican Woman*, October 1927, RWP scrapbook, 1925–27.

24 Hicks, *Republican Ascendancy*, 91–92.

25 "Interstate Conference of Republican Women," *Republican Woman*, June 1927, RWP scrapbook, 1925–27.

26 The independent tone of the RWP was echoed elsewhere. Like the RWP, the New Jersey Women's Republican Club (NJWRC), which grew out of the New Jersey Women's Suffrage Association, was also wary of any definition of partisanship that implied one had to support candidates deemed inferior for whatever reasons. As one of its members put it, the NJWRC formed not to elect candidates "selected . . . by a few men, but is interested in the principles for which those candidates stand." "The New Jersey Women's Republican Club," *Republican Woman*, February 1928, RWP scrapbook, 1928. The NJWRC, led by Lillian Feickert, had several early successes in achieving elements of its progressive legislative agenda, even working with state Democratic women to secure passage of legislation providing for the welfare of women and children. The NJWRC was not afraid to defy Republican leadership, winning a particularly difficult battle in 1923 when it helped push passage of a bill banning night work for women that Republicans in the state legislature had initially

opposed. "Back Where We Started From," *New Jersey Republican*, June 1929, Girl Scouts and Other Organizations, Women's National Republican Club, 1929–33, box 49, LHH papers; "Militant Women Frighten Jersey's Republican Bosses," *Searchlight*, January 1924, RWP scrapbook, 1920–24; F. Gordon, *After Winning*, 61, 82–84.

27 On machine politics in Philadelphia, see McCaffery, *When Bosses Ruled Philadelphia*; VandeCreek, "Unseen Influence," 33–43.

28 "Mrs. G. H. Lorimer Given G.O.P. Position," 4 September 1920, clipping in RWP scrapbook, 1920–24; Lorimer, "Republican Women of Pennsylvania," undated typescript, RWP scrapbook, 1920–24.

29 "Just What Can We Do for Our Country?," March 1926, clipping in RWP scrapbook, 1925–27.

30 Harriet Hubbs, "Our Women in the Field of Politics," *Philadelphia Public Ledger*, 1 September 1922, RWP scrapbook, 1920–24.

31 "Home and Politics One, Says Leader," *Philadelphia Inquirer*, 19 July 1921, RWP scrapbook, 1920–24.

32 "Mrs. Lorimer Hits G.O.P. Council Plan," *Philadelphia Bulletin*, 29 January 1923, RWP scrapbook, 1920–24.

33 "Urge Golden Rule on Women Voters," *Philadelphia Public Ledger*, 19 July 1921, RWP scrapbook, 1920–24. See also "Prepare G.O.P. Fund Drive," *Evening Bulletin* (Philadelphia), 11 September 1920, clipping in RWP scrapbook, 1920–24; "Study Candidates, Says Mrs. Lorimer," 13 October 1922, clipping in RWP scrapbook, 1920–24.

34 "Women at Odds in Pinchot Contest," *Philadelphia Public Ledger*, May 1924, RWP scrapbook, 1920–24; "The Women Voters," *Evening Public Ledger* (Philadelphia), 14 May 1928, RWP scrapbook, 1928; "Republican Women Call for Support of Full Party Ticket," unattributed clipping ca. fall 1926, RWP scrapbook, 1925–27. A handwritten note next to this last clipping states: "In the fall after Vare's nomination we ostensibly supported the Republican ticket though many voted for the Democrat William B. Wilson."

35 McCaffery, *When Bosses Ruled Philadelphia*, xv, 176–77.

36 Although Philadelphia's foreign-born population was smaller (percentagewise) than that of other large northern cities, it was still significant; between 1880 and 1930 one in two Philadelphians was a first- or second-generation immigrant. In 1930 more than 10 percent of Philadelphia's population was black. Ibid., 114–15.

37 Alma Lorimer, "A Message to the Republican Women of Pennsylvania," *Republican Woman*, October 1929, RWP scrapbook, 1929. This idea that political machines, liquor dealers, and big business together formed a united obstacle to the triumph of women's political values had been frequently expressed during the suffrage campaign. Kraditor, *Ideas of the Woman Suffrage Movement*, 60–61.

38 Alma Lorimer, "Women and Better Politics," *Republican Woman*, December 1925, RWP scrapbook, 1925–27. For a similar example, see "Republican Women Urge Union with Independents," *Philadelphia Public Ledger*, 13 October 1922, RWP scrapbook, 1920–24.

39 Alma Lorimer, "Home and Politics One, Says Leader," *Philadelphia Inquirer*, 19 July 1921, RWP scrapbook, 1920–24.

40 "Urge Golden Rule on Women Voters," *Philadelphia Public Ledger*, 19 July 1921, RWP scrapbook, 1920–24; "Women Opposing Bill on Jury Duty," *Philadelphia Public Ledger*, 19 February 1925, RWP scrapbook, 1925–27; "48-Hour Week Bill Is Women's Issue," clipping ca. April 1923, RWP scrapbook, 1920–24.

41 "Schofield Planning Policewomen Unit," *Philadelphia Inquirer*, 19 February 1929, RWP scrapbook, 1929.

42 "Feminine Voters to Be Instructed," undated clipping ca. April 1924, RWP scrapbook, 1920–24.

43 "'Coolidge Inn' Has New Crowd Daily," *Philadelphia Public Ledger*, 29 October 1924, RWP scrapbook, 1920–24.

44 "Mr. Hoover Approves Independent Republican Clubs," *Republican Woman*, February 1929, RWP scrapbook, 1929. Three years later, the RNC Women's Division claimed that thirty-three states had a statewide organization of Republican women, some of which were affiliated with the party machinery, and some of which were independent. Republican National Committee Women's Division, "Republican Women's Clubs, Councils, Leagues, and Federations," [1932], box 49, LHH papers. By 1928 Democratic clubwomen were also holding national conferences at the National Democratic Woman's Club headquarters in Washington, D.C. According to Emily Blair, the clubs she first helped found in 1924 were largely gone by 1932, when Molly Dewson began organizing women again. Blair blamed party infighting for the demise of the Democratic clubs in the twenties. Laas, *Autobiography of Emily Newell Blair*, 311–12, 345.

45 Cott, *Grounding of Modern Feminism*, 87; Terborg-Penn, "Discontented Black Feminists," 261–78.

46 Higginbotham, "Clubwomen and Electoral Politics," 138.

47 Hendricks, "African American Women as Political Constituents," 60–62.

48 Schechter, *Ida B. Wells-Barnett*, 221.

49 In 1926 NACW represented hundreds of black women's clubs in forty-one states. The activities of the NACW are discussed in Higginbotham, "In Politics to Stay," 205–8. See also Higginbotham, "Clubwomen in Electoral Politics," 134–55. The NACW, although founded as a nonpartisan organization, had long had loose ties to the GOP. Its founder, Mary Church Terrell, for example, was a "Republican loyalist." Gustafson, *Women and the Republican Party*, 78.

50 Higginbotham, "In Politics to Stay," 207; Higginbotham, "Clubwomen and Electoral Politics," 142–43.

51 Higginbotham, "In Politics to Stay," 208–9.

52 See letterhead in General Correspondence, Letters Received, Hert, Sallie (Mrs. Alvin T.), box 37; Minutes of the National League of Republican Colored Women Executive Committee, 6 August 1926, National League of Republican Colored Women Minutes, box 309, NHB papers.

53 This concern is reflected in a questionnaire conducted by the NLRCW and is discussed in Higginbotham, "In Politics to Stay," 210; Minutes of National

League of Republican Colored Women Executive Session, 12–14 May, ca. 1927, National League of Republican Colored Women, Miscellaneous, box 309, NHB papers.

54 Minutes of the Executive Committee of the National League of Republican Colored Women, 6 August 1926, National League of Republican Colored Women, Miscellaneous, box 309, NHB papers.

55 Gustafson, *Women and the Republican Party*, 12–13. Patricia Schechter makes a similar argument, suggesting that black women's clubs avoided the intense gender consciousness of many white women's clubs. Schechter, *Ida B. Wells-Barnett*, 221.

56 For concern about the black male Republican leadership, see Daisy Lampkin to Nannie Burroughs, 20 May [1928], General Correspondence, Letters Received, Lampkin, Daisy E., Sept. 1930–Jan. 1960, box 17; Nannie Burroughs to Daisy Lampkin, 23 May 1928, General Correspondence, Letters Sent, Lampkin, Daisy, 1927–59, box 39, NHB papers.

57 George W. Woodson, "Address to the Women's League of St. Paul," 11 March 1929, National League of Republican Colored Women, Miscellaneous, box 309, NHB papers.

58 Higginbotham, "Clubwomen and Electoral Politics," 144–45.

59 Nannie Burroughs to My Dear Co-Worker, ca. February 1929, National League of Republican Colored Women, Miscellaneous, box 309, NHB papers.

60 Daisy Lampkin to Fellow Republicans, 15 September 1928, General Correspondence—Republican National Committee, 1928–54, box 24, NHB papers.

61 Minutes of Executive Session of NLRCW, 12–14 May, ca. 1927, National League of Republican Colored Women, Miscellaneous, box 309, NHB papers.

62 Nannie Burroughs to Sallie Hert, 14 January 1929, General Correspondence, Letters Received, Hert, Sallie (Mrs. Alvin T.), box 37, NHB papers.

63 Sallie Hert to Nannie Burroughs, 10 November 1928, General Correspondence, Letters Received, Hert, Sallie (Mrs. Alvin T.), box 12, NHB papers.

64 F. Gordon, "After Winning," 21.

65 "Republican Women's Clubs, Councils, Leagues, and Federations," prepared by the Women's Division, [1932], Girl Scouts and Other Organizations, Miscellaneous, 1932–41 and undated, box 49, LHH papers.

66 Republican clubwomen, in their efforts to define partisanship for themselves, revealed an affinity with many of the political methods that were part of the voluntarist style described by Michael McGerr, such as voter education. McGerr, "Political Style and Women's Power," 867–68. Yet one of the most salient features of the voluntarist style was its existence outside the world of party politics. Kristi Andersen has also discussed the idea of a distinct female political culture or style, the features of which she identifies as "cooperation, gathering information, and building consensus." Andersen, *After Suffrage*, 163. These are useful features to note generally. Perhaps because my emphasis is on partisanship (and specifically *Republican* partisanship), rather than women's politics in general, I have identified different traits as most characteristic.

67 Schechter, *Ida B. Wells-Barnett*, 239.

68 Ella Taylor, Speech, Grundy Center, 8 June 1937, History Book, 1937–56, box 1, ICRW records.

69 Ella Taylor, "Value of Republican Women's Clubs," October 1936, History Book, 1937–56, box 1, ICRW records. Taylor raised similar concerns after Republican successes in 1938. Ella Taylor, "In Again Out Again," *Traer Star-Clipper*, 18 November 1938, TDRW scrapbook.

70 *Republican Daily News*, 25 August 1928, Republican National Committee—Daily News 7/23–9/20/28 file, Campaign and Transition period, box 162, HH papers.

71 Marilley, "Frances Willard and the Feminism of Fear"; Gifford, "Conversion to Woman Suffrage."

72 Burroughs is quoted in Daisy Lampkin to Fellow Republicans, 15 September 1928, General Correspondence—Republican National Committee, 1928–54, box 24, NHB papers. See also George W. Woodson, Address to the Women's League of St. Paul, 11 March 1929, National League of Republican Colored Women, Miscellaneous, box 309, NHB papers.

73 Schechter, *Ida B. Wells-Barnett*, 218, 239.

74 National League of Republican Colored Women—Colored Women in Politics questionnaire, box 308, NHB papers.

75 Rymph, "Keeping the Political Fires Burning," 120–21.

76 *Republican Daily News*, 20 September 1928, Republican National Committee—Daily News 7/23–9/20/28, Campaign and Transition period, box 162, HH papers.

77 Andersen, *After Suffrage*, 75.

78 On the Tama County Republican Women's Club, see Rymph, "Keeping the Political Fires Burning."

79 "Women Leaders Back Hoover and Urge Second Term," *Philadelphia Public Ledger*, 19 May 1931, RWP scrapbook, 1931.

80 Nannie Burroughs to Sallie Hert, 14 January 1929, General Correspondence, Letters Received, Hert, Sallie (Mrs. Alvin T.), box 37; Lenna Yost to Nannie Burroughs, 24 October 1932; Nannie Burroughs to Lenna Yost, 27 October [misdated as September] 1932, General Correspondence, Yost, Mrs. Ellis A., 1932–34, box 32, NHB papers.

81 Ella Taylor, Speech at Sixth District meeting in Des Moines, 1938, History Book, 1937–56, box 1, ICRW records.

82 Ella Taylor, Speech at Fourth District meeting, ca. 1938, ibid.

83 Ella Taylor, Speech at Third District meeting, 1937; Ella Taylor, Speech at Fourth District meeting, ca. 1938, ibid.

84 New Deal legislation such as the Agricultural Adjustment Act and the Farm Credit Act of 1933 were popular as were federal projects that surfaced and resurfaced Iowa roads and provided electricity to rural areas. From 1934 to 1938, cash farm income in Iowa was approximately double what it had been in 1932. Nonfarming Iowans also benefited from New Deal relief efforts such as the Federal Emergency Relief Administration and the Civil Works Administration. Jones, "New Deal Comes to Iowa," 24–26.

85 "Third District Republican Women's Club Formed," clipping ca. October 1936; "Third District Women Organize," clipping 23 October 1936; Ella Taylor, "A New Organization," *Traer Star-Clipper*, 6 November 1936, TDRW scrapbook; "'Candidates Night' in Traer Next Tuesday," *Traer Star-Clipper*, 20 March 1936; "County G.O.P. Rally at Dysart Monday," *Traer Star-Clipper*, 31 July 1936; "G.O.P. Rally to Be Held Wednesday at Traer Opera House," *Traer Star-Clipper*, 23 October 1936; "Hickenlooper Hits at 'Fifth Column' New Deal Tactics," *Gazette* (Cedar Rapids), 29 May 1940, TCRW scrapbook.

86 "Denver Meeting of Pro America Board Planned," *Denver Post*, 12 October 1941; Benowitz, *Days of Discontent*, 16; Bone, "New Party Associations in the West," 1119.

87 Benowitz, *Days of Discontent*, 16.

88 Transcripts of Republican National Committee meeting, 16 December 1931, frames 518–19, reel 3, RPP I-a.

89 Doris Fleeson, "Clash within the Party," *Washington Evening Star*, 17 December 1946. Fleeson herself was a supporter of the New Deal. Mary McGrory, "Doris Fleeson," in Sicherman and Green, *NAW: The Modern Period*, 239–41.

90 Ware, *Partner and I*, 168–69, 198–99, 203.

91 Ibid., 192. For more on women governmental workers in Washington during the 1930s, see Ware, *Beyond Suffrage*.

92 Badger, *New Deal*, 245–46, 275, 285–86.

93 Weed, *Nemesis of Reform*, 38–48.

94 Ibid., 114–15.

95 Goldman, *National Party Chairmen*, 396. Hamilton, who hailed from Landon's home state of Kansas, became chairman as the choice of the presidential candidate. Hamilton was a more strident anti–New Dealer than his fellow westerner, Landon, who approved of the New Deal's agriculture and conservation programs, endorsed the idea of Social Security, and supported the right of workers to organize. Weed, *Nemesis of Reform*, 99–101.

96 Goldman, *National Party Chairmen*, 401–3.

97 Cotter and Hennessy, *Politics without Power*, 194–95.

98 Remarks by John Hamilton, Transcripts of Republican National Committee meeting, 5 November 1937, frame 419, reel 5, RPP I-a.

CHAPTER 3

1 The next three paragraphs in the text describing Martin's life before becoming assistant chairman of the RNC are (except where otherwise noted) drawn from the following: "Progress of the Primary Campaign," 10 April 1930, clipping provided by William Martin (nephew of Marion Martin); Wellesley *Record Book* (1947); "Woman's Touch Works Well in Labor Mediation," *Bangor Daily News*, 20 February 1969, Martin Alumni file; "Political Victim Rebuilt State Labor Department," *Kennebec Journal*, 26 June 1972; Obituary, *Kennebec Journal*, 9 January 1987; Obituary, *New York Times*, 11 January 1987; "Maine's Joan of Arc," *Christian Science Monitor*, 13 January 1965. Marion Martin has received almost no attention from scholars. Jo Freeman is one exception. See J. Freeman,

A Room at a Time, 101–4. See also J. Freeman, "Marion Martin of Maine: A Mother of Republican Women," *Maine Sunday Telegram*, 14 May 2000. A copy of this article can be found at <http://www.jofreeman.com/polhistory/martin.htm> (accessed 4 January 2004). See also Candace A. Kanes, "Marion Martin," in Ware, *Notable American Women*, 415–16.

2 "Women in Maine Politics," *Evening Express* (Portland), 25 October 1936.

3 Marion Martin, "Our Job," *Tocsin*, November 1937, Republican Organizations, Women's Organizations, 1936–38, box 273, HH papers; "Republicans Switching from Barrows to Page," *Bangor Daily News*, 8 June 1936, MM scrapbooks, 1934–37.

4 Weed, *Nemesis of Reform*, 107, 112.

5 Report of Marion Martin, Transcripts of Republican National Committee Executive Session, 29 November 1938, frames 944–45, reel 5, RPP I-a.

6 When Republicans had held national power, however, they had not recognized women with high appointments. In 1928, Herbert Hoover had briefly considered Sallie Hert for appointment as secretary of the interior, a cabinet-level position. Although she had the support of the RNC chairman, Hubert Work, Hert was opposed by some women's groups from her home state of Kentucky and was not appointed in the end. "Women Protest Place in Cabinet for Mrs. Hert," *New York Herald Tribune*, 4 January 1929.

7 Report of Marion Martin, Transcripts of Republican National Committee Executive Session, 29 November 1938, frame 945, reel 5, RPP I-a.

8 Transcripts of Republican National Committee meeting, 17 December 1936, frames 253–354, reel 5, RPP I-a; D. L. Egnew to Gladys E. Knowles, 26 May 1944, NF-2 (a)(5) Mrs. W. Glenn Suthers, Gen'l Corres., 1943–46 #2, box 155, NFRW records.

9 Being "patted on the back," complained one committeewoman, was no longer enough. They were tired "of being told we are the backbone of the party and that your faith and hope lie in us," declared another. Transcripts of Republican National Committee meeting, 17 December 1936, frames 451, 447, reel 5, RPP I-a. In 1943, after several years of Federation existence, these kinds of complaints continued to emerge. "Something will have to be done by the National Committee, I think, to give women more of the feeling that they BELONG to the Party," wrote Federation president Marie Suthers. Women are "no longer satisfied with platform praise." Marie Suthers to Marion Martin, 2 July 1943, NF-2 (a)(2) Field Trips, Mrs. W. Glenn Suthers 1942–46, box 153, NFRW records.

10 Good, *History of Women in Republican National Conventions*, 24–26.

11 The status of the Women's Division had been somewhat confusing and tenuous since its creation in 1919. Although Harriet Taylor Upton and Sallie Hert had emphasized the necessity of a year-round women's organization, the Women's Division had operated primarily during campaign seasons. Often this was due to the budget priorities of the RNC. Women leaders were unsuccessful in persuading the RNC to devote large resources to organizing women in the off years. Will Hays had created the Women's Division in November

1919 with Ruth Hanna McCormick as chairman. Upton, as vice chairman of the RNC Executive Committee, had charge of the women's campaign in 1920. In 1924 women's activities were led by Sallie Hert (national committeewoman from Kentucky), whose title was vice chairman of the Republican National Committee. During the 1928 campaign, Hert retained the title of vice chairman but was assisted by Louise Dodson of Iowa, who served as director of the Women's Division. Dodson was not a national committeewoman, although she had served from 1920–24 as Iowa's associate (nonvoting) committeewoman. In 1930 Lenna Yost, committeewoman from West Virginia, became director of the Women's Division. Hert remained vice chairman of the RNC into the 1930s. In 1935 RNC chairman Henry Fletcher appointed Mrs. Robert Lincoln Hoyal of Arizona as director of the Women's Division. Hoyal resigned her post in early 1937, leaving the Women's Division without a leader until Hamilton's appointment of Martin as assistant chairman that fall. Good, *History of Women in Republican National Conventions*, 9–10, 20–22. Jo Freeman provides an overview of the Republican Women's Division in *A Room at a Time*, 96–107. See also Harvey, *Votes without Leverage*, 170–72.

12 Before she was elected to the Maine house, Martin had served as president of the Bangor Junior Welfare League, an organization that coordinated efforts of young women volunteers in providing services for the poor. In 1932 she was named to the executive committee of the Maine Conference on Social Welfare. "MacDonald to Head Welfare Conference," *Bangor Commercial*, 21 October 1932, MM scrapbook, 1931–33. The sketch of Dewson's life is taken from Paul C. Taylor, "Mary Williams Dewson," in Sicherman and Green, *NAW: The Modern Period*, 188–91. Ware, *Partner and I*, provides a book-length account.

13 Women's Division, *History of the National Federation of Republican Women*, 7.

14 Report of Marion Martin, Transcripts of Republican National Committee Executive Session, 29 November 1938, frames 942–43, reel 5, RPP I-a.

15 Marion Martin to Roselle Huddilston, 3 October 1941, 10/3/41 to Maine Clubwomen re: N.F.W.R.C., box 147, NFRW records. See also Report of Marion E. Martin, Transcripts of Republican National Committee Executive Session, 29 November 1938, frames 942–43, reel 5, RPP I-a.

16 Women's Division, *History of the National Federation of Republican Women*, 9–10, 13.

17 Lou Henry Hoover to Sue Dyer, 28 March 1938, Girl Scouts and Other Organizations, Miscellaneous, 1936–38, box 48, LHH papers.

18 Agnes Morley Cleveland to Lou Henry Hoover, 19 March 1938, Girl Scouts and Other Organizations, Miscellaneous, 1936–38, box 48, LHH papers.

19 Marion Martin to Marie Suthers, 19 June 1943, NF-2 (a)(5) Mrs. W. Glenn Suthers, Gen'l Corres., 1943–46 #7, box 155, NFRW records.

20 Women's Division, *History of the National Federation of Republican Women*, 11.

21 The bylaws for the Federation provided checks on the loyalty of clubs who wanted to join. All applications for club affiliation had to be approved by the

state's national committeewoman and vice chairman. Party regularity was ensured through a clause stating that no state Federation or local club would be accepted for membership in the national Federation if it had publicly endorsed ticket-splitting or a candidate of another party during the previous two gubernatorial campaigns. Dues were set at ten cents per capita to defray costs of study materials and other expenses and to begin to develop economic self-sufficiency. Women's Division, *History of the National Federation of Republican Women*, 12. Martin worried that as long as the men of the party could occasionally give small amounts of money to the women's organizations, they would feel they had adequately rewarded women and would then pass over women when it came to political appointments. A substantial part of the Federation's budget continued to come from the RNC. Marion Martin to All Presidents, 9 June 1939, Memo for dues, box 147, NFRW records; Marion Martin to Mrs. H. G. Nasburg, 24 October 1941, NF-9(c) Policy Developing letters from early days of Federation #1, box 253, NFRW records.

22 The results of the vote, which was conducted by mail, were twenty-eight in favor of the Federation plan and six opposed. Two committeewomen abstained and thirteen did not reply. Women's Division, *History of the National Federation of Republican Women*, 13–14.

23 Marguerite M. Wells, "A Portrait of the League of Women Voters," 1961, History, National League, box 48, LWVI records.

24 JHM interview, 15 October 1996.

25 Marion Martin to Judy Weis, 22 January 1941, NF-2 (a)(5) Mrs. Charles Weis, Gen'l Corres., 1941–42 #3, box 155; Judy Weis to Marion Martin, 3 September 1941, NF-2 (a)(2) Mrs. Charles Weis, 1941–42, Report on Field Trip 1941, box 153; Marion Martin to Judy Weis, 10 December 1941, NF-2 (a)(5) Mrs. Charles Weis, Gen'l Corres., 1941–42 #1, box 155, NFRW records.

26 Report of the Executive Director to the Advisory Committee, Covering the Period September 23, 1938 to June 15, 1940, NF-7 Advisory Board Phila.—June 1940—Report of Exec. Director, box 47; Report of the President, 10 March 1944, 3/44 N.F. Adv. Board Meeting Rept. of the Pres., box 52, NFRW records.

27 Marion Martin to Members of the National Federation, 22 January 1940, 1/22/40 to N.F. Members re Communications Comm., box 47, NFRW records.

28 Report of the Executive Director to the Advisory Committee, Covering the Period September 23, 1938 to June 15, 1940, NF-7 Advisory Board Phila.—June 1940—Report of Exec. Director, box 47, NFRW records.

29 For example, see Marie Suthers to Federation members, 27 January 1944, NF-9(a) To Nat'l Committeewomen & State V. Chm. re Chicago meeting 1/11/44, box 152, NFRW records.

30 Marion Martin to Joyce Arneill, 23 January 1939, NF-2 (a)(5) Mrs. James Arneill, Jr., Gen'l Corres., 1939–40 #2, box 154, NFRW records.

31 On the League of Women Voters Program in the 1930s, see League of Women Voters of the United States, "A History of the League Program," 1949, History—National League, box 48, LWVI records.

32 See, for example, "Women Are Urged to Back Parties," *Providence Journal*, 29 September 1946, Federation Convention Phila., Sept. 1946, box 58, NFRW records.

33 Sarah Pell to Marion Martin, 17 August 1938, NF-9(c) Policy Developing letters from early days of Federation #2, box 153; Margaret Sawyer to Marion Martin, 22 May 1940, NF-1(a) California—affiliated clubs "2," box 1, NFRW records.

34 Fleming, "Challenge Is Ours."

35 The last issue of *Women's Voice* ran in September 1940.

36 Marion Martin to Cecil Evans, 25 August 1938, NF-2(b) 2nd Vice Pres., Mrs. Wm. E. Evans 1939, box 156, NFRW records.

37 A tabulation of results from a questionnaire sent to state federations contains the category "C/BL." I have assumed that this category refers to "colored clubs" and that the numbers listed refer to the number of such clubs affiliated with the state federation in each state. The number of black women's clubs that did not affiliate with their state federations cannot be inferred from this questionnaire, nor can the number of black clubs that affiliated with both the Federation and the NARW. Digest of NFWRC Questionnaire of 9/39, Questionnaire, box 147, NFRW records.

38 Questionnaire, 26 October 1938, Digest of Replies to Questionnaire of Oct. 26, 1938, box 153, NFRW records.

39 Marion Martin to Irene Tribolet, 22 April 1940, NF-2(b) 3rd Vice Pres. Mrs. Ann Scott Wilson 1941–42, box 156, NFRW records. According to a notation regarding "colored club[s]" on a 1940 membership report, the ruling allowing black women's clubs to affiliate separately occurred on 5 June 1939. Growth of the National Federation of Women's Republican Clubs from September 24, 1938 to November 15, 1939, NF-9(c) Statistical Data and information re: NFWRC, box 153, NFRW records. Three black women's clubs did join the Federation separately: the Woman's Political Study Club of California; a black women's club in Kansas; and the Republican Women's Club of the District of Columbia (later called the Virginia White Speel Women's Republican Club). Although the same is not known regarding the Kansas club or the Women's Political Study Club, the D.C. club was also a member of the association. Its president, Julia West Hamilton, in explaining why her club joined the Federation, wrote of the importance of organizing women's power to restore constitutional principles and that she "pray[ed] for the cooperation of women everywhere." Hamilton, "Republican Women's Club of the District of Columbia."

40 Minutes of the Meeting of the Executive Committee, 5 September 1941, N.F. 7 Exec. Committee, Buffalo 9/5/41, Minutes, box 49, NFRW records.

41 Martin, "Minorities in Politics."

42 Press release, 25 March 1942, NF-7 Advisory Bd. Cleveland 3/24–25/42 Publicity and Releases, box 50, NFRW records.

43 Campbell, *Women at War with America*, 65–66, 71.

44 Marion Martin to Marjorie Tompkins, 8 January 1940, NF-9(c) Policy Developing letters from early days of Federation #1, box 153, NFRW records.

45 "May 1943–May 1944," Histories and Programs, box 47; League of Women Voters of the United States, "Forty Years of A Great Idea"; League of Women Voters of the United States, "A History of the League Program," History, National League, box 48, LWVI records.

46 "Supreme Sacrifice, Realism, and Vision Needed for War Effort," May 1942, clipping in scrapbook, 1938–43, box 2, ICRW records; Gladys Gordon to Marion Martin, 2 April 1942, NF-1(a) Ohio Affiliated clubs "2," box 11, NFRW records.

47 Marion Martin to the Advisory Board, 13 January 1942, NF-2(d) Letter to Advisory Bd. enclosing Treas. report 1/13/1942, box 148; Marion Martin to Wilma Bishop, 4 August 1942, NF-2(b) 1st Vice President, Mrs. Roy T. Bishop 1941–42, box 156; Excerpts from Speech of Mrs. W. Glenn Suthers, 7 May 1943, NF-2(a) Mrs. W. Glenn Suthers 1943–46 Speeches, box 156, NFRW records.

48 Rupp and Taylor characterize the NWP membership as "white, middle- or upper-class, well-educated and older women." Rupp and Taylor, *Survival in the Doldrums*, 25. The NWP was the main force behind the ERA in the 1940s, but the amendment was also endorsed at that time by various organizations of women professionals such as the National Federation of Business and Professional Women, the National Association of Women Lawyers, and the Association of American Women Dentists. The ERA was also endorsed by the National Association of Colored Women. Jane Todd, "Equal Rights Amendment," 28 December 1943, prepared for the National Federation of Women's Republican Clubs, Corres.— Nat'l Fed. Eq. Rights briefs, box 148, NFRW records.

49 Harrison, *On Account of Sex*, 19. Jo Freeman suggests that because the war necessitated new understandings of women's roles, there was a shift away from the view that women needed protection. This shift strengthened the NWP's arguments for the ERA. The GOP "led the way" in this regard, endorsing the ERA four years before the Democrats. J. Freeman, *A Room at a Time*, 211.

50 Caroline Huber to Marion Martin, 21 January 1944, Corres.— Nat'l Fed. Eq. Rights briefs— Todd & Huber, box 148, NFRW records. Later, after she was no longer with the Federation, Martin expressed her support for the "Women's Status Bill," which was endorsed by many women's groups (such as the LWV) as a compromise with the ERA because it called for an end to discrimination based on sex except where justified by physical difference, or biological or social function. On the Women's Status Bill, see Rupp and Taylor, *Survival in the Doldrums*, 62; Harrison, *On Account of Sex*, 26–30. There is no evidence that Martin's opposition to the ERA stemmed from concern about the fate of protective legislation, although she had worked for such laws as a Maine legislator. Martin explained her support for the Women's Status Bill as a belief that it would "carr[y] out our party platform," while being an "evolutionary rather than revolutionary way of accomplishing [the] ideal of equal rights for women." Marion Martin to Margaret Chase Smith, 17 February 1947; Marion Martin to Margaret Chase Smith, 20 February 1947, Martin, Marion–Smith Correspondence, MCS papers. By 1956 the Federation had endorsed equal rights planks in the Republican platform. Resolutions Adopted at Ninth Biennial Conven-

tion of the National Federation of Republican Women, 6–7 September 1956, Resolutions Committee, box 104, NFRW records.

51 Marion Martin to Judy Weis, 16 March 1942, NF-2 (a)(5) Mrs. Charles Weis Gen'l Corres. 1941–42 #2, box 155, NFRW records.

52 Marion Martin to Judy Weis, 2 October 1941, NF-2 (a)(5) Mrs. Charles Weis Gen'l Corres. 1941–42 #1; Marion Martin to Judy Weis, 16 March 1942, NF-2 (a)(5) Mrs. Charles Weis Gen'l Corres. 1941–42 #2, box 155, NFRW records.

53 This phrase is from the revised bylaws adopted at the Federation's 1940 Biennial Convention. Women's Division, *History of the National Federation of Republican Women*, 19.

54 The Federation did distribute briefs on both sides of the issue and conducted a survey, the results of which have not survived. The briefs were to be distributed only to those states in which the state club president requested the materials. Martin believed the state presidents could best decide whether introduction of the issue into their states would be advisable. Marion Martin to the Advisory Board, 28 January 1944, 1/28/44 to Adv. Board re: Equal Rights, box 148, NFRW records. A 1944 memo to the Federation's Advisory Board told members to urge local clubs to conduct secret polls of their members regarding their opinions of the ERA. Marion Martin to the Advisory Board, 30 March 1944, 3/30/44 to N.F. Adv. re: Equal Rights Poll, box 148, NFRW records.

55 Advisory Board Meeting, 21 January 1943, NF-2 (a)(5) Mrs. W. Glenn Suthers Gen'l Corres. 1943–46 #9, box 155; Marion Martin to Judy Weis, 26 January 1943, NF-2 (a)(5) Mrs. Charles Weis Gen'l Corres. 1941–42 #2, box 155, NFRW records.

56 Having noted that no women served on the Resolutions Committee in 1940, the RNC, shortly before the 1944 convention, recommended that the Resolutions Committee consist of a man and a woman from each state. Although the RNC recommendation did not have the force of a convention rule change, it established a custom that was generally followed at future conventions. Good, *History of Women*, 25–26.

57 Mary Donlon, vice chairman of the Resolutions Committee of the 1944 Republican National Convention, argued that the 1944 platform, the first on which women had real influence, contained planks reflecting the "three major issues that concern American women." These issues were ending the war and bringing the soldiers home as soon as possible; U.S. participation in a postwar international organization to prevent future wars; and the adoption of a program to put men who served in the armed forces to work in peacetime industries. Donlon's inclusion of the last issue is curious because it ignores the concern that some Federation leaders had with the fate of women workers after the war. Donlon did not include the ERA or the status of women workers as major issues concerning women. Excerpts from Speech of Miss Mary H. Donlon, 7 September 1944, N.F. Conv. 1944 Press Releases, box 54, NFRW records.

58 Weiss, *Farewell to the Party of Lincoln*, 270.

59 Dr. H. Claude Hudson, "Testimonial Address in Honor of Mrs. Betty Hill,"

Woman's Political Study Club convention pamphlet, 1940, NF-1(a) California Affiliated Clubs "2," box 1, NFRW records.

60 Speech by Betty Hill, 24 October 1940, ibid. A similar argument regarding African Americans and the New Deal was contained in the report of the RNC Program Committee released in February 1940. Weiss, *Farewell to the Party of Lincoln*, 270.

61 Barbara Whittiker to Marion Martin, 16 September 1946; Marion Martin to Barbara Whittiker, 18 September 1946, NF-1(a) California—Affiliated clubs, box 1, NFRW records.

62 On conflict within the GOP over the war issue during the 1940 campaign, see Cole, *Roosevelt and the Isolationists*, 390–92.

63 Judy Weis to Marion Martin, 3 September 1941, NF-2 (a)(2) Mrs. Charles Weis 1941–42, Report on Field Trip 1941, box 153, NFRW records. See also Judy Weis to Marion Martin, 5 August 1941; Marion Martin to Judy Weis, 7 August 1941, NF-2 (a)(5) Mrs. Charles Weis Gen'l Corres. 1941–42 #1, box 155, NFRW records.

64 Judy Weis to Marion Martin, 26 May 1941, NF-2 (a)(2) Mrs. Charles Weis, 1941–42, Report on Field Trip 1941, box 153; Judy Weis to Marion Martin, 7 August 1941, NF-2 (a)(5) Mrs. Charles Weis, Gen'l Corres., 1941–42 #1, box 155, NFRW records.

65 Minutes of Executive Committee meeting, 10 January 1941, NF-7 Exec. Committee Chicago, Jan. 10, 1941, Summary of Minutes, box 49, NFRW records.

66 On isolationist mothers' groups, see McEnaney, "He-Men and Christian Mothers"; Jeansonne, *Women of the Far Right*; Benowitz, *Days of Discontent*.

67 "Pro America Scores Waste in Government," *Denver Post*, 15 October 1941.

68 Marion Martin to Wilma Bishop, 4 August 1942, NF-2(b) 1st Vice President, Mrs. Roy T. Bishop 1941–42, box 156, NFRW records. See also Marion Martin to Joyce Arneill, 7 April 1942, NF-2 (a)(5) Mrs. James Arneill, Jr., Gen'l Corres. 1939–40 #2, box 154; Marion Martin to Judy Weis, 10 December 1941, NF-2 (a)(5) Mrs. Charles Weis Gen'l Corres. 1941–42 #1, box 155, NFRW records. On the response of leading Republican isolationists to the war after Pearl Harbor, see Cole, *Roosevelt and the Isolationists*, 502–7.

69 Gould, *Grand Old Party*, 265.

70 Linda Gordon, in her own work on social welfare policy during the New Deal, has acknowledged the problems of talking about feminism in this period but has opted for a definition of feminism that is loose and which can allow for a "wide variety of advocacy" across time. In Gordon's formulation, feminism is "a political perspective that considers women unjustly subordinated, finds that oppression to be humanly changeable, and strategizes for women's advancement." L. Gordon, *Pitied but Not Entitled*, 8.

71 Marion Martin to Judy Weis, 10 December 1941, NF-2 (a)(5) Mrs. Charles Weis Gen'l Corres. 1941–42 #1, box 155, NFRW records.

72 Lemons, *Woman Citizen*, 231.

73 Marion Martin to Judy Weis, 12 January 1943, NF-2 (a)(5) Mrs. Charles Weis

Gen'l Corres. 1941–42 #2, box 155, NFRW records. In 1944 the Federation's Advisory Board adopted a resolution favoring "job opportunities in the post-war world for men and women alike without discrimination in rate of pay because of sex." Resolutions Adopted, [March 1944], No. 53-A N.F. Adv. Board Meeting 3/44 Reports of Committees, box 52, NFRW records. Yet the 1944 Republican platform contained a plank endorsing the adoption of a program for putting veterans to work when they returned from the war without mention of sex discrimination. See note 57.

74 "Text of Address of Miss Marion E. Martin," 1 October 1940, NF-7 Convention Detroit Sept. 30–Oct. 1, 1940 #7, box 48, NFRW records.

75 Marion Martin to Judy Weis, 2 June 1941, NF-2 (a)(2) Mrs. Charles Weis 1941–42, Report on Field Trip 1941, box 153, NFRW records. "Women Are Urged to Back Parties," *Providence Journal*, 29 September 1946, Federation Convention Philadelphia 1946 clippings, box 58, NFRW records.

76 Marion Martin to Joyce Arneill, 15 January 1942, NF-2 (a)(5) Mrs. James Arneill, Jr., Gen'l Corres. 1939–40 #2, box 154, NFRW records.

77 Marion Martin to Mrs. George F. Frankberg, 24 October 1941, NF-9(c) Policy Developing letters from early days of Federation #1, box 153, NFRW records.

78 Helen Shorey to Marion Martin, 15 May 1938, NF-1(a) Maine—affiliated clubs "1," box 7, NFRW records.

79 Marion Martin to Mrs. Geo. F. Warren, 24 October 1941; Marion Martin to Mrs. G. W. T. Reynolds, 20 October 1939; Marion Martin to Mrs. John B. Crouch, 9 July 1941, NF-9(c) Policy Developing letters from early days of Federation #1, box 153; Emma Parsons to Judy Weis, 28 June 1941, NF-2 (a)(5) Mrs. Charles Weis Gen'l Corres. 1941–42 #3, box 155, NFRW records.

80 See, for example, Judy Weis to Marion Martin, 28 July 1941, NF-2 (a)(5) Mrs. Charles Weis Gen'l Corres. 1941–42 #1, box 155; Marion Martin to Judy Weis, 8 May 1941, NF-2 (a)(2) Mrs. Charles Weis 1941–42, Report on Field Trip, box 153, NFRW records.

81 Marion Martin to Joyce Arneill, 20 January 1939, NF-2 (a)(5) Mrs. James Arneill, Jr., Gen'l Corres. 1939–40 #2 file, box 154, NFRW records.

82 On women in right-wing movements in the late 1930s, see Jeansonne, *Women of the Far Right*; McEnaney, "He-Men and Christian Mothers"; Benowitz, *Days of Discontent*.

83 Marion Martin to Joyce Arneill, 11 September 1939, NF-2 (a)(5) Mrs. James Arneill, Jr., Gen'l Corres. 1939–40 #2, box 154, NFRW records. Martin did not always adhere to the subtle kinds of criticisms she advocated. On at least one occasion, she publicly argued that the New Deal was "based on Fascist principles including one man rule and a planned economy." "New Deal Fascistic, Marion Martin Says," 1937 clipping provided by William Martin. Generally, however, the danger that women would be carried away by alarmist rhetoric outweighed in her mind the appeals that same rhetoric could have. For an example of Martin's more typical (and more moderate) criticism of the New Deal, see Text of Address of Miss Marion E. Martin, 1 October 1940, box 48, NF-7 Convention Detroit Sept. 30–Oct. 1, 1940 #7, NFRW records.

84 "Handbook of Club Organization," 1940, box 157, NFRW records.

85 Marion Martin to Judy Weis, 29 April 1941, NF-2 (a)(2) Mrs. Charles Weis 1941–42, Report on Field Trip 1941, box 153, NFRW records.

86 Report by Marion Martin, Transcripts of Republican National Committee meeting, 7 December 1945, frames 796, reel 7, RPP I-a.

87 Molly Dewson to James Farley, 5 October 1933, quoted in Ware, *Partner and I*, 182.

88 Marion Martin to Judy Weis, 7 July 1941, NF-2 (a)(5) Mrs. Charles Weis Gen'l Corres. 1941–42 #3, box 155, NFRW records.

89 Marion Martin to All National Committeewomen, State Vice Chairmen and Members of the National Federation of Women's Republican Clubs, 7 April 1939, Memos 4/7/39 re: Wagner Act, box 147, NFRW records.

90 Mrs. E. G. Goddard to Board Members and Resolutions Committee, 6 September 1944, Resolutions Committee, Mrs. Green, Mass., Chairman, box 54, NFRW records.

91 Ibid.

92 Although at times it seemed that Martin was almost contemptuous of women, on a personal level she could be very supportive. Her correspondence with the women who served with her as Federation leaders was warm, encouraging, and frequently personal. Martin nourished talent where she saw it. Martin's assistant, Jane Hamilton Macauley, recalls how Martin rescued her when she was a young, incompetent secretary about to be fired from her job with the RNC Finance Division. Martin had intervened and offered to find Macauley a position in the Women's Division. Martin, as Macauley describes, nurtured the younger woman's talents and eventually made Macauley her assistant. JHM interview, 15 October 1996. Macauley later succeeded Martin as RNC assistant chairman and executive director of the Federation.

93 Remarks by Marion E. Martin, Transcripts of Republican National Committee meeting, 5 December 1946, frames 55–57, reel 8, RPP I-a.

94 "Political Victim Rebuilt State Labor Dept.," *Kennebec Journal*, 26 June 1972.

95 In a letter to one of Martin's supporters, Reece insisted that Martin had resigned voluntarily but in correspondence with his ally Irene Gerlinger he took a different tone. Irene Gerlinger to Carroll Reece, 21 January 1947; Carroll Reece to Janet Gould, 14 March 1947; Carroll Reece to Irene Gerlinger, 27 January 1947, folder 10, box 10, BCR papers.

96 Doris Fleeson, "Clash within Party," *Washington Evening Star*, 17 December 1946.

97 Margaret Chase Smith to Carroll Reece, 16 December 1946, MCS papers.

98 These chairmen were John Hamilton, who appointed Martin in 1937; Joseph Martin of Missouri; Harrison Spangler of Iowa; and Herbert Brownell of New York.

99 JHM interview, 15 October 1996.

100 Irene Gerlinger to Carroll Reece, 21 January 1947, BCR papers; Irene Gerlinger to Council of Oregon Republican Women Meeting, 16 March 1948, NF-1(f) Oregon—Correspondence with state officials, box 12, NFRW records; Wilma

Bishop to Elizabeth Farrington, 17 January 1949, box 19, Oregon—General "2," NFRW records.

101 Fleeson speculated that Brown would take over some of Martin's work in Doris Fleeson, "Clash within Party," *Washington Evening Star*, 17 December 1946; in an untitled clipping from the *Chicago Tribune*, ca. December 1946, Bertha Bauer is described as "licking her chops at the prospect" of receiving Martin's $12,000 job. Chicago Advisory Board Meeting Jan. 47—Program, box 61, NFRW records.

102 JHM interview, 15 October 1946.

103 "Maine Labor Is for Martin Appointment," *Maine State Labor News*, February 1950; "Maine Woman Has the Only Position of Its Kind in the Country," *Portland Telegram*, 7 May 1950, clippings provided by William Martin; "Political Victim Rebuilt State Labor Dept.," *Kennebec Journal*, 26 June 1972; "Scrappy Head of Maine's Labor Department Recalls Early Days," 27 June 1972, Martin alumni file.

104 See Martin's obituaries, *New York Times*, 11 January 1987; *Kennebec Journal*, 9 January 1987.

105 Wellesley, *Record Book* (1972), 23.

106 Those states that collected individual dues could determine statewide membership fairly accurately. Other states, however, paid a lump sum to the national Federation based on the estimated state membership. If a state were late in sending in its dues, its numbers would not appear in membership totals, although the state might have a healthy organization. Growth of the National Federation of Women's Republican Clubs from September 24, 1938, to November 15, 1939; Membership Growth of Statewide Federations, ca. 1943, NF-9(c) Statistical Data and information re: NFWRC, box 153, NFRW records.

107 Women's Division, *History of National Federation of Republican Women*, 19.

108 Report on Membership, 1 March 1944 to 31 December 1944, Exec. Committee Meeting Jan. 1945, box 55, NFRW records.

109 Marion Martin to All National Committeewomen and State Vice Chairmen, 20 August 1940, untitled folder, box 147; Report of the President, 10 March 1944, 3/44 N.F. Adv. Board Meeting Rept. of the Pres., box 52, NFRW records.

CHAPTER 4

1 Originally from Fort Madison, Iowa, the twenty-year-old Jane Hamilton moved to Washington, D.C., in 1937, in order to support herself and her widowed mother. Through her uncle, RNC chairman John Hamilton, Jane Hamilton secured a job first with Landon's campaign and eventually with the RNC Women's Division under Marion Martin. In 1946, after her old acquaintance Robert Macauley returned from the war, the two married. JHM interview, 15 October 1996; JHM interview, 12 August 1997; Entry for Mrs. Robert W. Macauley, in Rothe, *Current Biography*, 364–66.

2 Wilma Bishop to Betty Farrington, ca. February 1949, Oregon General "2," box 19, NFRW records.

3 Betty Farrington to Marie Suthers, 14 February 1950; Marie Suthers to Betty Farrington, 16 February 1950, Revisions and By-laws Committee, box 20, NFRW records.

4 Minutes of RNC Committee on Rules, 30 June 1952, frame 191, reel 12, RPP I-a; entry for Betty Farrington, NFRW Presidents, binder in NFRW-PR.

5 Report to the Advisory Board of the National Federation of Republican Women, Mrs. Robert W. Macauley, 27 June 1949, NF 7 Adv. Bd.-Exec Comm., Exec. Director's Report, box 69, NFRW records; Financial Statement, 16 January 1953, Minutes—Exec. Committee and Board of Directors Meetings, box 80, NFRW records. Farrington's successor, Nora Kearns, was a congressman's wife and also a Washington resident. She was therefore able to follow Farrington's precedent and run the Federation from Washington. Catharine Gibson, who followed Kearns as president in 1957, continued to reside in her home state of Michigan, but spent a great deal of time in Washington, continuing the practice of running the Federation personally from the nation's capitol. Catharine Gibson to Honorable Meade Alcorn et al., 25 July 1957, Republican Nat'l Committee, box 128, NFRW records.

6 Betty Farrington to Wilma Bishop, 25 February 1949, Oregon General "2," box 19, NFRW records; JHM interview, 12 August 1997.

7 Biographical sketch of Elizabeth Farrington in this and the subsequent paragraph has been compiled from the following: "Introducing: Mrs. Joseph R. Farrington," *Washington Newsletter*, October 1953, "Washington Newsletter," 1952–53, box 145; "Delegate from Hawaii Regarded as One of Nation's Most Influential Women," *St. Petersburg Times*, 8 December 1954, Florida "1," box 30, NFRW records; "Farrington Philosophy in Evidence," *Washington Post*, 14 October 1944, Mrs. William Culbertson President 1944–47, DC scrapbooks; "Did You Happen to See—Mrs. Joseph Farrington," July 1947, clipping in The Hon. Elizabeth Farrington President 1947–48, DC scrapbooks; Chapin, *Shaping History*, 232–33.

8 "Farrington Philosophy in Evidence," *Washington Post*, 14 October 1944.

9 Remarks by Mrs. Joseph Farrington, Transcripts of Western-Midwestern Regional Conference of the RNC, Joint Session, 12 May 1951, frame 212, reel 11, RPP I-a.

10 Marion Martin to Marie Suthers, 18 August 1945, NF-2 (a)(5) Mrs. W. Glenn Suthers Gen'l Corres. 1943–46 #2, box 155, NFRW records.

11 "Women's Lobby Is Slated for Investigation," *Chicago Daily Tribune*, 6 June 1949, reel 6, frame 726, WJCC records; "Congress to Pry into Ladies Club Lobbying," clipping, 26 June 1949, Public Relations, box 20, NFRW records; "Questions Have Two Sides except in 21 Women's Clubs," *Los Angeles Times*, 16 March 1949, in JHM scrapbook 1. For background on the WJCC, see Cott, *Grounding of Modern Feminism*, 97–99.

12 Mrs. Theodore O. Wedel to John Eklund, 9 August 1949, frame 202, reel 3, WJCC records. Such charges echoed the fears about radicalism in women's organizations (including the WJCC) that had been fueled in the 1920s by the distribution of "spider web charts," which purported to show how a host of

women's peace and welfare organizations were linked together in a subversive plot directed from Moscow. On the spider web charts, see J. Jensen, "All Pink Sisters"; Cott, *Grounding of Modern Feminism*, 242, 249–50; Nielsen, *Un-American Womanhood*, 75–84.

13 Address of Mrs. Joseph R. Farrington at the convention of the National Federation of Women's Republican Clubs, 30 August 1950, Original Copies of Committee Reports, box 72, NFRW records.

14 Minutes of Federation Advisory Board meeting, 15 January 1952, no folder, box 75, NFRW records.

15 Elizabeth Farrington to Nettie Stewart, 16 June 1950, Georgia General, box 17, NFRW records. See also exhibit material on public relations, which discusses the techniques of the CIO Women's Auxiliaries, box 20, Public Relations, NFRW records. For a description of efforts by Republican women in Pennsylvania to infiltrate nonpartisan women's organizations, see Remarks by Pennsylvania Vice Chairwoman Mrs. Sara Leffler, Transcripts of the Eastern Regional Conference of the RNC and Republican State Chairmen and Vice Chairmen Meeting, 1 October 1951, frames 440–41, reel 11, RPP I-a.

16 For a discussion of the CIO's efforts at community outreach, see Fones-Wolf, *Selling Free Enterprise*, 137–57.

17 "GOP School of Politics a Woman-Power Project," clipping ca. May 1950, Republican School of Politics, Small Exhibit of Publicity, box 116; see also undated public relations material, Public Relations, box 20, NFRW records.

18 McEnaney, "He-Men and Christian Mothers." See also Jeansonne, *Women of the Far Right*; Benowitz, *Days of Discontent*.

19 Jeansonne estimates that participants in the mothers' movement may have numbered as high as five to six million. Amy Swerdlow reasonably cautions that such numbers are probably too high and suggests that one million is more realistic. Swerdlow, "Playing the Mother Card for Fascism," 113. Even this lower number represented a quite successful movement at a time when other women's organizations boasted a much smaller number. In 1938 the League of Women Voters claimed 43,000 members. Marguerite M. Wells, "A Portrait of the League of Women Voters," 1961, History—National League, box 48, LWVI records. D'Ann Campbell suggests that Red Cross volunteers numbered in the "hundreds of thousands." Campbell, *Women at War with America*, 68–69.

20 McEnaney, "He-Men and Christian Mothers," 49–51.

21 Cole, *Roosevelt and the Isolationists*, 516–17.

22 On grass-roots conservatism in southern California, see McGirr, *Suburban Warriors*. McGirr concerns herself primarily with the 1960s, yet she does argue the importance wartime migration to California played in creating suburban communities where right-wing political groups (mostly mixed-gender groups in her work) would later flourish.

23 Nickerson, "Women, Domesticity, and Postwar Conservatism," 17.

24 Examples of such comments include copy of Niva Nichols to Guy Gabrielson, 9 December 1949, California General "1," box 16; Fanny Kelet to Betty Farrington, 1 December 1950, California General "2," box 16; Cecil Logan, "Will

Your Children Learn Too Late the Common End of Socialism and Communism?," attached to letter from Helen S. Walton to Betty Farrington, 25 April 1949, California General "1," box 16, NFRW records.

25 Jean Fuller to Betty Farrington, 28 November 1950, California General "2," box 16; Jean Fuller to Betty Farrington, 25 July 1951, California General "2," box 22; 2 October 1951, California General "1," box 22, NFRW records.

26 Helen Walton to Betty Farrington, 25 April 1949; Betty Farrington to Helen Walton, 3 May 1949, California General "1," box 16, NFRW records.

27 Jean Fuller to Members of the California Council of Republican Women, 26 September 1951, California General "1," box 22, NFRW records; Southern California Republican Women, *Special Bulletin*, October 1951, Republican Party, Women's Club Publications, 1931–32 and undated, Presidential papers, box 274, HH papers.

28 Scher, *Politics in the New South*, 95; Black and Black, *The Vital South*, 176–77.

29 Nettie Stewart to Marion Martin, 12 June 1945; Marion Martin to Nettie Stewart, 26 July 1945; Jane Macauley to Nettie Stewart, 13 February 1947, 22 March 1947; Nettie Stewart to Jane Macauley, 3 March 1947, 27 March 1947, NF-1(a) Georgia—Affiliated Clubs, box 3, NFRW records.

30 Scher, *Politics in the New South*, 144–45. Black and Black demonstrate that Republican candidates did best among southern white voters who had received some college education, as well as in urban areas. Black and Black, *The Vital South*, 183–84.

31 See, for example, Anne Hawkins to Jane Macauley, 5 April 1947; Jane Macauley to Anne Hawkins, 16 May 1947, NF-1(a) Georgia—Affiliated Clubs, box 3; Exchange between Mrs. J. D. Stratton and Bernard Lamb (Director of Field Organization for the RNC Congressional Committee), Transcripts of Meeting of Exec. Comm. & Bd. of Directors, 30 March 1957, untitled folder, box 98, NFRW records.

32 For state-by-state comparisons of the southern presidential vote 1900–1960, see Scher, *Politics in the New South*, 91–94 (Tables 4.1a–4.1d). Scher defines the "rim" South as encompassing Arkansas, Florida, North Carolina, Tennessee, Texas, and Virginia.

33 Black and Black, *The Vital South*, 183.

34 Remarks by Mrs. Joseph R. Farrington, Transcripts of Republican National Committee meeting, 26 January 1951, frame 685, reel 10, RPP I-a. See also Report of Mrs. Joseph R. Farrington, Transcripts of Midwest Regional Conference of the RNC, Executive Session, 15 September 1950, frames 265–66, reel 10, RPP I-a.

35 Jim McKillips to The Chairman [Leonard Hall], 25 November 1953, Southern Situation 1953, box 166, LWII papers.

36 Report of Mrs. Carroll D. Kearns to the National Federation of Republican Women, 6 September 1956, President's Report, 9th Biennial Conv., box 104, NFRW records. Although Kearns neglected to include North Carolina in the list of southern states with statewide federations, the North Carolina Federation of Women's Republican Clubs was formed in April 1953. Nora Kearns to

Mrs. Millard Teague, 15 April 1953, North Carolina 1953 (2), box 33, NFRW records.

37 Wilma Ver Meulen was appointed Federation chaplain around the end of 1953. In appointing a chaplain, the Federation followed the lead of the California Council of Republican Women, which did so in 1950, and the Republican National Committee, which did so in 1952. Mary Jasper to Betty Farrington, 9 October 1950, California General "2," box 16; Ella [illegible] to Nora Kearns, December 1953, Chaplain, box 128, NFRW records; Transcripts of Republican National Committee meeting, 18 January 1952, frames 863–66, reel 11, RPP I-a.

38 Elizabeth Farrington to Nettie Stewart, 16 June 1950, Georgia General, box 17, NFRW records.

39 Copies of the *Washington Newsletter* are found in boxes 144–47, NFRW records.

40 "Excerpts from Senator McCarthy's Address before Ohio Valley Women's GOP Clubs," *Intelligencer* (Wheeling), 10 February 1950. For local coverage of the Lincoln Day dinner, see also "M'Carthy Charges Reds Hold U.S. Jobs," *Intelligencer* (Wheeling), 10 February 1950; "Senator Joe McCarthy's Visit to Valley Area," *Intelligencer* (Wheeling), 11 February 1950. David Bennett describes this event as an "unlikely setting" for such an important speech. Bennett, *Party of Fear*, 293; David Halberstam characterizes the Ohio Women's Republican Club as not "prominent," suggesting that McCarthy's choice of forum was evidence that his remarks about communists in the State Department were not planned in advance. Halberstam, *The Fifties*, 49–50.

41 Many hesitated, for example, to embrace self-declared professional anticommunist Jessica Payne. Payne, president of the West Virginia Federation of Republican Women, was also a free-lance speaker on communism and subversion who had been active since the 1920s. Although Payne wanted to bring her expertise more closely to bear on the Federation, some found her to be overzealous and single-minded. "Like sin," Wilma Bishop complained to Betty Farrington, everyone was against communism. "[B]ut *why* have Payne take up the cudgel at every mile post?" Wilma Bishop to Betty Farrington, 21 February 1950, Oregon—General "1," box 19; Biographical Sketch of Mrs. E. Wyatt Payne, ca. 1949, West Virginia—General, box 20, NFRW records.

42 Mrs. Warren E. Moore to Ruth Thomas, ca. June 1949; Betty Farrington to Ruth Thomas, 12 July 1949; Betty Farrington to Mrs. Warren E. Moore, 12 July 1949, Florida "2," box 17, NFRW records.

43 Report by RNC Chairman Hugh D. Scott, Jr., Transcripts of Republican National Committee meeting, 27 January 1949, frame 85, reel 9, RPP I-a; Reinhard, *Republican Right*, 59–60.

44 Transcripts of Republican National Committee meeting, 26 January 1949, frame 22; Minutes of Republican Strategy Committee meeting, 13 December 1949, frames 565–82; Transcripts of RNC Policy Committee meeting, 18 January 1950, frames 604–999, reel 9, RPP I-a.

45 "G.O.P. Women's Chief Says Future of Party Rests with Congress," *Washington Evening Star*, 3 February 1949, DC scrapbooks, 1948–49.

46 Address of Mrs. Joseph R. Farrington to the National Federation of Women's Republican Clubs convention, 30 August 1950, Copies of Convention Reports, box 72, NFRW records; Remarks of Mrs. Joseph Farrington, Transcripts of RNC Policy Committee meeting, 18 January 1950, frames 656–59, reel 9, RPP I-a. For earlier expressions of Farrington's belief that unity could be achieved by adhering to simple principles, see "G.O.P. Women Start 1950 Vote Campaign Today," *Times-Herald* (New York), 3 February 1949, DC scrapbook, 1948–49.

47 Remarks by Mrs. Joseph Farrington, Transcripts of RNC Policy Committee, 18 January 1950, frames 657–58, reel 9, RPP I-a.

48 Remarks by Harold Mitchell, Transcripts of RNC Policy Committee meeting, 18 January 1950, frame 717, ibid.

49 Remarks by Mrs. LaFell Dickinson, Transcripts of RNC Policy Committee meeting, 18 January 1950, frame 647, ibid.

50 Transcripts of RNC Policy Committee meeting, 19 January 1950, frames 933–35, ibid.

51 Report of the Policy Committee on Republican Party Principles and Objectives by Clarence B. Kelland. Transcripts of Republican National Committee meeting, 6 February 1950, frames 68–79, reel 10, RPP I-a.

52 Frames 180–81, reel 10, RPP I-a; Reinhard, *Republican Right*, 65.

53 Address of Mrs. Joseph R. Farrington to the National Federation of Women's Republican Clubs convention, 30 August 1950, Copies of Convention Reports, box 72, NFRW records. See also speech by Farrington, 1951, Publicity, box 74; Suggested Report of the Public Relations Committee, 1950, Committees (1950) [1], box 71, NFRW records. Farrington introduced this argument to Republican strategists early in 1950. Remarks of Mrs. Joseph Farrington Transcripts of Policy Committee meeting, 18 January 1950, frame 657, reel 9, RPP I-a.

54 Suggested Report of the Public Relations Committee, 1950, Committees (1950) [1], box 71; Address of Mrs. Joseph R. Farrington to the convention of the National Federation of Republican Women, 30 August 1950, Original Copies of Committee Reports, box 72; Remarks of Mrs. Joseph R. Farrington, 1951, Publicity, box 73, NFRW records.

55 Program for "Women Who'll Work to Win," December 1948, DC scrapbooks, 1948–49.

56 "'School of Politics' Opened by Republicans," *Washington Post*, 2 May 1950, Republican School of Politics, Small Exhibit of Publicity, box 116, NFRW records; Remarks by Mrs. Joseph Farrington, Transcripts of Western-Midwestern Regional Conference of the RNC, Joint Session, 12 May 1951, frame 211, reel 11, RPP I-a.

57 *Washington Newsletter*, 30 November 1950, "Washington Newsletter," 1950–51, box 144, NFRW records.

58 Stouffer, *Communism, Conformity, and Civil Liberties*, 165–66, 169–70.

59 Porter and Johnson, *National Party Platforms 1840–1972*, 496–505.

60 On modern Republicanism, see Diggins, *The Proud Decades*, 130–32; Allen, *Eisenhower and the Mass Media*, 64–65; Andrew, *Other Side of the Sixties*, 32–36.

61 On the Bricker Amendment, see Tananbaum, *Bricker Amendment Controversy.*
62 Ibid., 119–20. Tananbaum argues that members of the Vigilant Women were not always well informed about the issue, and that the signatures obtained were in response to a very vaguely worded statement.
63 Ibid., x.
64 Betty Lou Atkins [Secretary to Nora Kearns] to Mrs. Neil Thackaberry, 22 April 1955, California [3], box 36, NFRW records.
65 Ruth Murray to Katharine Kennedy Brown, 8 September 1954, Committees—8th Biennial Convention, box 89, NFRW records. See also Mrs. Irl H. Marshall to Bertha Adkins, Illinois [2], box 37, NFRW records.
66 "GOP Unit Adopts 7 Measures," *Los Angeles Times,* 24 September 1954.
67 On the Girard case, see Packard, *Protest in Tokyo,* 35–36.
68 See ibid., 36, n. 2.
69 Vere de Vere Adams Hutchins to Catharine Gibson, 20 June 1957, California [3], box 42; 21 July 1957, California [2], box 42, NFRW records.
70 Ibid.
71 Minutes of National Federation of Republican Women Informal Board of Directors Meeting, 5 June 1957, Minutes—Exec. Com. and Bd. of Directors, box 99, NFRW records.
72 Scholarly accounts that have commented on the Federation's reputation in the late fifties and early sixties for being more conservative than other party organizations include Cotter and Hennessy, *Politics without Power,* 154; Kessel, *The Goldwater Coalition,* 144 n. 25.
73 Wallace, *Politics of Conscience,* 99–130.
74 Program for Women Who'll Work to Win, February 1949, DC scrapbooks, 1948–49.
75 Hofstadter, *American Political Tradition,* viii–ix; Hartz, *Liberal Tradition in America.*
76 Rossiter further classified conservatives as "ultra," "middling," and "liberal" based on the extent to which they accepted or rejected parts of what he called the New Economy (the New Deal), the United Nations, the Bricker Amendment, and Sen. Joseph McCarthy. Rossiter himself identified the middling conservatives as the best articulation of a true American conservatism. Rossiter, *Conservatism in America,* 170–75.
77 Samuel Stouffer's study of communism and civil liberties in 1954 consisted of interviews with a cross-section of about 5,000 Americans, based on a standard set of questions. In his study, Stouffer did not set out to explore views on communism per se. Rather, he sought to examine degrees of tolerance toward those who represented unpopular ideas. Conducting his study in the fifties, Stouffer logically chose to focus on tolerance of atheists, socialists, and communists—groups whose ideas garnered little sympathy among Americans at that time. His study, then, reveals much about American's perceptions about such "deviants." Because the Right levied charges of "godless communism" against supporters of liberal causes (such as the United Nations, public funding of schools, national health care, civil rights, etc.), one can cautiously infer

that a person's standing on Stouffer's scale of tolerance may have roughly conformed to his or her positions on some of these other issues. Stouffer, *Communism, Conformity, and Civil Liberties*, 13–25.

78 Stouffer's interest in examining women's attitudes separately from men's stemmed from concerns that would have been familiar to Republican clubwomen: if children were to learn tolerance and respect for the rights of others, they would do so first in their homes, from their mothers. Although concerned with the transmission of a different set of values, Stouffer and Republican clubwomen shared a belief that how women thought and acted could be of greater significance in the long run than the thoughts and actions of men. Ibid., 131.

79 Ibid., 132–55.

80 The "status anxiety" thesis arose in the 1950s out of an interest on the part of social scientists in studying movements of the political Right in the wake of McCarthyism. Writing as social critics, these scholars treated McCarthyism as an example of a pathology, marginal to American society, that needed to be exposed and explained. In 1955, Daniel Bell edited a collection of essays, written primarily by social scientists (including one historian, Richard Hofstadter), which would have enduring influence on the study of right-wing groups. Undertaking to explain the phenomenon of McCarthyism, Bell, Seymour Martin Lipset, and others developed in their essays the hypothesis that "status anxiety" was a major explanation for right-wing behavior. Bell, *Radical Right*. According to Lipset, while class conflicts produced leftist movements, concerns about status were the major source of American right-wing movements. In times of prosperity, Lipset argued, groups that were insecure about their social status (due to either a recent improvement in economic position or fear that current high status was being challenged by upwardly mobile groups) have sought to alleviate their frustration by targeting scapegoats and engaging in intolerant, antidemocratic behavior. Lipset, "Sources of the 'Radical Right,'" 260–61. The "status anxiety" thesis has been challenged by recent historians. William Hixson faults the thesis for its imprecision, whereas Leo Ribuffo objects to the tendency by proponents of the thesis to focus on beliefs as symptoms, rather than as ideas to be examined on their own terms. Hixson, *Search for the American Right Wing*, 310; Ribuffo, *Right Center Left*, 5.

81 Lipset, "Sources of the 'Radical Right,'" 303–4, n. 31.

82 Ibid. Lipset based his statement about women's concerns with morality on cross-national survey data.

83 Campbell, *Women at War with America*, 216–17.

84 Kerber, *Women of the Republic*, 199–200.

85 This was also the case in Nazi Germany and in Chile under Pinochet. See Koonz, *Mothers in the Fatherland*; Waylen, "Rethinking Women's Political Participation," 299–314.

86 Perelli, "Putting Conservatism to Good Use." Scholars of Latin American women's movements in particular have wrestled with the implications of the politicization of mothers' moral outrage. Mothers who organized around the disappearance of their sons played central roles in the movements against

dictatorships in Chile, Argentina, and elsewhere in the 1970s and 1980s. Some scholars have argued that these mothers' movements instilled in women the idea that politics could be a legitimate part of motherhood and thereby offered a socially acceptable way for traditional women to engage with politics. Yet others have also observed that, as democratization occurs in these countries, women appear largely to have demobilized. Perhaps, as Maria del Carmen Feijoó suggests, the political rhetoric of moral righteousness and nonnegotiability is appropriate for the politics of confrontation but is not so readily adapted to the "ordinary requirements of democratic politics which call for negotiation and bargaining." Feijoó, "Challenge of Constructing Civilian Peace," 73.

87 "Just a man looking at his party" to Catharine Gibson, 17 October 1957, Illinois, box 43, NFRW records.

CHAPTER 5

1 "Two Conventions? No, Three; One Is for Republican Women," *Star-Journal and Sunday Chieftain* (Pueblo, Colorado), 12 August 1956.

2 Noun, *More Strong-Minded Women*, 148.

3 Marvick and Nixon, "Recruitment Contrasts in Rival Campaign Groups," 205–6.

4 1954 Republican Speech Kit, prepared by the Republican Congressional Committee, Speech Kit, box 3, DCP papers.

5 Report of Clare B. Williams, Transcripts of RNC Executive Session, 10 June 1960, frames 655–56, reel 18, RPP I-a.

6 Report by Robert Humphreys, Transcripts of RNC Executive Committee meeting, 18 February 1955, frame 834, reel 14, RPP I-a.

7 For an example of these arguments, see Addams, "Why Women Should Vote."

8 Mayo, "Be a Party Girl," 156; Speech by Senator [?] [illegible], Program, General—Speakers, Music, Entertainment (1954), box 90, NFRW records.

9 Paula Baker describes the grass-roots work of Democratic and Republican women in Baker, "'She Is the Best Man on the Ward Committee.'"

10 Report on Organized Opposition by the Democratic Party, Transcripts of RNC Executive Committee meeting, 28 February 1953, frame 896, reel 13, RPP I-a; Remarks by Robert Humphreys, Transcripts of RNC Executive Committee meeting, 18 February 1955, frames 817–35, reel 14, RPP I-a; "Labor Looms as GOP's Opposition Party," *Washington Post*, 18 March 1958; Address by H. Meade Alcorn, Jr., Transcripts of RNC meeting, 22 January 1959, frame 97, reel 17, RPP I-a.

11 Foster, *The Union Politic*, 186–92, 178–81. Although labor was organizing for the Democrats, divisions between men's and women's political behavior existed in both parties. As Katie Louchheim, director of women's activities for the Democratic Party, said regarding the 1956 campaign, "You can be sure that most of the doorbells rung this fall will be rung by women's hands. . . . Campaign and elections headquarters will be manned by an even distribution of co-eds and grandmothers, while young matrons will transport voters to the

polls." "Women Voters, in Majority, Can Decide Elections," *New York Herald Tribune*, 15 October 1956, Political activities 1955–56, box 3, BA papers; Louchheim's assertion that "most" of the volunteer work for the party would be done by women contradicts the findings of Marvik and Nixon.

12 Lichtenstein, "From Corporatism to Collective Bargaining," 134–40; Foster, *The Union Politic*, 199–200.

13 "Idea Fest," Transcript of Board of Directors meetings, Bd. of Dir. Meeting & Exec. Comm., Charlotte, N. Carolina, Jan. 13–14–15, 1958, box 101, NFRW records.

14 On women's activism within progressive organizations, see Lynn, *Progressive Women in Conservative Times*. On women in the League of Women Voters, see Ware, "American Women in the 1950s." Democratic women's clubs also grew during the fifties. Although the Democrats did not have a national organization comparable to the Federation, the growth of Democratic women's clubs did disturb Federation leaders, who saw their twenty years of national organization as an advantage "we must hang on to at all costs." Finance Committee Report, 13–25 March 1958, meeting of the Exec. Comm. & Bd. of Dir., box 110, NFRW records.

15 Statement of Per Capita Dues & Service Charges Received thru February 29, 1956, Papers for Exec. Comm. and Bd. of Dir. 3/1–2–3, 1956, box 92, NFRW records.

16 "Women Democrats' Head to Hold Schools across Nation on Issues," *New York Times*, 26 April 1950; "GOP School of Politics a Woman-Power Project," ca. April 1950, clipping in Small Exhibit of Publicity, box 116, NFRW records.

17 "Have You Heard about . . . a Program-Planning Aid for the Modern Clubwoman," 10 March 1950, School of Politics, box 114; Arnilla Myhre to Guy Gabrielson et al., 16 May 1950, Repub. School of Politics — Letters of Commendation, box 116, NFRW records.

18 Report by Mrs. Gilford Mayes, Transcripts of Midwest Regional Conference of the RNC, Executive Session, 14 September 1950, frame 341, reel 10, RPP I-a.

19 Report of Albert Mitchell, Transcripts of RNC Executive Committee meeting, 8 December 1950, frame 549, reel 10, RPP I-a.

20 Priest, "The Ladies Elected Ike," 27.

21 Nora Lynch Kearns was married to Pennsylvania congressman Carroll D. Kearns. When the couple moved to Washington, she became involved with various civic and political organizations. She served as a leader of the Congressional Club, an organization of wives of members of Congress, and was a two-term president of the League of Republican Women of the District of Columbia. She became Federation president in 1953, serving through 1956. Introduction to Nora Kearns, Mrs. Roy E. James, 19 January 1954, Introductions (of Speakers), box 122, NFRW records.

22 Statement by Nora Kearns to Republican Women's Conference, Publicity — Board Meeting, Wash., D.C., Jan. 16–17, 1953, box 80, NFRW records. On the CIO-PAC's "marginal districts" campaign, see Foster, *Union Politic*, 177.

23 Address by Mr. Bernard Lamb, Transcripts of Meeting of the Executive Board

and the Board of Directors of the NFRW, 30 March 1957, box 98, NFRW records.

24 Texas Report, Aileen (Mrs. Robert D.) O'Callaghan, Minutes—Exec. Comm. & Bd. of Directors Meeting, June 5, 1957, box 99, NFRW records.

25 Baker, "'She Is the Best Man on the Ward Committee,'" 159.

26 "Work *Now* Win in November," Handbook from Republican National Women's Conference (March 1958), 27, Republican Women's Conference 1958, box 6, AL papers.

27 Report of Mrs. Ruth Parks, Transcripts of RNC meeting, 12 June 1962, frame 308, reel 1, RPP I-b.

28 May, *Homeward Bound*, 11.

29 National Federation of Republican Women News Release, 15 April 1955, Kitchen Kabinet Press Release, box 142; *Washington Newsletter*, April 1956 [supplement], Nominating Committee—1956, box 103, NFRW records.

30 Catharine Gibson to State Federation President, 8 April 1957, Campaign Projects—extra copies, box 127, NFRW records.

31 American Flag Project, Flag, box 122, NFRW records.

32 "Both Parties Creating Super Salesladies Staff," *Courier-News* (Plainfield), ca. fall 1956, unlabeled folder, box 129, NFRW records.

33 Report of Mrs. Ab Hermann to the National Federation of Republican Women Convention, 7 September 1956, 1956 GOP Convention, box 105; "'Operation Coffee Cup' Has National Kick-off," *Washington Newsletter*, August 1958; "Questions for Chicago Panel Discussion," Nat'l "Operation Coffee Cup"—1958, box 128, NFRW records.

34 Press Release, 5 January 1956, Press Release Announcing Nationwide Membership Drive, box 143, NFRW records. See also Nora Kearns, Report of the President to Board of Directors Meeting, 16 May 1956, Minutes—Bd. of Directors Meeting, box 92, NFRW records.

35 Operation Coffee Cup brochure, Nat'l "Operation Coffee Cup"—1958, box 128, NFRW records.

36 Catharine Gibson to State Federation Presidents, 9 May 1958, Campaign Projects—extra copies, box 127, NFRW records.

37 Patricia Luce, "A Republican Roundtable," 2 March 1956, unlabeled folder, box 129, NFRW records.

38 Statement by Sylvia Hermann to Republican Women's Conference, Publicity—Board Meeting, Wash., D.C., Jan. 16–17, 1953, box 80, NFRW records.

39 Statement of Miss Louise Gore, Publicity—Board Meeting, Wash., D.C., Jan. 16–17, 1953, box 80, NFRW records.

40 Address by Mrs. Carroll D. Kearns to the Republican Women of Pennsylvania, 1 April 1955, Repub. Women of Penn.—Phila., April 1 (1955), box 142, NFRW records.

41 Transcripts of NFRW Exec. Comm. & Bd. of Directors Meeting, 1 March 1955, box 94, NFRW records.

42 Foster, *The Union Politic*, 178–81.

43 Some separate working-class suburbs arose, though they would not likely have

been popular spots for Republican women's clubs. On the class structure of suburbia in this period, see Polenberg, *One Nation Divisible*, 141–44; Jackson, *Crabgrass Frontier*, 241–43. Although some Americans viewed suburbia as a breeder of Republicans, Polenberg debunks this perception, noting that Republican growth in the 1950s was less pronounced in the suburbs than in the cities and that the shift itself was more to Eisenhower than to the GOP. Polenberg, *One Nation Divisible*, 138–39.

44 Lisa McGirr suggests that mixed-gender anticommunist groups such as the John Birch Society served a similar purpose for suburban residents of Orange County, California, during the late 1950s and early 1960s. McGirr, *Suburban Warriors*, 77.

45 Zola Grahm to Whom It May Concern, 20 February 1958, Finance Committee, box 127, NFRW records; George Dixon, "GOP Women's Project Brings Scandalized Shock," *Washington Post*, 17 February 1958.

46 D'Ann Campbell has made a similar argument about the purpose of much of the volunteer work that middle- and upper-class women performed during World War II. Rolling bandages by hand, for example, was a "spectacular waste of volunteer time," but the Red Cross professional leadership, scornful of volunteers, needed a way to absorb the numbers of women who wanted to donate their time. Campbell, *Women at War with America*, 69, 71.

47 Mrs. William Burdick, "Your Club Meeting," Program Planning Committee, box 127, NFRW records; *Iowa Indicator*, December 1957, *The Indicator* newsletter, 1944–60, box 2, AL papers. See also Velma Rudd Hoffman to Mrs. Carroll D. Kearns, 8 March 1953, Arizona, box 28, NFRW records.

48 "Two Conventions? No, Three; One Is for Republican Women," *Star-Journal and Sunday Chieftain* (Pueblo, Colorado), 12 August 1956.

49 Speech by Senator Gordon Allott at National Federation of Republican Women Board of Directors Meeting, 1–2 March 1955, untitled folder, box 84, NFRW records; Speech by Barry Goldwater at National Federation of Republican Women Board of Directors Meeting, 1–2 March 1955, untitled folder, box 84, NFRW records; Remarks by Ray Bliss, Transcripts of Eastern Regional Conference of the RNC and Republican State Chairmen and Vice Chairmen Meeting, 1 October 1951, frames 434, 436, reel 11, RPP I-a.

50 The difficulty female politicians have had in defining their activism in terms other than altruistic is discussed in Witt, Paget, and Matthews, *Running as a Woman*, 30.

51 See Kerber, *Women of the Republic*, 199–200, 235.

52 1954 Republican Speech Kit, prepared by the Republican Congressional Committee, Speech Kit 1954, DCP papers. For an example of Dwight Eisenhower using similar language, see "Attention GOP Sales Ladies: This Is Your Role in Politics," *Washington Newsletter*, April 1956, Nominating Committee—1956, box 103, NFRW records. Adlai Stevenson is quoted in Friedan, *Feminine Mystique*, 60.

53 Report of Mrs. Carroll D. Kearns, 6 September 1956, President's Report, 9th Biennial Conv., Sept. 1956, box 104, NFRW records.

54 Remarks of Mrs. Peter Gibson to the 10th Annual Young Republican Convention Women's Brunch, 21 June 1957, Young Republicans, box 128, NFRW records. See also Mrs. William Burdick, "Women's Role in the Republican Party," ca. 1958, Program Planning Committee, box 127, NFRW records.

55 Republican Roundtables brochure, Convention Forms—1956—9th Biennial Convention, box 101, NFRW records.

56 Catharine Gibson, Report of the President, Board of Directors Meeting, 14–15 March 1958, Minutes of the Exec. Comm. & Bd. of Dir., box 100, NFRW records; Report by Mrs. Katherine [*sic*] Gibson, Transcripts of Republican National Committee meeting, 10 April 1959, frame 99, reel 18, RPP I-a.

57 Harrison, *On Account of Sex*, 58–60.

58 See Nora Kearns to Marjorie Zahrndt, 17 December 1952, 1953 Iowa, box 30; Ruth Jeffries telegram to Dwight Eisenhower, 26 November 1952, Arizona, box 28, NFRW records.

59 Ruth Gaddis Jeffries to Nora Kearns, 27 February 1953; Nora Kearns to Raymond Bowles, 10 March 1953, Recommendations of Federation Women for Appointive Positions, box 118; Edith Pierce to Nora Kearns, 28 November 1952, 1953 Iowa, box 30, NFRW records.

60 Gertrude Detweiler to Catharine Gibson, 11 March 1957, Recommendations of Federation Women for Appointive Positions, box 118; Catharine Gibson to Republican Colleagues, 2 March 1957, Exec. Committee, box 126; Edward Shattuck to Catharine Gibson, ca. March 1957, Exec. Committee, box 126; Wallace Townsend to Catharine Gibson, 11 April 1957, Exec. Committee, box 126, NFRW records.

61 Status of Women Committee, Iowa Women's Republican Club, "Flash Bulletin," 1953, Women in Political Service 53–56, box 6, AL papers.

62 Friedan, *Feminine Mystique*, 61–64.

63 Ware, "American Women in the 1950s," 291.

64 Arnilla Myhre to Guy Gabrielson, Joseph Martin, and Robert Taft, 16 May 1950, Repub. School of Politics—Letters of Commendation, box 116, NFRW records.

65 Meyerowitz, "Beyond the Feminine Mystique," 1458. Daniel Horowitz has shown that Friedan's own feminism emerged not purely from an awareness of being a bored housewife, but also from an earlier history of radical politics and engagement with working-class feminism. Horowitz, "Rethinking Betty Friedan." See also Horowitz, *Betty Friedan and the Making of "The Feminine Mystique."*

66 Basic biographical information in this and subsequent paragraphs is taken from the finding aid to the BA papers and BA interview. An early statement of her views on society's responsibilities toward social welfare is found in Remarks by Bertha Adkins, Transcripts of RNC Policy Committee meeting, 18 January 1950, frame 637, reel 9, RPP I-a.

67 May, *Homeward Bound*, 82.

68 "G.O.P. Names 2 to Committee, Plans Staff Cut," clipping, Repub. Nat'l Comm. 1953 (2), box 119, NFRW records.

69 BA interview, 51.

70 "Top-Ranking Republican Woman Launches Whirlwind Texas Tour," *Dallas Morning News*, 10 June 1958, Political Activities April–June 1958, box 5, BA papers; BA interview, 42, 50–51.

71 "Republican Women's Club Will Hear Bertha Adkins," *Cecil Whig* (Elkton), 13 June 1957; "Democrats Came, Too," *Washington Post and Times Herald*, 14 June 1957, Political Activities April–August 1957, box 3, BA papers. For a comparison of Eisenhower and Truman appointments of women, see Harrison, *On Account of Sex*, 62.

72 Issues of *Women in Politics* are found in various collections including Women in Political Service, box 5, AL papers; *Women in Politics* (RNC Bulletin), box 125, NFRW records.

73 "Eisenhower to Have Breakfast with 20 Key G.O.P. Women," *Washington Sunday Star*, 23 January 1955, A-19, Breakfasts—Pres. Eisenhower & Republ. Women Leaders 1955, box 121, NFRW records; BA interview, 46–49.

74 Thank You, Mr. President brochure, "Thank You, Mr. President" Project, box 125, NFRW records. Together with other women's fundraising campaigns, women raised over $2 million for the party from over 500,000 contributors, according to Adkins. Report of Bertha Adkins, Transcripts of RNC Executive Committee meeting, 11 March 1957, frame 662, reel 15, RPP I-a.

75 "Casual Art of Politics Is Defined," *Richmond New Leader*, 17 September 1957, Political Activities Sept. 1957–March 1958, box 4, BA papers.

76 BA interview, 8.

77 For examples of Federation complaints about the Women's Division, see Wilma Bishop to Nora Kearns, 7 December 1955, Corres. with Chairman Hall—RNC, box 125; Nora Kearns to Bernard M. Shanely, Appointment Secretary to the President, 25 April 1956; Gladys Penland to Leonard Hall, 21 September 1956, White House 1953 [*sic*], box 120, NFRW records.

78 Wilma Bishop to Nora Kearns, 23 March 1953, 1953 Oregon, box 33; Katharine Kennedy Brown to Bertha Adkins, 19 March 1954, Women's Div. 1953 (RNC), box 119, NFRW records.

79 Report made by Catharine Gibson at meeting Nov. 1 with Len Hall; Report of Mrs. Gladys Leggett Penland on Interview Held with Hon. Leonard W. Hall, 4 November 1955, Corres. with Chairman Hall—RNC, box 125, NFRW records.

80 Wilma Bishop to Nora Kearns, 7 December 1955, Corres. with Chairman Hall—RNC, box 125, NFRW records. Gladys Penland gave a similar account. Report of Mrs. Gladys Leggett Penland on Interview Held with Hon. Leonard W. Hall, 4 November 1955, Corres. with Chairman Hall—RNC, box 125, NFRW records.

81 Katharine Kennedy Brown to Nora Kearns, 19 November 1955; Wilma Bishop to Nora Kearns, 7 December, 1955, Corres. with Chairman Hall—RNC, box 125, NFRW records.

82 Cotter and Hennessy, *Politics without Power*, 154.

83 Ibid., 153; Katharine Kennedy Brown to Nora Kearns, 19 November 1955, Corres. with Chairman Hall—RNC, box 125, NFRW records.

84 Report of Nora Kearns, 6 September 1956, President's Report, 9th Biennial Conv., Sept. 1956, box 104, NFRW records.

85 National Federation of Republican Women, Press Release, ca. August 1955, Remarks by Mrs. Carroll D. Kearns at Dinner Given by Calif. Federation, box 144, NFRW records. Unfortunately, the raw data are not available, and I have had to rely on the sometimes imprecise categories the Federation used in its summaries of the data. For example, it created lump categories, such as "PTA and Civic Organizations" and "Women's Clubs," yet listed many clubs separately that would seem to fall into one of those categories. Furthermore, questions about education, age, marital status, race, and income apparently were not asked. Some of that information can be inferred from occupation but, in the absence of data on husbands' occupations, is of limited value in determining economic and social background of Federation members. Although the overwhelming majority of women delegates were club members, the data on those who were not have not been separated from the rest. Despite these caveats, the survey does offer some information about Republican women who used the club movement as an entree into politics.

86 Farrington held her seat until 1956. Chapin, *Shaping History*, 233; Holmes, *Specter of Communism in Hawaii*, 217–18. Judy Weis, who was Federation president under Marion Martin, served in Congress from 1959 until 1963. In 1961 she was named to President Kennedy's Commission on the Status of Women. Finding Aid to the JW papers; Harrison, *On Account of Sex*, 229.

87 Report of Nora Kearns, 6 September 1956, President's Report, 9th Biennial Conv., Sept. 1956, box 104, NFRW records.

88 Cecil Kenyon to Catharine Gibson, 13 November 1956; Cecil Kenyon to Catharine Gibson, 10 January 1957, California [4], box 42; Cecil Kenyon to Catharine Gibson, 9 March 1957, California [3], box 42, NFRW records.

CHAPTER 6

1 Gladys Penland to Catharine Gibson, 9 May 1958, Citizens for Eisenhower— 1956, box 126, NFRW records.

2 Rae, *Decline and Fall of the Liberal Republicans*, 46–47; Reinhard, *Republican Right*, 140.

3 Brennan, *Turning Right in the Sixties*, 31–32.

4 Speech to National Federation of Republican Women Board of Directors Meeting by Barry Goldwater, 1–2 March 1955, untitled folder, box 84, NFRW records.

5 Report of Anne-Eve Johnson, transcripts of RNC Executive Session, 23 January 1959, frames 383–84, reel 17, RPP I-a; Speech by Barry Goldwater to the D.C. League of Republican Women, 7 May 1962, Speeches, Releases, News Stories and Books, frame 820, reel 6, magazine 6, BG papers. See also Barry Goldwater, Speech to California Federation of Republican Women, 3 October 1963, frame 955, reel 6, magazine 6; Speech to National Federation of Republican Women Board of Directors Meeting by Barry Goldwater, 1–2 March 1955,

untitled folder, box 84, NFRW records. On Goldwater's reelection bid in 1958, see R. Goldberg, *Barry Goldwater*, 125–32.

6 NFRW press release, ca. 1955, Press Release Hometown, Citizens for Eisenhower—1956, box 142, NFRW records.

7 Brennan, *Turning Right in the Sixties*, 33; Andrew, *Other Side of the Sixties*, 27–31, 47.

8 Brennan, *Turning Right in the Sixties*, 34–35; Andrew, *Other Side of the Sixties*, 52.

9 R. Goldberg, *Barry Goldwater*, 162.

10 In 1962 Goldwater supporter Clif White formed a Young Republican Caucus in an effort to ensure "control" of that organization. 1962 Report, December Meeting, box 9, FCW papers. Mary Brennan is one historian who has noted the efforts of the Goldwater forces to control the Young Republicans. Brennan, *Turning Right in the Sixties*, 38. For a contemporary account, see Rusher, "Plot to Steal the GOP," 669. Conservatives were also successful in capturing the traditionally liberal California Republican Assembly. See McGirr, *Suburban Warriors*, 124–27.

11 White, *Suite 3505*, 73–74. The pro-Goldwater slate included Dorothy Camp of Iowa, Connie Armitage of South Carolina, Martha Whitehead of Indiana, and Jean Leveton of Oregon.

12 Ibid., 74; "Don't Surrender Defenses, GOP Women Told," *Arizona Republic*, 28 September 1963.

13 George F. Hobart, "Inside the Goldwater Draft," *Advance* (Spring 1963), Chapter X—"Secret Meeting," box 9, FCW papers.

14 Rusher, "Plot to Steal the GOP," 669.

15 White, *Suite 3505*, 136–37.

16 Ibid., 138.

17 Ibid., 137.

18 F. Clifton White to Barry Goldwater, 7 June 1963, Goldwater correspondence, box 18, FCW papers.

19 White, *Suite 3505*, 138.

20 Ibid., 139.

21 Ibid., 138–40.

22 Progress Report #2, Peter O'Donnell, Jr., to Goldwater State Chairman and Key Goldwater People, 25 September 1963, Steering Committee Reports, box 9; "Women at Parley Favor Goldwater," *New York Times*, 13 September 1963, Mothers for a Moral America, box 6, FCW papers.

23 Report of Ione Harrington on Women's Activities, Minutes—National Draft Goldwater Steering Committee, 6 October 1963, Steering Committee Reports, box 9, FCW papers.

24 See Special Report: California, 28 February 1964, Polls, box 8; undated field report, State Contacts, box 10, FCW papers.

25 Rockefeller's support in a race against Kennedy before the news of his remarriage was 36 percent nationally (35 percent among men, and 37 percent among

women). After his remarriage, Rockefeller's support in the same race was 32 percent nationally (37 percent among men, and 27 percent among women). George Gallup, "Rockefeller's Remarriage: Poll Surprise," *New York Herald Tribune*, 28 May 1963, Public Opinion Poll, box 19, FCW papers.

26 Press release, transcript of "Brunch with Barry," nationwide television program, NBC, 12 October 1964, 1964 Presidential Campaign Newsletters: July–Nov. 1964, box 19, BG papers.

27 Commencement Address by Senator Barry Goldwater, Pennsylvania Military College, 7 June 1964, Goldwater Campaign Speeches 1964 vol. 1, BG papers.

28 Jessie Owens to Barry Goldwater, 23 October 1964; Sarah Jane Oarr to Barry and Peggy Goldwater, 16 October 1964, folder 8, box 7, Goldwater Political series, BG papers.

29 Sarah Jane Oarr to Barry and Peggy Goldwater, 16 October 1964; Anna Paveglio to Barry and Peggy Goldwater, 27 October 1964, folder 8, box 7, Goldwater Political series, BG papers.

30 Brennan, *Turning Right in the Sixties*, 2–3.

31 McGirr, *Suburban Warriors*, 81–98. Michelle Nickerson examines women's activism in Southern California in Nickerson, "Moral Mothers and Goldwater Girls." See also Nickerson, "Domestic Threats."

32 Undated material summarizing different parts of the campaign, ca. fall 1964, Personal, box 4, FCW papers.

33 Information about the creation of Mothers for a Moral America is contained in the "women's division" section of an undated summary of different parts of the campaign, ca. fall 1964, Personal, box 4, FCW papers. See also "Mothers for Moral America Join Goldwater-Miller Forces," News Release from Citizens for Goldwater-Miller, 15 October 1964, Miscellaneous releases, box 5, FCW papers.

34 Undated drafts of campaign strategy, Personal, box 4, FCW papers.

35 See "Mothers for Moral America Blueprint for Action," Mothers for Moral America, box 6, FCW papers.

36 "Mothers for Moral America Join Goldwater-Miller Forces," News release from Citizens for Goldwater-Miller, 15 October 1964, Miscellaneous releases, box 5, FCW papers.

37 "Mothers Fight Moral Decay," *Goldwater-Miller Freedom Special*, 1 October 1964, Citizens News—Freedom Specials, box 5, FCW papers.

38 Memo from Thomas W. Benham to the RNC, 28 August 1964, Opinion Research Polls, box 6, FCW papers.

39 In 1952, 58 percent of women had voted for Eisenhower, compared with 53 percent of men. In 1956 the corresponding percentages were 61 percent and 55 percent. In 1960, 51 percent of women had voted for Nixon compared with 48 percent of men. Thus the 1964 drop in women's support for the Republican nominee was considerable. Percentage of Vote by Groups in Presidential Elections—1952–64 [based on Gallup Poll data], Ripon Society, *Election '64*, January 1965, Ripon Society Report, copy in box 112, MLS papers.

40 Republican National Committee Research Division, *1964 Elections*, 56.

41 Ripon Society, *From Disaster to Distinction*, 38.

42 Rae, *Decline and Fall of the Liberal Republicans*, 75; Ripon Society, *Election '64*, 19.

43 "Ripon Society Offers Twelve 'First Steps' for Rebuilding Republican Party," Ripon Society Press Release, 18 January 1965, Ripon Society Report, box 112, MLS papers.

44 Ripon Society, *From Disaster to Distinction*, 84.

45 On RNC discussions of Burch and Bliss, see RNC Executive Committee Executive Session, 21 January 1965, frames 367–98, reel 4, RPP I-b.

46 Rusher, "Plot to Steal the GOP"; Schlafly, *Safe—Not Sorry*, 148–49.

47 Ripon Society, *From Disaster to Distinction*, esp. 23–27.

48 R. Goldberg, *Barry Goldwater*, 235–37. For other recent arguments about the links between the Goldwater campaign and Reagan's later victory, see Schoenwald, *A Time for Choosing*; Brennan, *Turning Right in the Sixties*, 138–42; Diamond, *Roads to Dominion*, 64–65; Andrew, *Other Side of the Sixties*, 205–20.

49 Background on Schlafly is taken from Felsenthal, *Sweetheart of the Silent Majority*, 9–102. See also Critchlow, "Phyllis Schlafly and Grassroots Conservatism."

50 Felsenthal, *Sweetheart of the Silent Majority*, 152–62.

51 Van Ingen, "Gender, Race, and the Politics of Power," 5.

52 Schlafly, *A Choice Not an Echo*, 23–26. Quotation is from p. 25.

53 Ibid., 107–9. Quotation is from p. 107.

54 Ibid., 110.

55 Ibid., 81.

56 Felsenthal, *Sweetheart of the Silent Majority*, 170–71.

57 Shadegg, *What Happened to Goldwater?*, 266.

58 Schlafly, *A Choice Not an Echo*, 117–19. Quotation is from pp. 118–19.

59 Unlike others, such as California's Cecil Kenyon, who had spoken previously of the potential political power of the moral force of grass-roots women, Schlafly did not focus on women voters in her book. *A Choice Not an Echo* translated the insider-outsider language of intraparty resentment into gender-neutral terms.

60 Rusher, "Plot to Steal the GOP," 669.

61 N. Freeman, "V-Day in Omaha."

62 Report by Mrs. Dorothy A. Elston, transcripts of RNC Executive Session, 28 June 1965, frame 802, reel 4, RPP I-b; Report by Mrs. Dorothy A. Elston, transcripts of RNC Executive Session, 8 September 1967, frame 282, reel 6, RPP I-b; Remarks by Mrs. Dorothy A. Elston, transcripts of RNC Executive Session, 20 June 1966, frame 410, reel 5, RPP I-b.

63 "Bliss Learning That the Center Sometimes Is the Storm Center," *Los Angeles Times*, 2 July 1965. For additional discussion of the 1967 Federation presidency battle, see Critchlow, "Conservatism Reconsidered," 122–23.

64 Mrs. Iven Kinchloe to Mrs. A. E. Benton, 14 October 1965; Elly Peterson to Mrs. Iven Kinchloe, 26 October 1965; "Romney Women Win Control," undated clipping; Elly Peterson to Dorothy McHugh et al., 30 September 1965, Republican Women's Federation, 1965–67, box 14, EP papers.

65 Elly Peterson to Janet Tourtellote, 17 March 1965, Correspondence Mar. 1965, box 6, EP papers.

66 Rhoda Lund to Elly Peterson, 10 October 1965, Republican Women's Federation, 1965–67, box 14, EP papers. See also Janet Tourtellote to Elly Peterson, 29 May 1966, Correspondence May 21–30, 1966, box 7, EP papers.

67 Biography of Gladys O'Donnell in binder labeled "NFRW Presidents," NFRW-PR. On O'Donnell's career as an aviator, see O'Brien, "Gladys O'Donnell."

68 Reagan, *First Father, First Daughter*, 148.

69 Gladys O'Donnell to Elly Peterson, 13 August 1965, Correspondence Sept. 1–15, 1967 [*sic*], box 7, EP papers.

70 Gladys O'Donnell, *Build!*, [July–August 1966], NFRW, misc. (1967–77), box 118, MLS papers.

71 "Bitter Fight Sees GOP Women Tap Coalition Choice," *Washington Post*, ca. May 1967, clipping in NFRW Biennial Convention—1967, NFRW, misc. (1967–77), box 118, MLS papers. See also Gladys O'Donnell, "I Believe," NFRW Biennial Convention—1967, NFRW misc. (1967–77), box 118, MLS papers.

72 Elly Peterson to George Anna Theobald, 11 December 1966, Correspondence Dec. 1966, box 7, EP papers.

73 Rhoda Lund to Elly Peterson, 10 October 1965, Republican Women's Federation, 1965–67, box 14; Gladys O'Donnell to Elly Peterson, 21 August 1965 [postscript dated 22 August], Correspondence Sept. 1–15, 1967 [*sic*], box 7; Elly Peterson to Gladys O'Donnell, 27 August 1965, Correspondence Sept. 1–15, 1967 [*sic*], box 7; Janet Tourtellote to Elly Peterson, 13 March 1965, Correspondence March 11–20, 1966, box 6, EP papers.

74 "Goldwater Denies Mrs. Schlafly Is Target of Purge Attempt," *St. Louis Post-Dispatch*, 6 April 1967.

75 Ibid.; Schlafly, *Safe—Not Sorry*, 151.

76 This had been the case with Judy Weis (second vice president), Marie Suthers (treasurer), Peg Green (second vice president), Catherine Gibson (first vice president), Ruth Parks (first vice president), and Dorothy Elston (first vice president). Women's Division, *History of the National Federation of Republican Women*, 39–40. Elizabeth Farrington and Nora Kearns had not been Federation officers but had each served as president of the D.C. League of Republican Women.

77 Biography of Dorothy Elston in binder labeled "NFRW Presidents," NFRW-PR.

78 Schlafly, *Safe—Not Sorry*, 153–54. Schlafly was not the only one to see sinister motives behind these changes. George Embrey, Washington Bureau reporter for the *Columbus Dispatch*, made similar charges. "Young Republicans Are Next Target of Bliss 'Silencers,'" *Columbus Dispatch*, 14 May 1967.

79 Schlafly, *Safe—Not Sorry*, 158; "Goldwater Denies Mrs. Schlafly Is Target of Purge Attempt," *St. Louis Post-Dispatch*, 6 April 1967.

80 O'Donnell had supported California favorite son Earl Warren on the first ballot in 1952, as required by provisions of the California Election Law. At the convention that year she had demonstrated her support for Taft as one of the nine delegates who voted for the seating of Taft delegates in contested states.

O'Donnell was also defended in 1967 by California senator George Murphy, a fellow delegate in 1952. Press Release of the Gladys O'Donnell for President Unity Team, 3 May 1967; Report from Elly Peterson of NFRW's Convention, 8 May 1967, NFRW Biennial Convention—1967, box 118, MLS papers; "Murphy Takes Sides in GOP Women Dispute," *Los Angeles Times*, 5 May 1967.

81 *Time*, 12 May 1967, 21.

82 "Mrs. O'Donnell Elected to Head GOP Federation," *Los Angeles Times*, 7 May 1967.

83 Ruth Jackson, Suppressed Minority Report of Credentials Committee; "Who Is Responsible?" memo from Republicans for Schlafly; Report from Elly Peterson of NFRW's Convention, 8 May 1967, NFRW Biennial Convention—1967, box 118, MLS papers; "Bitter Fight Sees GOP Women Tap Coalition Choice," *Washington Post*, clipping, NFRW Biennial Convention—1967, box 118, MLS papers.

84 Report by Mrs. Gladys O'Donnell, Transcripts of RNC Executive Session, 23 February 1968, frame 591, reel 6, RPP I-b; "GOP Woman Foresees End to Bloodletting," *Los Angeles Times*, 30 June 1967.

85 *Time*, 12 May 1967; "Bitter Fight Sees GOP Women Tap Coalition Choice," *Washington Post*, clipping, NFRW Biennial Convention—1967, box 118, MLS papers.

86 Like Schlafly's other books, *Safe—Not Sorry* contains numerous footnotes to back up her charges but also demonstrates Schlafly's penchant for quoting selectively and occasionally out of context. Schlafly's biographer, Carol Felsenthal, tells roughly the same story in Felsenthal, *Sweetheart of the Silent Majority*, 179–97.

87 Schlafly, *Safe—Not Sorry*, 168–69.

88 "See Fight for Leadership of G.O.P. Women," *Chicago Tribune*, 26 January 1967.

89 Schlafly, *Safe—Not Sorry*, 155–56.

90 Ibid., 156.

91 Carl Greenberg, "Mrs. Schlafly Aims at Bliss," *Los Angeles Times*, 20 June 1967.

92 FOCUS, May 1969, folder 12, RG papers.

93 Mary McGrory, "G.O.P. Gals Storm," 10 May 1967, *Gazette* (Cedar Rapids); Reagan, *First Father, First Daughter*, 161; "Bitter Fight Sees GOP Women Tap Coalition Choice," *Washington Post*, clipping, NFRW Biennial Convention—1967, box 118, MLS papers.

94 "Bitter Fight Sees GOP Women Tap Coalition Choice," *Washington Post*, clipping, NFRW Biennial Convention—1967, box 118, MLS papers; "Mrs. O'Donnell Elected to Head GOP Federation," 7 May 1967; "GOP Woman Foresees End to Bloodletting," *Los Angeles Times*, 30 June 1967. Apparently there was some discussion among board members of censoring Schlafly and removing her from her position as Illinois Federation president, but it was decided to allow her to remain until the end of her term. "GOP Woman Foresees End to Bloodletting," *Los Angeles Times*, 30 June 1967.

CHAPTER 7

1 Evans, *Born for Liberty*, 274–79.

2 J. Freeman, "Whom You Know versus Whom You Represent," 223–29; Wandersee, *On the Move*, 20–22; Melich, *Republican War against Women*, 25–32, 58–72.

3 Rosemary Lucas Ginn began her local GOP work in the 1940s, helping to build the county Republican organization in a heavily Democratic area. She became president of the Boone County Republican Women's Club in 1948 and later served as president of the Federation of Republican Women's Clubs of Missouri from 1959 to 1961. She was also RNC committeewoman from Missouri beginning in 1960 and a member of the RNC Executive Committee from 1962 to 1964. Biographical material on Ginn taken from finding aid to the RG papers; "Life Stories: Rosemary Bewick Lucas Ginn," *Missourian* (Columbia), 5 February 2003; "Obituary: Rosemary Ginn," *Columbia Daily Tribune*, 4 February 2003.

4 "GOP Wars Quietly on Convention Disorders, Discrimination," *Miami Herald*, 24 August 1970.

5 "Half of Republican Delegates in '72 May Be Women," *New York Times*, 23 July 71; "GOP Reform Committee Holds Closed Session," undated clipping ca. 1970, folder 39, RG papers.

6 Rae, *Decline and Fall of the Liberal Republicans*, 99; Ripon Society, *Election '64*.

7 Biography—Elly M. Peterson, 15 June 1973, Peterson, Elly (Personal), box 16; "Elly Peterson Builds Urban GOP," *Washington Evening Star*, 15 September 1969; "Elly's Task: Change Image of Republicans," *Lansing State Journal*, 18 May 1969; "Elly an Activist from Word 'Go,'" *Charlotte Observer*, 11 July 1969, Scrapbook April 1969–December 1969, box 22, EP papers.

8 Quoted in Burrell, "Party Decline, Party Transformation and Gender Politics," 297. For background on the Democratic Party reforms of the late sixties and early seventies, see Ranney, *Curing the Mischiefs of Faction*.

9 Ranney, *Curing the Mischiefs of Faction*, 2.

10 Although the exact wording changed, the general thrust of these proposals remained the same. I refer to them generally as DO 7, 8, and 9.

11 See Skrentny, *Minority Rights Revolution*.

12 Good, *History of Women*, 41–42.

13 "GOP Unit Delays Ruling on Ratio of Minority Delegates," *Washington Sunday Star*, 25 July 1971; DO Committee recommendations, ca. 1970, folder 110, RG papers.

14 National Women's Political Caucus, "D.O. 8," 1972, 10, folder 406; DO Committee recommendations, ca. 1970, folder 110, RG papers.

15 Surveys and questionnaires sent to Republican activists by the DO committee are found in folders 111–53, RG papers.

16 Rowland Evans and Robert Novak, "The GOP's McGovern Reforms," 19 July 1972, folder 176, RG papers.

17 "Gabby Delegates," *Washington Daily News*, 28 July 1971.

18 Martha Metcalf to Robert Dole, 14 April 1972, folder 174, RG papers.

19 Beryl Buckley Milburn to RNC members, 2 February 1972, folder 174, RG papers. See also Milburn to William Cramer, 17 November 1971, folder 175, RG papers.

20 Wilma Rogalin to Rosemary Ginn, 26 July 1972, folder 175, RG papers.

21 Press Release of the Ad Hoc Committee on Delegate Selection and Reform, 9 August 1972, folder 176; Recommendation of Republican Ad Hoc Committee on Delegate Selection and Reform, ca. August 1972, folder 177, RG papers.

22 Gene Snyder form letter to Members of Congress, 4 August 1972, folder 175, RG papers.

23 Durward G. Hall to Rosemary Ginn, 8 August 1972, folder 175, RG papers.

24 Philip Crane to Republican Delegates, 2 August 1972, folder 175, RG papers.

25 "Half of Republican Delegates in '72 May Be Women," *New York Times*, 23 July 1971.

26 "Recommendations of Republican Ad Hoc Committee on Delegate Selection Reform," ca. August 1972, folder 177, RG papers.

27 Senator Bill Brock press release, 9 August 1972, folder 187, RG papers.

28 Williams, "Private Sector Origins of Affirmative Action," 204–6.

29 Recommendations of Republican Ad Hoc Committee on Delegate Selection Reform, folder 177, RG papers.

30 Bobbie Greene Kilberg, "A Republican Woman Looks at Her Party," *Washington Post*, 15 August 1972.

31 Birmingham, "Jill Ruckelshaus," 121.

32 On the political battles over women's rights legislation during the Nixon years, see Kotlowski, *Nixon's Civil Rights*, 222–58. See also Skrentny, *Minority Rights Revolution*, 230–62.

33 Anne Armstrong Reports on Progress of Women in the Nixon Administration, ca. 1972, Anne Armstrong, box 47, AA papers.

34 Jill Strickland was born 19 February 1937 in Indianapolis. She earned an A.B. from Indiana University and an M.A. in English from Harvard. She married fellow Hoosier William Ruckelshaus in 1962. The couple had five children. Biography of Mrs. William Doyle Ruckelshaus, National Commission—Principal Candidates (I), box 28, L–H files.

35 On the formation of the NWPC, see Wandersee, *On the Move*, 22–24; J. Freeman, "Whom You Know versus Whom You Represent," 222–23.

36 Wandersee, *On the Move*, 24; J. Freeman, "Whom You Know versus Whom You Represent," 223–24; Young, *Feminists and Party Politics*, 88–95.

37 National Women's Political Caucus, "D.O. 8," 19, folder 406, RG papers.

38 This was actually a several-step process. First, on Monday, 14 August, the 50-member RNC Rules Committee began meeting and hearing testimony. On Thursday, this committee presented its report to the full RNC. On 20 August, the 105-member Rules Committee of the convention itself began its consideration of the new rules. Elizabeth Griffith Deardourff, "Those 'Not So Gentle' Republican Ladies," [typescript], ca. September 1972, folder 405, RG papers.

39 Ibid.

40 Statement of Senator James L. Buckley before the Committee on Rules, 14 August 1972, folder 185, RG papers. For a discussion of Buckley's role in opposing affirmative action during congressional hearings in 1974, see Skrentny, *Minority Rights Revolution*, 295.

41 Young Republicans' testimony is found in folder 185, RG papers.

42 Elizabeth Griffith Deardourff, "Those 'Not So Gentle' Republican Ladies," [typescript], ca. September 1972, folder 405, RG papers.

43 Ibid.

44 Rules Committee Testimony of Ms. Jessie Sargent, 14 August 1972, folder 185, RG papers.

45 Bobbie Green Kilberg, "Republican Women Assessing Their Gains and Losses," *Washington Post*, 2 September 1972. See also Elizabeth Griffith Deardourff, "Those 'Not So Gentle' Republican Ladies" [typescript], ca. September 1972, folder 405, RG papers.

46 Kilberg, "Republican Women Assessing Their Gains and Losses," *Washington Post*, 2 September 1972. See also Elizabeth Griffith Deardourff, "Those 'Not So Gentle' Republican Ladies" [typescript], ca. September 1972, folder 405, RG papers; Melich, *Republican War against Women*, 25–27.

47 "The Republican Women's Attempt at Semi-Activism," *Washington Post*, 24 August 1972.

48 Elizabeth Griffith Deardourff, "Those 'Not So Gentle' Republican Ladies" [typescript], ca. September 1972, folder 405, RG papers.

49 Smith discusses her discovery of feminism in an interview in Noun, *More Strong-Minded Women*, 146–57. Crisp tells her story in Crisp, "My Journey to Feminism," 25–32.

50 Statement attached to Greetings to a Fellow Republican (from Jill Ruckelshaus), ca. August 1972, folder 63, RG papers.

51 List of Women Signing Statement, Rule 30, box 105, MLS papers.

52 "The Republican Women's Attempt at Semi-Activism," *Washington Post*, 24 August 1972.

53 Ibid.

54 Quoted in Ranney, *Curing the Mischiefs of Faction*, 138. For a discussion of feminist demands at the Democratic convention, see Brodkin, "Power in Numbers," 6–7.

55 "The Republican Women's Attempt at Semi-Activism," *Washington Post*, 24 August 1972.

56 Ibid. On feminist achievements at the two conventions, see J. Freeman, "Whom You Know versus Whom You Represent," 223–25.

57 Elizabeth Griffith Deardourff, "Those 'Not So Gentle' Republican Ladies" [typescript], ca. September 1972, folder 405, RG papers.

58 Summary of the First Meeting of the Republican Women's Task Force of the National Women's Political Caucus, 18 April 1975, Republican Women's Task Force, box 69, MLS papers.

59 On Nixon's veto of day-care legislation, see Kotlowski, *Nixon's Civil Rights*, 248–50.

60 "The Republican Women's Attempt at Semi-Activism," *Washington Post*, 24 August 1972.

61 In 1964 the ERA was dropped from the Democratic platform. Although it technically remained part of the Republican platform, it was not printed as part of that document. In 1968 neither party included the ERA in its platform. J. Freeman, *A Room at a Time*, 209–10.

62 For background on the divisions over the ERA before the emergence of second-wave feminism, see Cott, *Grounding of Modern Feminism*, 117–42; Harrison, *On Account of Sex*.

63 Rae, *Decline of the Liberal Republicans*, 130–33; Kilberg, "A Republican Woman Looks at Her Party," *Washington Post*, 15 August 1972.

64 Melich, *Republican War against Women*, 40.

65 Senator Pete Domenici and Congressman Tom Railsback to Members of the Republican National Committee, February 1975, folder 211, RG papers.

66 "New Republican Chief—an Ability to Organize," *Charlotte Observer*, 6 September 1974; "Ford's Choice for GOP Post a Shrewd Move," *Washington Star-News*, 5 September 1974.

67 "New Republican Chief—an Ability to Organize," *Charlotte Observer*, 6 September 1974; "Ford's Choice for GOP Post a Shrewd Move," *Washington Star-News*, 5 September 1974. The Democratic National Committee briefly had a woman chair in 1972. Jean Westwood was appointed chair at the suggestion of Democratic nominee George McGovern, but she resigned after his defeat, having served only a few months.

68 Doug Bailey to Bob Gable, 1 August 1975, Women—Equal Rights Amendment-General, General Subject files, box 47, SW files.

69 Evans, *Personal Politics*, 221–22; RWTF newsletter June 1976, Women—Republican Women's Clubs 74–76, box 75, MLS papers.

70 Mansbridge, *Why We Lost the ERA*, 20.

71 The meeting was initiated by Pat Goldman, who enlisted Heckler and Ginn to send out invitations. Pat Goldman to Rosemary Ginn, ca. April 1975, folder 405, RG papers.

72 Attending the NWPC's initial conference were 148 Democrats, 18 Republicans, 1 Independent, and 38 of no party affiliation. Report of the Organizing Conference of the National Women's Political Caucus, July 10–11, 1971, [National Women's Political Caucus] [1 of 4], box 65, AA papers.

73 Cathy Bertini to Mary Louise Smith et al., 10 July 1975, National Women's Political Caucus, box 48, MLS papers.

74 Paula Page, Keynote Address to the NWPC Organizing Conference, undated, ca. 1971, [National Women's Political Caucus] [1 of 4], box 65, AA papers.

75 Elly Peterson to Anne Armstrong and Gladys O'Donnell, 17 September 1971, National Women's Political Caucus, box 20, EP papers.

76 Jill Ruckelshaus to Mrs. Stephen A. Birch, 12 March 1973, Staff Correspondence and Memoranda File [Chron file February–May 1973], box 11, AA papers.

77 Form letter [drafted by Pat Goldman], 9 April 1975, folder 405, RG papers.

78 "Positive Action Plan Devised by Republicans," *Washington Post*, 16 June 1974;

"GOP Leaders Debate Rules on Delegates," *St. Louis Post-Dispatch*, 17 June 1974; "Both Parties Press Role of Minorities," *Washington Post*, 9 December 1974; "GOP Urged to Enlist Youth, Minorities," *Washington Post*, 15 June 1974; Summary of the First Meeting of Republican Woman's Task Force, 18 April 1975, Republican Women's Task Force, box 69, MLS papers.

79 1975–1976 Progress Report, Republican Women's Task Force, box 119, MLS papers.

80 Proposal: Republican Women's Task Force, 16 May 1975, Republican Women's Task Force, box 69; RWTF newsletter December 1977, Republican Women's Task Force newsletters, box 119; Republican Women for I.W.Y. [International Women's Year] to Bill Brock [undated, ca. November 1977], Non-partisan Women's organizations, IWY—Republican Women for IWY, box 122, MLS papers.

81 Cathy Bertini to Mary Louise Smith, 21 April 1975, National Women's Political Caucus, box 48; Summary of the First Meeting of the Republican Women's Task Force of the National Women's Political Caucus, 18 April 1975, Republican Women's Task Force, box 69, MLS papers.

82 Summary of the First Meeting of the Republican Women's Task Force of the National Women's Political Caucus, 18 April 1975, Republican Women's Task Force, box 69, MLS papers.

83 Statement of Patricia A. Goldman, RWTF press release, 23 January 1976, Republican Women's Task Force, box 69, MLS papers.

84 1975–1976 Progress Report, Republican Women's Task Force, box 119, MLS papers.

85 Proposal: Republican Women's Task Force, 16 May 1975, Republican Women's Task Force, box 69, MLS papers.

86 1975–1976 Progress Report, Republican Women's Task Force, box 119, MLS papers.

87 J. Freeman, *A Room at a Time*, 24.

88 Statement of Jill Ruckelshaus [undated, ca. 1976], Republican Women's Task Force, box 119, MLS papers.

89 J. Freeman, "Whom You Know versus Whom You Represent," 235–36.

90 Ibid.

CHAPTER 8

1 A number of scholars have explored Nixon's Southern Strategy. See, for example, Carter, *Politics of Rage*, 324–70; Rae, *Decline and Fall of the Liberal Republicans*, 98–99, 103.

2 Reinhard, *Republican Right*, 210–12, 216–17.

3 Rae, *Decline and Fall of the Liberal Republicans*, 108, 112–13.

4 Himmelstein, *To the Right*, 80–84; Rae, *Decline and Fall of the Liberal Republicans*, 136. Among the New Right's core leaders were Richard Viguerie, Howard Phillips, Paul Weyrich, John Dolan, and Jesse Helms. Other leaders included Patrick Buchanan and Phyllis Schlafly.

5 For explorations of the struggles over the ERA in the 1970s, see Mansbridge, *Why We Lost the ERA*; Mathews and De Hart, *Sex, Gender, and the Politics of ERA*.

6 Felsenthal, *Sweetheart of the Silent Majority*, 203–4.

7 Ibid., 239–40.

8 Ibid.

9 Nielsen, *Un-American Womanhood*, 9, 136. Not everyone would agree that Schlafly's social conservatism and antifeminism were sincere. Andrea Dworkin, for example, has interpreted Schlafly's leadership of socially conservative women as an attempt to create a constituency that would enable her to fulfill higher political ambitions, namely to gain access to the "upper echelon of right-wing male leadership." Dworkin, *Right-Wing Women*, 30.

10 Felsenthal, *Sweetheart of the Silent Majority*, 195, 266.

11 Ibid., 269–71.

12 On Schlafly's relationship with Ervin, see Mathews and De Hart, *Sex, Gender, and the Politics of ERA*, 50–53.

13 Phyllis Schlafly, "The Fraud Called the Equal Rights Amendment," *Phyllis Schlafly Report*, May 1972; Phyllis Schlafly, "The Right to Be a Woman," *Phyllis Schlafly Report*, November 1972, Anti-ERA stuff, box 32, AA papers.

14 Phyllis Schlafly, "The Right to Be a Woman," *Phyllis Schlafly Report*, November 1972, Anti-ERA stuff, box 32, AA papers. Freund also influenced the ERA's best-known male opponent (and Schlafly ally), Senator Sam Ervin, Democrat of North Carolina. For more on Ervin's opposition to ERA, see Mathews and De Hart, *Sex, Gender, and the Politics of ERA*, 36–53.

15 Phyllis Schlafly, "The Fraud Called the Equal Rights Amendment," *Phyllis Schlafly Report*, May 1972, Anti-ERA stuff, box 32, AA papers. The *Yale Law Journal* article asserted that the ERA would have made sex a "prohibited classification," except in the case of the right to privacy (including public toilets) and laws that addressed one sex's unique physical attributes. Other feminists and legal scholars insisted it was the intent of Congress and the likely interpretation of the courts that sex be viewed under the ERA as a "suspect classification" (a lower standard of scrutiny). Jane Mansbridge details these views in *Why We Lost the ERA*, 51–52, 250–53 [nn. 23, 25]. The authors of the *Yale Law Journal* article, Barbara A. Brown, Thomas I. Emerson, Gail Falk, and Ann E. Freedman, did argue that the ERA would require women to be drafted for combat duty. Others, however, insisted that while the ERA was likely to have required women to be drafted for military service, the question of whether female draftees would serve in combat would have continued to be left to the military itself. According to Mansbridge, "If the President, Congress, and the military were to decide, especially in wartime, that it was in the military interest of the country not to send women draftees into combat on the same basis as men, the justices of the Supreme Court would be unlikely to order such an outcome if there were a plausible constitutional reason for not doing so. The Court's deference to the military in the past and the legislative history of the

amendment clearly gave the Court such an alternative." Mansbridge, *Why We Lost the ERA*, 65; Brown et al., "The Equal Rights Amendment."

16 Phyllis [Schlafly] to [STOP] ERA State Coordinators, 2 February 1973, Anti-ERA stuff, box 32, AA papers.

17 Phyllis Schlafly, "The Fraud Called the Equal Rights Amendment," *Phyllis Schlafly Report*, May 1972; Resolution from the Martha Washington Council of Republican Women, 20 December 1972, Anti-ERA stuff, box 32, AA papers. Also similar is an unfavorable discussion of the ERA in "The Arlington Republican Women's Club Newsletter," November 1972, Equal Rights Amendment [2], box 7, AA papers.

18 Statement by Mrs. Gladys O'Donnell to the Constitutional Amendments Subcommittee of the Judiciary Committee, ca. spring 1970, Equal Rights Amendment, box 39, AA papers.

19 Gladys O'Donnell to All Club Presidents, [ca. spring 1970], Equal Rights Amendment, ibid.

20 Gladys O'Donnell to All State Presidents and Board Members, 15 June 1970, Equal Rights Amendment, ibid.

21 Gladys O'Donnell to All Club Presidents, [ca. spring 1970], Equal Rights Amendment, ibid.

22 "Distaff Vote for Reagan Claimed," *Milwaukee Sentinel*, 24 March 1975, General Subject files, Betty Ford—campaigning, box 37, SW files; NFRW newsletter, 21 November 1975, Republican Women's Clubs, 1974–76, box 75, MLS papers.

23 Jane Robinson to Anne Armstrong, 20 December 1972, Equal Rights Amendment [3], box 7, AA papers.

24 California Federation of Republican Women, Resolutions, November 1975, Chairman—Women's Federation September 1974–November 1975, box 48, MLS papers.

25 Reagan, *First Father, First Daughter*, 117–18.

26 Anne Armstrong, "Draft Op-Ed," undated ca. 1973, Op-Ed, box 22, AA papers.

27 "Feminist Recalls Road to Credo," unattributed clipping, ca. 1975, NWPC (I), box 37, L–H files.

28 Elly Peterson to George and Lenore Romney, 9 January 1980, Romney, George (position on ERA), box 19, EP papers.

29 Noun, *More Strong-Minded Women*, 148–51.

30 Crisp, "My Journey to Feminism," 28–29.

31 Reagan, *First Father, First Daughter*, 213–16. Reagan discusses her experiences as an abused wife in chapter 6 of her book, pp. 120–34.

32 See unattributed clipping [labeled "Jill Ruckelshaus"] in National Commission—Principal Candidates (1), box 29, L–H files. See also Speech by Mrs. Jill Ruckelshaus, 14 March 1973, Jill R's Speeches, box 15, AA papers.

33 J. Freeman, *A Room at a Time*, 20, 24–25.

34 Bobbie Greene Kilberg, "Republican Women Assessing Their Gains and Losses," *Washington Post*, 2 September 1972.

35 "Will It Be Stopped?," undated clipping, Clippings—STOP ERA Campaign, ED papers; "ERA R.I.P.," *Detroit News*, 27 June 1982.

36 Lenore Romney to Elly Peterson, 6 January 1980; Elly Peterson to Lenore and George Romney, 9 January 1980; "ERA Group Pickets Romney," unattributed clipping, 19 January 1980; Elly Peterson to Laura [sic] [Carter Callow], 26 January 1980, Romney, George (position on ERA), box 19; Lara Carter Callow to Elly Peterson, 21 January 1980, ERAmerica Romney, George (position on ERA), box 18, EP papers.

37 On conservative views of Ford, see Critchlow, "Mobilizing Women," 296, 298–99.

38 Harris Survey for release, 9 August 1976, Ford, Betty—Women, box 21, L–H files.

39 President Ford Committee press release, 27 May 1976, Peterson, Elly (Personal), box 16, EP papers.

40 Melich, *Republican War against Women*, 53.

41 "G.O.P. Women Irked at Party," *New York Times*, 29 July 1976.

42 Pat Goldman to Rogers Morton, 8 March 1976, Republican Women's Task Force, box 37, L–H files; Pat Goldman to Mary Louise Smith, 21 July 1976; Pat Goldman to Ody J. Fish, 31 July 1976, Chairman—ERA, box 28; 1975–1976 Progress Report, Republican Women's Task Force, box 119, MLS papers.

43 Pat Goldman to Mary Louise Smith, 26 May 1976, Chairman—ERA—Jan.–December 1976, box 28, MLS papers.

44 Young, *Feminists and Party Politics*, 36, 97.

45 Sara Fritz, unattributed clipping, ca. August 1976, Women—Clippings (2), box 47, SW files.

46 Maureen Reagan, Testimony before the Republican Platform Committee Hearing, 14 June 1976, Statements (others), box 19, EP papers.

47 1975–1976 Progress Report, Republican Women's Task Force, box 119, MLS papers; "The Women: Rights Issues Splits Their Ranks in K.C.," *New York Post*, ca. August 1976, in RWTF newsletters, box 119, MLS papers; J. Freeman, "Whom You Know versus Whom You Represent," 226–27. For additional background on feminists at the 1976 convention, see Melich, *Republican War against Women*, 58–72.

48 Republican Women's Task Force Newsletter, August–September 1976, Republican Women's Task Force, box 37, L–H files.

49 On the 1976 Republican Convention, see Reinhard, *Republican Right since 1945*, 230–34; Gould, *Grand Old Party*, 404–12.

50 1975–1976 Progress Report, Republican Women's Task Force, box 119, MLS papers.

51 Melich speculates about why Crisp was selected in *Republican War against Women*, 75. Crisp discusses her role in getting the Republican Party to support an extension for ERA ratification in "My Journey to Feminism," 29.

52 Speech by Mary Louise Smith to the NWPC Convention, 11 September 1977, reprinted in RWTF newsletter, September–October 1977, RWTF newsletters, box 119, MLS papers. Smith went on to note that Republican feminists were "no more responsible" for Schlafly than Democrats were for Jimmy Carter's opposition to abortion.

53 Melich, *Republican War against Women*, 82.

54 For a fuller discussion of the National Women's Conference, see Wandersee, *On the Move*, 175–96.

55 Republican Women for I.W.Y. Press release, 19 November 1977, IWY — Republican Women for IWY, box 122, MLS papers; "Ex-GOP Head Smith Chides Schlafly," *Des Moines Register*, 21 November 1977.

56 "GOP Feminists Seek Way to Support Reagan," *Washington Post*, 30 May 1980.

57 "ERA Supporters March at the 1980 National Republican Convention," Press Release, National Organization for Women, 13 July 1980, ERA miscellaneous, box 18, EP papers.

58 On the 1980 convention, see J. Freeman, "Whom You Know versus Whom You Represent," 230; Melich, *Republican War against Women*, 102–17.

59 Carl T. Rowan, "Mary Crisp and the GOP," undated clipping, ca. July 1980, ERA miscellaneous, box 18, EP papers.

60 On Crisp's ousting, see Melich, *Republican War against Women*, 115–16; Crisp, "My Journey to Feminism," 30–31; Rae, *Decline and Fall of the Liberal Republicans*, 144.

61 Remarks by Mary Louise Smith to the Republican National Convention, 15 July 1980, Correspondence — General, July, box 93, MLS papers.

62 "Reagan Seeks to Mollify Women on ERA," *Washington Post*, 16 July 1980; Maureen Reagan to the California Republican Women's Task Force, ca. August 1980, Women's Policy Advisory Board memoranda, box 109, MLS papers.

63 For speculations on this point, see Melich, *Republican War against Women*, 156.

64 Maureen Reagan to the California Republican Women's Task Force, ca. August 1980, Women's Policy Advisory Board Memoranda, box 109, MLS papers. See also Reagan, *First Father, First Daughter*, 251–53.

65 Mary Louise Smith quoted in Melich, *Republican War against Women*, 138.

66 Helen Milliken to Elly Peterson, 13 August [1980], Correspondence 1980–85 [IV], box 17, EP papers.

67 Lynne Arena to Lorelei Kinder, 29 September 1980, Women's Policy Advisory Board Memoranda, box 109, MLS papers. Minutes of the WPAB's meetings indicate that many of the board's proposals were not given serious consideration. See box 109, MLS papers.

68 "GOP Feminists Seek Way to Support Reagan," *Washington Post*, 30 May 1980.

69 Ibid.

70 "Mary Louise Smith's Political Dilemma," *Des Moines Register*, 30 September 1980.

71 Ibid.

72 Young, *Feminists and Party Politics*, 46.

73 Rae, *Decline and Fall of the Liberal Republicans*, 144; "Women's Votes Are a Reagan Woe," *New York Times*, 19 November 1981. For recent scholarly work analyzing the gender gap, see A. Greenberg, "Deconstructing the Gender Gap"; Levitt and Naff, "Gender as a Political Constant," 67–85.

74 "Women Voters Are a Reagan Woe," *New York Times*, 19 November 1981.

75 "Changing Electorate Is Wild Card in Race," *Washington Post*, 5 August 1984.

76 Witt, Paget, and Matthews, *Running as a Woman*, 163–80. See also Davis, *Moving the Mountain*, 427.

77 J. Freeman, "Whom You Know versus Whom You Represent," 232.

78 "The Women in Bush's Brigade: Tasks Accomplished, Obstacles Overcome, Questions Raised aboard the Campaign," *Washington Post*, 11 August 1988.

79 A. Greenberg, "Deconstructing the Gender Gap." Levitt and Naff, "Gender as a Political Constant."

80 Levitt and Naff, "Gender as a Political Constant."

81 Senator Trent Lott, *All Things Considered*, National Public Radio, 6 June 1995. Quoted in Ducat, *Wimp Factor*, 174.

82 Ducat, *Wimp Factor*, 6.

83 Arnold Schwarzenegger, Republican governor of California, used the term "girlie men" (taken from a Saturday Night Live sketch) to denounce Democratic opponents during the state's budget negotiations in the summer of 2004. The comment, which received considerable media attention, was revived by Schwarzenegger to great applause during his remarks to the Republican National Convention several weeks later. Mocking critics of President Bush's approach to the American economy, Schwarzenegger goaded them not to be "economic girlie men," a phrase that has now entered the political lexicon. "Schwarzenegger Calls Budget Opponents 'Girlie Men,'" *New York Times*, 19 July 2004. See "Text of Schwarzenegger's Speech," 31 August 2004, <http://www.cbsnews.com/stories/2004/08/31/politics/main639869.shtml> (accessed 9 January 2005); see also Frank Rich, "How Kerry Became a Girlie-Man," *New York Times*, 5 September 2004.

84 This commitment to state action to ensure equal opportunity distinguishes Republican feminists from the laissez-faire conservative women interviewed by Rebecca Klatch. Klatch, *Women of the New Right*, 53.

85 On Smith's work with the Civil Rights Commission, see boxes 124–26, MLS papers.

86 National Federation of Republican Women, *NFRW: Fifty Years of Leadership*, 35.

87 Dillard, *Guess Who's Coming to Dinner* Now? Quotation is from p. 14.

88 "The Women in Bush's Brigade," *Washington Post*, 11 August 1988.

89 Bobbie Greene Kilberg, "Republican Women Assessing Their Gains and Losses," *Washington Post*, 2 September 1972.

90 Lakoff, *Moral Politics*, 303–7.

91 "'Mother' of New GOP Endorses Blanchard," *Detroit News*, 6 October 1982. For more information on Peterson's involvement in this campaign, see documents in Michigan Gubernatorial Campaign, 1982, box 17, EP papers.

92 Maxine Swanson to Spencer Abraham, 6 July 1983, Correspondence 1980–85 (folder III), box 17, EP papers.

93 [Peterson's remarks], A Tribute to Elly Peterson, 1984, box 20, EP papers.

94 Melich, *Republican War against Women*.

95 See <http://www.thewishlist.org/FAQs.htm> (accessed 10 November 2004).

96 E-mail to author from Pat Carpenter, 8 November 2004.

1 Ranney, *Curing the Mischiefs of Faction*, 139–41.

2 Both Jane De Hart and Rebecca Klatch have noted that socially conservative women use their belief in the different roles of men and women and the moral superiority of women to justify public roles for women. De Hart and Klatch also point out that socially conservative women see men's and women's interests as fundamentally at odds and exhibit a distrust of men. It is for these reasons that these women oppose reforms such as the ERA that would seem to relieve men of the responsibility of caring for their wives and families. Far from acting politically out of a selfless desire to help society as they claim, these women have a keen sense of their own interests within the traditional, religiously based gender systems in which they live. Klatch, "The Two Worlds of Women of the New Right"; De Hart, "Gender on the Right."

3 William Hixson has advanced a similar argument in his suggestion that members of the contemporary American Right are the heirs of Victorian modernizers whose values had helped transform American society from a premodern to a modern society in the nineteenth century. Modernization in that period depended on Victorian values such as hard work, postponement of gratification, repression of sexuality, and the desire to improve oneself. It was women in the nineteenth century who bore the burden of transmitting those values. Thus modernization, according to Hixson, can be said to have been "consummated in a society that carefully restricted women's roles in order to provide stability for their competitive husbands and guidance for their children." Feminism in the 1970s challenged the ideal of separate spheres that had been central to the values of the late nineteenth-century modernizers. If the anti-ERA activists were truly "traditional," they would not participate in public life at all. In fact, Hixson argues, these women are modernists who believe that a separate women's sphere is central to the proper functioning society. Hixson, *Search for the American Right Wing*, 318–26. Quotation is from p. 324.

4 J. Freeman, "Whom You Know versus Whom You Represent," 224–25.

5 For a helpful discussion of the impact of socially conservative women on American politics in the 1980s, see Critchlow, "Mobilizing Women."

6 Young, *Feminists and Party Politics*, 44.

7 In the 1980s, sociologist Rebecca Klatch explored the worldviews of what she calls "laissez-faire" women, noting that they, in contrast to socially conservative women, "do not act as members of a sex; rather they seek to protect their freedom as self-interested 'members' of the market." Klatch notes the irony of the fact that while "laissez-faire" women were closer to feminist women in their views of gender roles, it was socially conservative women who acted according to their interests as women. One area in which the groups differed was in the "laissez-faire" group's general acceptance of and support for gender egalitarianism. The "laissez-faire" women did not identify as feminists, however. They rejected arguments that sexism was institutionally based, or that government action or collective responses on the part of women are required to address such problems. Instead, they focused on the responsibility of

individual women to bring about change in their own circumstances. Klatch, *Women of the New Right*, 10.

8 Rossiter, *Conservatism in America*, viii–ix.

9 Scholars and feminists disagree over the merits of such labels. For a discussion of "radical" versus "cultural" feminism, see Echols, *Daring to Be Bad*; for "liberal" versus "radical" feminism, see B. Ryan, *Feminism and the Women's Movement*, 40–44. Jo Freeman prefers the terms "younger" and "older." J. Freeman, "Whom you Know versus Whom You Represent," 221. Other scholars who have written histories of second-wave feminism include Evans, *Personal Politics*; Davis, *Moving the Mountain*; Rosen, *The World Split Open*. Lisa Young emphasizes that the women's movement in the United States has been noteworthy when compared with movement's in other countries for the "hegemonic liberal feminism" of the American experience. Young, *Feminists in Party Politics*, 184. See also Lakoff, *Moral Politics*, 301–3.

10 Ferree, "Equality and Autonomy," 175–77.

11 For a discussion of efforts by feminists to change the law and to change constitutional interpretation, see Daughtrey, "Women and the Constitution."

12 Ferree, "Equality and Autonomy," 177–80.

13 J. Scott, *Only Paradoxes to Offer*, 17.

14 J. Freeman, "Whom You Know versus Whom You Represent," 236.

BIBLIOGRAPHY

PRIMARY SOURCES
Manuscript Collections
Abilene, Kansas
    Dwight D. Eisenhower Presidential Library
        Bertha S. Adkins Papers
        National Federation of Republican Women Records
        Republican National Committee, Office of the Chairman (Leonard W. Hall)
            Records
Ann Arbor, Michigan
    Bentley Historical Library, University of Michigan
        Elaine Chenevert Donnelly Papers
        Elly Peterson Papers
    Gerald R. Ford Presidential Library
        Betty Ford Papers
        Bobbie Greene Kilberg Papers
        Patricia Lindh and Jeanne Holme Files
        Sheila Weidenfeld Files
College Park, Maryland
    National Archives
        Anne Armstrong Papers, Nixon Presidential Materials, White House
            Central Files: Staff Members and Office Files
Columbia, Missouri
    Western Historical Manuscript Collection, University of Missouri
        Forrest C. Donnell Papers
        Rosemary Lucas Ginn Papers
Iowa City, Iowa
    Iowa Women's Archives, University of Iowa Libraries
        Anna Cochrane Lomas Papers
        League of Women Voters of Iowa Records
        Sue M. Reed Papers
        Mary Louise Smith Papers
    Special Collections Department, University of Iowa Libraries
        Lester L. Kluever Papers
        Don C. Pierson Papers
        James S. Schramm Papers
    State Historical Society of Iowa
        Iowa Council of Republican Women Records
Ithaca, New York
    Rare and Manuscripts Divisions, Carl A. Kroch Library, Cornell University
        F. Clifton White Papers

Johnson City, Tennessee
    Archives of Appalachia, East Tennessee State University
        B. Carroll Reece Papers
Orono, Maine
    Fogler Library Special Collections, University of Maine
        Alumni Files (1935), Marion Martin
Philadelphia, Pennsylvania
    Historical Society of Pennsylvania
        Republican Women of Pennsylvania Scrapbooks
St. Paul, Minnesota
    Minnesota Historical Society
        Carrie S. Jorgens Fosseen Papers
Skowhegan, Maine
    Margaret Chase Smith Library, Northwood University
        Margaret Chase Smith Papers
Tempe, Arizona
    Arizona Historical Foundation, Hayden Library, Arizona State University
        Barry Goldwater Papers
Washington, D.C.
    Library of Congress, Manuscripts Division
        Nannie Helen Burroughs Papers
West Branch, Iowa
    Herbert Hoover Presidential Library
        Herbert Hoover Papers
        Lou Henry Hoover Papers

Collections on Microfilm

*Papers of the Republican Party. Part I: Meetings of the Republican National
    Committee, 1911–1980. Series A: 1911–1960; Series B: 1960–1980.* Bethesda, Md.:
    University Publications of America, 1988.

*Jessica Weis Papers. Women's Studies Manuscript Collections from the Schlesinger
    Library, Radcliffe College. Series 2: Women in National Politics, Part B:
    Republicans.* Bethesda, Md.: University Publications of America, 1994.

Women's Joint Congressional Committee Records. Washington, D.C.: Library of
    Congress Photoduplication Service, 1983.

Privately Held Collections

Jane Hamilton Macauley
    Jane Hamilton Macauley Scrapbooks
William Martin
    Marion Martin Clippings and Photographs
National Federation of Republican Women
    League of Republican Women of the District of Columbia Scrapbooks
    Marion Martin Scrapbooks
    National Federation of Republican Women Records

Joyce Wiese
  Tama County [Iowa] Republican Women Scrapbook
  Third District [Iowa] Republican Women Scrapbook

Oral Histories and Interviews
Bertha Adkins. Interview with John T. Mason Jr. 18 December 1967. Columbia
  University Oral History Project. Transcript at Dwight D. Eisenhower
  Presidential Library, Abilene, Kansas.
Jane Hamilton Macauley. Interviews with author. 15 October 1996; 12 August
  1997. Fairfax, Virginia.
Marion Martin. Videotaped interview with Ann Becker and Polly Bloedern.
  30 June 1986. Republican National Committee Production, Communications
  Division.

Newspapers
Arizona
  Arizona Republic
California
  Los Angeles Times
Colorado
  Denver Post
  Star-Journal and Sunday Chieftain (Pueblo)
Florida
  Miami Herald
  St. Petersburg Times
Illinois
  Chicago Daily Tribune
Iowa
  Des Moines Register
  Gazette (Cedar Rapids)
  Traer Star-Clipper
Maine
  Bangor Daily News
  Evening Express (Portland)
  Kennebec Journal
  Maine State Labor News
  Maine Sunday Telegram
  Portland Telegram
Maryland
  Cecil Whig (Elkton)
Massachusetts
  Christian Science Monitor
Michigan
  Detroit Free Press
  Detroit News

Lansing State Journal
Missouri
    Columbia Daily Tribune
    Missourian (Columbia)
    St. Louis Post-Dispatch
New Jersey
    Courier-News (Plainfield)
New York
    New York Herald Tribune
    New York Post
    New York Times
    Times-Herald (New York)
North Carolina
    Charlotte Observer
Ohio
    Columbus Dispatch
Pennsylvania
    Evening Bulletin (Philadelphia)
    Evening Public Ledger (Philadelphia)
    Philadelphia Bulletin
    Philadelphia Inquirer
    Philadelphia North American
    Philadelphia Public Ledger
    Times Herald (Norristown)
Rhode Island
    Providence Journal
Texas
    Dallas Morning News
Virginia
    Richmond New Leader
Washington, D.C.
    Washington Daily News
    Washington Evening Star
    Washington Post
    Washington Post and Times Herald
    Washington Star-News
    Washington Sunday Star
West Virginia
    Intelligencer (Wheeling)
Wisconsin
    Milwaukee Sentinel

Published Works
Addams, Jane. "Why Women Should Vote." *Ladies Home Journal* 27 (January 1910): 21–22.

Birmingham, Frederic. "Jill Ruckelshaus: Lady of Liberty." *Saturday Evening Post* (March–April 1973): 50–51, 120–21.

Bradford Academy. *Annual Catalogue.* Bradford, Mass.: Bradford College, 1916–17.

———. *Bradford Annals.* Bradford, Mass.: Bradford College, 1915, 1916, 1917.

Crisp, Mary Dent. "My Journey to Feminism." In *True to Ourselves: A Celebration of Women Making a Difference,* edited by Nancy M. Neuman, 24–32. San Francisco: Jossey-Bass Publishers, 1998.

Fleming, Lethia. "The Challenge Is Ours." *The Women's Voice: A National Women's Magazine Published in the Interest of Republican Policies,* June 1939, 7.

Freeman, Neal B. "V-Day in Omaha." *National Review,* 11 July 1967, 747.

Good, Josephine. *The History of Women in Republican National Conventions and Women in the Republican National Committee.* Washington, D.C.: Republican National Committee Women's Division, 1963.

Hamilton, Julia West. "Republican Women's Club of the District of Columbia Joins National Federation of Republican Women's Clubs." *The Women's Voice: A National Women's Magazine Published in the Interest of Republican Policies,* June 1940, 9.

Laas, Virginia Jeans, ed. *Bridging Two Eras: The Autobiography of Emily Newell Blair, 1877–1951.* Columbia: University of Missouri Press, 1999.

Martin, Marion. "Minorities in Politics." *The Women's Voice: A National Women's Magazine Published in the Interest of Republican Policies,* June 1939, 4–5.

National Federation of Republican Women. *NFRW: Fifty Years of Leadership, 1938–1988.* Washington, D.C.: National Federation of Republican Women, 1987.

National Women's Political Caucus. *Democratic Women Are Wonderful: A History of Women at Democratic National Conventions.* Washington, D.C.: National Women's Political Caucus, 1980.

———. *Republican Women Are Wonderful: A History of Women at Republican National Conventions.* Washington, D.C.: National Women's Political Caucus, 1980.

O'Brien, Pamela. "Gladys O'Donnell." *Southwesterly Newsletter,* September/October 2001, <http://www.ninety-nines.org/odonnell.html> (accessed 10 January 2005).

Pond, Sara Jean. *Bradford: A New England School.* Bradford, Mass.: Bradford Academy Alumnae, 1954.

Porter, Kirk H., and Donald Bruce Johnson, comps. *National Party Platforms, 1840–1972.* Urbana: University of Illinois Press, 1973.

Priest, Ivy Baker. "The Ladies Elected Ike." *American Mercury* 76 (February 1953): 27.

Reagan, Maureen. *First Father, First Daughter: A Memoir.* Boston: Little, Brown, 1989.

Republican National Committee Research Division. *The 1964 Elections: A Summary Report with Supporting Tables.* Washington, D.C.: Republican National Committee, October 1965.

Ripon Society. *Election '64: A Ripon Society Report.* Cambridge, Mass.: Ripon Society, January 1965.

———. *From Disaster to Distinction: A Republican Rebirth*. New York: Pocket Books, 1966.

Rusher, William A. "The Plot to Steal the GOP." *National Review*, 12 July 1966, 668–71.

Schlafly, Phyllis. *A Choice Not an Echo*. Alton, Ill.: Pere Marquette Press, 1964.

———. *Safe—Not Sorry*. Alton, Ill.: Pere Marquette Press, 1967.

Wellesley College. *Record Book*. Wellesley, Mass.: Wellesley College, 1947, 1958, and 1972.

White, F. Clifton. *Suite 3505: The Story of the Draft Goldwater Movement*. New Rochelle, N.Y.: Arlington House, 1967.

Women's Division of the Republican National Committee. *The History of the Founding and Development of the National Federation of Republican Women*. Washington, D.C.: Women's Division of the Republican National Committee, 1963.

SECONDARY SOURCES

Allen, Craig. *Eisenhower and the Mass Media: Peace, Prosperity, and Prime-Time TV*. Chapel Hill: University of North Carolina Press, 1993.

Andersen, Kristi. *After Suffrage: Women in Partisan and Electoral Politics before the New Deal*. Chicago: University of Chicago Press, 1996.

———. "Women and Citizenship in the 1920s." In *Women, Politics, and Change*, edited by Louise A. Tilly and Patricia Gurin, 177–98. New York: Russell Sage Foundation, 1990.

Anderson, Kathryn. "Evolution of a Partisan: Emily Newell Blair and the Democratic Party, 1920–1932." In *We Have Come to Stay: American Women and Political Parties, 1880–1960*, edited by Melanie Gustafson, Kristie Miller, and Elisabeth Israels Perry, 109–20. Albuquerque: University of New Mexico Press, 1999.

Andrew, John A., III. *The Other Side of the Sixties: Young Americans for Freedom and the Rise of Conservative Politics*. New Brunswick, N.J.: Rutgers University Press, 1997.

Badger, Anthony J. *The New Deal: The Depression Years, 1933–1940*. New York: Noonday Press, 1989.

Baker, Paula. "The Domestication of Politics: Women and American Political Society, 1780–1920." *American Historical Review* 89 (1984): 620–47.

———. *The Moral Frameworks of Public Life: Gender, Politics, and the State in Rural New York, 1870–1930*. New York: Oxford University Press, 1991.

———. "'She Is the Best Man on the Ward Committee': Women in Grassroots Party Organizations, 1930s–1950s." In *We Have Come to Stay: American Women and Political Parties, 1880–1960*, edited by Melanie Gustafson, Kristie Miller, and Elisabeth Israels Perry, 151–60. Albuquerque: University of New Mexico Press, 1999.

Bell, Daniel, ed. *The Radical Right: The New American Right, Expanded and Updated*. Freeport, N.Y.: Books for Libraries Press, 1963.

Bennett, David H. *The Party of Fear: From Nativist Movements to the New Right in American History.* New York: Vintage Books, 1988.

Benowitz, June Melby. *Days of Discontent: American Women and Right-Wing Politics, 1933–1945.* Dekalb: Northern Illinois University Press, 2002.

Black, Earl, and Merle Black. *The Vital South: How Presidents Are Elected.* Cambridge, Mass.: Harvard University Press, 1992.

Blee, Kathleen. *Women of the Klan: Racism and Gender in the 1920s.* Berkeley: University of California Press, 1991.

Bone, Hugh A. "New Party Associations in the West." *American Political Science Review* 45 (December 1951): 1115–25.

Bordin, Ruth. *Woman and Temperance: The Quest for Power and Liberty, 1873–1900.* Philadelphia: Temple University Press, 1981.

Braitman, Jacqueline R. "A California Stateswoman: The Public Career of Katherine Philips Edson." *California History Magazine* 65 (June 1986): 82–95.

Breckinridge, Sophonisba P. *Women in the Twentieth Century: A Study of Their Political, Social and Economic Activities.* New York: McGraw-Hill, 1933.

Brennan, Mary C. *Turning Right in the Sixties: The Conservative Capture of the GOP.* Chapel Hill: University of North Carolina Press, 1995.

Brinkley, Alan. *The End of Reform: New Deal Liberalism in Recession and War.* 1995. Reprint, New York: Vintage Books, 1996.

———. "The Problem of American Conservatism." *American Historical Review* 99 (1994): 409–29.

———. "Response to the Comments of Leo Ribuffo and Susan Yohn." *American Historical Review* 99 (1994): 450–52.

Brodkin, Kimberly Anne. "For the Good of the Party: Gender, Partisanship, and American Political Culture from Suffrage to the 1960s." Ph.D. diss., Rutgers University, 2002.

———. "Power in Numbers: Democratic Women in Pursuit of Political Equity." Paper presented at the Social Science History Association annual meeting, Baltimore, 15 November 2003.

Brown, Barbara A., Thomas I. Emerson, Gail Falk, and Ann E. Freedman. "The Equal Rights Amendment: A Constitutional Basis for Equal Rights for Women." *Yale Law Journal* 80 (1971): 955–62.

Buhle, Mari Jo. *Women and American Socialism, 1870–1920.* Urbana: University of Illinois Press, 1983.

Burner, David. *Herbert Hoover: A Public Life.* New York: A. A. Knopf, 1979.

Burnham, Walter Dean. *The Current Crisis in American Politics.* New York: Oxford University Press, 1982.

Burrell, Barbara C. "Party Decline, Party Transformation and Gender Politics: The USA." In *Gender and Party Politics,* edited by Joni Lovenduski and Pippa Norris, 291–308. London: Sage Publications, 1993.

Campbell, D'Ann. *Women at War with America: Private Lives in a Patriotic Era.* Cambridge, Mass.: Harvard University Press, 1984.

Carter, Dan T. *The Politics of Rage: George Wallace, the Origins of the New*

Conservatism, and the Transformation of American Politics. New York: Simon and
Schuster, 1995.

Chafe, William H. *The American Woman: Her Changing Social, Economic and
Political Roles, 1920–1970.* New York: Oxford University Press, 1972.

———. "Women's History and Political History: Some Thoughts on
Progressivism and the New Deal." In *Visible Women: New Essays on American
Activism,* edited by Nancy A. Hewitt and Suzanne Lebsock, 101–18. Urbana:
University of Illinois Press, 1993.

Chapin, Helen Geracimos. *Shaping History: The Role of Newspapers in Hawai'i.*
Honolulu: University of Hawai'i Press, 1996.

Cole, Wayne S. *Roosevelt and the Isolationists, 1932–45.* Lincoln: University of
Nebraska Press, 1983.

Cook, Fred J. *Barry Goldwater: Extremist of the Right.* New York: Grove Press,
1964.

Cook, Blanche Wiesen. *Eleanor Roosevelt.* Vol. 1. New York: Viking Penguin, 1992.

Coontz, Stephanie. *The Way We Never Were: American Families and the Nostalgia
Trap.* New York: Harper Collins, 1992.

Cott, Nancy F. "Across the Great Divide: Women in Politics before and after
1920." In *Women, Politics, and Change,* edited by Louise A. Tilly and Patricia
Gurin, 153–76. New York: Russell Sage Foundation, 1990.

———. "Early-Twentieth-Century Feminism in Political Context: A Comparative
Look at Germany and the United States." In *Suffrage and Beyond: International
Feminist Perspectives,* edited by Caroline Daley and Melanie Nolan, 234–51.
New York: New York University Press, 1994.

———. *The Grounding of Modern Feminism.* New Haven, Conn.: Yale University
Press, 1987.

———. "What's in a Name: The Limits of 'Social Feminism': or Expanding the
Vocabulary of Women's History." *Journal of American History* 76 (1989):
809–29.

Cotter, Cornelius P., and Bernard C. Hennessy. *Politics without Power: The
National Party Committees.* New York: Atherton Press, 1964.

Critchlow, Donald T. "Conservatism Reconsidered: Phyllis Schlafly and
Grassroots Conservatism." In *The Conservative Sixties,* edited by David Farber
and Jeff Roche, 108–26. New York: Peter Lang Publishing, 2003.

———. "Mobilizing Women: The 'Social Issues.'" In *The Reagan Presidency:
Pragmatic Conservatism and Its Legacies,* edited by W. Elliot Brownlee and
Hugh Davis Graham, 293–326. Lawrence: University Press of Kansas, 2003.

Daughtrey, Martha Craig. "Women and the Constitution: Where We Are at the
End of the Century." *New York University Law Review* 75 (April 2000): 1–23.

Davis, Flora. *Moving the Mountain: The Women's Movement since 1960.* 1991.
Reprint, Urbana: University of Illinois Press, 1999.

De Hart, Jane. "Gender on the Right: Meaning behind the Existential Scream."
Gender and History 3 (1991): 246–67.

Degler, Carl. *At Odds: Women and the Family in America from the Revolution to the
Present.* New York: Oxford University Press, 1980.

Diamond, Sara. *Roads to Dominion: Right-Wing Movements and Political Power in the United States.* New York: Guilford Press, 1995.

Diggins, John Patrick. *The Proud Decades: America in War an Peace, 1941–1960.* New York: W. W. Norton, 1988.

Dillard, Angela D. *Guess Who's Coming to Dinner Now?: Multicultural Conservatism in America.* New York: New York University Press, 2001.

Dinkin, Robert J. *Before Equal Suffrage: Women in Partisan Politics from Colonial Times to 1920.* Westport, Conn.: Greenwood Press, 1995.

DuBois, Ellen. *Feminism and Suffrage: The Emergence of an Independent Women's Movement in America, 1848–1869.* Ithaca, N.Y.: Cornell University Press, 1978.

———. "Woman Suffrage around the World: Three Phases of Suffragist Internationalism." In *Suffrage and Beyond: International Feminist Perspectives,* edited by Caroline Daley and Melanie Nolan, 252–74. New York: New York University Press, 1994.

Ducat, Stephen J. *The Wimp Factor: Gender Gaps, Holy Wars, and the Politics of Anxious Masculinity.* Boston: Beacon Press, 2004.

Dworkin, Andrea. *Right Wing Women.* 1978. Reprint, New York: Coward-McCann, Inc., 1983.

Echols, Alice. *Daring to Be Bad: Radical Feminism in America, 1967–1975.* Minneapolis: University of Minnesota Press, 1989.

Edwards, Rebecca. *Angels in the Machinery: Gender in American Party Politics from the Civil War to the Progressive Era.* New York: Oxford University Press, 1997.

Evans, Sara. *Born for Liberty: A History of Women in America.* New York: Free Press, 1989.

———. *Personal Politics: The Roots of Women's Liberation in the Civil Rights Movement and the New Left.* 1979. Reprint, New York: Vintage Books, 1980.

Farber, David, and Jeff Roche, eds. *The Conservative Sixties.* New York: Peter Lang, 2003.

Feijoó, Maria del Carmen. "The Challenge of Constructing Civilian Peace: Women and Democracy in Argentina." In *The Women's Movement in Latin America: Feminism and the Transition to Democracy,* edited by Jane S. Jacquette, 72–94. Boston: Unwin Hyman, 1989.

Felsenthal, Carol. *The Sweetheart of the Silent Majority: The Biography of Phyllis Schlafly.* Garden City, N.Y.: Doubleday, 1981.

Ferree, Myra Marx. "Equality and Autonomy: Feminist Politics in the United States and West Germany." In *The Women's Movements of the United States and Western Europe: Consciousness, Political Opportunity, and Public Policy,* edited by Mary Fainsod Katzenstein and Carol McClurg Mueller, 172–95. Philadelphia: Temple University Press, 1987.

Fisher, Betty, and Marguerite J. Whitehead. "American Government and Politics: Women and National Party Organizations." *American Political Science Review* 38 (October 1944): 895–903.

Fite, Gilbert C. "The Agricultural Issue in the Presidential Campaign of 1928." *Mississippi Valley Historical Review* 37 (1951): 653–72.

Flexner, Eleanor. *Century of Struggle: The Woman's Rights Movement in the United States.* 1959. Reprint, New York: Athenaeum, 1968.

Foner, Eric. *Free Soil, Free Labor, Free Men: The Ideology of the Republican Party before the Civil War.* New York: Oxford University Press, 1970.

Fones-Wolf, Elizabeth A. *Selling Free Enterprise: The Business Assault on Labor and Liberalism, 1945–1960.* Urbana: University of Illinois Press, 1994.

Foster, James Caldwell. *The Union Politic: The CIO Political Action Committee.* Columbia: University of Missouri Press, 1975.

Freedman, Estelle. "Separatism as Strategy: Female Institution Building and American Feminism, 1870–1930." *Feminist Studies* 5 (1979): 512–29.

Freeman, Jo. *The Politics of Women's Liberation: A Case Study of an Emerging Social Movement and Its Relation to the Policy Process.* New York: McKay, 1975.

———. *A Room at a Time: How Women Entered Party Politics.* Lanham, Md.: Rowman and Littlefield, 2000.

———. "Whom You Know versus Whom You Represent: Feminist Influence in the Democratic and Republican Parties." In *The Women's Movements of the United States and Western Europe*, edited by Mary Fainsod Katzenstein and Carol McClurg Mueller, 215–44. Philadelphia: Temple University Press, 1987.

Friedan, Betty. *The Feminine Mystique.* 1963. Reprint, New York: Dell, 1983.

Gerson, Judith M., and Kathy Peiss. "Boundaries, Negotiation, Consciousness: Reconceptualizing Gender Relations." *Social Problems* 32 (April 1985): 315–29.

Gifford, Carolyn DeSwarte. "Frances Willard and the Woman's Christian Temperance Union's Conversion to Woman Suffrage." In *One Woman, One Vote: Rediscovering the Woman Suffrage Movement*, edited by Marjorie Spruill Wheeler, 117–34. Troutdale, Ore.: NewSage Press, 1995.

Goldberg, Michael Lewis. *An Army of Women: Gender and Politics in Gilded Age Kansas.* Baltimore: Johns Hopkins University Press, 1997.

———. "Non-Partisan and All-Partisan: Rethinking Woman Suffrage and Party Politics in Gilded Age Kansas." *Western Historical Quarterly* 64 (Spring 1994): 21–44.

Goldberg, Robert Alan. *Barry Goldwater.* New Haven, Conn.: Yale University Press, 1995.

Goldman, Ralph M. *The National Party Chairmen and Committees: Factionalism at the Top.* Armonk, N.Y.: M. E. Sharpe, 1990.

Gordon, Ann D., ed. *African American Women and the Vote, 1837–1965.* Amherst: University of Massachusetts Press, 1997.

Gordon, Felice D. *After Winning: The Legacy of the New Jersey Suffragists, 1920–1947.* New Brunswick, N.J.: Rutgers University Press, 1986.

———. "After Winning: The New Jersey Suffragists in the Political Parties, 1920–1930." *New Jersey History* 101 (Fall/Winter 1983): 12–35.

Gordon, Linda. *Pitied but Not Entitled: Single Mothers and the History of Welfare.* Cambridge, Mass.: Harvard University Press, 1994.

Gould, Lewis L. *Grand Old Party: A History of the Republicans.* New York: Random House, 2003.

Graham, Otis. *An Encore for Reform: The Old Progressives and the New Deal.* New York: Oxford University Press, 1967.

Greenberg, Anna. "Deconstructing the Gender Gap." Working paper of the Kennedy School of Government's Politics Research Group, Harvard University, 1998, <www.ksg.harvard.edu/prg/greenb/gengap.htm#> (accessed 13 June 2001).

Greenberg, J. "The Limits of Legislation: Katherine Philips Edson, Practical Politics, and the Minimum-Wage Law in California, 1913–1922." *Journal of Policy History* 5 (1993): 207–30.

Gustafson, Melanie. "Partisan and Nonpartisan: The Political Career of Judith Ellen Foster, 1881–1910." In *We Have Come to Stay: American Women and Political Parties, 1880–1960,* edited by Melanie Gustafson, Kristie Miller, and Elisabeth Israels Perry, 1–12. Albuquerque: University of New Mexico Press, 1999.

———. "Partisan Women in the Progressive Era: The Struggle for Inclusion in American Political Parties." *Journal of Women's History* 9 (Summer 1997): 8–30.

———. *Women and the Republican Party, 1854–1924.* Urbana: University of Illinois Press, 2001.

Gustafson, Melanie, Kristie Miller, and Elisabeth Israels Perry, eds. *We Have Come to Stay: American Women and Political Parties, 1880–1960.* Albuquerque: University of New Mexico Press, 1999.

Halberstam, David. *The Fifties.* New York: Ballantine Books, 1993.

Harrison, Cynthia. *On Account of Sex: The Politics of Women's Issues, 1945–1968.* Berkeley: University of California Press, 1988.

Hartz, Louis. *The Liberal Tradition in America: An Interpretation of American Political Thought since the Revolution.* New York: Harcourt Brace, 1955.

Harvey, Anna L. *Votes without Leverage: Women in American Electoral Politics, 1920–1970.* New York: Cambridge University Press, 1998.

Hawley, Ellis, ed. *Herbert Hoover as Secretary of Commerce: Studies in New Era Thought and Practice.* Iowa City: University of Iowa Press, 1981.

Hendricks, Wanda A. "African American Women as Political Constituents in Chicago, 1913–1915." In *We Have Come to Stay: American Women and Political Parties, 1880–1960,* edited by Melanie Gustafson, Kristie Miller, and Elisabeth Israels Perry, 55–64. Albuquerque: University of New Mexico Press, 1999.

Hewitt, Nancy A., and Suzanne Lebsock, eds. *Visible Women: New Essays on American Activism.* Urbana: University of Illinois Press, 1993.

Hicks, John D. *Republican Ascendancy, 1921–1933.* New York: Harper Torchbooks, 1960.

Higginbotham, Evelyn Brooks. "Clubwomen and Electoral Politics in the 1920s." In *African American Women and the Vote, 1837–1965,* edited by Ann D. Gordon, Bettye Collier-Thomas, John H. Bracey, Arlene Voski Avakian, and Joyce Avrech Berkman, 134–55. Amherst: University of Massachusetts Press, 1997.

———. "In Politics to Stay: Black Women Leaders and Party Politics in the

1920s." In *Women, Politics, and Change*, edited by Louise A. Tilly and Patricia Gurin, 199–220. New York: Russell Sage Foundation, 1990.

Himmelstein, Jerome L. *To the Right: The Transformation of American Conservatism*. Berkeley: University of California Press, 1990.

Hixson, William B., Jr. *Search for the American Right Wing: An Analysis of the Social Science Record, 1955–1987*. Princeton, N.J.: Princeton University Press, 1992.

Hoff-Wilson, Joan. *Herbert Hoover: Forgotten Progressive*. Boston: Little, Brown, 1975.

Hofstadter, Richard. *The American Political Tradition*. New York: A. A. Knopf, 1948.

Holmes, T. Michael. *The Spector of Communism in Hawaii*. Honolulu: University of Hawai'i Press, 1994.

Horowitz, Daniel. *Betty Friedan and the Making of "The Feminine Mystique": The American Left, the Cold War, and Modern Feminism*. Amherst: University of Massachusetts Press, 1998.

———. "Rethinking Betty Friedan and *The Feminine Mystique*: Labor Union Radicalism and Feminism in Cold War America." *American Quarterly* 48 (1996): 1–42.

Howes, Durwood. *A–L*. Vol. 1 of *American Women, 1935–1940: A Composite Biographical Dictionary*. Detroit: Gale Research Company, 1981.

Iowa Press Association. "Ella Taylor." *The Iowa Press Association's Who's Who in Iowa*, 1168–69. Des Moines: Iowa Press Association, 1940.

Jackson, Kenneth T. *Crabgrass Frontier: The Suburbanization of the United States*. New York: Oxford University Press, 1985.

Jacquette, Jane S., ed. *The Women's Movement in Latin America: Feminism and the Transition to Democracy*. Boston: Unwin Hyman, 1989.

James, Edward T., ed. *Notable American Women: A Biographical Dictionary*. 3 vols. Cambridge, Mass.: Belknap Press of Harvard University Press, 1971.

Jeansonne, Glen. *Women of the Far Right: The Mothers' Movement and World War II*. Chicago: University of Chicago Press, 1996.

Jensen, Joan M. "All Pink Sisters: The War Department and the Feminist Movement in the 1920s." In *Decades of Discontent: The Women's Movement, 1920–1940*, edited by Lois Scharf and Joan M. Jensen, 199–222. Westport, Conn.: Greenwood Press, 1983.

Jensen, Richard. *The Winning of the Midwest: Social and Political Conflict, 1888–1896*. Chapel Hill: University of North Carolina Press, 1971.

Jones, Alan. "The New Deal Comes to Iowa." In *The New Deal Viewed from Fifty Years: Papers Commemorating the Fiftieth Anniversary of the Launching of President Franklin D. Roosevelt's New Deal in 1933*, edited by Lawrence E. Gelfand and Robert J. Neymeyer, 21–53. Iowa City: University of Iowa Press, 1983.

Katzenstein, Mary Fainsod, and Carol McClurg Mueller, eds. *The Women's Movements of the United States and Western Europe: Consciousness, Political Opportunity, and Public Policy*. Philadelphia: Temple University Press, 1987.

Kazin, Michael. "The Grass-Roots Right: New Histories of U.S. Conservatism in the Twentieth Century." *American Historical Review* 97 (1992): 136–55.

Kerber, Linda K. "Separate Spheres, Female Worlds, Woman's Place: The Rhetoric of Women's History." *Journal of American History* 75 (1988): 9–39.

————. *Women of the Republic: Intellect and Ideology in Revolutionary America.* New York: W. W. Norton, 1980.

Kessel, John H. *The Goldwater Coalition: Republican Strategies in 1964.* Indianapolis: Bobbs-Merrill, 1968.

Klatch, Rebecca E. "Coalition and Conflict among Women of the New Right." *Signs* 13 (1988): 671–94.

————. "The Two Worlds of Women of the New Right." In *Women, Politics, and Change,* edited by Louise A. Tilly and Patricia Gurin, 529–52. New York: Russell Sage Foundation, 1988.

————. *Women of the New Right.* Philadelphia: Temple University Press, 1987.

Kleppner, Paul. *The Third Electoral System, 1853–1892: Parties, Voters, and Political Cultures.* Chapel Hill: University of North Carolina Press, 1979.

————. "Were Women to Blame?: Female Suffrage and Voter Turnout." *Journal of Interdisciplinary History* 12 (1982): 621–43.

Koonz, Claudia. *Mothers in the Fatherland: Women, the Family and Nazi Politics.* New York: St. Martin's Press, 1987.

Kotlowski, Dean J. *Nixon's Civil Rights: Politics, Principle, and Policy.* Cambridge, Mass.: Harvard University Press, 2001.

Kraditor, Aileen S. *The Ideas of the Woman Suffrage Movement, 1890–1920.* 1965. Reprint, New York: W. W. Norton, 1981.

Lakoff, George. *Moral Politics: What Conservatives Know That Liberals Don't.* Chicago: University of Chicago Press, 1996.

Lamb, Karl A., and Paul A. Smith. *Campaign Decision-Making: The Presidential Election of 1964.* Belmont, Calif.: Wadsworth Publishing, 1968.

Lebsock, Suzanne. "Woman Suffrage and White Supremacy: A Virginia Case Study." In *Visible Women: New Essays on American Activism,* edited by Nancy A. Hewitt and Suzanne Lebsock, 62–100. Urbana: University of Illinois Press, 1993.

————. "Women and American Politics, 1880–1920." In *Women, Politics, and Change,* edited by Louise A. Tilly and Patricia Gurin, 35–62. Ithaca, N.Y.: Russell Sage Foundation, 1990.

Lemons, J. Stanley. *The Woman Citizen: Social Feminism in the 1920s.* Urbana: University of Illinois Press, 1973.

Levitt, Melissa, and Katherine C. Naff. "Gender as a Political Constant: The More Things Change, the More They Stay the Same." In *The Election of the Century and What It Tells Us about the Future of American Politics,* edited by Stephen Wayne and Clyde Wilcox, 67–85. New York: M. E. Sharpe, 2002.

Lichtenstein, Nelson. "From Corporatism to Collective Bargaining: Organized Labor and the Eclipse of Social Democracy in the Postwar Era." In *The Rise and Fall of the New Deal Order, 1930–1980,* edited by Steve Fraser and Gary Gerstle, 122–52. Princeton, N.J.: Princeton University Press, 1989.

Link, Arthur S., and Richard L. McCormick. *Progressivism*. Arlington Heights, Ill.: Harlan Davidson, 1983.

Lipset, Seymour Martin. "The Sources of the 'Radical Right'—1955." In *The Radical Right: "The New American Right," Expanded and Updated*, edited by Daniel Bell, 259–312. Freeport, N.Y.: Books for Libraries Press, 1963.

Lovenduski, Joni, and Pippa Norris, eds. *Gender and Party Politics*. London: Sage Publications, 1993.

Lynn, Susan. *Progressive Women in Conservative Times: Racial Justice, Peace, and Feminism, 1945 to the 1960s*. New Brunswick, N.J.: Rutgers University Press, 1992.

Mansbridge, Jane J. *Why We Lost the ERA*. Chicago: University of Chicago Press, 1986.

Marilley, Susan M. "Frances Willard and the Feminism of Fear." *Feminist Studies* 19 (1993): 123–45.

Marvick, Dwaine, ed. *Political Decision-makers*. New York: Free Press of Glencoe, 1961.

Marvick, Dwaine, and Charles Nixon. "Recruitment Contrasts in Rival Campaign Groups." In *Political Decision-Makers*, edited by Dwaine Marvick, 193–217. New York: Free Press of Glencoe, 1961.

Mathews, Donald, and Jane Sherron De Hart. *Sex, Gender and the Politics of ERA: A State and the Nation*. New York: Oxford University Press, 1990.

Matthews, Glenna. *The Rise of Public Woman: Woman's Power and Woman's Place in the United States, 1630–1970*. New York: Oxford University Press, 1992.

May, Elaine Tyler. *Homeward Bound: American Families in the Cold War Era*. New York: Basic Books, 1988.

Mayo, Edith. "Be a Party Girl: Campaign Appeals to Women." In *Hail to the Candidates: Presidential Campaigns from Banners to Broadcasts*, edited by Keith Melder, 149–59. Washington, D.C.: Smithsonian Institution Press, 1992.

McCaffery, Peter. *When Bosses Ruled Philadelphia: The Emergence of the Republican Machine, 1867–1933*. University Park: Pennsylvania State University Press, 1993.

McEnaney, Laura. "He-Men and Christian Mothers: The America First Movement and the Gendered Meanings of Patriotism and Isolationsim." *Diplomatic History* 18 (Winter 1994): 47–57.

McGerr, Michael E. *The Decline of Popular Politics: The American North, 1865–1928*. New York: Oxford University Press, 1985.

———. "Political Style and Women's Power, 1830–1930." *Journal of American History* 77 (1990): 864–85.

McGirr, Lisa. *Suburban Warriors: The Origins of the New American Right*. Princeton, N.J.: Princeton University Press, 2001.

Melich, Tanya. *The Republican War against Women: An Insider's Report from Behind the Lines*. New York: Bantam Books, 1996.

Meyerowitz, Joanne. "Beyond the Feminine Mystique: A Reassessment of Postwar Mass Culture, 1946–1958." *Journal of American History* 79 (1993): 1455–82.

Miller, Kristie. *Ruth Hanna McCormick: A Life in Politics.* Albuquerque: University of New Mexico Press, 1992.

Mink, Gwendolyn. "The Lady and the Tramp: Gender, Race, and the Origins of the American Welfare State." In *Women, the State, and Welfare,* edited by Linda Gordon, 92–122. Madison: University of Wisconsin Press, 1990.

Moos, Malcolm. *The Republicans: A History of Their Party.* New York: Random House, 1956.

Morone, James A. *Hellfire Nation: The Politics of Sin in American History.* New Haven, Conn.: Yale University Press, 2003.

Moskowitz, Eve. "'It's Good to Blow Your Top': Women's Magazines and a Discourse of Discontent, 1945–1955." *Journal of Women's History* 8 (1996): 66–98.

Muncy, Robyn. *Creating a Female Dominion in American Reform, 1890–1935.* New York: Oxford University Press, 1991.

Nichols, Carole. *Votes and More for Women: Suffrage and After in Connecticut.* New York: Haworth Press, 1983.

Nickerson, Michelle. "Domestic Threats: Women, Gender and Conservatism in Cold War Los Angeles, 1945–1966." Ph.D. diss., Yale University, 2003.

———. "Moral Mothers and Goldwater Girls." In *The Conservative Sixties,* edited by David Farber and Jeff Roche, 51–62. New York: Peter Lang, 2003.

———. "Women, Domesticity, and Postwar Conservatism." *OAH Magazine of History* 17 (January 2003): 17–21.

Nielsen, Kim E. "Doing 'the Right' Right." *Journal of Women's History* 16 (2004): 168–72.

———. *Un-American Womanhood: Antiradicalism, Antifeminism, and the First Red Scare.* Columbus: Ohio State University Press, 2001.

Nieman, Donald G. *African Americans and Southern Politics from Redemption to Disfranchisement.* New York: Garland, 1994.

Noun, Louise R. *More Strong-Minded Women: Iowa Feminists Tell Their Stories.* Ames: Iowa State University Press, 1992.

O'Neill, William L. *Everyone Was Brave: The History of Feminism in America.* 1969. Reprint, New Brunswick, N.J.: Transaction Publishers, 1989.

Packard, George R., III. *Protest in Tokyo: The Security Treaty Crisis of 1960.* Princeton, N.J.: Princeton University Press, 1966.

Palermo, Patrick F. "The Rules of the Game: Local Republican Political Culture in the Gilded Age." *Historian* 47 (August 1985): 479–96.

Perelli, Carina. "Putting Conservatism to Good Use: Women and Unorthodox Politics in Uruguay, from Breakdown to Transition." In *The Women's Movement in Latin America: Feminism and the Transition to Democracy,* edited by Jane S. Jacquette, 95–113. Boston: Unwin Hyman, 1989.

Perry, Elizabeth. *Belle Moskowtiz: Feminine Politics and the Exercise of Power in the Age of Alfred E. Smith.* New York: Oxford University Press, 1987.

———. "Defying the Party Whip: Mary Garrett Hay and the Republican Party, 1917–1920." In *We Have Come to Stay: American Women and Political Parties,*

1880–1960, edited by Melanie Gustafson, Kristie Miller, and Elisabeth Israels Perry, 97–107. Albuquerque: University of New Mexico Press, 1999.

Polenberg, Richard. *One Nation Divisible: Class, Race, and Ethnicity in the United States since 1938.* 1980. Reprint, New York: Penguin Books, 1985.

Polsby, Nelson W., and Aaron Wildavsky. *Presidential Elections: Strategies of American Electoral Politics.* 6th ed. New York: Charles Scribner's Sons, 1984.

Rae, Nicol C. *The Decline and Fall of the Liberal Republicans: From 1952 to the Present.* New York: Oxford University Press, 1989.

Ranney, Austin. *Curing the Mischiefs of Faction: Party Reform in America.* Berkeley: University of California Press, 1975.

Reinhard, David W. *The Republican Right since 1945.* Lexington: University Press of Kentucky, 1983.

Ribuffo, Leo. *Right Center Left: Essays in American History.* New Brunswick, N.J.: Rutgers University Press, 1992.

———. "Why Is There So Much Conservatism in the United States and Why Do So Few Historians Know Anything about It?" *American Historical Review* 99 (1994): 438–49.

Riley, Denise. *"Am I That Name?": Feminism and the Category of "Women" in History.* Minneapolis: University of Minnesota, 1988.

Rosen, Ruth. *The World Split Open: How the Modern Women's Movement Changed America.* New York: Viking, 2000.

Rossiter, Clinton. *Conservatism in America.* 1955. Reprint, New York: A. A. Knopf, 1982.

Rothe, Anne, ed. *Current Biography: Who's News and Why, 1949.* New York: H. W. Wilson, 1949.

Rupp, Leila J., and Verta Taylor. *Survival in the Doldrums: The American Women's Rights Movement, 1945 to the 1960s.* New York: Oxford University Press, 1987.

Ryan, Barbara. *Feminism and the Women's Movement: Dynamics of Change in Social Movement Ideology and Activism.* New York: Routledge, 1992.

Ryan, Mary. *Women in Public: Between Banners and Ballots, 1825–1880.* Baltimore: Johns Hopkins University Press, 1990.

Rymph, Catherine. "'Keeping the Political Fires Burning': Women's Republican Clubs and Female Political Culture in Small-Town Iowa, 1928–1938." *Annals of Iowa* 56 (Winter/Spring 1997): 99–127.

Scharf, Lois, and Joan M. Jensen, eds. *Decades of Discontent: The Women's Movement, 1920–1940.* Westport, Conn.: Greenwood Press, 1983.

Schechter, Patricia A. *Ida B. Wells-Barnett and American Reform 1880–1930.* Chapel Hill: University of North Carolina Press, 2001.

Scher, Richard K. *Politics in the New South: Republicanism, Race and Leadership in the Twentieth Century.* 2nd ed. Armonk, N.Y.: M. E. Sharpe, 1992.

Schlesinger, Arthur M., Jr. *The Vital Center.* Boston: Houghton Mifflin, 1949.

Schoenwald, Jonathon. *A Time for Choosing: The Rise of Modern American Conservatism.* New York: Oxford University Press, 2001.

Scott, Anne Firor. *Natural Allies: Women's Associations in American History.* Urbana: University of Illinois Press, 1992.

Scott, Joan Wallach. *Only Paradoxes to Offer: French Feminists and the Rights of Man.* Cambridge, Mass.: Harvard University Press, 1996.

Shadegg, Stephen. *What Happened to Goldwater: The Inside Story of the 1964 Republican Campaign.* New York: Holt, Reinhart, and Winston, 1965.

Sherman, Richard B. *The Republican Party and Black America from McKinley to Hoover.* Charlottesville: University Press of Virginia, 1973.

Sicherman, Barbara, and Carol Hurd Green. *Notable American Women: The Modern Period.* Cambridge, Mass.: Belknap Press of Harvard University Press, 1980.

Skrentny, John D. *The Minority Rights Revolution.* Cambridge, Mass.: Belknap Press of Harvard University Press, 2002.

Stouffer, Samuel A. *Communism, Conformity, and Civil Liberties: A Cross-Section of the Nation Speaks Its Mind.* 1955. Reprint, New Brunswick, N.J.: Transaction Publishers, 1992.

Swerdlow, Amy. "Playing the Mother Card for Fascism." *Dissent,* Spring 1997, 112–15.

Tananbaum, Duane. *The Bricker Amendment Controversy: A Test of Eisenhower's Political Leadership.* Ithaca, N.Y.: Cornell University Press, 1988.

Terborg-Penn, Rosalyn. "Discontented Black Feminists: Prelude and Postscript to the Passage of the Nineteenth Amendment." In *Decades of Discontent: The Women's Movement, 1920–1940,* edited by Lois Scharf and Joan M. Jensen, 261–78. Westport, Conn.: Greenwood Press, 1983.

Testi, Arnaldo. "The Gender of Reform Politics: Theodore Roosevelt and the Culture of Masculinity." *Journal of American History* 81 (1995): 1509–33.

Tilly, Louise A., and Patricia Gurin. "Women, Politics, and Change." In *Women, Politics, and Change,* edited by Louise A. Tilly and Patricia Gurin, 3–34. New York: Russell Sage Foundation, 1990.

———, eds. *Women, Politics, and Change.* New York: Russell Sage Foundation, 1990.

Tingsten, Herbert. *Political Behavior: Studies in Election Statistics.* London: P. S. King & Son, 1937.

VandeCreek, Drew E. "Unseen Influence: Lucretia Blankenburg and the Rise of Philadelphia Reform Politics in 1911." In *We Have Come to Stay: American Women and Political Parties, 1880–1960,* edited by Melanie Gustafson, Kristie Miller, and Elisabeth Israels Perry, 33–43. Albuquerque: University of New Mexico Press, 1999.

Van Ingen, Linda. "Gender, Race, and the Politics of Power in the Electoral Campaigns of Charlotta Bass, Phyllis Schlafly and Helen Gahagan Douglas, 1944–1952." Paper presented at the Organization of American Historians annual meeting, Boston, 26 March 2004.

Varon, Elizabeth. "Tippecanoe and the Ladies, Too: White Women and Party Politics in Antebellum Virginia." *Journal of American History* 82 (1995): 494–521.

———. *We Mean to Be Counted: White Women and Politics in Antebellum Virginia.* Chapel Hill: University of North Carolina Press, 1998.

Wallace, Patricia Ward. *Politics of Conscience: A Biography of Margaret Chase Smith.* Westport, Conn.: Praeger Publishers, 1995.

Wandersee, Winifred. *On the Move: Women in the 1970s.* Boston: Twayne Publishers, 1988.

Ware, Susan. "American Women in the 1950s: Nonpartisan Politics and Women's Politicization." In *Women, Politics, and Change,* edited by Louise A. Tilly and Patricia Gurin, 281–99. New York: Russell Sage Foundation, 1990.

———. *Beyond Suffrage: Women in the New Deal.* Cambridge, Mass.: Harvard University Press, 1981.

———. *Partner and I: Molly Dewson, Feminism, and New Deal Politics.* New Haven, Conn.: Yale University Press, 1987.

———, ed. *Notable American Women: A Biographical Dictionary: Completing the Twentieth Century.* Cambridge, Mass.: Belknap Press of.Harvard University Press, 2004.

Wattenberg, Martin P. *The Decline of American Political Parties: 1952–1988.* Cambridge, Mass.: Harvard University Press, 1990.

Waylen, Georgina. "Rethinking Women's Political Participation and Protest: Chile, 1970–1990." *Political Studies* 40 (1992): 299–314.

Weed, Clyde P. *The Nemesis of Reform: The Republican Party during the New Deal.* New York: Columbia University Press, 1994.

Weiss, Nancy J. *Farewell to the Party of Lincoln: Black Politics in the Age of FDR.* Princeton, N.J.: Princeton University Press, 1983.

Welter, Barbara. "The Cult of Domesticity, 1820–1860." *American Quarterly* 18 (Summer 1966): 151–74.

Wheeler, Marjorie Spruill, ed. *One Woman, One Vote: Rediscovering the Woman Suffrage Movement.* Troutdale, Ore.: NewSage Press, 1995.

Williams, Benton. "Title VII and the Private Sector Origins of Affirmative Action: 1964–1996." Ph.D. diss., University of Missouri, 2005.

Witt, Linda, Karen M. Paget, and Glenna Matthews. *Running as a Woman: Gender and Power in American Politics.* New York: The Free Press, 1995.

Yohn, Susan. "Will the Real Conservative Please Stand Up?: Or, the Pitfalls Involved in Examining Ideological Sympathies: A Comment on Alan Brinkley's 'Problem of American Conservatism.'" *American Historical Review* 99 (1994): 430–37.

Young, Lisa. *Feminists and Party Politics.* Vancouver: UBC Press, 2000.

California Federation of Republican
  Women, 164, 178, 179, 186, 217;
  Council of Republican Women,
  83, 107, 108, 159, 180, 287 (n. 44);
  Southern California Republican
  Women's Task Force, 209
Carpenter, Liz, 226
Carter, James E. (Jimmy), 224, 226,
  230, 231, 303 (n. 52)
Carter, Jeanette, 77
Catt, Carrie Chapman, 15, 17,
  255 (n. 14)
Childcare, 203, 234
Christian Right, 237–38, 242
Christiansen, Dorothy, 143
Civil rights, 236, 213; and American
  politics, 7, 12, 197, 212; Republican
  Party and, 7, 12, 82, 84, 173, 193,
  195, 242; and Federation, 83, 85,
  119; Democratic Party and, 108,
  210; relationship to feminism, 218,
  245–46
Civil Rights Act of 1964, 173, 196, 203
Clubwomen: versus party women, 2,
  7, 39, 40, 247; Democratic, 38, 263
  (n. 44), 285 (n. 14); African American, 40, 46, 59, 65, 247, 264 (n. 55),
  270 (nn. 37, 39) (See also National
  Association of Colored Women;
  National Association of Republican Women; National League of
  Republican Colored Women); in
  nineteenth century, 41–42; diversity
  of, 55, 65, 263 (n. 44); political style
  of, 55–59. See also National Federa-
  tion of Women's Republican Clubs /
  National Federation of Republican
  Women; Republican Women of
  Pennsylvania; Woman's Political
  Study Club
Cold War, 98, 114, 118, 124; and
  détente, 222. See also Soviet Union
College Republicans, 146, 163, 224
Colom, Audrey Rowe. See Rowe,
  Audrey

Commission on the Status of Women.
  See President's Commission on the
  Status of Women
Committee on Political Education
  (COPE). See AFL-CIO
Congress of Industrial Organizations.
  (CIO), 105, 134, 137, 141, 162
Congressional Union. See National
  Woman's Party
Conservatism: social, 1, 213, 214, 217,
  244; women and, 9–10; defined,
  124, 282 (n. 62); versus "right-
  wing," 125; and gender, 169, 214;
  versus liberalism, 171, 182; multi-
  cultural, 235; laissez-faire, 244;
  European, 245; and Federation (See
  National Federation of Women's
  Republican Clubs / National Fed-
  eration of Republican Women). See
  also Republican Party
Coolidge, Calvin, 51, 52
Cramer, William, 195, 198
Crane, Philip, 195
Crisp, Mary Dent: at 1972 Republican
  Convention, 200; as party official,
  204, 248; political background of,
  217; and feminism, 218, 200, 228,
  237; as RNC cochairman, 224, 303
  (n. 51); and 1980 presidential campaign, 228, 242; efforts to change
  party, 237, 228, 303 (n. 51)
Crusading style. See Political style

Dawes, Charles, 51
Deardourff, Elizabeth (Betsy) Griffith,
  198, 200, 202, 205
Deardourff, John, 205, 206
Delegates and Organization Committee (DO Committee), 191–92,
  195, 197, 198, 297 (n. 38); DO 7,
  193, 196, 198–99; DO 8, 193–96,
  198–99, 201, 203; DO 9, 193, 196,
  198–99. See also Rule 32
Delegates to presidential conventions
  —Republican women as, 29, 208; in

99, 112; and political training for
women, 135–36, 150, 243; and religion, 111–12, 114, 117; and women's
political crusade, 112, 114, 116–17,
118, 128, 169; as President of Federation, 99–102, 114, 135, 147, 184,
294 (n. 76); and outreach, 103–5,
107–8, 110–11; and women's difference, 103, 118; and nonpartisan
groups, 103; and political style, 169;
and right-wing women, 107–8; and
southern Republicans, 108, 110–
11; and party strategy, 114–15; and
RNC, 114; and conservatism, 124
Farrington, Joseph, 103, 158
Federation. *See* National Federation
of Women's Republican Clubs /
National Federation of Republican
Women
Feickert, Lillian, 261 (n. 26)
"Female" political style. *See* Political
style
Feminine Mystique, The, 149, 150, 151,
218, 288 (n. 65)
Feminism, 7, 231, 248; and Republican Party, 1, 3, 7, 12, 156, 186,
189–90, 202, 203, 206, 212, 213,
219–39 passim, 243, 245; definitions of, 86, 273 (n. 70), 307 (n. 9);
second-wave, 156, 188, 197, 206,
233, 234, 236, 306 (n. 3); "radical"
("women's liberation"), 188, 200,
215, 245, 246; Republican, 189, 207,
209, 225, 230; bipartisan, 189, 236,
244; and liberal tradition, 244–45,
307 (n. 9); "liberal" ("rights-based"),
245; West German, 246; history of,
248, 273 (n. 70)
Feminists: conservative, 235–36; and
laissez-faire conservative women,
244, 305 (n. 84), 306–7 (n. 7)
—in Democratic Party, 1, 200, 202,
207, 210, 223, 236, 237, 242, 244
—in Republican Party, 1, 3, 205, 245,
246, 247; at 1972 presidential con-

vention, 197, 200–202, 203, 204,
207; and RWTF, 207, 208, 209,
210, 211, 224, 225, 244; at 1976
presidential convention, 222–24;
and National Women's Conference,
226–27, 246; at 1980 presidential
convention, 227, 230; since 1980s,
235, 236, 237, 238, 244; and house-
work of government, 242–43, 244.
See also Republican Women's Task
Force; Women's Political Advisory
Board
Ferraro, Geraldine, 231
Fernald, Judy, 165
50-50 laws, 27, 28, 32, 69, 93
Fleming, Lethia, 21, 77
Ford, Betty, 1, 222, 223, 226
Ford, Gerald, 204, 205, 226; and femi-
nism, 1, 105, 223, 226; challenged
by Reagan, 211, 217, 222, 223, 224
Fosseen, Carrie, 21
Foster, Ellen, 14
"Free labor" ideology, 245
Freund, Paul, 215, 301 (n. 14)
Friedan, Betty. See *Feminine Mystique,
The*

Gabrielson, Guy, 136, 152
Gender boundaries, 36–37, 259 (n. 63)
Gender consciousness, 5, 8–9, 12, 59,
232, 244, 264 (n. 55)
Gender gap, 231–33, 292 (n. 39)
Gerlinger, Irene, 95, 95 (n. 3)
Gibson, Catharine, 122, 145, 146,
277 (n. 5)
Ginn, Rosemary: and feminism, 189;
and DO Committee, 191, 192, 197;
as party official, 204, 248; political
background of, 217, 296 (n. 3)
Girard case, 121, 122
Goddard, Mrs. E. G., 92, 93, 241
Goldman, Patricia, 208
Goldwater, Barry: and 1964 presiden-
tial campaign, 4, 129, 160, 163–64,
167–68, 170–72, 173–74, 212, 214,

217; appeal to women, 9, 58, 162, 167, 172; and 1958 Senate campaign, 161, 162; versus "modern" Republicans, 161; and Federation, 162, 164–66, 181; and 1960 presidential campaign, 163; *Conscience of a Conservative*, 175

Goldwaterism, 161, 167–68; and Federation, 6, 291 (n. 11); and gender, 11, 161

Gore, Albert, Jr., 232

Grand Old Party (GOP). *See* Republican Party

Great Depression, 55, 124. *See also* New Deal

Griffith, Elizabeth. *See* Deardourff, Elizabeth

Hall, Leonard, 152, 155, 186

Hamilton, Jane. *See* Macauley, Jane Hamilton

Hamilton, John, 63, 64, 65, 69, 70, 266 (n. 95), 275 (n. 98), 276 (n. 1)

Harding, Warren G., 23–24, 49, 77

Harrington, Ione, 164–66

Hay, Mary Garett, 15–16, 18, 21–22, 191, 256 (n. 25)

Hays, Will, 14, 15, 99, 267–68 (n. 11)

Headlee, Richard, 237

Heckler, Margaret, 195, 197, 200–202, 204, 208, 217, 229, 299 (n. 71)

Hermann, Sylvia, 141

Hert, Sallie, 35, 54, 62, 267–68 (nn. 6, 11)

Hill, Betty, 83. *See also* Woman's Political Study Club

Hiss, Alger, 113

Hobbs, Ruth, 178

Hoover, Herbert, 35, 57, 59–60, 267 (n. 6)

Hopper, Heda, 171

Hosmer, Lucille, 164

Housework of government, 4, 11, 132–34, 150; shortcomings of, 183, 189, 243–44

Hoyal, Mrs. Robert Lincoln, 267–68 (n. 11)

Hubbs, Harriet, 32, 33, 35, 44

Humphreys, Robert, 133, 134, 137

Hutchins, Vere de Vere Adams, 121, 122, 123, 130, 146, 241

Hyde, Jeannette, 21

Illinois suffrage bill (1913), 15, 52

Independent Republican women. *See* Political style: of independent clubwomen

Iowa Council of Republican Women, 143, 149, 205, 239

Isolationist mothers groups, 85, 106–7, 278 (n. 19)

John Birch Society, 169, 287 (n. 44)

Johnson, Henry Lincoln, 26

Kearns, Nora, 141, 145, 157, 158, 277 (n. 5), 285 (n. 21)

Kemp, Jack, 195

Kennedy, John F., 164, 188, 291–92 (n. 25)

Kenyon, Cecil, 159, 160, 293 (n. 59)

Kerry, John, 233

Kilberg, Bobbie, 196, 198–200, 204, 219, 229–30

Kissinger, Henry, 222

Kitchen Kabinet, 138

Laissez-faire conservatism, 244

Lampkin, Daisy, 35, 54

Landon, Alfred, 64, 266 (n. 95)

League of Nations, 14, 15, 23

League of Women Voters (LWV), 23, 27, 105, 255 (n. 14), 256 (n. 20)

Lend-Lease Act, 84, 85

Lippincott, Miriam, 29, 31

Lipset, Seymour Martin, 125, 126, 127, 283 (n. 80)

Livermore, Henrietta, 21, 37, 38, 46, 47, 56

Lodge, Henry Cabot, 163

Lorimer, Alma, 99, 120; on men and women in politics, 30, 33–34, 59, 91, 257–58 (n. 48); and political independence, 46, 230, 237, 248; and Republican Women of Pennsylvania, 48–50; vision of women in politics, 56–57, 91, 241

Lott, Trent, 233

Macauley, Jane Hamilton, 96, 100, 102, 109, 275 (n. 92), 276 (n. 1)

"Male" political style, 247. See also Political style

Martin, Joseph, 136, 275 (n. 98)

Martin, Marion: and founding of Federation, 6, 11, 71–72, 243, 248; and women's political advancement, 6, 67, 68–69, 75, 86, 88, 95, 132, 241, 242, 243; and women's political style, 6, 67, 70, 87, 91–92, 97, 112, 118, 169; and party loyalty, 6, 67, 75, 99, 108, 112, 242, 246; as RNC Assistant Chairman, 65, 69; biography of, 67–68, 69–70, 96, 268 (n. 12), 275 (n. 92); and Maine politics, 68, 70, 96; and RNC, 68, 88, 91, 94; as head of Federation, 71, 73, 132; opposition to, 72, 94–95; and race, 78, 83, 85, 92, 93; and two-party system, 80; and New Deal, 80, 87, 88, 90, 274 (n. 83); and ERA, 81–82, 85, 271 (n. 50); and isolationism, 84–85; and women's rights agenda, 86, 87, 88, 93, 94, 246–47; and political philosophy, 86–87, 92; and Republicanism, 86, 87, 93–94; and feminism, 86, 94, 96; and "alarmism", 89–90, 118; firing of, 94–96; and male allies, 95; as Maine secretary of labor, 96; and individualism, 247

Matalin, Mary, 232

McCarran Act (1950), 98

McCarthy, Joseph, 113, 123, 125, 280 (n. 40), 282 (n. 76)

McCarthyism, 113, 283 (n. 80)

McCormick, Medill, 15

McCormick, Ruth Hanna, 15–16, 18, 21, 35

McGovern, George, 299 (n. 67)

McGovern-Fraser Commission. See Democratic Party: and reform

Melich, Tanya, 198, 217, 226, 237

Michigan Federation of Republican Women, 51, 178

Milburn, Beryl, 194

Millikan, Helen, 229

Mitchell, Harold, 115

Modern Republicanism. See Republican Party

Mothers for a Moral America, 171, 292 (n. 33)

Multicultural conservatism, 235. See also Conservatism

Murray, Ruth, 121, 123, 130

Myhre, Arnilla, 150

National American Woman Suffrage Association (NAWSA), 15, 255 (n. 14)

National Association of Colored Women (NACW), 35, 51–54, 57, 263 (n. 49), 271 (n. 48). See also Burroughs, Nannie; National League of Republican Colored Women

National Association of Republican Women (NARW), 77, 270 (n. 37)

National Consumers League, 70

National Federation of Women's Republican Clubs / National Federation of Republican Women: and ERA, 1, 81–82, 217; and Federation presidency fight (1967), 4, 177–82, 184, 186–87, 216 (See also Schlafly, Phyllis: and Federation presidency fight); and relationship to Women's Division, 7, 154–56; and right wing, 11, 97, 119–20, 123–24, 128–30, 134; and Goldwater movement, 11, 162–67, 172, 179; history and founding

ministration of, 197, 204; and
childcare, 203; and Watergate, 204;
reliance on party outsiders, 205;
and Southern Strategy, 212; and
Goldwater supporters, 213, 222; and
conservatives, 227

Novak, Robert, 177

Nye, Gerald P., 107

O'Connor, Sandra Day, 229

O'Donnell, Gladys, 80, 242; and Federation presidency fight, 177–82,
184, 186–87, 214, 217, 295 (n. 94)

O'Neill, William, 259 (n. 60)

Operation Coffee Cup, 138–39

Packwood, Bob, 195

Page, Paula, 207

Park, Maude Wood, 23

Parks, Ruth, 137, 294 (n. 76)

Partisanship: as corrupt, 17, 38, 43,
44–45, 76; as respectable, 57, 75–
76, 80, 176; defined, 253 (n. 1), 261
(n. 26). *See also* Party loyalty
—and women: study of, 7–8, 41;
before 1920, 7, 10, 41, 44

Party loyalty, 6, 21, 40, 119; versus
independence, 6, 22, 37–38, 160;
and feminism, 12, 240, 243; criticism of, 21, 37, 239, 241; as political
"test" for women, 37, 86, 240

Party of Lincoln. *See* Republican
Party: as "Party of Lincoln"

Party of Mars. *See* Republican Party:
as "Party of Mars"

Party of the Open Door. *See* Republican Party: as "Party of the Open
Door"

Party politics, women's entry into, 2,
13, 15–16, 27–28, 29, 149, 188, 248;
and separatism versus integration,
2, 6–7, 13, 14–17, 18, 29, 90–92,
242, 247, 255 (n. 13); club movement as strategy for entering, 4, 11,
45, 55, 132, 149, 243, 248–49; "seats

for women" strategy, 26, 28, 29, 30,
31–33, 258 (n. 54)

Party women, 3–4, 7, 19, 37–38, 41, 45,
241, 248–49; versus club women,
2, 5, 253 (n. 2); and feminism, 3; and
male allies, 8; African American, 13,
21, 23, 24, 34, 35, 52, 53, 54, 77

Paul, Alice, 14, 29, 81

Pell, Sarah, 76

Penland, Gladys, 161, 289 (n. 80)

Pennsylvania Republicans, 43–44;
and Philadelphia politics, 49–50.
See also Republican Women of
Pennsylvania

Percy, Charles, 225

Peterson, Elly: and Federation presidency fight, 177–82, 184, 186–87,
214, 217, 295 (n. 94); at 1972 presidential convention, 198, 204; and
Michigan politics, 217–18, 221–23,
237; and George Romney, 221–22;
as RNC assistant chairman, 191–
92, 223; and ERA activism, 225–26;
and Ford campaign, 233; and Republican identity, 237; and Reagan
campaign, 242

Pinchot, Gifford, 43, 44, 49

Political education, 25, 50–55, 74, 243

Political realignment, 98, 213, 219,
222, 244

Political socialization, 7, 46–55, 97,
243, 261 (n. 19)

Political style, 245; voluntarist, 4, 41–
42, 260 (n. 7), 264 (n. 66); "male"
versus "female," 4–5, 10, 11, 42–
46, 137, 140–41, 144, 168–69, 247;
"crusading," 5, 6, 55, 57–58, 59, 60,
66, 90, 112, 113, 126–27, 128, 129;
of independent clubwomen, 40,
55–59, 66, 90, 97, 241–48, 264
(n. 66); defined, 260 (n. 1)

Presidential campaigns/elections, 119;
of 1920, 23, 24, 48, 77; of 1924, 50–
51, 52, 54; of 1928, 54, 59–60; of
1936, 57, 64, 68; of 1940, 77, 86;

Republican Women: Feminism and
Conservatism from Suffrage through
the Rise of the New Right, by
Catherine E. Rymph (2006)

Women and Patriotism in Jim Crow
America, by Francesca Morgan
(2005).

Relative Intimacy: Fathers, Adolescent
Daughters, and Postwar American
Culture, by Rachel Devlin (2005).

The Freedom of the Streets: Work,
Citizenship, and Sexuality in a
Gilded Age City, by Sharon E. Wood
(2005).

Home on the Rails: Women, the
Railroad, and the Rise of Public
Domesticity, by Amy G. Richter
(2005).

Worrying the Line: Black Women
Writers, Lineage, and Literary
Tradition, by Cheryl A. Wall
(2005).

From Welfare to Workfare: The
Unintended Consequences of Liberal
Reform, 1945–1965, by Jennifer
Mittelstadt (2005).

Choice and Coercion: Birth Control,
Sterilization, and Abortion in Public
Health and Welfare, by Johanna
Schoen (2005).

Closer to Freedom: Enslaved Women and
Everyday Resistance in the
Plantation South, by Stephanie
M. H. Camp (2004).

Masterful Women: Slaveholding Widows
from the American Revolution
through the Civil War, by Kirsten E.
Wood (2004).

Manliness and Its Discontents: The

Black Middle Class and the
Transformation of Masculinity,
1900–1930, by Martin Summers
(2004).

Citizen, Mother, Worker: Debating
Public Responsibility for Child Care
after the Second World War, by
Emilie Stoltzfus (2003).

Women and the Historical Enterprise in
America: Gender, Race, and the
Politics of Memory, 1880–1945, by
Julie Des Jardins (2003).

Free Hearts and Free Homes: Gender
and American Antislavery Politics,
by Michael D. Pierson (2003).

Ella Baker and the Black Freedom
Movement: A Radical Democratic
Vision, by Barbara Ransby (2003).

Signatures of Citizenship: Petitioning,
Antislavery, and Women's Political
Identity, by Susan Zaeske (2003).

Love on the Rocks: Men, Women, and
Alcohol in Post–World War II
America, by Lori Rotskoff (2002).

The Veiled Garvey: The Life and Times
of Amy Jacques Garvey, by Ula
Yvette Taylor (2002).

Working Cures: Health, Healing, and
Power on Southern Slave
Plantations, by Sharla Fett (2002).

Southern History across the Color Line,
by Nell Irvin Painter (2002).

The Artistry of Anger: Black and White
Women's Literature in America,
1820–1860, by Linda M. Grasso
(2002).

Too Much to Ask: Black Women in the
Era of Integration, by Elizabeth
Higginbotham (2001).

Imagining Medea: Rhodessa Jones and Theater for Incarcerated Women, by Rena Fraden (2001).

Painting Professionals: Women Artists and the Development of Modern American Art, 1870–1920, by Kirsten Swinth (2001).

Remaking Respectability: African American Women in Interwar Detroit, by Victoria W. Wolcott (2001).

Ida B. Wells-Barnett and American Reform, 1880–1930, by Patricia A. Schechter (2001).

Taking Haiti: Military Occupation and the Culture of U.S. Imperialism, 1915–1940, by Mary A. Renda (2001).

Before Jim Crow: The Politics of Race in Postemancipation Virginia, by Jane Dailey (2000).

Captain Ahab Had a Wife: New England Women and the Whalefishery, 1720–1870, by Lisa Norling (2000).

Civilizing Capitalism: The National Consumers' League, Women's Activism, and Labor Standards in the New Deal Era, by Landon R. Y. Storrs (2000).

Rank Ladies: Gender and Cultural Hierarchy in American Vaudeville, by M. Alison Kibler (1999).

Strangers and Pilgrims: Female Preaching in America, 1740–1845, by Catherine A. Brekus (1998).

Sex and Citizenship in Antebellum America, by Nancy Isenberg (1998).

Yours in Sisterhood: Ms. Magazine and the Promise of Popular Feminism, by Amy Erdman Farrell (1998).

We Mean to Be Counted: White Women and Politics in Antebellum Virginia, by Elizabeth R. Varon (1998).

Women Against the Good War: Conscientious Objection and Gender on the American Home Front, 1941–1947, by Rachel Waltner Goossen (1997).

Toward an Intellectual History of Women: Essays by Linda K. Kerber (1997).

Gender and Jim Crow: Women and the Politics of White Supremacy in North Carolina, 1896–1920, by Glenda Elizabeth Gilmore (1996).

Delinquent Daughters: Protecting and Policing Adolescent Female Sexuality in the United States, 1885–1920, by Mary E. Odem (1995).

U.S. History as Women's History: New Feminist Essays, edited by Linda K. Kerber, Alice Kessler-Harris, and Kathryn Kish Sklar (1995).

Common Sense and a Little Fire: Women and Working-Class Politics in the United States, 1900–1965, by Annelise Orleck (1995).

How Am I to Be Heard?: Letters of Lillian Smith, edited by Margaret Rose Gladney (1993).

Entitled to Power: Farm Women and Technology, 1913–1963, by Katherine Jellison (1993).

Revising Life: Sylvia Plath's Ariel Poems, by Susan R. Van Dyne (1993).

Made from This Earth: American Women and Nature, by Vera Norwood (1993).

Unruly Women: The Politics of Social and Sexual Control in the Old South, by Victoria E. Bynum (1992).

The Work of Self-Representation: Lyric Poetry in Colonial New England, by Ivy Schweitzer (1991).

Labor and Desire: Women's Revolutionary Fiction in Depression America, by Paula Rabinowitz (1991).

Community of Suffering and Struggle:
Women, Men, and the Labor
Movement in Minneapolis, 1915–
1945, by Elizabeth Faue
(1991).

All That Hollywood Allows: Re-reading
Gender in 1950s Melodrama, by
Jackie Byars (1991).

Doing Literary Business: American
Women Writers in the Nineteenth
Century, by Susan
Coultrap-McQuin (1990).

Ladies, Women, and Wenches: Choice
and Constraint in Antebellum
Charleston and Boston, by Jane H.
Pease and William H. Pease
(1990).

The Secret Eye: The Journal of Ella
Gertrude Clanton Thomas, 1848–
1889, edited by Virginia Ingraham
Burr, with an introduction by Nell
Irvin Painter (1990).

Second Stories: The Politics of Language,
Form, and Gender in Early
American Fictions, by Cynthia S.
Jordan (1989).

Within the Plantation Household: Black
and White Women of the Old South,
by Elizabeth Fox-Genovese (1988).

The Limits of Sisterhood: The Beecher
Sisters on Women's Rights and
Woman's Sphere, by Jeanne
Boydston, Mary Kelley, and Anne
Margolis (1988).